# THE SUN

# THE SUN

## IN MYTH AND ART

COMPILED AND PRESENTED BY

**MADANJEET SINGH**

WITH CONTRIBUTIONS BY

**AHMAD HASAN DANI:** PAKISTAN • **MIRANDA GREEN:** UNITED KINGDOM
**JEANNINE DAVIS-KIMBALL:** U.S.A. • **JACQUES LACARRIÈRE:** FRANCE
**BORIS I. MARSHAK:** RUSSIA • **ANATOLY IVANOVICH MARTYNOV:** RUSSIA
**MARY ELLEN MILLER:** U.S.A. • **EDUARDO MATOS MOCTEZUMA:** MEXICO
**RAMIRO MATOS MENDIETA:** PERU • **GREGORY NAGY:** U.S.A.
**JAN L. PERKOWSKI:** U.S.A. • **YURI A. PIATNITSKY:** RUSSIA
**ALLEN F. ROBERTS:** U.S.A. • **JAMES F. ROMANO:** U.S.A.
**CHRISTOPHER D. ROY:** U.S.A. • **JAMES R. RUSSELL:** U.S.A.
**ELIZABETH SCHULTZ:** U.S.A. • **EDI SEDYAWATI:** INDONESIA
**MADANJEET SINGH:** INDIA • **HUA TAO:** CHINA
**PANOS D. VALAVANIS:** GREECE • **FUMIKO YAMAMOTO:** JAPAN
**ATSUHIKO YOSHIDA:** JAPAN • **VERA N. ZALESSKAYA:** RUSSIA

IN COOPERATION WITH

**HELEN DICKINSON BALDWIN:** U.S.A. • **PETER BRYDER:** SWEDEN
**PAULINA LEDERGERBER:** ECUADOR • **YEVGENY V. MAVLEEV:** RUSSIA
**LYUDMILA PIROGOVA:** RUSSIA • **MOIRA TAMPOE:** SRI LANKA

UNESCO

WORLD DECADE FOR CULTURAL DEVELOPMENT

THAMES AND HUDSON

First published in Great Britain in 1993
by Thames and Hudson Ltd, London



British Library Cataloguing-in-Publication Data

A catalogue record for this book is available from the British Library

ISBN 0-500-01598-8

Printed and bound in Italy by Amilcare Pizzi s.p.a., Milan

# CONTENTS

3

1. *Madhavi Mudgal and her companions performing a sun dance in front of the Indian solar deity Sûrya, a thirteenth-century sculpture from the Temple of the Sun, Konarak, India.* **(National Museum, New Delhi)**

2. *The sun in gold-thread embroidery. Seventeenth century. Rewa, India.*

3. *Taperet with raised hands worshipping the Egyptian sun god Horakhty, who gives out sunrays of lily flowers. Painted on wood. Ninth century.* **(Musée du Louvre, Paris)**

# PREFACE

*"All that exists was born from Sûrya, the God of gods," states the* Rg Veda *of ancient India, thus articulating the primeval homage all civilizations spontaneously paid to the sun since the dawn of history. Like the devotees in India who seek the sun god Sûrya's blessing on the banks of holy rivers, thousands of Japanese in their own "land of the rising sun" go to pray on the Futamigaura seashore at Ise, the Shinto shrine of the "Heaven Shining" sun goddess Amaterasu.*

*As the bestower of light and life, ancient cultures generally identified the sun as the symbol of Truth, the all-seeing "one eye" of justice and equality, the fountainhead of wisdom, compassion, and enlightenment, the healer of physical and spiritual maladies, and, above all, the fundamental source of fecundity, growth, and fruition, as well as of death and the renewal of life. Most religious rituals, social functions, cultural pageants, festivals, and sports can be traced back to the ancient worship of the sun or related to it through agriculture and fertility rites. The lighting of fires, jumping over them, and dancing around a tree or central pole during the winter and summer solstices have connotations similar to the lighting of the Olympic torch and to the runner carrying this sun symbol from one location of the games to another.*

*Several magnificent sun-temples and shrines as well as museums and archaeological sites all over the world contain exquisite works of art with sun motifs, and sun patterns are reflected in beautiful textile designs, embroidered mantles, engraved gourds, decorated bowls, and other objects of wood, silver, and gold. These art forms transcend both time and space, showing how the deep-rooted solar cultures manifest themselves in our everyday life, as a complex totality of artistic inventiveness and identity on the one hand and in cultural interaction between different civilizations on the other.*

*"He who dwells in man and who dwells in the sun is one and the same," states* Taittiriya Upanishad. *It was in this spirit that Madanjeet Singh conceived and compiled this volume in cooperation with several scholars hailing from different regions of the world—some of whom also participated with him in the* UNESCO *project: "Integral Study of the Silk Roads"—within the framework of the World Decade for Cultural Development.*

**Federico Mayor**
Director-General, UNESCO, Paris

***4. Traditional Japanese painting of the New Year celebration at the Futamigaura seashore, Ise, Japan.***

5

# INTRODUCTION

MADANJEET SINGH

Thousands of people in the "land of the rising sun" go annually to the Futamigaura seashore at Ise and await the dawn on New Year's Day in order to pay homage to the sun goddess Amaterasu. The silence of darkness is interrupted only by the rhythmical breaking of waves against the shore. Gradually the hazy outline of a pair of *Mateo-iwa* rocks in the sea, one larger than the other, come into focus as the sky begins to glow with a spectacular crimson. The larger rock is said to represent a male and the smaller a female principle, while a sturdy rope binding them together is the eternal bond that unites the divine couple. The Gateway of Heavenly Deities, *Shin-mai-Dorii*, on the larger rock, is the universal sun-door symbol of immortality. [**5**]

As the hazy outline of mountain ranges across the sea becomes clearer, the excitement grows and the people, their hands joined, lean over the gigantic frog sculptures of bronze and stone [**86**] in order to see the sunrise. Finally the brilliant halo of the

---

5. *The pair of* **Mateo-iwa** *rocks at the Futamigaura seashore represents the divine couple. The Gateway of Heavenly Deities on top of the larger rock is the universal sun-door of life and death.*

6

7

sun goddess appears above the mountain peaks, and the silence is suddenly broken as the anxious devotees clap their hands sharply twice and bow in order to draw the attention of the goddess toward themselves. The sun's spectrum continues to change color and they close their eyes and pray until the sun rays are no longer red. They clap again, this time to take leave of the sun goddess. The devotees then walk toward the shrine of Amaterasu on the seashore, while others gather around the celestial cave from which the goddess is said to have emerged to illuminate the world with the sunlight of spiritual salvation. [**6, 7**]

The sun icon in the austere wooden shrine is a small round mirror, which, together with jade jewelry and the bronze dagger, form the three sacred objects of Japanese mythology. The solar connotation of the mirror which lures Amaterasu out of the cave is rooted in the ancient practice of making convex polished discs of bronze with solar symbols incised on the nonreflecting side; a Siberian origin is evident, as bronze mirrors, daggers, and perforated pole finials were widely used by the Scythian peoples of the Eurasian steppe. Bronze mirrors with geometric patterns of circles, wheel-shaped bands, thatched triangles, dots, and oblique intaglio lines (symbolizing sun rays) were also popular throughout the vast Eurasian continent, from Hallstatt in Austria to Minusinsk in the upper Yenisey River Valley of Siberia, as well as in Korea. [**9** to **13**]

---

**6.** *The sun goddess Amaterasu emerges out of the cave in a Shinto ritual dance called* **Takachiho-Kagura.**

**7.** *The emergence of Amaterasu from the cave is depicted in a wood engraving called* **Origin of Iwato-Kagura** *(1844), by Toyokuni III.* **(Asai Collection, Tovonaka City, Japan)**

8

Models of bronze mirrors can be traced back to the Hui-style mirrors of pre-Han China. Several small discs excavated from the tomb at Shang-ts'un-ling in Honan (eighth century BC) are believed to be the earliest mirrors in China, and the sun symbolism on the Honan mirrors is often shown by dragons interwoven with zoomorphs whose tails turn into volutes. Cast in high relief or repoussé, bronze mirrors with zoomorphic solar motifs became very popular in China during the Sui and T'ang dynasties. They include directional indications and the "five elements" of Taoist imagery, as well as the twelve zodiacal animals. Zodiac signs were already popular in the West under Roman influence, as seen in the Zodiac Tyche depicting a second-century Nabataean Goddess of Fortune which was excavated at Khirbet Tannur in Jordan. [**14**] During the seventh and eighth centuries, a "lion-and-grapes" motif was apparently introduced by the Uighurs from Central Asia and became closely associated with the Manichaean faith, which is the reason this kind of mirror abruptly disappeared following the persecution of Manichaeism in China in AD 843. Egyptian and Aegean bronze mirrors as well as similar Etruscan solar discs of pre-Roman Italy (tenth–ninth centuries BC) also relate mirrors with the sun.

The pair of *Mateo-iwa* rocks and the celestial cave at Futamigaura, out of which the sun goddess is said to emerge, recall the solar-eclipse myths found among Austro-Asian peoples and similar sun-related cave and netherworld legends in several cul-

**8.** ***A Japanese devotee praying in the Shinto shrine at Ise.***

tures. Australian aborigines believe that during *wongar*, or "dreaming times," there was a cave in which slept a beautiful woman, the sun. The "Origin People" of the Incas in Peru were also thought to have come out of a cave, as their deity, Viracocha, created them from painted stone dolls. The Ayarmaca in northern Chile—who share with the Incas the hero-creator, Viracocha—believe that after men and women showed disrespect to the deity, he turned them into stone, but as they could not survive in complete darkness, he re-created the sun and brought them back to life. The sun god Utu, in a Sumerian myth, helped Dumuzi, the young husband of the deity Inanna, to escape from the netherworld by changing him into a stone. Only one man and one woman survived the great flood unleashed by the enraged Zeus in Greek mythology, and that couple, Deucalion and Pirra, re-created humankind by throwing stones over their shoulders on the mountain of Parnassus, frequented by Apollo. *Bhavisya Purana* states that it was out of the orb of the sun that Vishvakarma, the divine sculptor of the Hindus, chiselled the human form. Indeed, humankind could be said to have been literally chiselled from the solar orb during the Paleolithic or Old Stone Age period, when people living in caves or beneath overhanging rocks used wooden sticks and unpolished, chipped stones for hunting wild beasts.

The tool-making hominids, as anthropologists call them, emerged about one-and-a-half million years ago. But the sun's identification with the animals they hunted became evident much later as in the striking circular engravings representing the sun, discovered in the Central Asian regions (thirteenth millennium BC) in Siberia and western Turkistan. They seem to have eventually influenced the earliest artifacts

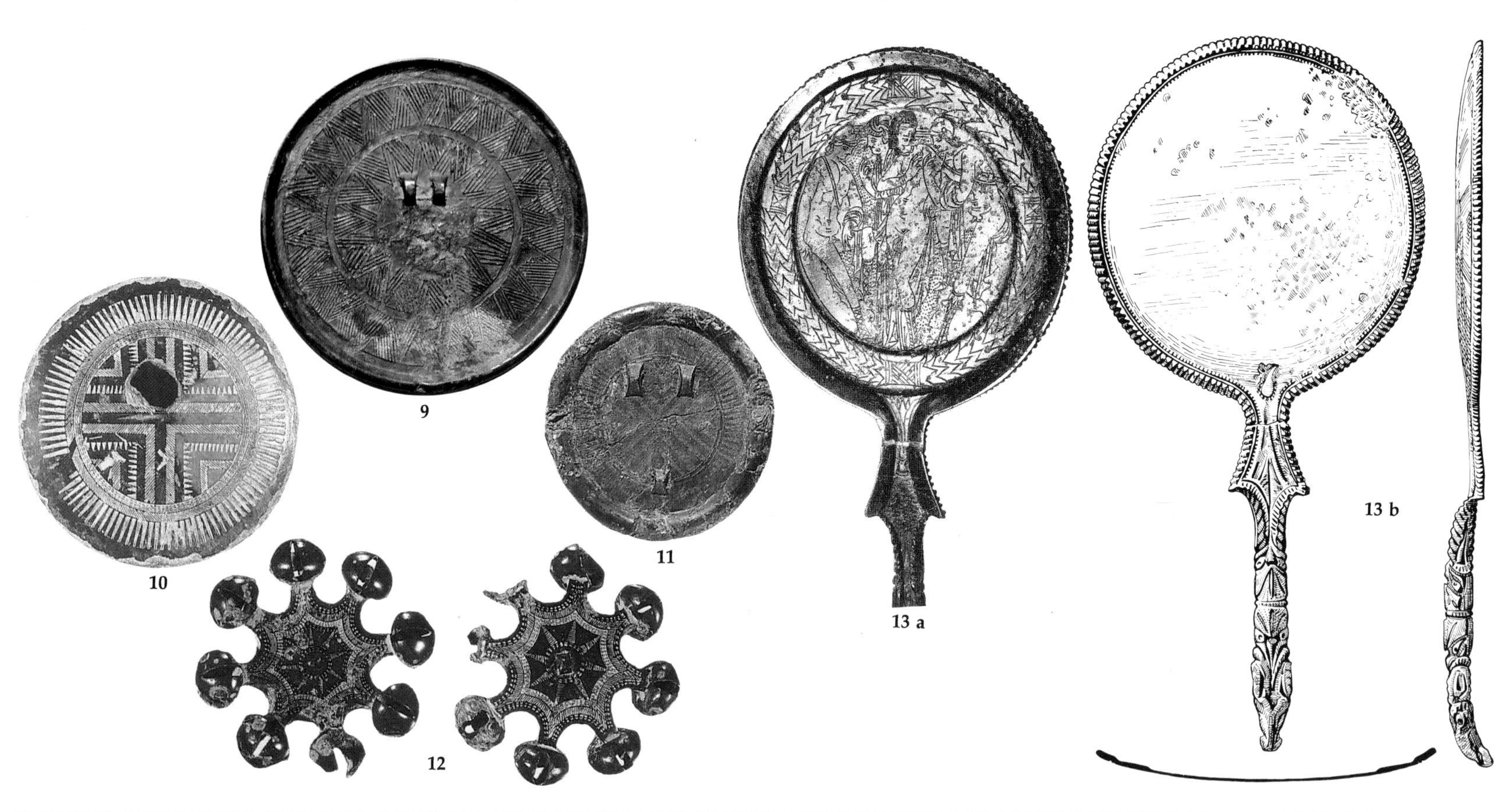


**9.** *Bronze mirror (8½″). Early Iron Age, c. third–second century* BC. *Kangwon province, Republic of Korea.* **(Sungjon University Museum, Republic of Korea)**

**10.** *Bronze disc (5″), with motifs showing rays of the sun as in the Shamanic folk arts of Siberia. End of the fourth century* BC. *Iksan province, North Chola, Republic of Korea.* **(National Museum of Korea, Seoul)**

**11.** *Multihandled mirror (4¾″) with cruciform sunray motifs. Beginning of the second century* BC. *Ch'op'o-ri, South Chola province, Republic of Korea.* **(National Museum of Korea, Seoul)**

**12.** *Ritual handbell (5¾″) with eight crotals and star design, representing the sun. First half of the third century* BC, *from Nonsan in South Ch'ungch'ong province, Republic of Korea.* **(National Museum of Korea, Seoul)**

made in Iran and Mesopotamia, while others became linked to eastern and central Europe through the Volga River and Kazakhstan. The sun in a variety of anthropomorphic forms, such as a nimbus surrounding a head, rays emanating from a circle, concentric circles with dots, and so on, is seen in petroglyphs found at Zaraut Say in the Babatag Range east of Termez, in Tamgaly near Alma Ata in Kazakhstan, and at Saimaly Tash, high in the Kyrgyzstan Tien Shan. [**16, 17, 18**] Apart from the animals depicted in the Lascaux caves in France, at Altamira in Spain, at Adduara in Sicily (15,000 to 10,000 BC), and at the prehistoric Tassili N'Ajjer in the Sahara region (7000 to 4000 BC), are also strange human figures such as the dancing man with horns on his head and a stallion tail, as in the cave paintings at Trois Frères in Ariège. These are comparable to similar figures seen on the third-millennium-BC Mohenjo-daro seals found in the Indus Valley—symbols that are identified with the sun. Among the more explicit Mohenjo-daro solar motifs is a seal showing a number of animals emerging out of a sun disc. [**15**]

The "magic drawings" that trace the contours of rock surfaces in the "womb of the living earth" also inaugurated the later fertility cults of earth-mother and mother-goddess. The original bulbous rotundity and egg-shaped forms of ancient fertility figurines, such as the Venus of Willendorf from Austria (c. 25,000 to 20,000 BC), can be compared with the so-called "sacred pebble." In India, the stone has a parallel in the Salagrama ammonite, representing the solar deity Vishnu, as well as the Brahmanda stone, polished by the flowing water, and identified with *hiranya-garbha*, "the golden egg" (or womb) of Brahma, described in the *Rg Veda* as "the resplendent sun." [**19, 20**]

14

15

**13 a,b.** *Etruscan bronze mirror showing the two Dioscuri with Minerva, wife of Herkle, the "energy of fire." Fifth century* BC. *Etruria.* **(Hermitage Museum, St. Petersburg)**

**14.** *Zodiac Tyche, representing the Nabataean goddess of fortune, excavated in 1937–38 at Khirbet Tannur sanctuary site in Jordan. Early second century.* **(Cincinnati Art Museum, Ohio)**

**15.** *A Mohenjo-daro seal with several animals emerging out of a sun disc. First millennium* BC. **(National Museum of India, New Delhi, India)**

Hindu mythology has it that *hiranya-garbha* emerged from the lotus flower (a sun symbol) growing out of the navel of Vishnu, who is also called Sûrya-Narayana or the "sun god." In another form, as Vikrantamurti, Vishnu crossed the universe in three steps, variously interpreted as: the three locations of the sun at dawn, midday, and sunset; fire, lightning, and the sun; as well as Heaven, earth, and the Underworld. [**21**]

Fire appears to have become identified with the sun and fertility soon after it was discovered some one-and-a-half million years ago by the peoples of the tropical and subtropical Old World—probably in Africa or southern Asia. Initially, it is said to have been produced by friction caused by rubbing two pieces of wood together; a tree called *tau* (the sun) is the totem of the subtribe Tau of the Kenyahs in Indonesia, who believe that coitus is the result of rubbing a liana of the *lurek* plant against a tree. Australian aborigines and the indigenous peoples of Papua and New Guinea trace the origin of fire to the sexual act. In India, Mexico, and several African countries, the ancient ritual of igniting fire with the aid of "male and female" firewood is still observed. The Maoris believe that fire was seized by their hero Maui from his ancestress Mahuike in the depths of the earth before it was put in a tree—the reason fire can be ignited from wood. The Tlingit of the Pacific northwest tell a tale of magical conception of virgins by sawdust from the fire-borer. In the West African empire of Loango, the act of boring to ignite the new state fire is represented by the public coitus of a young couple, a custom also observed by the people of Monomotapa in Africa.

17

18

**16.** *Petroglyphs with sun symbols. Bronze Age. Saimaly Tash, Kyrgyzstan.*

**17,18.** *Anthropomorphicized sun-god images in Saimaly Tash rock drawings. Bronze Age. Tien Mountains, Kyrgyzstan.*

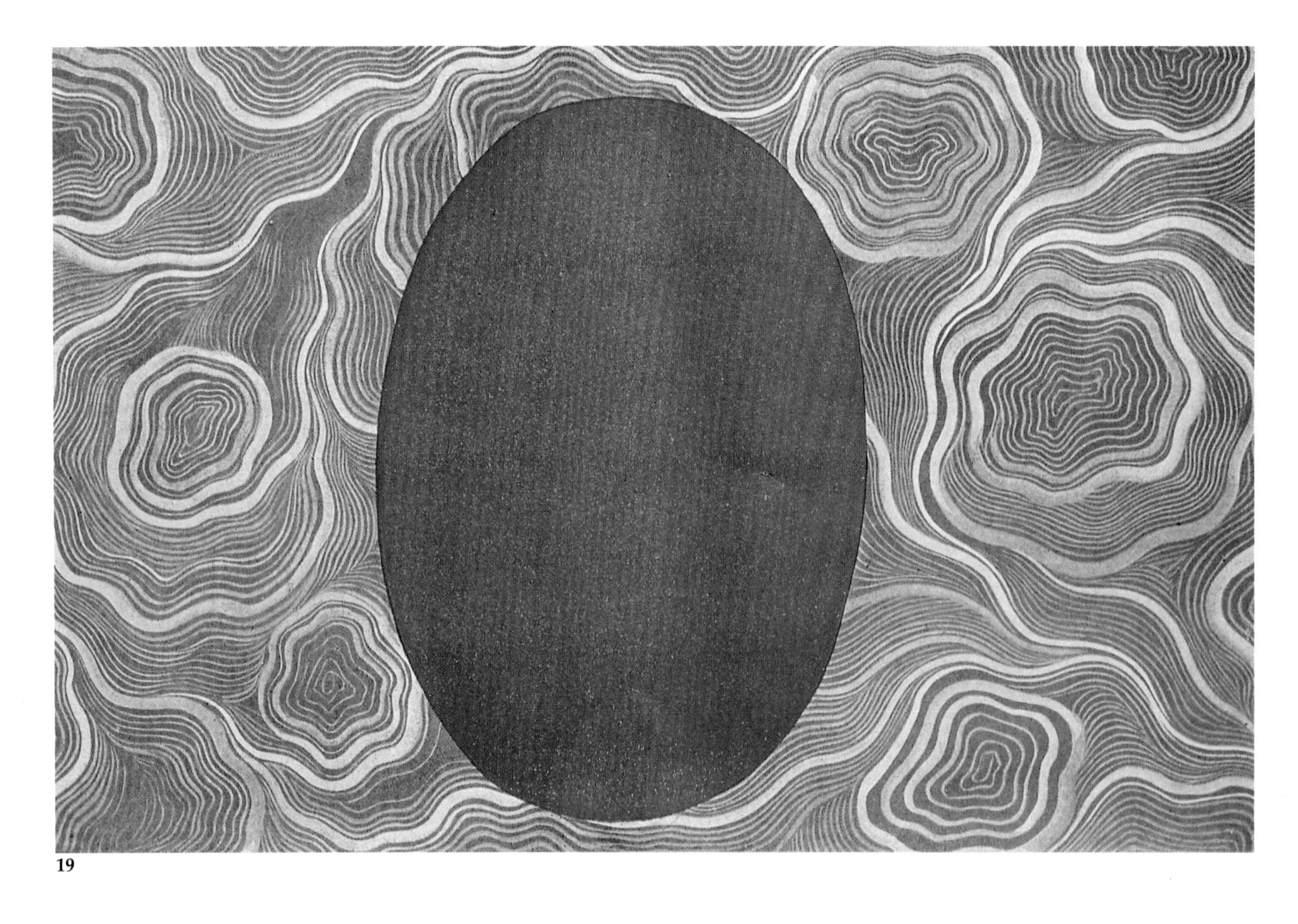

19

"Water gave birth to Agni [fire]," states the *Rg Veda*, and in most archaic civilizations fire and water (like Heaven and earth) are brought together in a unity of opposites and are connected with the sun's cosmic powers of fertility. In Etruria (central Italy), the Etruscans worshipped Herakles, "the energy of fire," and as the solar deity of fertility he was usually represented as swimming in water along with his wife, Minerva, commonly identified with the Greek Athena. In India a barren woman desiring a child was advised to stand naked in water facing the sun; and even today it is a common sight to see childless women go to the well-known Dharma temple in the Burdwan district, Bengal, hoping that a drop of fertility sun-water will fall on their heads while an effigy of the solar deity Dharma Thakur is being bathed in the holy water of the river. [**23**] A fourth-century BC Greek orator, Aeschines, tells of a similar custom in ancient Greece in which, on their wedding eve, girls went naked on a sunny morning to bathe in the river Skamandros and requested that its water accept their virginity.

In several cultures, fire (the sun) is usually personified as male, and water (the moon) as female. On the other hand, when "preserved in the womb of the earth," fire becomes female, while rainwater, "the semen of heaven," takes on a male character. That is perhaps the reason that in several cultures the sun is considered both male and female, such as the Hebrew sun, Shemesh, as well as in eastern Indonesia where the sun is said to

**19. Hiranya-garbha** *in Hindu mythology is the golden egg of Brahmā, described as the "resplendent sun" in the* **Rg Veda.**
*Seventeenth-century Kangra school of painting.* **(Bharat Kala Museum, Varanasi, India)**

20

be bisexual. The gender of Amaterasu is currently under debate in Japan, and in China the sexuality of Hsi-ho, called "the Mother of Ten Suns," is also under scrutiny. Irrespective of gender, however, the sun and the moon are conceived as brother and sister in most cultures and as the progenitors of humankind.

Amaterasu's parents, Izanagi and Izanami, for example, are brother and sister, and the sun goddess herself begets children from her brother Susanowo. Tefnut is the twin sister and wife of the Egyptian god of air and light, Shu, just as the divine king Osiris ruled with his sister-spouse Isis. In Indian mythology a son of the sun, Yama, is prevailed upon by his twin sister, Yami (the River Yamuna), to perpetuate humankind by cohabiting with her. Njord, the father of the Scandinavian-Germanic god of sunshine and fertility, Freyr, is married to his own sister. Ugaritic texts speak of fertility aspects of the supreme god Baal in context with his relations with Anath, his sister and consort. Rhea, a goddess of Heaven and earth in later Crete (recalling Riyat, the Egyptian female personification of the sun) marries her brother Cronus, the father of Zeus.

A Sumerian goddess Inanna later identified as Ishtar, the sister of Shamash, is also the consort of the sun god of the Semitic pantheon. Cohabitation between the sister sun and her brother moon is also echoed in the Native American mythology as far away as the region between Greenland and the Mackenzie River in northern

**20.** *Devotees paying homage to the sun, depicted as* **Hiranya-garbha.** *Eighteenth-century Mughal school of painting, India.*

Canada, and in the Andean culture the moon deity Mama-Kilya is the sister and consort of the sun god Inti.

Living in the midst of all-embracing nature, "ethnographic" (a term now commonly used in lieu of the derogatory word "primitive") societies did not distinguish between such perceptions as our modern analytical minds tend to discern, such as: *animism*, the notion that all objects have a soul; *totemism*, that security of human life depends on guardianship of animals; *fetishism*, that magical powers can be infused in the representation of objects; and *shamanism*, the revelation of the unseen world of nature by "medicine men," the shamans. Their notions were similar to the Shinto concept of *kami*, which is not an easy one for the modern mind to comprehend. Wrote Motoori Norinaga, an eighteenth-century Japanese scholar: "I do not understand it myself; the *kami* are both the deities of Heaven and earth who appear in ancient records and they are also human beings as well as birds, beasts, plants, seas, mountains, trees, water, and so forth." It is in tune with the Chinese legend of Hsi-ho, "the Mother of Ten Suns," each of whom represents an element of nature, as the sun, clouds, water, rocks, the stag, the tortoise, the crane, the pine tree, bamboo, and the herb of eternal life. The Ten Suns are depicted in a Korean Yi-Dynasty colored screen of ten panels. [**30**]

Our prehistoric ancestors seemed to know instinctively (as the Indian *sutratma* doctrine states), that all things are connected with the sun. They must have noticed how beasts and birds, insects and fish, all use the sun as a point of reference and so adapted the same technique in order to orient themselves when hunting or when searching for pasture. They did not have to "invert the cosmic fig tree" in order to comprehend that its roots draw physical and spiritual nourishment directly from the sun, as the *Vedas* and *Upanishads* later tried to explain: "The threefold Brahman has its root above," states *Maitreya Upanishad*. The relationship between the sun and the tree is similarly explained in Jewish kabbalistic literature: "The Tree of Life extends from above downwards, and it is the sun which illuminates all." The sun's equation with trees can be seen in several exquisite pieces of ancient Mesopotamian ivory. [**27, 28, 29**] It is a motif that has been depicted, reinterpreted, or elaborated in most cultures over the centuries. Its classical projection is the beautiful sculpture by Bernini in the Borghese Gallery, Rome, showing Daphne transforming herself into a tree as she is pursued by Apollo, the Greek solar deity.

In time almost all elements of nature such as stones, mountains, trees, plants, flowers, birds, beasts, water, and fire turned into solar deities in anthropomorphic or theriomorphic forms and/or transformed into sun-related cult objects. The tree in Vedic literature, for example, became the Sacrificial Post *(Yupa)* representing the trinity of Fire, Gale and Sun *(Agni, Vayu,* and *Aditya)*. Similar symbolism came to be established in the parasol shaft *(chattravalli)* of the stupa and other Hindu and Buddhist reliquary objects, such as the perpendicular column *(stambha* or *laat)*; in the sacred pillar *(matzewa)* of the ancient Hebrews; and in the imposing Egyptian obelisks, as well as the pillar-tree *(djed)*. In Serbia and Russia, as well as among the Slavs living near the Elbe river, the sun is identified with old trees which are venerated by erecting fences around them. The birch tree in Siberia and Central Asia has a similar connotation in shamanist rituals as it passes through the "sun" in the roof-opening of

**21.** ***Vishnu Vikrantamurti covered the universe in three steps, placing them in Heaven, earth, and the Underworld, as well as in fire, lightning, and the sun. Stone bas-relief.* AD *467. Kathmandu, Nepal.***

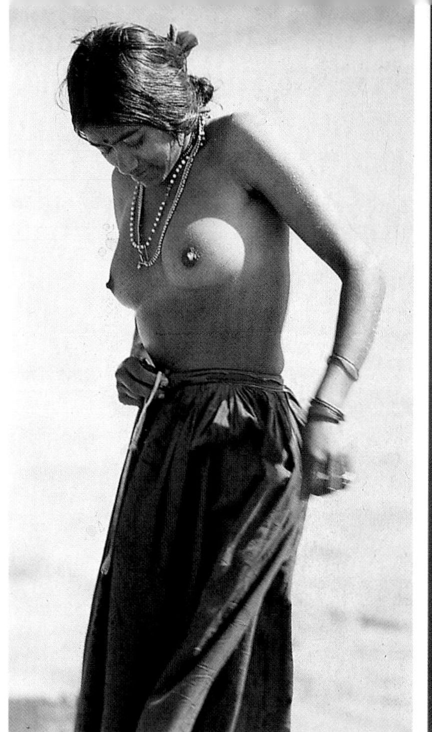

22. *Isis, the Egyptian sky goddess of fertility, cuddling the sun god Horus. Late Bronze period.* (Musée du Louvre, Paris)

23. *Barren women desiring children were advised to stand naked in water facing the sun, an ancient practice still followed in India.*

24. *Woman with a Mirror (sun symbol) carved on a medieval sun temple in India.*

25. *Hittite goddess in gold with a sun-disc headdress sits on a throne holding an infant on her lap. Thirteenth century* BC. *Central Anatolia. (National Geographic Society, Washington, D.C.)*

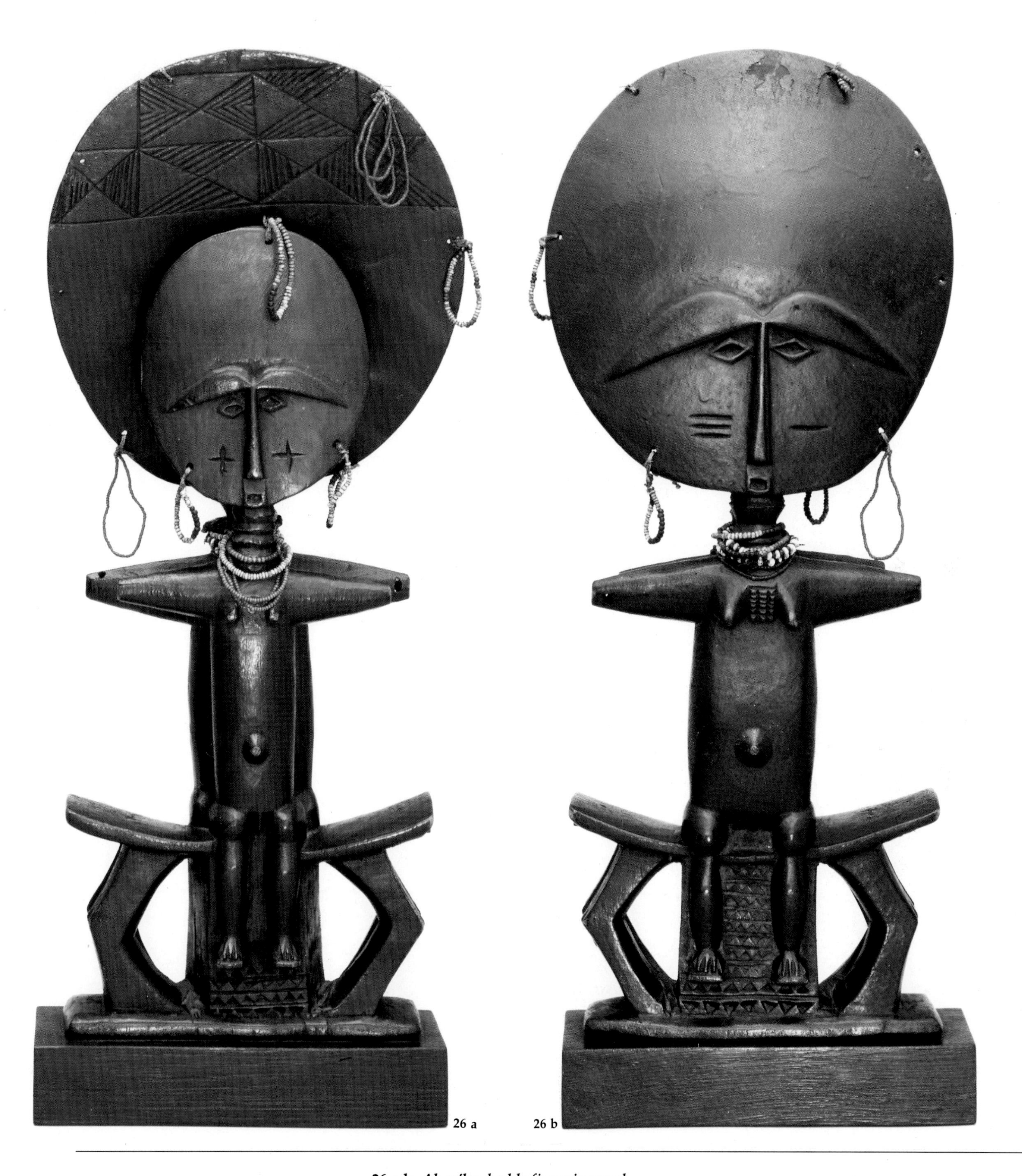


**26 a,b.** *Akua'ba double figure in wood of a male and female on either side, joined together by a sun-disc-shaped headdress. Asante group, Ghana.* **(Smithsonian Institution, National Museum of African Art, Washington, D.C.)**

27

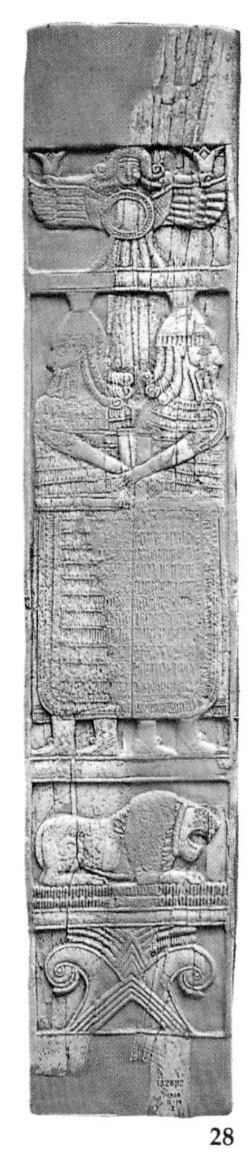

28

29

30

27,28. *Furniture with ivory panels showing a goddess with a winged sun disc above two guardian spirits (28).* **(British Museum, London)**

29. *Each of the two outer panels (27, 29) shows a stylized tree with a sun disc above. Eighth century* BC. *Phoenician.* **(British Museum, London)**

30. *The sun is among the ten elements of nature symbolizing longevity, as in this Korean painting called sehwa. Eighteenth century. Yi Dynasty.* **(Hoam Art Museum, Yongin)**

the nomadic *yurt*. In Meso-America Maya kings erected stelae called "stone trees" in the belief that they confirmed their royal status at the center of the cosmos. The practice in Japan of felling a sacred tree on a mountain, dragging the log down to the village, [**31, 32**] and erecting it as a holy pillar *(mi-hashira)*, recalls the ancient sun-related annual festival of Cybele, the mountain mother of the Greco-Romans, at which a pine tree was similarly felled and brought to her shrine and worshipped, along with her lover Attis.

The mountain as cult symbol became the "heavenly ladder" needed to reach Heaven where the sun god and other solar deities supposedly lived. In Egypt "the ladder of Horus" notion became identified with the earliest mastaba-like constructions over which the step pyramids (such as the one at Saqqara) were erected. Shamash, the sun god of the Semitic pantheon, rose from the eastern mountains and inaugurated the practice of building elevated citadels such as the ziggurats of the Babylonian moon god Nanna. Hebrews erected the High Places *(bamot)*, and the Greeks tried to imitate their highest mountain, Olympus. Pausanias, a Greek traveller in the second century, relates how he saw the sun altars of worship on the highest acropolis at Corinth, called Akrocorinth. The Aztecs related the Teotihuacan pyramids in Mexico to the sun and the moon, [**39**] and similar meaning is attributed by the Amerindians to their sacred Chimborazo mountains in "the heart of the Andes."

The mountain-like Buddhist temple at Borobudur in Indonesia is called Kailasha after the mountain peak in the Himalayas which the Hindu and Buddhist pilgrims climb in order to reach even higher to the abode of the gods on the mythical Mount Meru; *panchajanah*, or the five kins in the *Rg Veda*, represent "mind at its ascending levels towards the sun." The mountain at Bojonegoro in Java is venerated because

31

32

**31,32.** *A festival called Okibiki is celebrated in Japan in which a huge log of wood, symbolizing the sun, is carried in a procession to the Zingu Shicho Kohoka at Ise.*

34

33

35

33. *Victory stele of the Akkadian king Naram-Sin from Susa, c. 2250* BC.
**(Musée du Louvre, Paris)**

34. *The Andes Mountains of south-central Peru are identified with the sun, and at Machu Picchu, the "lost city of the Incas," many sun temples were built.*

36

"the sun comes out of it" and in Sri Lanka, Saman "the deity of the morning sun," is worshipped on Samanolakanda Mountain, also called Adam's Peak. The Chinese Emperor Wu-di of the Han Dynasty (140–87 BC) frequented the Cheng mountain at the eastern end of the Shandong peninsula in order to worship the sun rising from the sea. The mountain deity of ancient Japan, Yama-no-kami, is worshipped as "the sun of forests and animals."

The holy mountain Obong is depicted alongside the sun and the moon, with which the Korean kings of the Yi Dynasty identified themselves, on an eight-paneled colored screen which was installed behind the beds of the royal couple. [37] Identification of the holy mountain with the sun in Mexico is graphically depicted in the

**35.** *Identification of the sun with mountains is graphically depicted in the Aztec sculpture* **Teocalli de la Guerra Sagrada** *(1500), showing the sun disc in place of the usual shrine on top of the pyramid.* **(Museo Nacional de Antropologia, Mexico City)**

**36.** *Temples in Asia are modeled after the holy Mount Kailasha in the Himalayas, such as the sun temple at Khajuraho. Mid-tenth to mid-eleventh century AD. India.*

37

Aztec sculpture *Teocalli de la Guerra Sagrada* (1500), in which, at the top of a steep staircase, the customary shrine is replaced by the image of the sun. [**35**] Like the Maya Temple of Inscriptions at Palenque, at Cerros, Belize, [**490, 491**] the solar concept of a mountain-like tiered construction with its steep staircase and smallish temple with soaring roof on top, seen also at Tikal in Guatemala, and at the Cambodian Baksei Chamkrong Temple at Angkor, show amazing architectural similarities between widely separated civilizations flourishing at opposite ends of the world.

Birds flying in the sky naturally became identified with the sun, and the symbolism appears in a fantastic variety of mythologies and forms among different cultures. Russian folklore endows extraordinary powers in a mythical firebird that "even one of its feathers could flood the whole world with sunlight of happiness." In ancient Egypt another fabulous bird was known as the *bennu*, a heron, associated with the worship of the rising sun and of life after death. Also called the phoenix, this golden bird with brilliant scarlet plumage was said to live for five hundred years, making a nest of aromatic boughs and spices, which it set on fire when its end approached, consuming itself in the flames. The legend went on to say that out of the pyre, a new phoenix miraculously sprang which, after embalming its «father's» ashes in the golden egg of myrrh *(hiranya-garbha?)*, flew with them to Heliopolis, where it deposited them on the altar in the Temple of the Sun.

The image of the phoenix appears on the coinage of the late Roman Empire, a theme depicted also on the Kushana Dynasty coins in India from about the late first to the third century, as the "sun-like" *Khvarenah* in the shape of a bird leaving Yima, the Iranian underworld deity (Yama in Hindu mythology). Probably the myth originated in Arabia or India, where there were plentiful spices for its nest. The Chinese bird is *pheng* or *ch'i-lin*, and in Arabic mythology it is called *rukh* or *anqâ* (Persian *sîmorgh*). The huge bird, according to the thirteenth-century cosmographer al-Qazwini, "darkened the sky with the spread of its enormous wings." The theme is

**37.** ***The sun represents the king, and the moon, the queen, in a Korean eight-panel screen depicting Mount Obon. Yi Dynasty. Second half of the eighteenth century.*** **(Hoam Art Museum, Yongin)**

38

39

represented on several Islamic monuments, such as at Bukhara, showing mythical birds flying toward the sun. [42] The "all-seeing eye" of the sun is identified with the bird in many parts of the world; during the UNESCO Silk Route expedition in Kyrgyzstan a native told me that he could ride his horse with closed eyes because the falcon he held was "the sun of my eyes." [44] The very popular Asian solar deity Garuda in the Indian epic *Râmâyana*, is portrayed as the "sun-eye of Râma" in an episode in which his wife Sita is abducted by the demon Râvana. [49] In another faraway corner of the world the notion is symbolized in the beautiful Aztec sculpture, *The Sun* (1480), in which a man is shown in the hide of an eagle, excavated at the site of the Templo Mayor Museum in Mexico City. [47]

The eagle/falcon image on the palette of the King Narmer from Hierakonpolis (c. 3000 BC), representing the sun god Horus, is among the earliest works of art which, together with the lion, [53, 54] became the regal sun symbols *par excellence* of classical cultures in Egypt and Mesopotamia, as well as of other great civilizations. The lion was identified with the sun as early as 2500 BC when the famous Egyptian Sphinx, with a lion's body and a human head, was created for Pharaoh Khafre as "the living image of the sun god." [55] Matching the royal zoomorphic symbols of the sun, nomadic cultures had their own sun-related animals, specially those with horns and antlers. A Siberian myth relates:

> The wild deer Miandash has left the womb of the Mother Earth
> Miandash is the source of all life on earth.
> On and on he runs, showing the way to the sun. . .

Among the earliest Siberian myths is a popular legend in which the gigantic cosmic hunter Arom-Tell (Tjermes) shoots his fiery arrows of lightning, as he is forever chasing a huge reindeer or elk. The celestial reindeer (depicted with circular

---

**38.** ***The Book of Wonders by the thirteenth-century cosmographer al-Qazwini depicts the connection between the sun, the moon, and the mountains.***

**39.** ***The Sun Pyramid of Teotihuacán "the city of the gods." Beginning of the Christian era. Mexico.***

symbols of the sun in some early neolithic representations) runs from East to West during the day, and descends to the "subterranean sea" at night. The moral of the story is that the hunter must not succeed in killing the solar animal, for otherwise "the sun shall drown in blood, the stars shall fall down from the sky, and all living creatures on earth shall perish." Later, Scythian legends (seventh to second century BC) introduced totemic concepts of the race having descended from the deer; for example, the magical impregnation of a young girl by a deer results in the birth of a deer-man.

Among the cult objects found in the ancient burial mounds and vaults in Central Asia are round bronze mirrors bearing representations of the sky-riding reindeer and other sun symbols such as goats, rams, snakes and birds. The gold-plated bronze reindeer with arched antlers found in the Chelintin and Issyk burial mound in Kazakhstan belong to the same tradition of craftsmanship which inspired the talented Hittite metalsmiths from central Anatolia to shape the elegant *rhyton*, or drinking horn. The stag at rest is engraved with a beautiful frieze showing a sun goddess holding a falcon with one hand as she sits before an altar or brazier. [**65**] Another figure, probably the god-protector of wildlife, stands on an antler while holding a bird of prey, and behind whom are devotees with offerings.

The goat in particular was identified with the sun. Peoples in North Africa, for example, associate the animal with mountain worship, and perform goat-related cult

**40.** ***One of the earliest sun gods, in the shape of a falcon, is depicted on the palette of King Narmer from Hierakonpolis. c. 3000 BC.*** **(Egyptian Museum, Cairo)**

**41.** ***Funerary papyrus of the high-ranking priestess Anhai, showing the sun god as falcon. Twentieth Dynasty, c. 1100 BC.*** **(British Museum, London)**

42

rituals to bring rain. Thor, the Germanic solar deity of fertility and thunderstorms, travels in a chariot drawn by goats. The *Rg Veda* of the nomadic Aryans tells of the one-legged goat *Aja-ekapad* (swift-one-foot), the draft animal of the solar deity Pûshan. The golden-bearded deity is the "good shepherd" who glows in the midnight pit where he was born and found by Agni (fire). He is the "herdsman born on the path of paths, the child of the way, the wanderer, the steady guide who never loses his herd and helps in finding treasures." He eats *karambha*, "the food of life," and the goat that pulls his seven-wheeled golden chariot represents the power of solar movement which "precedes Sûrya's sun-horses and climbs up to Heaven in its yearly cycle. The notion was literally demonstrated by "the Sun King" Sûryavarman II, the builder of the famous Angkor Wat temple, [**61**] who was taken in "a spectacular procession of carriages drawn by goats and horses, all of them ornamented with gold." The fabulous ceremony, held in the kingdom of Khmer during the first half of the twelfth century, was recorded by a Chinese visitor, Chou Ta-kuan.

The *Rg Veda* identified the deity Varuna with "the horse of the yonder sun who rises from the water like a spark of life at daybreak, and then dies at sunset before rising again the next morning." The symbolism is echoed in Europe by the horse pulling the Bronze Age sun chariot from Trundholm, Denmark, carrying a sun disc which is gilded on one side to represent the day-sun, while the plain obverse side

**42.** ***The mythical sun-bird, depicted here on the gateway of the seventeenth-century Bukhara monument, manifests under different names and in many forms all over the world.***

43. The Great Solar Eagle *(1720) by the Korean painter Chong Hong-Nae, was painted on silk in gold during the Yi Dynasty period.* (National Museum of Korea, Seoul)

44. *"The eagle is the sun of my eyes," stated this native of Kyrgyzstan, articulating a notion commonly held in many cultures.*

45. *The owl in Central Asia represents the nocturnal sun as the eagle symbolizes the day sun.*

46

connotes the night-sun. [60] The horse as a solar symbol has been claimed both by rulers and their subjects alike, but the admittance of the nomadic goat into the royal court was comparatively a later development. In terms of art, the merger of two cultures, the high and the low, is symbolized in a unique Etruscan bronze showing a goathead springing out of the flaming back of a roaring lion whose tail ends in a serpent (early fourth century BC). The so-called Mythical Beast, unearthed at Arezzo in 1533 and bought by Cosimo de Medici, ingeniously combines three important solar motifs into one fascinating sculpture representing the sun. [57] The discovery of another famous sculpture, *Goat in the Thicket*, excavated in the Royal Cemetery at Ur in Iraq (c. 2600 BC), also alludes to the goat's "royal status." [66]

Thus goats and antlered beasts were not only assimilated into high society, but worshipped as solar deities, as seen in the Mesopotamian ritual-object from Larsa (c. 1800 BC), representing a worshipper beside a "trinity" of goats. This was perhaps the beginning of the Holy Trinity concept in anthropomorphic religious worship, a transitional symbol of which is the Kashmiri *Vyuha*-form of Vishnu, showing a triple combination of lion-man-boar heads surmounted by three human heads and culmi-

**46.** ***The eagle is a popular sun motif in Himalayan Buddhist monasteries, as depicted in this sixteenth-century Thikse shrine. Ladakh, India.***

**47.** *The sun symbolized as an Aztec warrior with eagle's hood. c. 1480.* **(Templo Mayor Museum, Mexico City)**

**48.** *The traditional bird-man from the Sepik River, New Guinea.* **(Washington University Gallery of Art, St. Louis, Missouri)**

**49.** *Winged Garuda from central Java. c. eighth century.* **(Museum Nasional, Jakarta, Indonesia)**

50. *The solar bird-man in Tolima style.* **(Museum of Gold, Bogotà, Colombia)**

51. *The Egyptian sun god Horakhty. c. ninth century* BC. **(Egyptian Museum, Cairo)**

52. *The Buddhist version of Garuda. Sixteenth century. Thimphu monastery, Bhutan.*

54

nating on top in a horse head. Vishnu is incarnated in several man-animal configurations, such as the horse-headed Kalkî, the boar-headed Varaha, Narasimha with the head of a lion, Kûrma as the tortoise, and Matsya, the fish. Christian iconography, too, eventually incorporated not only the sun-inspired halo but also animals, as for example the symbolic winged Evangelists: the eagle for St. John, the lion for St. Mark, and the bull for St. Luke.

An extraordinary Chinese piece combining anthropomorphic and zoomorphic sun symbols is a ritual bronze vessel for keeping coins (206 BC), found at Jinning in the Shi-zhai mountains of Yunnan province. [70] The gilded man riding a horse on a central pedestal is evidently a sun deity, as he is surrounded by solar symbols of the four oxen representing the four directions, while the two leonine figures in place of the vessel's handles symbolize the two horizons. Solar deities were generally depicted in gold, "the sun-metal," and the practice was widespread in Central Asia as, for example, with the Gold Man, now in the Archaeological Museum in Alma Ata, Kazakhstan. [71] This piece was found among several hundred gold, silver, wood, and ceramic artifacts excavated in 1969 from Issyk Kurgan, a fifth-fourth-century-BC treasure trove of Saka culture which was contemporaneous with the solar cultures of the Scythians living in the Black Sea coastal regions, as well as with the Sauromatians in the Volga River area.

The sun's complex symbolic peculiarities were largely derived from ancient beliefs in which horned animals, reptiles, bird and plants, as well as anthropomorphic gestures were assigned special powers or meaning. Like the one leg of Pûshan's goat, the three-legged bird (crow) usually engraved in a circle on the crown of the bodhisattva Sûryaprabha, or "Light of the Sun," is a sun symbol that became popular in Korea and Japan with the advent of Buddhism. The image is seen in the crown of a

---

**53.** *Lion's head with solar symbols. Detail of Etruscan bronze statue of Chimera guarding the Sepulchre against intruders. Late sixth century BC. Etruria.* **(Hermitage Museum, St. Petersburg)**

**54.** *Ivory panel carved on both sides showing a seated lion crowned with a sun disc and uraeus. Ninth century BC. Phoenician.* **(British Museum, London)**

**55.** *Following pages. The Great Sphinx with a lion's body and human head at Giza in Egypt was created around 2500 BC for Pharaoh Khafre as "the living image of the sun god," and the colossal pyramids represented the "heavenly ladder of the sun god Horus."*

53

56

fifteenth-century gold-and-bronze sculpture discovered in a stone pagoda in the Sujong temple at Yangsu-ri, South Korea. [72] It was apparently derived from Chinese mythology in which the golden three-legged crow is the "spirit of the sun"—recalling also the three steps of Vishnu which the Hindu solar deity planted in three places as he strode across the universe. [21] Buddhism was introduced into Korea from China during the fourth century, carrying in its wake some of the sun-related notions that China itself had absorbed from India and Central Asia. Tradition has it that Buddhism was brought to China from India after the Han Emperor Ming (AD 58–76) dreamt of a flying golden deity which he interpreted as a vision of the Buddha.

The gesture of reassurance *(abhaya-mudra)* in which the Buddha shows the palm of his hand is also an important sun symbol, [**73, 315**] a motif depicted on prehistoric petroglyphs in many parts of the world. In Africa the solar connotation of the outstretched open hand can be traced back to hand-impressions seen on the rock-faces at

57

56. *Imdugud, a Sumerian solar deity, was a composite, a lion-headed eagle with a fish-like tail. This beautiful amulet made of gold and lapis lazuli was given by the Sumerian king of Ur (c. 2500 BC) to the neighboring king of Mari, who controlled the vital trade route to Sumer.*

57. *Three solar symbols are ingeniously combined in an Etruscan bronze called* **Mythical Beast**, *in which a goat head springs out of the flaming back of a roaring lion whose tail ends in a serpent. Fourth century BC.* **(Museo Archeologico, Florence)**

58

59

Tassili N'Ajjer in the Sahara region, representing the rising sun—a tradition which is evident from the hand carved on a wooden Kuba-Bushoong drum, decorated with sun-disks *(phila)*. [**76**] Prehistoric hand symbols are also found in the Bohuslän region of southern Sweden, and on the Danish island of Bornholm. The fingers of outstretched hand-impressions in Danish petroglyphs are shown like the arms of a cross pointing in four directions; and at Pech-Merle, in southern France, a handprint is significantly depicted above the image of a horse. The sunrise symbolism is evident from the large, upraised hands with fingers resembling sun rays or antlers, as depicted in the Val Camonica rock art of northern Italy, [**78**] as also in similar petroglyphs of Anasazi origin found in the petrified forest of Arizona (c. 700–1300). [**77**] A bronze panel at Wismar in Germany (c. 1200 BC) shows a disk with three-pronged stylized hands as solar symbols.

Outstretched hands pointing downward usually connote sunset or the "night sun," as represented by the Etruscan sun god Cautha or Uzil. [**75**] The fifth-century-BC piece from Etruria is a winged youth with the body and skin of a reptile as he emerges from water, invoking a kind of solar theology with dualistic beliefs represented by the day and the night sun. Such Oriental notions of immortality and the reincarnation of the soul in which opposing forces of fiery elements, emerging from

**58.** *The sun shines through the "roof box" into the passage of the tomb at Newgrange, Ireland, during the winter solstice. Megalithic period.*

**59.** *The massive stone pillars of the great megalithic monument at Stonehenge in England were positioned in such a way as to allow observation of the rising and setting sun, particularly during the winter and summer solstices.*

60

water, soar upward toward Heaven, became a universal theme in mythologies of many cultures and their art. One outstanding example, combining sun and water motifs, is the lion-headed eagle with a fishlike tail, called Imdugud. [**56**] This fantastic amulet made of gold and lapis lazuli was sent by the Sumerian king of Ur (c. 2500 BC) to the neighboring King of Mari in order to secure the use of trade routes in the adjoining territories that he controlled.

Moving in primeval waters, Vishnu eternally sleeps on the "endless" serpent Ananta, during the periodic annihilation and renewal of the world by Agni. [**83**] His equivalent in Vajrayana Buddhism is the serpentine Pancharaksha goddess with many heads against a flaming nimbus and "a thousand eyes" covering her whole body, as she lifts herself from the churning water toward the sky. [**74**] In China this concept of fecundity and renewal is embodied in the serpentine sun and moon bodies of Fu-xi and Nu-wa in the creation myths of Tao tradition. [**82**] On the opposite side of the globe the Aztecs of Mexico worshipped Xiuhcoatl, the Serpent of Fire, [**90**] and the Hopi Indians of Arizona paid homage to the sun by performing the snake-antelope dance, in which a number of snakes were released in four directions to seek rain.

A sacred serpent *(uraeus)* rising in front of a canine figure was among the golden

**60.** ***The sun disc on the Trundholm Chariot is gilded on one side, while the other side is plain, representing the day and the night suns. Bronze Age.*** **(Nationalmuseet, Copenhagen)**

61

ornaments with solar symbols excavated in the kingdom of Kush. [84] The Meroitic civilization in Africa flourished along the River Nile from before 700 BC to about AD 350, and even though it was remote from classical centers of civilization, an intermingling of several cultures is evident from the discovery at the site of inscriptions in Greek and Latin besides Egyptian and the native Meroitic language. The universality of the concept in which the sun and water are thus symbolized is effectively represented also in the twelfth-century-BC Babylonian stone relief from Susa showing a serpent coiled around the World Mountain, its head resting on the summit. [89]

Nommo, the companion of the supreme being Amma in the tradition of the Dogon people of Mali in Africa, is a hermaphrodite with snakelike arms and legs. He stole "a piece of the sun" used for forging Amma's creations, in order to provide fire for Dogon blacksmiths. A similar legend in Greek mythology tells how the Titan Prometheus, the Greek god of fire, stole the sun from the blacksmith Hephaestus—a myth which is still celebrated annually during the Promethean Festival in Greece. Perhaps the Nommo mythology is invoked in the wooden sculpture of the celebrated blacksmith Kuba Chief Mbop Pelyeeng aNce. [91] The universality of the tradition is evident in other parts of the world, as in the smithy depicted at the Indonesian fifteenth-century sanctuary of Candi Sukuh, situated along the slopes of Mount Lawu in central Java. In this beautiful frieze, both cloud-and-lightning as well as sun-fire finials are shown on the upper-right-hand

**61.** *Aruna, the charioteer of the sun god Sûrya, drives the sun chariot, in the magnificent Angkor Wat temple built by the "sun king" Sûrya Varman II. Twelfth century. Cambodia.*

62

corner by a blacksmith in his workshop. [92] Sun-Fire-Finial [319] is especially interesting as it is very much like the headgear worn by the Kazakhstan Gold Man. [71]

With the consolidation of agricultural communities the emphasis on fecundity and fruition shifted to the soil and inevitably started the struggle for the control of water, a recurring mythological theme among farmers, fruit-growers, herdsmen, and marsh people who inhabited, particularly, the regions stretching from the Nile valley in Africa, the area between the Euphrates and Tigris rivers, all the way to the Indus valley in the Indian subcontinent. As in real life, mythical battles were now fought in order to liberate fertilizing waters from the clutches of beasts and monsters and to revive agriculture and vegetation after the dry season or a drought. In Palestinian and Syrian mythology, Baal, the god of fertility, battles with Leviathan, the water monster; and, in an Indian myth, Indra, the god of the firmament, slays Vritra, the demon of drought. Such sun-related myths symbolizing death and regeneration became very popular among the Egyptians, Babylonians, Assyrians, Aramaeans, Canaanites, Phoenicians, Sumerians, and Aryans, as well as in Aegean, Etruscan, Greek, Roman and Celtic communities, and were echoed in the mythology of the North American Huron Indians, in which the spring-hero, Joskeha, kills the frog that prevented the water from flowing freely.

Thus, the thunderstorm gods living on cloud-covered mountains came into prominence and, even though their task was to administer the sun's "heavenly semen of

**62.** ***Aruna drives the five-horse-drawn chariot of the sun god Sûrya. Eighteenth-century Pahari miniature.*** **(Bharat Kala Museum, Varanasi, India)**

63 a

63 b

fertility," they tried to usurp some of the sun's prerogatives. As custodians of rainwater, they began claiming a status comparable to that of the almighty sun. The envious Zephyr, the god of the west wind in Greek mythology, maliciously deflected the throw of Apollo's discus (associated with the sun) and killed his lover Hyacinthus, [93] the prehistoric solar deity whom the Greeks replaced with Apollo during the classical period with Apollo. [94] Among the rebels were such solar deities as Ninurta, the Mesopotamian god of thunderstorms, Indra in India, the Sumero-Akkadian deity Enlil, the Greco-Roman god Zeus/Jupiter, Perkons of the Latvians, Taranis of the Celts, Thor/Donner of the Germans, Perkunis of the Slavs, and so on. The Basque god Orko, the Finnish god Ukko, and the West Asian thunder gods Teshub and Hadad also joined the fray.

But the shrewd sun knew how to curtail the ambitions of his solar subordinates by making alliances with powerful kings and emperors for mutual benefit. So the Pharaohs of Egypt cast themselves in the image of the sun god Re; the Greeks claimed descent from the sun deity Helios, or Apollo; the Romans imagined themselves to be as unconquerable as their sun god Sol Invictus. Like the royal devotees of the Sumerian sun god Utu, the Semitic rulers in Mesopotamia became identified with their sun god Shamash. Iranian monarchs invoked Mithra, the ancient fire deity representing the sun, and the medieval royal families in India claimed descent from "Sûrya-Vansha," the solar race.

**63 a,b.** *Etruscan solar theology is depicted on this tripod censer from Etruria, in which the fiery element of nature is struggling to free itself from chaos, symbolized by the solar energy god Herkle defeating the water ox (63b). Etruria. Sixth century* BC. **(Hermitage Museum, St. Petersburg)**

64

Across the Atlantic, the king of the Natchez Indians in America was known as the "Great Sun," whom the "people of the sun" worshipped; Aztec rulers identified themselves with the sun god Huitzilopochtli; Maya kings bore the title "the Sun-faced Lord" Kinich Ahau; and the Inca rulers of Peru traced their descent from the sun god, Inti. In sub-Saharan Africa, too, early court historians compared the sun to Moro Naba, the king of Ouagadougou (Mossi Empire). In cultures where the sun was regarded as female, she became the consort of powerful rulers; the sun goddess Xihe is the wife of Emperor Dijun in Chinese mythology.

As a consequence, royal thrones as well as the preaching altars of the prophets

**64.** ***A lion overpowering a deer (without horns in spring) had similar connotations in Irano-Sogdian style to Herkle defeating the water ox, or as Mithra killing the bull. Seventh-century silver dish from Khurasan.*** **(Hermitage Museum, St. Petersburg)**

became identified with the sun all over the world. The *Mahâvamsa* Buddhist scriptures refer to the Buddha's second-century-BC ivory throne which was "embellished with the sun in gold and the moon in silver." In Egypt the throne, like the sun, became the creator of the Pharaohs themselves, since the name Isis is the Greek form of the ancient Egyptian hieroglyph meaning "throne" and the sun goddess was the mother of the king. "The weapons of the gods and kings were forged from pieces trimmed from Sûrya," state the *Purânas* (ancient Indian tales) and such notions in most cultures unleashed a plethora of art forms in which not only arms and shields but almost everything regal such as royal robes, jewelry, horses, and elephants (including their saddles and *haudas*), and so on, all became associated with the sun. [**101** to **114**]

The common people, too, identified their everyday objects with the sun as the wide-brimmed hat with a conical crown used in China, Korea, Japan, and in other parts of the world. [**127**] In Greece a similar hat is called *petasos*, after the winged hat of the Greek deity Hermes. Not far from the thirteenth-century Sun Temple at Konarak in India, there is a village called Pipli where almost everyone is engaged in handicrafts incorporating sun motifs—textiles, embroideries, engraved gourds, and other artifacts using leather, wood, lacquer, gold, silver, and other metals. Pipli women weave beautiful textiles inlaid with round mirrors, representing the sun, [**115**] patterns which are so incredibly similar to the embroideries woven by Meso-American Indians, especially in Guatemala.

The sun in different shapes and forms is also the main theme in a colorful variety of Baltic as well as Slavonic handicrafts, embroidery in clothes, head-scarfs, belts, footwear, tablecloths, towels, and so on, which play an important role at weddings, christenings and funerals. It is the focus of attention in the Suzani textiles of Uzbekistan, an exquisite selection of which is exhibited in the Tashkent Museum of Handicrafts. [**123, 124, 125**] In Europe, a beautiful selection of "Creation of the World" tapestries is preserved in the Cathedral Museum of Gerona in Spain; [**130**] and in France artists like Lurçat have created some outstanding pieces with solar motifs. [**131**] The dragon in China is the protector of the sun (and people), and hence motifs of the sun and other planets are incorporated into stylized logograms, as seen on the ceremonial garment of Lin Putian, now in the Museum of the Celestial Empress at Quanzhou in China. [**129**]

Among the duties of the rulers in ancient civilizations was the responsibility of preventing the sun from deviating from its path, especially when it changed its seasonal cycle (the solstice). It was the king's responsibility to keep the sun moving on its stipulated course in order to ensure good harvests for his subjects. The connection between the sun and agriculture resulted in the formulation of the first ever solar calendar of 365 days in Egypt (fifth millennium BC), its cycle related to the annual inundation of the Nile delta and the celestial movement of the sun. Even more ingenious was the two-track Maya calendar combining the sacred round of 260 days and an approximate year of 360 days. The Maya, like the Aztecs, were farmers, and the solar calendars that they formulated for marking agricultural cycles were functional life-sustaining aids for predicting seasons, which at the same time consolidated the sacred position of their kings at the center of the cosmos. [**142**] The Neolithic monuments at Stonehenge in England and the eighteenth-century Jaipur "Jantar Mantar" in India, served a similar function as the sun helped in calculating the correct dates for solar

65 a

65 b

**65 a,b.** *A Hittite silver rhyton, or drinking horn, engraved with a frieze showing solar deities holding birds of prey, and worshippers with offerings. Thirteenth century* BC. *Central Anatolia*

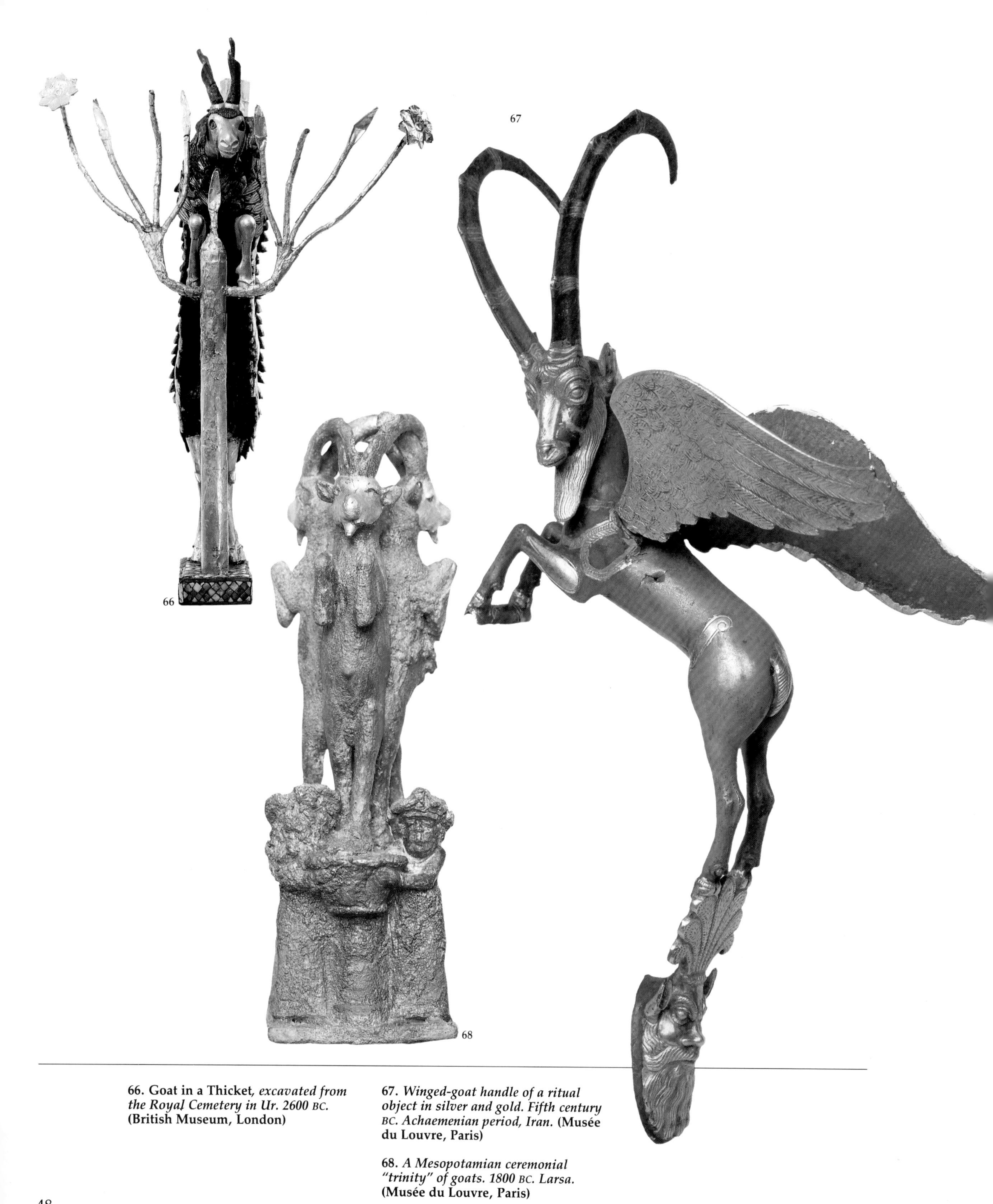

**66. Goat in a Thicket,** *excavated from the Royal Cemetery in Ur. 2600 BC.* **(British Museum, London)**

**67.** *Winged-goat handle of a ritual object in silver and gold. Fifth century BC. Achaemenian period, Iran.* **(Musée du Louvre, Paris)**

**68.** *A Mesopotamian ceremonial "trinity" of goats. 1800 BC. Larsa.* **(Musée du Louvre, Paris)**

69

festivals and in instructing farmers on the seasonal rhythm of their work. [**143, 144, 145**]

So the "all-seeing sun" could not deviate from its set course across the sky and in that position assumed the duties of upholding law and order by witnessing and enforcing treaties and covenants. Accordingly, ancient boundary stones were often engraved with images of the sun disc as tokens of irrevocable guarantee against territorial encroachment. [**146, 147**] In the Roman empire oaths were required to be taken in the name of Mithra, and royal treaties were generally inscribed on metal plates bearing the image of the sun god. [**148, 149**] Myths and legends strengthened this notion. It was the omnipresent Helios in Greek mythology who witnessed the well-kept secret when Hades abducted Persephone and carried her down to the Underworld. Likewise, Sûrya was the one who detected Rahu, the demon who had gate-crashed into the assembly of the gods and stolen some of the *Amrita*, which Vishnu was distributing among his guests. So Vishnu (in form of Mohini) cut off Rahu's head. But Rahu, having tasted the *Amrita*, had already become immortal and so could not be killed. Thus as a truncated dragon head he became the ascending node of the sun while his body, Ketu, representing the dragon's tail, was transformed into the descending node.

With the development of metaphysical thought the sun's spiritual responsibilities also multiplied. The sun god Mithra (Vedic Mitra) became the charioteer of Ahura Mazda, the Zoroastrian Creator God of Light who is opposed by the evil darkness of

***69.** The goat symbolizing the sun punishes a sinner, in a sixteenth-century wall painting depicting the Buddhist Wheel of Existence, in the Himalayan monastery of Thikse. Ladakh, India.*

70

**70.** ***A ritual bronze vessel showing a gilded sun deity riding a horse surrounded by four oxen representing the four directions, and two leonine figures symbolizing the two horizons. 206 BC. Found in the Shi-zhai Mountains, Jinning, Yunnan Province, China.*** **(Museum of Yunnan Province, Kumming, China)**

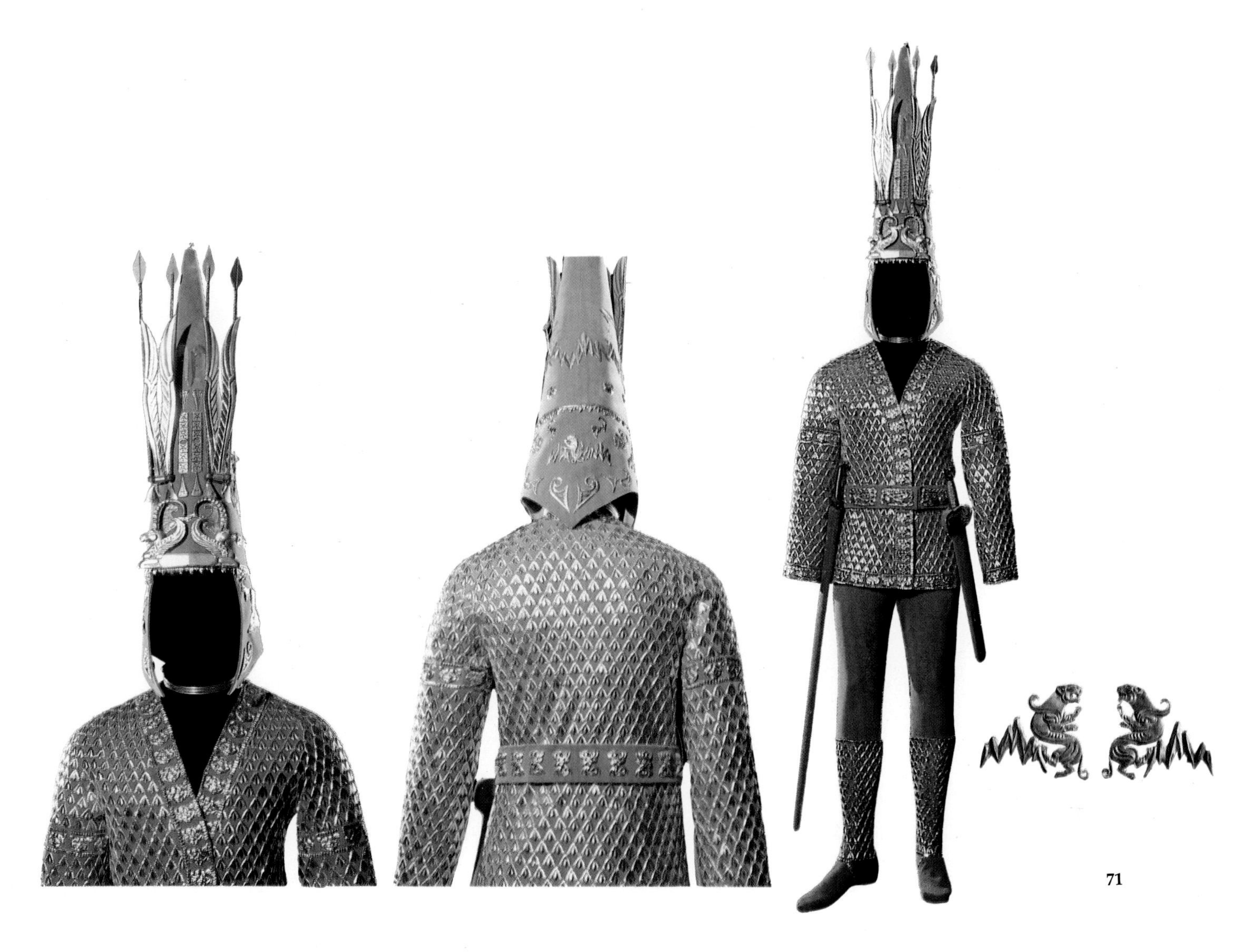

Angra Mainyu or Ahriman. Ahura Mazda is "like the sun to behold—for the sun is the greatest of all visible, earthly fire," stated Zoroaster (c. 628–551 BC); and to this day in several eastern Iranian languages the word for the sun is simply "of Ahura Mazda." Zoroastrianism and Manichaeism were among the great dualistic world religions which the sun inspired and, even though Manichaeism has since all but disappeared, the religion was once professed by many peoples, from Spain in the west to the eastern coast of China where there is a beautiful image of Mani (AD 216–274) in a temple called Cao'an which is still in use in Fujian Province near Quanzhou. [**152**] It was truly an "ecumenical" faith, embracing all people, as Mani tried to integrate diverse religions such as Gnostic Christianity, Zoroastrianism, and Buddhism, in a strongly dualistic philosophy based on the eternal struggle between good and evil, light and darkness. The Manichaean sun god, also known as the Third Messenger *(Neryosang)*, resides in the sun along with the Mother of Life and the Living Spirit ("Holy Trinity"). Among other things, the Third Messenger sets the sun and the moon in motion, thus creating the changes of seasons on earth.

"Sûrya is the ultimate Truth," states *Aditya-Hrydya Sûtra*, and this is beautifully depicted in the miniature painting, *Heart of Sûrya*, in which Vishnu and his consort Lakshmi are seated in the sun. [**159**] The Buddha calls the sun "the fiery heart, my kith and kin," as stated in the *Samyutta Nikaya*, and Buddhists in India, China, Korea, and

**71.** ***Among the sun-related artifacts excavated in 1969 from the Issyk Kurgan in Kazakhstan was the Gold Man. Saka Period, fifth–fourth century*** **BC. (Archaeological Museum, Alma Ata, Kazakhstan)**

Japan believe that the palace of bodhisattvas, such as Ekadasamukhavalokitesvara (One-Ten-Faced Deity) [**251**] and the popular Chinese Avalokitesvara Kouan-yin (Sahasrabhujasahasranetravolekitesvara), "a-thousand-hands-and-thousand-eyes," is located in the sun, the Truth. [**156**] Pancharaksha goddess of Vajrayana Buddhism, depicted in Himalayan monasteries, are assigned similar virtues. [**74**]

In Persian mystic poetry and folklore the sun is a round-cheeked girl *(khorshid)*, [**353**] and in Japan, children with round rosy cheeks are said to be blessed by the sun. The Greeks went so far as to model the shape of Truth on the sun so that Truth literally became round like the sun. This was elaborated in a mystical journey which the philosopher Parmenides made in the sun's chariot, accompanied by the daughters of Helios. As he crossed the divine threshold of Night and Day guarded by "avenging justice," he finally realized "the unshakeable heart of *well-rounded* Truth." The massive marble monolith in the shape of a circular sun disc called *Bocca della Verità*, "the Mouth of Truth," is a remarkable Greco-Roman interpretation of Plato's identification of the sun with Truth and its "avenging justice." The solar deity (fourth century BC) was originally conceived as Pan, the son of the Greek god Hermes, who, as patron of pasture and fertility, was depicted with the horns, legs, and ears of a goat. The Romans adopted him later as their rural deity Faunus. His icon in the shape of a huge marble disc is now displayed in the portico of the church of Santa Maria in Cosmedin in Rome, where it was originally found

**72.** *Bodhisattva Sûryaprabha is identified by the three-legged-bird sun symbol in his crown. The fifteenth-century gold and bronze "Light of the Sun" was discovered in a Korean stone pagoda of the Sujong temple, Yangsu-ri. Republic of Korea.* **(National Museum of Korea, Seoul)**

**73.** *The swirling-flame-nimbus design and hand gestures* **(mudras)** *of the Korean gilded bronze Buddha (Kongdokmyongbul) are both solar motifs. AD 539. Koguryo.* **(National Museum of Korea, Seoul)**

74

*74. Oriental notions about reincarnation, in which forces of fiery elements emerging from water soar toward heaven, are represented by Pancharaksha, goddess of Vajrayana Buddhism. Sixteenth century. Tayul monastery, Ladakh, India.*

in a pagan shrine. [154] People who tell lies are advised not to insert their hand in the Mouth of Truth, for the "avenging justice" of the sun is said to bite it off.

The "avenging justice" of the sun in Vajrayana Buddhism is depicted by a goat swallowing a sinner in a wall painting, the Wheel of Existence, in the Himalayan monastery of Thikse in Ladakh. [69] Hindu mythology interpreted the theme through a popular legend in which Vishnu, as Nara-simha (man-lion), suddenly appears from a pillar and tears Hiranya-kasipu to pieces because the tyrant king would not permit his son Prahalada to worship the solar deity. [155] It is a variation of the Greek legend in which the god Dionysus urged the Maenads to tear Orpheus to pieces because he worshipped the rival god Apollo. The superstition continues to live; it is generally believed that King Charles I of Great Britain (1625–49) was executed because he deprived his subjects of freedom, in the name of the sun, [183] just as Hitler met with a similar fate for abusing the swastika emblem.

The sun is associated with Truth in sub-Saharan oral traditions as well and invoked through incantations that play a major role in African cultures. As translated by Romanus Egudu in *Black Orpheus*, an Ibo diviner chants:

> What will it be today?
> Success or failure? Death or Life?
> Ha! The flood cannot run uphill.
> What is the evil spirit that throws its shadow
> between me and the truth?
> I hold my sacred staff against it.

---

**75.** ***The Etruscan sun god Cautha, or Uzil, is a winged youth with the body and skin of a reptile, as he emerges out of water with stretched hands, representing the sun. Fifth century*** **BC.** ***Etruria.*** **(Hermitage Museum, St. Petersburg)**

76. *The open hand is a universal solar symbol, as seen in this African Kuba-Bushong drum depicted with sun* **(phila)** *motifs.* **(Museum of Mankind, London)**

77. *Arizona petrified-forest petroglyphs of Anasazi origin. c. 700–1300* AD.

78. *Bronze Age rockcarvings in the Camonica valley, northern Italy.* **(Drawing: Paul Jenkins, after Anati)**

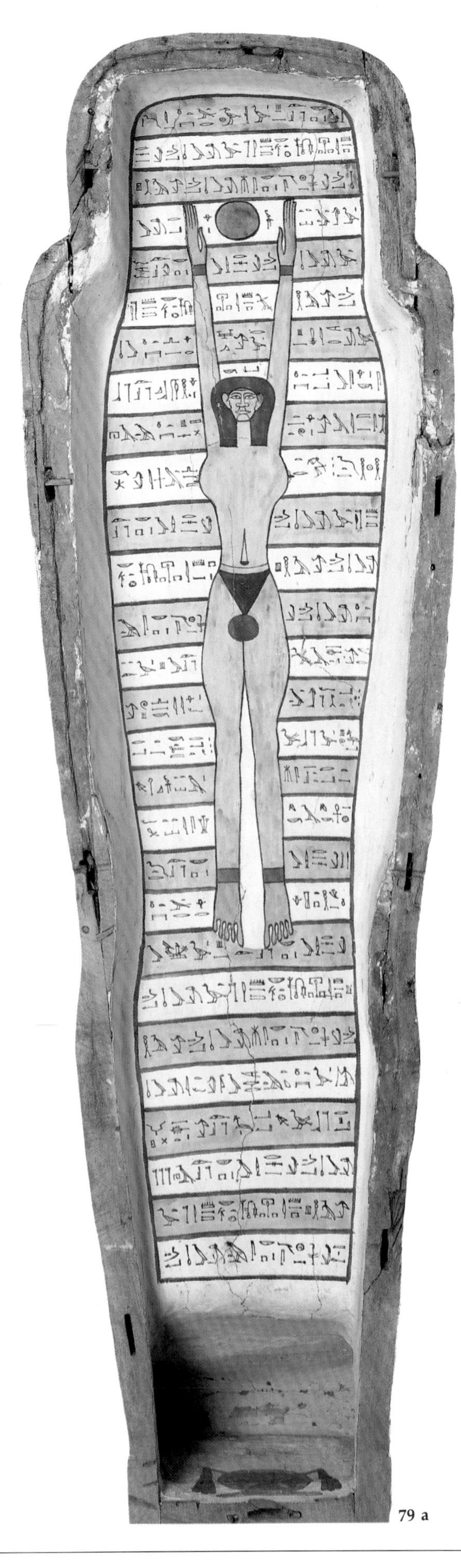

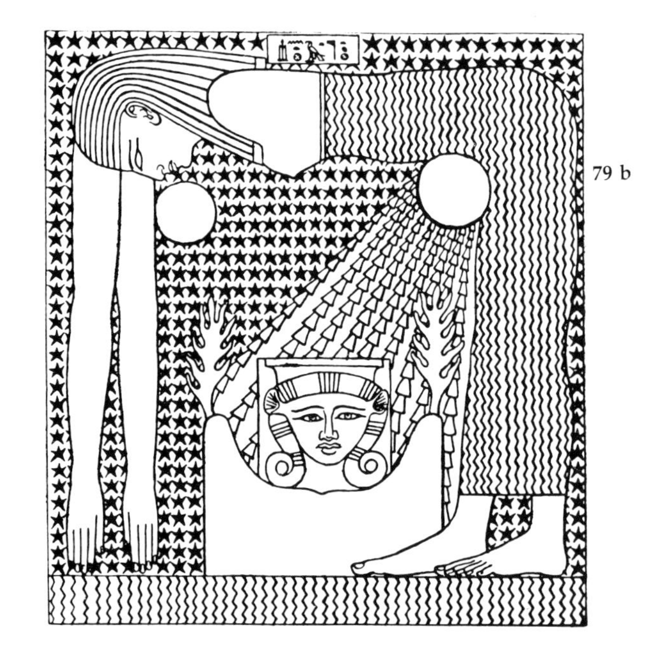

79 a

79 b

80

**79 a.** *The sun's journey during a twenty-four-hour day is symbolically portrayed by the sky goddess Nut, painted on the coffin of Udjaersen. The daughter of a Theban priest holds the sun between her hands preparatory to swallowing it (sunset, death); at the same time she is shown giving birth to the sun disc (sunrise, life). Twenty-sixth Dynasty, c. 656–525* BC. **(Metropolitan Museum of Art, New York)**

**79 b.** *Nut giving birth to the sun. Sketch after a painting in the temple of Hathor at Dendéra. First century* AD, *Egypt.*

**80.** *Fertility is symbolized by the sun disc between the thighs of an Aztec terra-cotta figure. c. 1500.* **(Museo Nacional de Antropologia, Mexico City)**

Here is the East, there is the West;
Here the sun rises. . . .
See the Truth come riding on the rays of the sun.

In sub-Saharan Africa the image of the sun is rarely represented, though its transformative power is pervasive in most aspects of life. As in ancient ethnographic societies, the sun's light and warmth is cherished for its fecundity and fruition but equally feared for its power to scorch and kill, especially in the Sahara. Congo tribesmen beat on the drum and chant at sunrise in fear of the sun whom they believe to be a lion whose roar (thunderstorms) scatters their animals. The sun does not appear in anthropomorphic form but makes its potency felt as part of the overall cosmic power through a variety of fantastic masks symbolizing animal and ancestral spirits invoked in an all-embracing life of rituals, incantations, divinations, protecting spirits, fertility rites, circumcision ceremonies, dance, and music, all in tune with the sun's rhythm. [**465** to **473**]

The tradition of ancient "magic drawings in the womb of the living earth" was carried forward by several cultures in one form or another and, similarly, the sun's healing and protecting powers were ascribed to them. The Navajo Indians, inhabiting the arid southwest of the United States, believe that drawing a ritualistic image of the sun in sand can cure all kinds of maladies. [**161**] In India floor-drawing is generally called *dhûli-chitra* and these "magic diagrams" came to be depicted under different names such as *kolam, alpana, rangoli, aripan, mandana, sanjhi,* and so forth. They are related to the course of the sun during the year as well as to the morning and evening sun (the two horizons). Their protective powers are ritually invoked at each sacrament of life *(samskara),* the passage from one state of life to another, such as at childbirth, at a boy's investiture with the sacred thread, at a wedding, and at other such auspicious occasions. Mostly drawn by women using wet rice paste, red vermillion, turmeric powder, and in some cases cow dung, and with the sun in an especially prominent role, taking-the-vow *(vrata)* drawings, represent the whole cosmos integrated with the sun, the moon, and the stars. Such paintings are especially popular in Mithila, Bihar, where a newly wed girl is

**81.** ***Bronze Age petroglyphs from all over the world depict connections between the sun and fecundity, as with this drawing from the Camonica valley in Italy of a male figure with the solar disc attached to his phallus.*** **(Sketch: Paul Jenkins, after Anati)**

82

expected to paint the walls of her entire bridal room [**166**] and then for a month after her marriage to draw the sun's image in front of the house every morning, noon, and evening. [**162**]

The sun in *dhûli-chitra* is not only a circle but also depicted as a square, a tradition that can be traced back to the swastika sun symbol conceived by the Indus Valley civilization (c. 2500–c. 1750 BC). Subsequently the four sides of the square Vedic altar became identified with the four directions and later personified as the four World Guardians or the Heavenly Kings (*Lokapâla* in Sanskrit). They appear on the Hindu and Buddhist temple-sculptures and reliquary objects all over Asia, such as the beautiful gilt-bronze casket now in the National Museum of Korea, Seoul. [**98**] Its abstract representation is the Chinese concept of Heaven and Earth in the shape of ritual objects of jade; the *pi*, which is circular, [**261**] and the *ts'ung*, which is externally square and internally tubular. [**262**] Shamanist drums display a similar combination of circular and square symbols of the sun. [**229**]

The baffling complexity of solar symbolism is essentially rooted in barely a handful of fundamental motifs, such as the rudimentary shapes of plain or radiate circles, and concentric circles with dots, spirals, wheels, and other nimbus-like shapes, as seen in

83

**82.** *The serpentine bodies of Fuxi and Nu-wa represent the sun and the moon in the creation myths of the Chinese Tao tradition and symbolize fecundity and renewal. Seventh-century painting on hemp from Turfan, China.* **(National Museum of Korea, Seoul)**

**83.** *The Hindu solar deity Vishnu eternally sleeps on the endless serpent Ananta in primeval waters during the periodic annihilation and renewal of the world by Agni (fire). Late seventeenth century, Buddha Nilakantha, Nepal.*

84. *A composite canine figure in gold with the sacred serpent Uraeus was found among the gold ornaments with solar symbols at Kush. The Meroitic Kingdom flourished along the River Nile from before 700* BC *to about* AD *350.*

85. *The sun symbolized by the seven-headed serpent halo of Vishnu Balarama. Sixth century. Kashmir, India.*

86. *The gigantic toads in bronze and stone squatting on the Futamigaura seashore at Ise in Japan relate the sun with water and fecundity.*

87 a

87 b

87 c

88

89

90

87 a. *Indian folk drawing depicts Sûrya Mandala with a cobra, symbolizing the sun, water, and vegetation.*

87 b. *Silver amulet of coiled serpents. Eighteenth century. Gujarat, India.*

87 c. *A fifteenth-century stone representing Saint Guga Pir in the shape of a cobra. Trivambaka, India.*

88. *Cobra-worship at the tenth-century Liugaraj temple, Bhuvaneshwar, India.*

89. *A serpent coiling around the World Mountain. Beginning of the twelfth century BC, from Susa, Mesopotamia.* **(Musée du Louvre, Paris)**

90. *Xiuhcoatl, the Aztec Serpent of Fire, AD 1500.* **(Museo Nacional de Antropologia, Mexico City)**

petroglyphs all over the world. [16, 333] Notations such as these might well have inspired the earliest forms of hieroglyphic writing or "sacred carving," which Egyptian theology traces back to Thoth (toward the end of the fourth millennium BC) and were identified with the sun god Re. In India, "cipher-shaped" *(Sunya-mûrti)* was one of the pre-Vedic names of the sun and perhaps it germinated the Indian concept of zero in mathematics. Some Chinese scholars believe that the sun images on the Neolithic pottery of the Da-wen-kou culture (4300–2500 BC) could have been the basis of primitive Chinese script. Writing, in Norse mythology, is also attributed to the wisdom of Odin's "one eye" (the sun), which enabled him to write secretly on picture-stones.

The revolutionary invention of the wheel dating back to about 3500 BC, is among the greatest technological achievements of all time, and it is possible that the idea was originally conceived from the circular image of the sun. A variety of wheel-shaped rock drawings at several Neolithic and Early Bronze Age sites show that, before the wheel was actually invented, imaginative people in Sumer might have anticipated its shape from

**91 a.** *Wood figure (ndop) of a Kuba Bushong chief, Mishoa Pelyeeng aNce, playing on a drum, a sun symbol. Late eighteenth century.* **(Museum of Mankind, London)**

**91 b.** *The blacksmith's profession is universally identified with the sun, as also represented by the eighteenth-century African Kuba-Bushong chief, Mbop Pelyeeng aNce.* **(Museum of Mankind, London)**

92

the image of the ever-rolling sun disc in the sky. Even the spoked wheel, invented around 2000 BC, was apparently designed after petroglyphs in which the circle is either crossed in the middle or actually spoked. The "chariot of the sun" notion and its mythology in most cultures appears to be its obvious corollary.

The spiral, a very common architectural motif and a popular design in art was probably derived from the antlers of quadrupeds, related to the sun. [**334**] Its fertility connotation is indicated by the incised geometric spiral designs on the back and buttocks of the female "Venus" figurines in ivory (c. 24,800 BC), found in Moravia, Czech Republic. Similar spiral sun symbols are seen elsewhere, as on ancient bronze mirrors, particularly on Honan discs from China (eighth century BC) in which dragons are interwoven with zoomorphs whose tails turn into volutes. The "mystic spiral" seen in the *ûrnâ* of the Buddha's curly hair, on the volutes of ancient gateways, as well as on the capitals of Ionic and Corinthian columns in Greece which influenced architectural designs in many countries, testifies to the motif's widespread popularity.

**92.** ***Cloud-and-lightning and sun-fire finials are depicted in this beautiful fifteenth-century frieze of a smithy in the Sanctuary of Candi Sukuh, Indonesia.*** **(Courtesy, Directorate of Museums, Jakarta)**

While artists, architects, and technicians benefited from useful ideas inspired by the sun, and prophets, such as Zoroaster and Mani, invoked the sun's divine light of virtue over the darkness of evil, great conquerors and rulers employed the spirit of solar universality in order to ensure the loyalty and undivided allegiance of their subjects. Confronted with the ever-growing number of antagonistic sects which engendered social tensions, ethnic hatred, and religious animosity, emperors such as Akhenaton in Egypt, Aurelian in Rome, Alexander the Great, Ashoka and Akbar in India, Louis XIV in France, and others—albeit widely separated in time and space—attempted in their own way to create stable governments through norms of unity symbolized by the sun. The "Sun King" of France stated that "L'Etat c'est moi," and across the Atlantic, all that lay under the sun was claimed by the "Sun King" of the Incas.

Akhenaton (c. 1353 BC) sought to unite his people under the all-embracing light emanating from his solar disc, the Aton. A hymn inscribed in the tombs at El-Amarna states: "Thou art beautiful, great, shining and high above every land, and thy rays enfold

93. *Hyacinthus, the prehistoric Greek solar deity, was killed by the envious west wind Zephyr by deflecting Apollo's discus throw as the two lovers were playing with the sun symbol. Roman copy of original Greek statue. c. fourth century* BC. **(Hermitage Museum, St. Petersburg)**

**94. Apollo Belvedere,** *a Roman copy of the original Greek statue, which was probably by Leochares. Fourth century* BC. **(Vatican Museum, Rome)**

the lands to the limit of all that thou hast made, thou being the sun and thou reachest their limits and subjectest them to thy beloved son." Akhenaton did not create a new god but rather singled out Aton from among several others, such as the hawk-headed sun god Horus. With his emphasis upon *maat*, or Truth, he created the first-ever "realistic" artistic style, at Tell-el-Amarna in Egypt, ordering the artists and craftsmen to depict faithfully what they actually saw rather than follow the tradition-bound rules and canons glorifying the Pharaoh's personality. Thus in a style associated with the sculptor Totmes, a revolutionary transformation occurred in Egyptian art in which even the peculiar, deformed physiognomy of Akhenaton himself was shown in the unique and extremely original Amarna style. [**168**] Here, artists did not confine themselves to official themes only but portrayed the king in daily life, as he caressed his wife, played with his children, or rewarded subordinates and common people. At this site the famous portrait of Nefertiti of the New Kingdom period was also excavated, showing that the queen must have been as stunningly beautiful as "truly" depicted in her portraits. [**167**]

Likewise, Alexander the Great (356–323 BC) aspired to rule the world "like the sun," especially after his conquest of Egypt, when he chose to become the "son of the Sun-god Amon." He attempted to fuse together the many different beliefs and practices existing in his rapidly growing empire, establishing or consolidating a number of Hellenistic colonies following his eastern campaigns, where he encouraged a hybrid culture and style in art. Among the artifacts excavated at Ai Khanum, on the left bank of the river Oxus (modern Amu Darya in Afghanistan), is also the beautiful Medallion of Cybele. [**170**] The plaque, made of chased silver plated with gold shows the Greek goddess of nature, Cybele, accompanying a winged victory in a chariot as they drive toward an altar on which stands a sun deity with what appears to be an hourglass. Here is a fascinating synthesis between art styles of three ancient civilizations: Cybele's Indian-style chariot is pulled by lions (instead of a quadriga), while the Greek-style Helios shines in the sky together with a moon and star conceived in the Mesopotamian fashion.

The medallion makes an interesting comparison with the seventeenth-century Indian miniature from Rajasthan; [**171**] the latter incorporates several additional ele-

95

**95.** *The rising sun-god Shamash is cutting his way through the mountains of the east on this greenstone cuneiform cylinder seal showing the major solar deities of the Akkadian dynasty, which ruled in Mesopotamia from about 2350 to 2200 BC.* **(British Museum, London)**

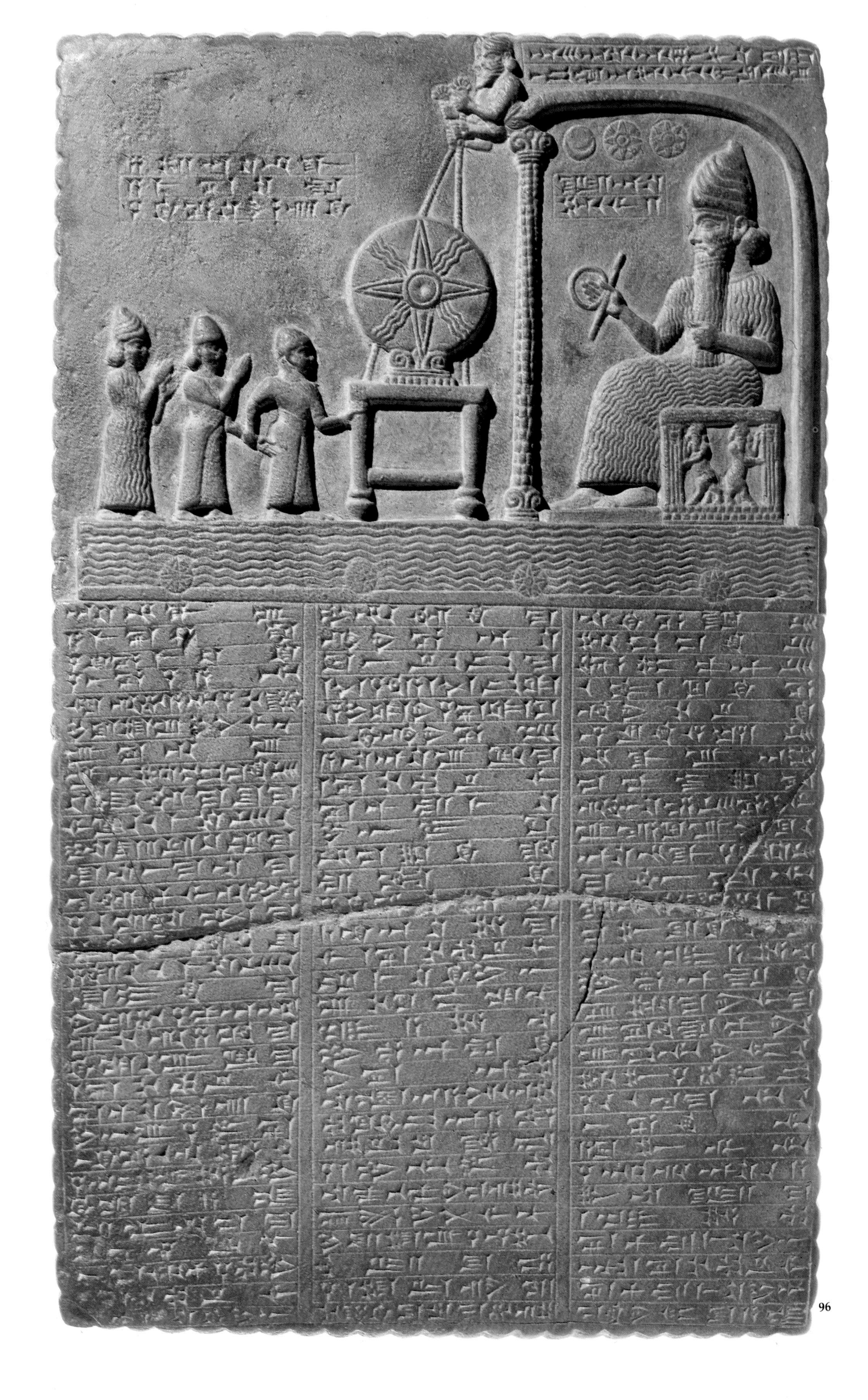



96

97

98

99

**96.** *The Babylonian King Nabu-apla-iddina worshipping the sun god Shamash in his shrine resting on the heavenly ocean. A sun disc on a stool is lowered by two gods, and smaller symbols represent the moon god, sun god, and goddess Ishtar (Venus). About 870* BC. *Sippar, Iraq.* **(British Museum, London)**

**97.** *A Semitic ritual tray with a sun emblem and mythological scenes. Phoenician (Northwest Syria). Eighth–seventh century* BC. **(Musée du Louvre, Paris)**

**98.** *The circular sun was also depicted as a square, like the Vedic altar and its four directions identified with the four World Guardians* **(Lokapalas)**, *as depicted on the Korean gilt-bronze casket.* AD *682.* **(National Museum of Korea, Seoul)**

**99.** *Laminated sun disc in gold showing the four solar deities of direction. c. sixth–seventh century* AD. **(National Museum of Costa Rica, San José)**

68
100

101

102

103

ments from Hindu mythology, such as the bull-headed Rahu (eclipse), trying to stop the sun-chariot from the rear, while Hanuman, the monkey god, holds a banner in front as he leads the carriage, the wheels of which are supported by snakes. In Asia, the number of horses pulling Sûrya's sun-chariot, was not confined to a quadriga of horses, but varied from two, [**61**] five, [**62**], or seven horses, as commonly seen in Indian sculptures and paintings.

The Mauryan emperors in India were inspired to emulate the example set by Alexander's brief incursion into India in 326 BC, which helped in reviving the ancient sun-related Vedic concepts. Chandragupta Maurya (c. 321–297 BC) cast himself in the "sun-guardian" *(Chakravartin)* image of Universal Emperor. Ashoka (d. 238 BC), the last major emperor of the Mauryan Dynasty, erected numerous pillars inscribed with sun symbols; [**173**] the Indian motif of a lotus with a thousand petals represents the immortal rays of the sun, the Egyptian lions symbolize the four quarters of the universe, the bulls and horses on its abacus are of Mesopotamian import, while the honeysuckle and acanthus leaf follow the Hellenistic style. He also installed several rock edicts, and repeatedly emphasized "unity" or "coming together" *(samavayo)* as the Imperial motto. The Roman Emperor Aurelian (AD 215–275) sought similarly to bring divergent sects and tribal minorities in his empire under the aegis of the Unconquerable Sun (Sol Invictus) and, surrounding himself with an aura of the divine sun as the Restorer of the World *(resitutor orbis)*, he convinced his armies that Sol Invictus was the principal source of his authority.

---

**100.** ***The diorite stela inscribed with the Code of Hammurabi, showing the Babylonian King before the sun god Shamash. Bas-relief from Susa. Eighteenth century*** BC. **(Musée du Louvre, Paris)**

**101.** ***The throne of the Sri Lankan Nayakkar kings is adorned with solar symbols. Eighteenth century.*** **(National Museum of Sri Lanka, Colombo)**

**102.** ***The throne, like the sun, became the creator of Pharaohs themselves, as with that of Akenaton. c. 353*** BC. **(Egyptian Museum, Cairo)**

**103.** ***A Roman throne in marble found in the shrine of Mithra. c. second century, now in the Basilica of San Clemente, Rome.***

104

105

The "Divine Sun" was at the center of the syncretic cult, Din-i-Ilahi, around which the Mughal Emperor Akbar (1542–1605), tried to rally the diverse peoples of his vast Indian empire. On the basis of ancient traditions, including the sanctity of the cow, Din-i-Ilahi encouraged the intermingling of Islamic, Hindu, Zoroastrian, Buddhist, Jain, and even Christian faiths "with the great advantage of not losing what is good in one religion while gaining whatever is better in the other," as explained by Abul Fazl, the emperor's close companion and chronicler. Akbar was influenced by the Sufi mysticism of Islam, particularly the *Ishraki*, or the "illuminist" school, which the twelfth-century visionary Shihab al-Din Suhravardi founded in Iran and on which the Zoroastrian and Manichaean adoration of the sun had left its imprint; he based his philosophy on the verses of the Qur'an in which God is qualified as "Light on Light." In pre-Islamic Central Asia the sun and the moon were worshipped in conjunction with other important deities. In the Sogdian iconography (seventh to eighth century), Khvar, the sun, was a charioteer-archer and apparently a subordinate of Nanaya, the goddess of both day and night—as indicated by the sun and moon discs she holds in her raised hands. [**343**] These pre-Islamic luminaries and their zoomorphic symbols later found their way into the Islamic arts and crafts of Iran and India.

During Akbar's time a distinctly Indian style of painting was essentially inspired by his open-ended "solar vision." It is characterized by a vivid treatment of the physical

**104.** *Elephants adorned with solar symbols are taken out annually in a religious procession in Trichurpuram, South India.*

**105.** *A marble elephant with the sun image on its forehead stands at the entrance to the palace of the Maharaja of Jaipur, India.*

**106.** *The universal association of the sun with hunting is depicted in a frieze in the Palace of the Marquis of Fronteira. AD 1670. Portugal.*

**107.** *The sun and the moon embellish the famous "hunting dishes" of the Sassanids in Iran. Third–seventh century.* **(Hermitage Museum, St. Petersburg)**

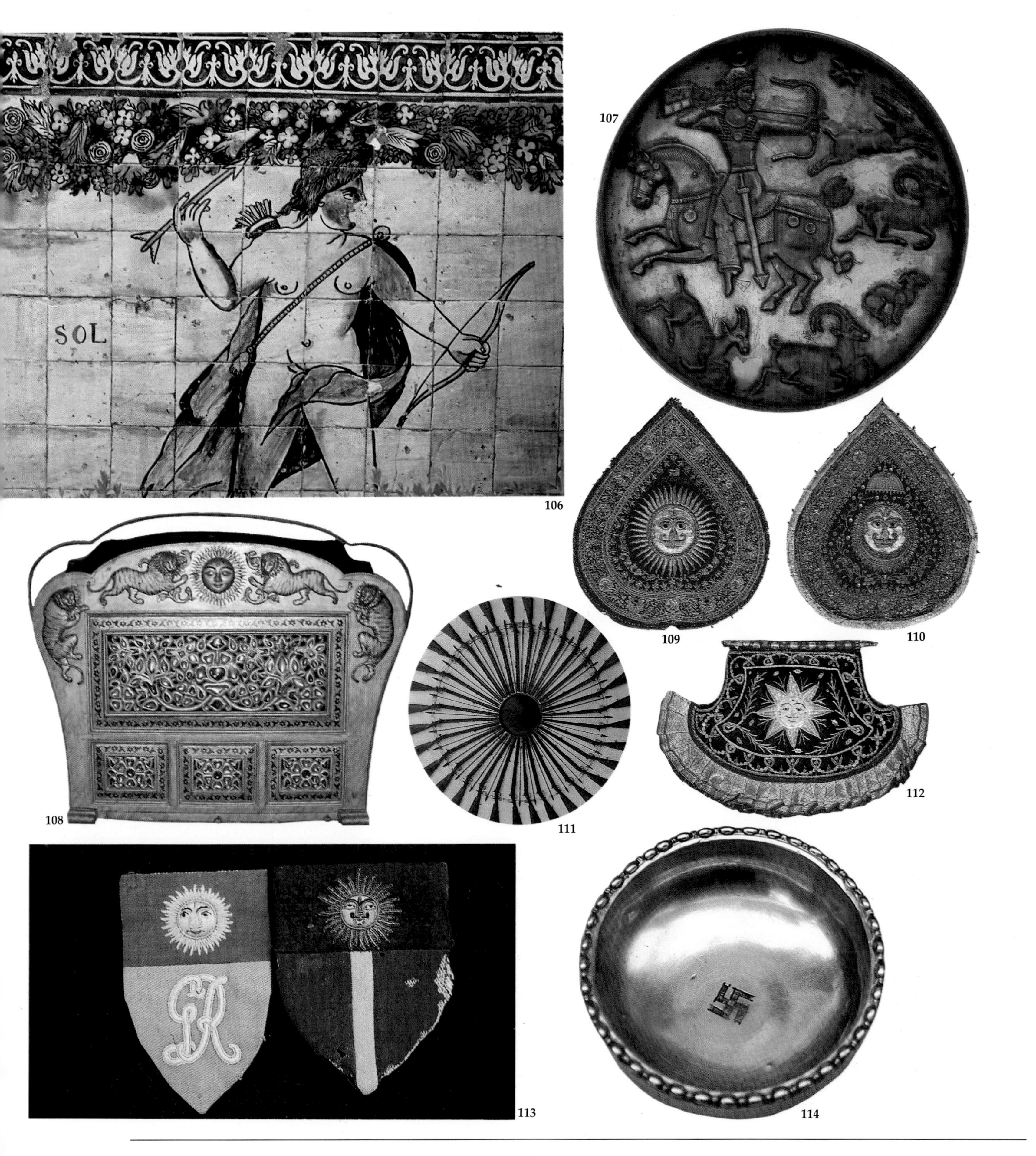


106

107

108

109

110

111

112

113

114

**108.** *"Hauda" seats on elephants in South Asia are generally decorated with solar motifs. Fifteenth century. Jaipur.*

**109,110.** *The sun and moon buntings. Eighteenth century. Udaipur, India.*

**111.** *Rifles arranged to represent the sun in the eighteenth-century Jaipur Palace, India.*

**112.** *Eighteenth-century hand-fan with silver handle. Jaipur.*

**113.** *Regal emblems of Jaipur. Eighteenth century.*

**114.** *A Roman cup with a central swastika. c. AD 230–260. Chatuzange in Gaul.* **(British Museum, London)**

115

**115.** *A circular, sun-like mirror embedded in a Pipli textile design recalls the Japanese icon of Amaterasu; it floats besides two lotuses which the sun god Sûrya holds in the nearby Konarak sun temple.*

116

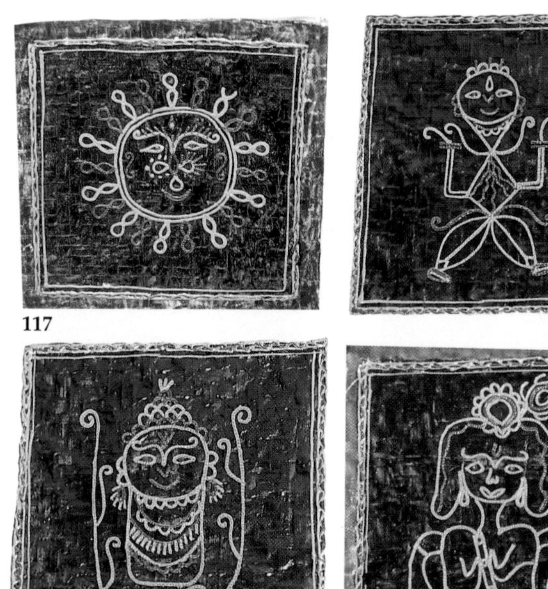

117 118 119 120

121

122

**116.** *A sun-face on a seventeenth-century silk scarf from Kullu, India.*

**117–120.** *Lacquer handicrafts, depicting the sun and solar deities. Bhuvaneshwar, India.*

**121.** *A woman at work in the village of Pipli, India.*

**122.** *Against the image of the solar deity Jaganath, a traditional Indian artisan paints the sun on the bottom of the earthenware pot "to help the fire in cooking faster."*

123

124

125

126

127

128

123–125. *Eighteenth-and nineteenth-century Suzani textiles, named after a village in Uzbekistan, are famous for their solar designs.* **(Tashkent Museum, Uzbekistan)**

126. *Stylized sun symbol on the turban of a Kyrgyz woman.*

127. *Conical hats worn by Japanese peasants symbolize the sun.*

128. *Wearing a traditional conical "hat of the sun," a bride in Kazakhstan sits beside a stream of water.*

**129 a,b.** *The ceremonial garment of the "Celestial Empress" Lin Putian, with sun symbols.* AD *1680.* **(Shrine Museum Quanzhou, China)**

**130. Creation of the World** *tapestry. Eleventh century.* **(Museo-Tesoro Catedralico, Gerona, Spain)**

**131.** *Solar tapestry created by the French artist Jean Lurçat.*

**132.** *A Latvian woman with traditional solar jewelry.*

**133,134,138,141.** *Gold ornaments with solar motifs excavated in the Kingdom of Kush, the Meroitic civilization that flourished along the River Nile from before 700 BC to about AD 350.*

**135.** *Gold necklace with pendants showing sun motifs. Mesopotamia. c. nineteenth–eighteenth century BC.* **(Metropolitan Museum of Art, New York)**

136 a,b. *Gold ornaments of Paekche kings in Korea, with solar motifs of flames and lotus leaves and buds on the top. Early sixth century.* **(Kyongju National Museum, Republic of Korea)**

137. *The headpiece, the* **bindu** *on the forehead, and the nose-ring are all sun symbols, worn in India since time immemorial.*

139,140. *Achaemenian gold ornaments with winged horned griffins and other solar symbols. Fifth–fourth century* BC. **(British Museum, London)**

142

143

142. *The great stone calendar of the Aztecs.* AD *1500.* (Museo Nacional de Antropologia, Mexico City)

143. *The Neolithic monuments of Stonehenge in England.*

144,145. *The Jaipur observatory, Jantar Mantar, was one of the five built of stone and marble by Maharaja Jai Singh II (1699–1743). Much like the Aztec and Maya calendars, some of its instruments are still used by* pandits, *wise men, to determine auspicious dates for festivals and seasonal rhythms.*

144

145

world and hence quite different from the Safavid miniatures of Iran on which Mughal painting was based. Unlike the Iranian style, in which the emphasis was on line and detail, Akbar encouraged his painters to incorporate techniques of realism and perspective which he admired in works of art imported by Christian missionaries from Europe. The "naturalistic" Mughal style can be seen in the celebrated manuscript *Hamzeh-nameh* (c. 1567), a technique in which the image acquired greater expressive power through added emphasis on mass rather than on line. [**174**] The miniature painting on ivory in which women are seen playing the game of polo also shows a new sensuous mood glorifying the female and her body, a secular style of art that audaciously ignored Islamic injunctions excluding women from such male-dominated outdoor activities. [**185**]

The shining spirit of the sun also inspired Japanese painting. The Imperial edicts of the seventh and eighth centuries which formed the basis of Japanese political, legal, and ethical values refer repeatedly to "the sun's bright, pure, honest, and sincere heart," and these virtues were also incorporated into the realm of aesthetics so that purity, directness, and brightness became the essence of Japanese art and literature. In *The Vocabulary of Japanese Aesthetics*, by Hisamatsu Sen'ichi, the quality of art is likened to "high noon on a brilliant sunny day." The auspicious image of a rising sun was often depicted on the first page of a book or print series like those designed by masters of the wood-block print, Hiroshige (1797–1858) and Eisen (1790–1848); and the picture of the sun at the end of the work was a guarantee that truth, justice, and virtue had finally triumphed. [**245**] The pervasive influence of the sun in Japanese culture is evident also in *haiku* poetry,

**146.** *Sealed with solar images of guarantee, Babylonian boundary stones, called* **kuduwu**, *were set up in temples to record land grants. This 1100 BC* **kuduwu** *is unusual, as a snake sun symbol hangs down its one side.* **(British Museum, London)**

**147.** *A commemorative stela with cuneiform inscription was set up in honor of the "dagger-bearer" of the Babylonian god Marduk. Ninth century BC.* **(British Museum, London)**

148

149

150

calligraphy, and ink-drawn scrolls, as well as in the tea ceremony, in flower arrangements, and in garden design.

In the field of architecture, too, it is impossible to encapsulate in a brief introduction the enormous influence which the sun exercised all over the world as a result of inventive genius or through interaction between different civilizations. Just as it is difficult to imagine a huge, magnificent tree actually sprouting from a tiny seed, so it is amazing how the simple sun motif in a nomadic yurt in the shape of a small circular opening in the roof ultimately developed into as grand and marvelous a source of luminosity as the one seen in the dome of Hadrian's Pantheon in Rome (AD 117–126) and its rotunda. [**175**] Apparently, the Roman baths and similar structures built to serve as tombs for pagan emperors were also "glorified yurts" and it was not until the fourth century that a Christian meaning was given to light-oriented architecture in the baptisteries and funerary chapels linked with basilican churches. The manner of orienting pagan shrines toward the sunrise was also adopted by Christian churches, built either with the altar at the east end or more accurately in the direction where the sun rose on the feast day of their patron saint. The sun also inspired the circular urban plan which encircles the central shrines in many medieval towns in Europe—as the Roman town of Bram in France (founded in AD 333). [**176**] Its plan recalls the ancient Zoroastrian townships in Central Asia, conceived as they were either on a circular design *(kukeldash)* or in the shape of a crossed-circle *(shashtepa).*

Fascinating interiors "wearing" velvet garments of sunlight can be admired also in

**148,149.** ***The seven sunrays emanating from Mithra's halo symbolize his triumph over the forces of darkness. The Latin text is a dedication by fellow priests to Sextus Pompeius Maximus. Roman period.*** **(British Museum, London)**

**150.** ***The head of the Statue of Liberty is adorned with Mithra's seven rays, and the flame she holds is also a sun symbol.***

151

Hagia Sophia in Istanbul (AD 532-537) and in a number of other monuments, such as the château of Castel del Monte, constructed by Emperor Fredrick II of Hohenstaufen (1194–1250), as well as in the famous Taj Mahal, built (1632–1654) by a consortium of architects from India, Persia, Central Asia, Turkey, and beyond. The *Casa del Sol,* built by the Solis family in the Spanish town of Cáceres, and its sun emblem, [**520**] is another beautiful product of architectural interaction among different cultures. One of the Solis ancestors in the sixteenth century had served the Spanish Crown in Peru and on his return from Tahuantinsuyu built "the House of the Sun." "Our eyes are constructed to see things in terms of light," commented the architect Le Corbusier; and in a manifesto of the Athens Charter, formulated in 1940 at the International Congress of Architecture, "a place in the sun" is recognized "as among the fundamental human rights of every individual."

"The Sun King" of France, Louis XIV (1638–1715)—whom Voltaire compared to the Egyptian Sesostris kings—was another outstanding ruler who effectively used sun imagery and also built the great palace of Versailles and its enchanting gardens. Marly, one of his favorite palaces, represents the solar system, with one central building representing the sun, surrounded by satellite pavilions. The monarch glorified the myth of Apollo and, dressed as the sun deity, often appeared with his baroque entourage at the lavish feasts he organized in the vast gardens of Versailles. A sculpture of Apollo stands in the grotto of Tethys, much like the king himself who was similarly served by his mistresses. [**177**] Another figure of the sun seated in a chariot is also said to represent the king. [**178**] In his *Memoirs for the Instruction of the Dauphin,* the king states the reason why the sun emblem was chosen: "It is because in constantly producing life, joy, and activity everywhere, the sun never departs or deviates from its steady and invariable course."

**151.** ***The agate cylinder-seal depicts the Achaemenid Persian King Darius the Great (522–485 BC) hunting lions under the winged disc of the Zoroastrian god Ahura-Mazda.*** **(British Museum, London)**

154

**154.** *The monolith called* **Bocca della Verità** *is a massive marble sun disc. People who tell lies are advised not to insert their hand in the Mouth of Truth for the "avenging justice of the sun" will bite it off. c. second century* BC. *The church of Santa Maria in Cosmedin, Rome.*

**155.** *The sun's "avenging justice" in Hindu mythology is portrayed by Nara-simha (man-lion) Avatara, who appeared from a pillar and killed the tyrant king for not letting his son Prahalada worship the solar deity Vishnu. Changu Narayan, Nepal.*

156

157 158

A detailed account of the sun temple at Konarak in India by Akbar's chronicler, Abul Fazl, perhaps inspired him to build Diwan-i-Khas, the magnificent palace at Fatehpur Sikri; its circular throne represents the sun from which four diagonally arranged passages with pillars, symbolizing planets, fan out towards the four quarters. Akbar's son and successor Jahangir (1569–1627) commissioned a Frenchman, Augustine Heriart, to design and build for him a royal throne on which, as Heriart wrote to one of his friends, "the King will sit once a year when the sun enters the House of Aries." He was rewarded with a house, horse, and stable and perhaps also given some gold coins with the sun's imprint. [**181**] The sun-and-lion motif engraved on Jahangir's coins is seen also on monuments in Samarkand and Bukhara, for the Mughals, who were descended from the Timurids, were in continuous contact with that part of the world. [**180**]

The sport of polo, which was apparently known in some form to the Persians at the time of Darius I (reigned 522–486 BC) and played in India since the time of the Huns (fifth century), was restored to its original "sun game"significance by Akbar. Known as the *Chaughan*, it was played during his time with a "lighted fire-ball" *(chakkar)*. [**184**] Agile horsemen riding swift horses moved the "sun-ball" across the "sky-field" and scoring a

**156.** ***The Chinese solar deity Kouan-yin, with a thousand hands and eyes, is located in the sun.*** *AD* ***981. Dun-huang, China.*** **(Musée Guimet, Paris)**

**157, 158.** ***Sûryaprabha, the Buddhist sun deity and Chandraprabha, the moon deity, from the Tokoin temple, Japan. Twelfth century.*** **(Fukuoka Art Museum, Japan)**

goal was equated with the triumph of light over darkness, good over evil. In fact the ball is very much a sun symbol in all such sports as football, hockey, basketball, and cricket. The very popular game of baseball is related to the sun in the sundial-like shape and pattern of its circular field, as well as in its rules of play and scoring. Like all other sports, baseball also embodies the sun's seasonal cycles in much the same way as ancient ceremonial contests were held as a part of fertility rites.

The sun's association with sport can be traced far back to the "epic" of the Sumerian hero Gilgamesh, inscribed in cuneiform writing on clay tablets (c. 2100 BC). It narrates how the sporting equipment—a stick and a ring or a ball—which Gilgamesh had carved out of an uprooted tree, had fallen into the netherworld as he began oppressing his people by repeated athletic competitions, and how eventually it was the sun god who opened a hole in the ground in order to recover them. The Olympic torch which the runner carries to mark the sun's cyclic movement throughout the "Olympiad," the four-year period until the next games, is also related to the sun's cyclic rhythm. First celebrated in the eighth century BC at Olympia in Greece, the games were ceremonial contests in honor of Zeus, the thunderbolt-hurling sky-and-weather god. They are said

159

**159.** *Heart of Sûrya. Indian miniature painting. Maharatha school.* AD *1725.* **(Bharat Kala Museum, Varanasi, India)**

**160.** *The sun and the moon are among the gods paying obeisance to the "Thousand Buddhas" in the Raja Mahavihara rock-temple. Eighteenth century. Dambulla, Sri Lanka.*

160

to to have been founded by Herakles in Olympia, while the Pythian Games at Delphi were related to Apollo. [**186, 187**]

As in sport, the sun is omnipresent in practically all aspects of life, whether it be art, architecture, literature, philosophy, religion, festivals, folklore, dance, or music. Every morning a "pagan" god of the day wakes us up, for the Romans in the early centuries of the Christian era named each day after the seven planets—Sun, Moon, Mars, Mercury, Jupiter, Venus, and Saturn. Monday was the moon's day, and with the assimilation of Anglo-Saxon and Scandinavian pagan gods, Tyr, one of the oldest gods of Norse mythology, became identified with Mars and thus we have *Tys dagr* or Tuesday; Wednesday is derived from Woden, also known as Odin; and Thor, the thunder god of the early Germanic peoples became synonymous with Thursday, equated as he was with the Roman god Jupiter; while Friday is named after Frigg, the wife of Odin and the mother of another pagan god, Balder. The day of Saturn or Saturday was followed by Sunday, the day of rest and recreation, as it is observed today. The Romans identified the seven planets with the sun's seven rays emanating from Mithra's halo and thus elevated the sanctity of number *seven* to the level of other auspicious numbers such as the sun's *one*

---

**161.** *A Navajo medicine man curing a sick child by drawing a sand-painting of the sun, in the arid south-west of the United States.* **(American Museum of Natural History, New York)**

**162–165.** *The "magic diagrams" of the sun and other planets (163), drawn on the floor or walls of houses are invoked for therapeutic purposes or for blessing each sacrament of life such as weddings (164), childbirth (165), and so on.*

166

eye of Truth and Justice, the *two* horizons, the *three* worlds, and the *four* directions.

Similar beliefs were cherished by other cultures all over the world, such as the seven steps of Ziggurats; the Babylonian belief in hebdomadism; the holy number seven in Mithraic initiation in pre-Islamic Iran; *saptami*, or the seventh day of the month of *Magha* (January) when the devotees in India go to bathe in one of "the seven holy rivers" *(sapta-sindhava)*; the seven wheels of the solar deity Pûshan's chariot; the seven tongues of Agni—a tradition which created the cult of the seven sisters, seven mothers, and the seven virgins in South Asia. The seven superimposed "umbrellas" over Buddhist stupas, represent the succession of seven heavens, as do the seven sacred steps of the Buddha. There are seven notches of shamanic rituals; and the nocturnal sun god Jaguar of the Underworld in Maya culture was identified with the number seven.

"God created seven firmaments" according to the Qur'an, and the Zoroastrian Parsi community in India believes that the "seven holy beings" *(Amesha Spentas)* emanated from Ahura Mazda "like torches lit from a torch." The Jewish seven-branched candelabrum known as the *menorah* was similarly interpreted by the Jewish philosopher Philo of Alexandria (c. 30 BC–AD 50) as the paths of the seven planets around the sun; for the lamp

**166.** ***"Dhûli-Chitra" drawings of the sun are especially popular in Mithila, Bihar, where a newlywed girl is expected to paint the walls of her entire bridal room.*** **(Crafts Museum, New Delhi)**

**152.** *The granite stone relief depicting Mani against a Turfan-style aureole was carved during the Yuan Dynasty (AD 1279–1368) in the temple of Cao'an near Quanzhou in China.*

**153.** *Mani is still worshipped in the temple of Cao'an but some Chinese devotees confuse the prophet with Sakyamuni Buddha.*

167

168

on the vertical shaft of the lampstand represents the Light of God from which the other six derive their reflected glory. The *menorah* itself was fashioned on Mesopotamian models, which probably inspired Philo in his attempt to unite the Mosaic law and Plato's Greek philosophy with Oriental thought, based on the universality of solar cultures.

Most pageants and festivals all over the world can be traced back either directly to the sun or indirectly to it through agricultural and fertility rites, even though, over a period of time, their individual features have become blurred and diffused and, in some cases, completely reinterpreted. In a place called Tsutsu, on the Japanese island of Tsushima, a special kind of red rice is cultivated, and the rice-field is regarded as the divine body of the solar deity Tentô. A bag full of rice is ritually hung from the ceiling of a house for worship, and every year it is taken down and carried in a procession to another house for a similar ceremony. The head of the village carrying the bag on his back covers it with his own garments as if it were a baby and, as the holy procession passes through the streets, people kneel down and pray with folded hands.

Processions involving animal and reptile solar symbols in many Asian, African, and native American societies, have equivalents in Europe as well; until recently a fat ox was paraded through the streets of Paris on Mardi Gras (Shrove Tuesday), like Roman

**167–168.** *The Egyptian king Akhenaton created a new Amarna style in art based on* **maat**, *or Truth of the Sun, ordering artists not to glorify even the Pharaoh's own personality. Thus his deformed physiognomy was depicted as such, and the queen Nefertiti was portrayed as beautiful, as she truly was. c. 1360* BC. **(Ägyptisches Museum, Berlin)**

**169.** *Pharaoh Akhenaton sought to unite his people under the all-embracing light emanating from his solar disc, the Aton. c. 1353* BC. **(Egyptian Museum, Cairo)**

sacrificial processions. The once popular carnival giants in Douai and Dunkirk in France, and Antwerp in Belgium, actually originated in sacrificial rituals of ancient solar cults, in which huge osier frames of greenery were carried—much like the Jack-in-the-green-basket-clad figures in English May Day parades (which are essentially fertility celebrations). Christians in Wales adopted another pagan ritual of fertility and conception in which the link between the sun and water was invoked by "walking sunwise" around a holy well three times, just as pagan pageants such as the Bacchanalia, Lupercalia, and Saturnalia were precursors of the carnival processions that precede Lent in many Roman Catholic countries.

Sun-related rituals were also performed in order to "encourage and assist" the sun when it seemed to "hesitate and waver" at the turn of the seasons (solstice) and to quell

169

170

**170.** ***The Medallion of Cybele, excavated at the Hellenistic City of Ai Khanum (Afghanistan), combines Greco-Roman, Mesopotamian, Persian, and Indian art styles, which Alexander the Great (356–323 BC) created as he aspired to rule "like the sun."***

171

the fear that it might be extinguished during an eclipse. The Ojibway Indians of North America and the Sencis in eastern Peru shoot burning arrows at the sun in order to rekindle its darkening orb during an eclipse, and the Plains Indians of North America erect and dance around a central pole symbolizing the sun's power. In some agricultural communities in South Asia, the *Cadak*, or hook-swinging ceremony, is still performed, in which a man hooked to a tall pole swings around it as an act of magic in order to help the sun to move from its position in Sagittarius to Capricorn. In French villages in the Thur and Thann valleys, nine-feet-tall towers of fire *(chavandes)* are built in order to provide the sun with sufficient fire energy, thus enabling it to resume its journey around the earth during the critical rest periods before changing its direction from the longest night (December 21) to the shortest (June 21). [**445, 446**] A "helping hand" during midsummer day is similarly extended in Slav, Baltic, and other northern cultures where the custom of dancing around a pole or jumping over fire is now identified with the Christian message. [**415**]

Solar rites in Aquitaine in the fourth century, in which a flaming sun-wheel was rolled down a hillside, were also adapted by Christianity and celebrated as the birth of St. John the Baptist. Syncretic assimilation between pagan solar festivals and Christian feasts is especially popular in Latin American countries. The ancient Inca sun festival of Inti-raymi, marking the start of the summer solstice, has come to be identified with Corpus Christi and St. John. The two events fall at about the same time, and are celebrated with a great deal of fanfare, songs, and dances in colorful costumes. [**192**] The presence of the Andean sun god is also felt in secular functions, as it was in the spectacular fashion show arranged by a modern American fashion house at one of the

**171.** ***The Medallion of Cybele makes an interesting comparison with seventeenth-century Indian miniature painting from Rajasthan, in which Sûrya replaces Cybele, besides incorporating several elements of later Hindu mythology.*** **(Santi Choudhary Collection, Jaipur)**

172

173

**172.** *Signs of the Zodiac inspired the Akbar school of miniature painting, as depicted by a ram, the sign of Aries. Sixteenth century.* **(Bharat Kala Museum, Varanasi, India)**

**173.** *The capital of commemorative pillars erected by the Mauryan emperor Ashoka is a composite solar symbol deriving its style from several cultures. Sarnath, India. c. 240 BC.* **(Sarnath Museum, India)**

174

ancient sun-temple ruins in Ecuador. [193] The scenario was inspired by the magnificent golden mask of the Inca sun god, now exhibited in the Archaeological Museum of the Central Bank of Ecuador in Quito. [511]

In Russia the solar deity Yaril is celebrated during the Maslenitsa feast, as well as at another equally popular spring festival connected with the fertility rite, when a maiden dressed in white with a wreath on her head rides a white horse through a sown field while dancers in procession sing praises in honor of the sun god. [194] The white horse is linked to the cult of the sun in the Slav tradition as well, and it is believed that in the past a naked woman used to ride the horse—much like the legendary Lady Godiva who rode through the crowded marketplace of Coventry in England (1057). The Godiva Procession is still held every seven years, as a part of the Coventry Fair. One of Francisco de Goya's sketches, *Disparate Desenfrenado,* [196] in which the horse (symbolizing the sun) appears to be undressing a woman on its back, perhaps belongs to the same tradition.

The Romans in their religion of Sol Invictus held a colorful festival on the day of the winter solstice because the increase in the length of the day was regarded as the time of life's renewal, comparable to the rebirth of the sun god Mithra. It was in place of the Day of the Invincible Sun *(Dies Invicti Solis)* festival—introduced by Emperor Aurelian in Rome in the third century—that the birth of Jesus Christ, the "sun of righteousness"

**174.** ***Akbar's "solar vision" created the celebrated manuscript* Hamzeh-nameh *(c. 1567), with added emphasis on mass rather than line, as seen in* The Prince Worshipping the Sun. (Museum für augewandte Kunst, Vienna)**

175

**175.** ***The nomadic*** **yurt** ***inspired "the sun" in the dome of Hadrian's pantheon and its rotunda. Rome.*** **AD** ***117–126. Painting by Giovanni Paolo Pannini. c. 1740.*** **(National Gallery of Art, Washington, D.C., Samuel H. Kress Collection)**

(Mal. 4:2), came to be celebrated as Christmas. The gifts and seasonal greetings which jolly Santa Claus brings to children do not come from Christ's birthplace in Judaea but from the opposite direction, toward the North Pole. That is why opposition by religious orthodoxy to celebrating pagan festivals by proxy continued as late as the seventeenth century; in Calvinist Geneva, anyone celebrating Christmas was imprisoned and in the British colonies of America a Massachusetts magistrate proclaimed a law (1640) levying a five-shilling fine on such culprits.

The halo, now taken so much for granted in art, is also a gift of pagan artists, who first conceived the figure of the sun in human form, as seen in numerous petroglyphs. [**16, 17, 18**] The "visage" of the sun on rock drawings appears to have been replaced subsequently by actual faces of holy personages, the sun-face receding to become the halo. Originally only representations of solar deities, such as the Babylonian Shamash and the Sumer-

**176**

***176.** The sun determined circular habitations and the orientation of buildings, such as the Roman town of Bram in France, founded in AD 333.*

177

ian Asakku, were depicted with radiate heads. The mannerism was later adopted in Hellenistic and Roman sculpture as well, portraying Greek Helios and Roman Sol Invictus with a halo, before the Roman emperors themselves came to be depicted with the sun disc. By then Asian cultures were familiar with the halo, but its popularity grew with the creation of the first Gandhara-style image of the Buddha under Greco-Roman influence. Earlier the sun (as a swastika) was depicted on the Buddha's foot-impressions [**286**] as an iconographic proxy, before his figure was created in the first century. Hindu iconography elaborated it further by identifying Vishnu's nimbus with the hood of the serpent with seven heads (like the seven rays emanating from Mithra's halo) as seen in Vishnu Balarama, a fifth-century Kashmiri bronze. [**85**]

Early Christian art avoided the halo, as clerics such as Clement of Alexandria, Origen, and Epiphanius objected to its pagan origin. But eventually from about the middle of the fourth century, Christ was allowed to wear a crown of sun rays, somewhat like the Roman emperors. Around the sixth century, the Virgin Mary and other Christian saints came to be depicted with haloes, but opposition to the use of the halo continued as late as the ninth century—until Carolingian art came into vogue and pagan sun symbols became identified with the Christian message. As seen in several manuscripts and their jewelled ivory-and-gold bindings, the nimbus now became fully accepted as the symbol of spiritual luminosity. [**197, 198**] This style of realistically rendered supernatural light in

**177.** ***A sculpture of Apollo stands in the grotto of Tethys in the gardens of Versailles, built by the Sun King of France, Louis XIV (1638–1715).***

art became popular all over Europe, particularly in Byzantine and Russian icons, as well as in Spanish Christian art following several centuries of Moorish domination. With its emphasis on movement, the vigorous style set the tone of early-twelfth-century Spanish Romanesque sculpture, best known through such monuments as the portal of Las Platerias in the Cathedral of Santiago de Compostela and the tympanum and capitals of the Church of St. Isidoro, Leon. Oriental influences are evident in the strong features on the faces of the sun and the moon, comparable to those of Christ and other personages seen in the bas-relief, The Descent from the Cross, [**200**] and also from the use of the black lignite fossil stone called *azabache*, a Spanish word of Arabic origin.

During this period the ancient Paleo-Christian personage Elijah or Ilya (c. ninth century) came to be venerated in place of the lightning-wielding solar deity Perun (Perkunas of the Lithuanians) [**201**]; in Byzantium his name Ilyos blended with Gelyos, the ancient sun god. Legend has it that Eliyyahu, the Hebrew prophet, also recognized by Islam, remained in dire seclusion in a cave (like the one of Amaterasu) where he was fed by a crow (Chinese "spirit of the sun"), until an angel showed him the way to Heaven in a fiery chariot (of Helios), drawn by fiery steeds. The theme is often depicted in Byzantine and Russian icons as well as in Palekh *papier-mâché* artifacts, combining both secular and Christian motifs. The Russian Palekh art forms originated in the center of the Vladimir Suzdal estate in the seventeenth century and derive their inspiration from Old

**178.** ***Helios in his sun chariot at Versailles is also said to represent the Sun King of France.***

179

180

181 a b

Slavonic folklore in which the sun god Yaril was "the giver of life and bounty."

The changing perception is demonstrated by the "christening" of the polychrome mosaic representing the sun god Helios as Christo Sole. [**204**] The image was discovered in 1574 during excavations of the second-century pagan tombs beneath the basilica of St. Peter in the Vatican. Wearing a Greek tunic, "Christ the Sun" stands with his cloak flying, in a chariot drawn by white horses (quadriga), depicted against a nimbus from which seven sun rays shoot out. The pagan origin of the mausoleum (built by the parents of the deceased Julius Tarpeianus) is evident also in its cinerarium and the grapevine decorations associated with Dionysus. The basilica of St. Clemente in Rome was also built over a second-century pagan shrine in the basement of which a statue depicting the birth of Mithra still stands alongside the sun deity killing a bull. The aura of the sun is also very visible in the twelfth-century basilica built over the Mithra shrine in which the Cross of Christ is depicted with birds and surrounded by other sun motifs on the walls and floor. [**203, 205**]

By the twelfth century, the movement called "European Humanism" succeeded in "externalizing" the nature of the sun so that it began shining once again, sparkling with the freshness and beauty of earthly life while at the same time delighting in God's cosmic glory. Its forerunners were intellectuals such as Alain de Lille, Bernard of Sylvestris, and John of Salisbury. Later the comparative freedom of expression won by artists, writers, and poets during the Renaissance further strengthened the exalted status of the sun that it had enjoyed in the Orient as well as in Italy during the Roman period. Its parallel in

**179,180.** *The sun-and-lion motif depicted on the eighteenth-century Shirdar Madrasa gateway is an ancient sun symbol, first seen at Mohenjo-daro in the Indus Valley.*

**181 a,b.** *The sun-and-lion motif is also engraved on the gold coins of the Mughal emperor Jahangir (1569–1627).* **(Bharat Kala Museum, Varanasi, India)**

Asia was the Sufi mysticism of Islam which interacted also with similar *bhakti* ideas in India, as in the writings of both male and female poet-saints, such as Mirabai, Kabir, and Nanak, who rejected sectarian worship of God and upheld secular ideals in a simple, comprehensible vernacular rather than highbrow Sanskrit. The mystic Chaitanya in Bengal (fifteenth to sixteenth centuries) exalted the passionate yearning of a woman for her beloved, while his contemporary Vallabha delighted in the exploits of the divine lover Krishna (Vishnu's incarnation)—thus giving life to a new surge of superb art.

In Europe the adoration of the sun by Romantic artists such as J.M.W. Turner, Philipp Otto Runge, and Eugène Delacroix, to name but a few, laid the foundations of the Impressionist school of painting. The sun-drenched landscapes of Turner (1775–1851) were influenced not only by Claude Lorrain (1600–1682), the greatest master of ideal-landscape painting, but also by the poems of John Milton and James Thomson. Echoing Milton's "May I Sing to Thee?" Thomson extolled the sun in numerous passages of *Spring and Summer*—how at sunrise the sun lit up the "dew-bright earth" and colored the sky at sunset—an atmosphere beautifully depicted in Turner's paintings in which the sun mysteriously emerges from clouds or mist in the colorful splendor of dawn and dusk. The German painter Runge (1777–1810), overcame the *Melancholia* [**210**] of his compatriot Albrecht Dürer (1471–1528), and delighted instead in the separation of light from dark. He was inspired by St. John's description of the revelation as "the light shining in darkness," and equated the Holy Trinity with the three prime colors—blue, red, and yellow.

---

**182,183.** ***Gold medal (1633) by Nicolas Briot, issued to mark the return to London of Charles I of Great Britain (1625–1649).*** **(Sotheby's Collection, New York)**

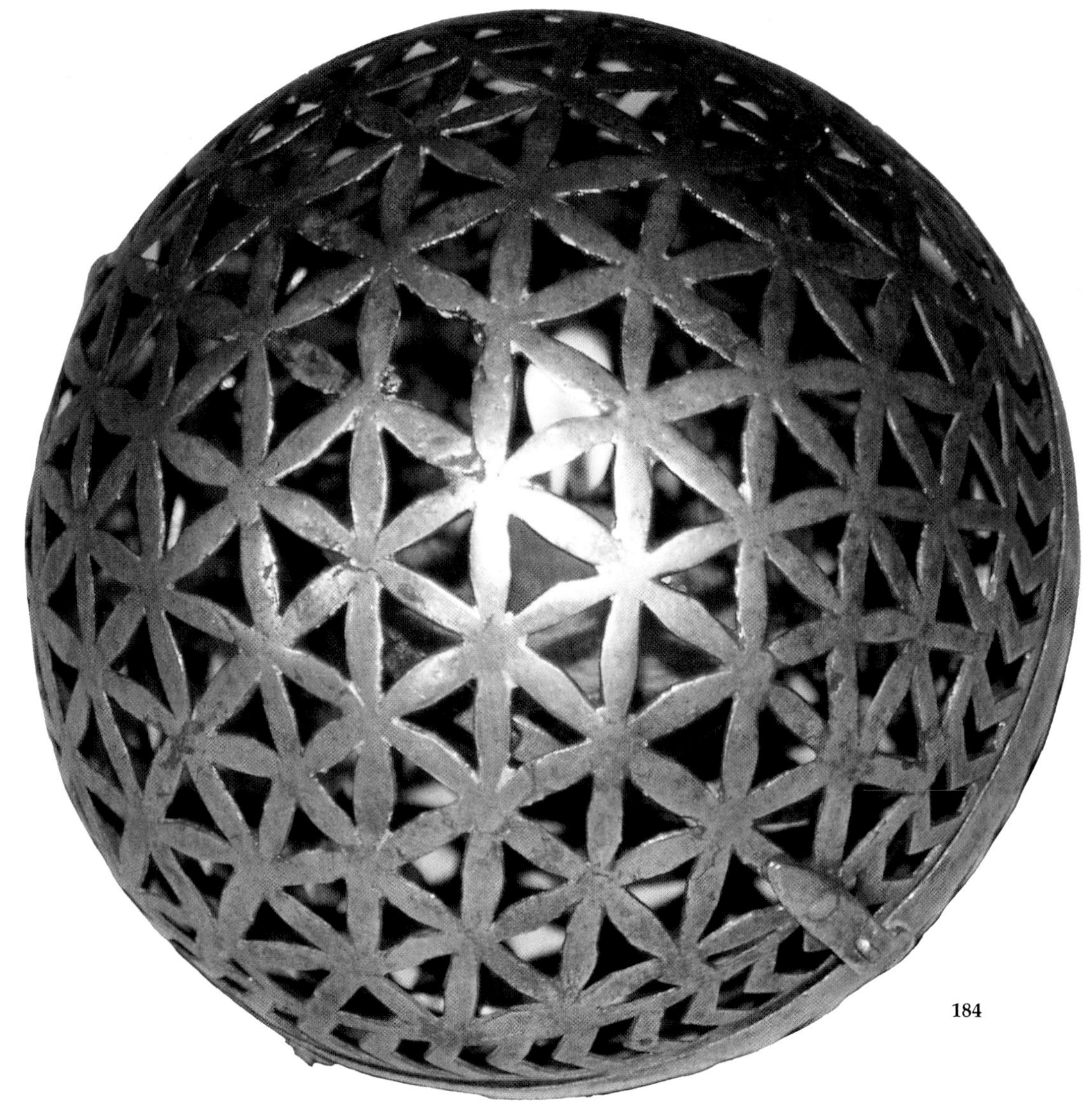

184

185

**184.** *The "sun game" of polo was actually played with an ignited "sun ball" during Akbar's time (1542–1605).* **(Sawai Man Singh Museum, Jaipur, India)**

**185.** *A Rajasthan-school miniature painting on ivory showing women playing polo. Seventeenth century.* **(Maharaja Sawai Man Singh II Museum, Jaipur, India)**

186

187

**186,187.** ***The sun, moon, and other planets float overhead at the 1992 Barcelona Olympic games. The sun's association with sports predates the deities Herakles and Apollo in Greece, as is evident from the epic tale of the Sumerian hero Gilgamesh (c. 2100 BC).***

189

**188.** *Wall painting (1810), depicting the seven planets worshipping Sûrya, as his sun chariot is driven by his charioteer Aruna.* **(Traditional Jaipur house of Santi Choudhary, India)**

**189.** *The sun chariot of Sûrya. Indian miniature painting. Mewar school, eighteenth century.*

The bold initiative taken by post-Renaissance painters thus released the sun's spectrum of colors from the bondage of medieval orthodoxy, producing a number of Impressionist painters obsessed with the sun who, like Georges Seurat and Paul Signac, sought to distinguish rays of the sun through the so-called "Divisionist technique." Camille Pissarro (1830–1903) also came under their sway as seen in his *Winter Sunset at Eragny.* [**209**] Its natural development was a marvelous new current of Expressionism in modern art as interpreted by some of the greatest painters, such as Vincent Van Gogh (1853–1890). [**212**] The trend in painting that gave priority to color for its own sake came to be called "Orphism" by the French poet Guillaume Apollinaire (1912), and among the leaders of this style of abstract Cubism was Robert Delaunay who painted *Simultaneous Composition: Sun Disks,* the cosmic aura of which is effectively enhanced by the circular format of the painting. [**211**]

Throughout history, the sun's image remained central to the heart of world literature. A paradigm attributed to the Sumerian priestess Enheduanna, history's earliest known author (c. 2300 BC), envisaged paradise as "the place where the sun rises." From Homer's *Odyssey* and Sophocles' *Œdipus Rex* to Dante's *Divine Comedy,* the sun is the leitmotiv of European literature: in Milton's *Comus,* Cyrano de Bergerac's *The Other World,* John Keats's *Ode to Apollo,* Marcel Proust's *A la Recherche du Temps Perdu,* Charles Dickens's *A Christmas Carol,* Bram Stoker's *Dracula,* Ernest Hemingway's *The Sun Also Rises,* to mention but a few. Eleven days before Johann W. Goethe died (March 22, 1822), he spoke in the same breath of Christ and the sun as the most sublime revelations of godliness: "If you ask me whether it be in my nature to show him [Christ] adoring reverence, then I say: Thoroughly! I bow before him as the divine revelation of the highest principle of morality. And if you ask me whether it be in my nature to revere the sun, then I say again: Thoroughly! For it is likewise a revelation of the most high and to be sure the most powerful one granted us earthly children to perceive. I worship in it the light and the creative power of God, by which alone we live, act and exist, as well as all plants and animals with us."

Goethe expressed similar ideas in his greatest drama, *Faust,* the second part of which he completed just before his death. His adoration of the sun had much to do with his prodigious knowledge of world literature and philosophy as, for example, the writings of Kalidasa, whom Goethe admired as an outstanding Indian poet and dramatist. One of the "nine gems" at the court of the fabulous King of Ujjain, Vikramaditya, "sun of valor," Kalidasa's Sanskrit writings such as *Garland of the Seasons,* also inspired Max Muller and his controversial belief that all solar myths could be traced back to Sanskrit originals.

*The Sun* (1920) by D. H. Lawrence is a modern version of the sun mythology as an emblem of the life force of fertility behind the principle of resurrection and renewal through sexual awakening. In this charming story, set in a Mediterranean resort, Lawrence poignantly describes the feeling of an exhausted American housewife as she encounters the sun, personified as the warm, unselfish lover: "The sun lifted himself naked and molten, sparkling over the sea's rim. Juliet lay in her bed and watched him rise. It was as if she had never seen the naked sun stand up pure upon the sealine, shaking the night off himself." It is the kind of feeling one experiences looking at the lavish carvings of *mithuna,* or the "state of being a couple," depicted on the walls of medieval temples in India; for example, the exceptionally frank, erotic sculptures seen on

---

**190. Birth of the Sun and Triumph of Dionysus.** *Painting by Corrado Giaquinto (1700–1765).* **(Museo del Prado, Madrid)**

190

191

the walls of the sun temples at Khajuraho and at Konarak. [**213** to **216**] This tradition became identified with Tantric mysticism in South Asia, and its Buddhist counterpart is the Yab-Yum divine couple, symbolizing the cosmic union of the sun and the moon, heaven and earth. [**218**] The Chinese depicted the two complementary forces or principles in an abstract sun-disc design called the Yin-Yang. [**219, 220**]

How ancient traditions in widely diverse regions of the world interacted and themes repeatedly re-emerged in different civilizations is shown in the sphere of music as well. Among the most ancient musical instruments are the flute and the drum. The flute, as a phallic symbol, is universally identified with the male, while the drum represents the female's womb; together they symbolize the sun and hence fecundity, happy life, and rebirth. The flute was used for virginity tests in cultures as remote as those of the Panamanian Indians and the ancient Greeks. Its aphrodisiac power over women was widely employed by the cowherd Krishna, the Hindu solar deity, [**222**] in order to lure milkmaids—just as the Bacchantic followers of Dionysus danced by torchlight to the rhythm of his flute and *tympanon* (kettledrum).

In China the connection between the sun, water, and fertility was represented through the well-known bronze drums, the earliest of which, with similar solar motifs as on bronze mirrors, were excavated at Chuxiong in Yunnan province (seventh century

**191.** ***Donning robes with a sun emblem, the New Year spring festival ceremony is performed by priests in the temple of the "Celestial Empress" Lin Putian. Quanzhou, China.***

192

BC). But it was not until the first century BC that the image of the shining sun as such came to be depicted in the center surrounded by a number of toads (representing water) squatting at the outer rim of the drum. [**230**] In Africa drums were also associated with the sun as seen in the wooden Kuba drums decorated with sun *(phila)* motifs. [**76**] The drum or tambourine of the shaman in Siberia is a major source of information concerning solar symbols. The circular form of the drum symbolizes the universe, which is divided into three parts: Heaven, earth, and the Underworld. The sun and the moon live in the upper world and can be invoked by the sound of the drum which is painted with solar and zodiacal symbols. [**229**]

The flute and drum are the principal musical accompaniment to sun-dances in most cultures, which are performed generally with four dancers representing the four quarters of the universe. [**223**] In Japan the four dancers, *yorozuimai*, perform with similar musical instruments at ceremonial dances called *bugaku*. [**227**] At the Inti-raymi sun-festival of the Incas in Peru the traditional flute, the *pincullo*, with two holes at the top and two below, also represents the four directions; it is played in tune with the booming sound of the leather-covered drum called the *tinya*. The festival coincides with the harvest season and young unmarried damsels vie with each other in order to become pregnant by the four principal dancers called "sons of the sun," and identified as angels of the fertilizing

**192.** *Inti-Raymi sun-festival in Peru combines Inca solar traditions with Christian beliefs.*

**193.** *Following pages. A fashion show among ancient sun-temple ruins in Quito, Ecuador.*

194

195

union between the sun and the earth. [228] The Maya also believed that their sun god Kinich Ahau was the personification of the number four.

The folk culture inspired such Andean musical works of the late nineteenth century as Valle-Riestra's *Ollanta* and Vicente Stea's *Aboriginal Symphony*. Daniel Alomia Robles also used folk material in his works, such as the *Hymn to the Sun*, incorporating local solar motifs into Western forms. The flute's cosmic significance is evident also in European classical works as, for example, Mozart's opera, *The Magic Flute*. In it, two "realms" are separated by light and darkness, and the struggle is to possess the powerful Sevenfold Solar Circle which the "husband" of the Queen, ruling the Realm of Night, had bequeathed to Sarastro (Zoroaster?), high priest of the cult of Isis and Osiris. The Queen is assisted by three ladies (the Trinity) who kill the serpent pursuing the young prince Tamino and give him the magic flute. Tamino's name recalls that of Tammuz, the Syrian and Phoenician equivalent of Adonis, a beautiful youth very much like Orpheus and Krishna. The magic flute played by Tamino finally helps him and Pamina, his beloved and daughter of the Queen, to pass through the trial of fire and water. Mozart's genius has beautifully created through music the fire-water trial of the flute, and the composition is as enchanting, though differently interpreted, as Haydn's *Creation*, in which

**194. The Song of the Sun God Yaril** ***(1954), painted by B.M. Yermolaev. The traditional Palekh miniatures in lacquer originated at the Vladimir Suzdal estate in eighteenth-century Russia.*** **(Museum of Decorative Arts, Moscow)**

**195.** ***Based on Slavonic folklore, Palekh art combines both secular and religious beliefs in sun-related festivals such as the Maslenitsa. Painted by Valentina Malahova. Mstera, Russia.*** **(Museum of Decorative Arts, Moscow)**

196

the birth of light out of darkness explodes with one stunning sunburst of sound.

Most traditional cultures believe that the sun is capable of both compassion and vengeance; while it creates and nourishes life it is also the harbinger of death. "This sun" *(si saule)* in Baltic terminology means light and life while "that sun" *(vina saule)* implies darkness and death. The thin dividing line between life and death is no more than the universal threshold of the "Sun Door at World's End," which Ananda Coomaraswamy described in his treatise, *Svayamatrnna: Janua Coeli.* He explained that in most ancient cultures an aspirant could obtain salvation only by "passing over by way of the sun door," thus crossing over from mortality to immortality. Vishnu's third stride, according to the *Rg Veda,* passes through *Sûryaloka* (the abode of the sun), the final destination of life after death. It is symbolized by the Vedic fire altar in which three stones represent the "universal lights" of Fire, Gale and the Sun (Agni, Vayu, and Aditya) on which the deities, infused with Sûrya's breath of life, stride up and down between Heaven and Earth.

In this scheme the uppermost stone is the "self-perforate" or the "Sun Door of Truth," without which the way is barred by the sun, the Janitor of Heaven. *Brahmanas Upanishads* states: "He reaches the sun; it opens out there for him like the hole of the drum; through it he mounts higher."

---

**196.** ***Fecundity is symbolized by a horse (the sun), undressing a woman on his back, in*** **Disparate Desenfrenado,** ***a sketch by Francisco Goya (1746–1828).*** **(Museo del Prado, Madrid)**

**197.** *Carolingian art is represented by the* **Gospel Book of Francis II,** *in which the king is depicted as the sun, and his queen by the image of the moon, on either side of the Cross. Late ninth century. Northern France.* **(Bibliothèque Nationale, Paris)**

**198.** *The ivory cover for* **Pericopes** *of Henry II (c. 870) is another Carolingian piece, showing the sun in his chariot drawn by four horses, while on the left of Christ is the moon goddess riding in a chariot driven by bullocks.* **(Bayerische Staatsbibliothek, Munich)**

**199.** *A mosaic after Achilli, showing Irish monks raising hands in the ancient Egytian manner of paying homage to the sun. Cave-chapel of St. Columbanus, St. Peter's Basilica, Vatican City.*

200

**200.** ***Sun and moon images flanking the Cross symbolize the cosmic implication of the Redemption. Mid-twelfth century. Northern Spain.*** **(Metropolitan Museum of Art, New York. Gift of Ella Brummer)**

201

**201.** *Revered by Christianity and Islam alike, the Fiery Ascension of the Hebrew Prophet Elijah (c. ninth century) was cast in the image of the solar deity Perun in the mythology of northern Slavs. Sixteenth-century Russian icon. Moscow school.*
**(Madanjeet Singh Collection)**

**202,203.** *The twelfth-century basilica of San Clemente, Rome, is embellished with sun motifs, as originally it was a second-century Mithra shrine. The sun is symbolized by the birds on the Cross (203).*

**204.** *A second-century polychrome mosaic of the sun god Helios in the pagan tomb, discovered in 1574 beneath St. Peter's Basilica in the Vatican, is now known as Cristo Sole.*

**205–208.** *How cultures transcend religions is seen in this twelfth-century mosaic with sun motifs in the basilica of San Clemente, Rome, built over the Mithra temple (206). The birth of the sun god is shown in a statue of Mithra emerging from a cloud in the shape of a snake (207), and another in which he is killing a bull (208).*

209

210

With some variations, the Indian sun-door concept is similar to those in Chinese, Egyptian, Greek, Hebrew, and other cultures. In China the sun door is symbolized by "two perforates" (instead of the Vedic three); the earth symbol, *ts'ung,* is internally tubular and externally square, and the solar symbol, *pi,* is a perforated circular disc. *Ts'ung* in Chinese literature *(Ku yu t'u p'u)* is described as "wheel hubs of the ancient jade chariot reserved for the Son of Heaven, the Emperor," and *pi* is compared with Neolithic flattened mace-heads and with spindle-whorls. Both *pi* and *ts'ung* are made of jade, which stands for immortality.

A pair of annular symbols of the Siberian shamans also consists of a perforated disc representing the earth, but the sun is the circular opening in the roof of the yurt. In the shamanic rites of the Altai people, a young birch tree *(Axis Mundi)* is set up in the yurt, symbolizing the door god *(udesi-burchan),* and at the bottom of the tree seven steps are cut out with an axe as the "ladder to Heaven." The tree passes through "the sun" in the roof of the yurt, thus opening the way of the shaman to Heaven, from one world into another.

Several paintings and bas-reliefs on Egyptian monuments were made in accordance with the *Book of the Dead,* as they depict the sun door either as an open door mounted

**209. Winter Sunset at Eragny** ***(1898).*** ***Oil painting by Camille Pissarro.*** **(Galerie Schmit Collection, Paris)**

**210.** ***The sun-inspired Renaissance influence in the works of Albrecht Dürer (1471–1528) superseded the orthodoxy of Gothic elements, as seen in his well-known painting*** **Melancholia** ***(1514).*** **(Metropolitan Museum of Art, New York)**

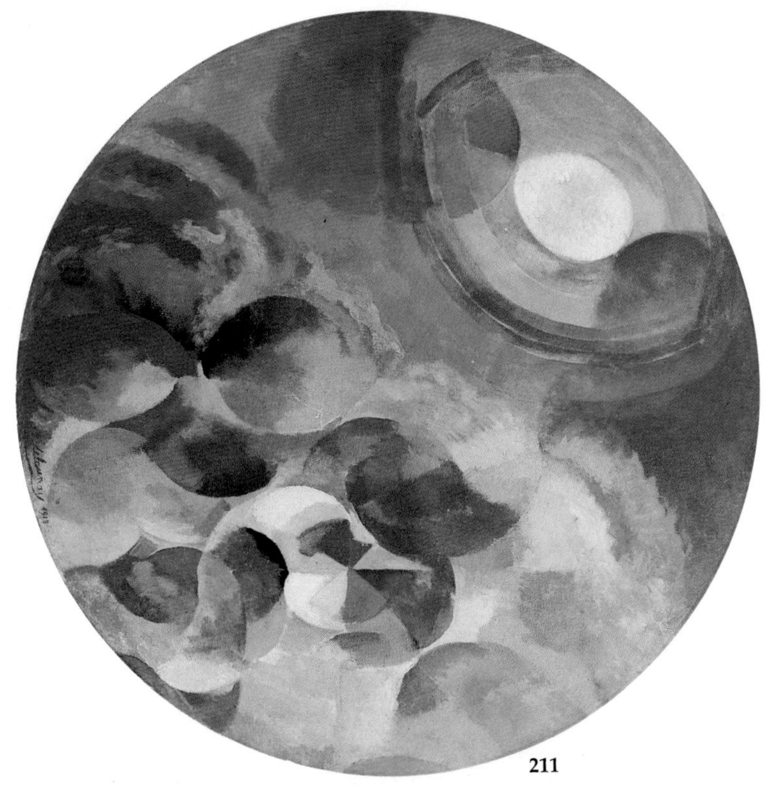

211

212

211. *Simultaneous composition:* Sun Discs *(1912) by Robert Delaunay.* (Museum of Modern Art, New York. Simon Guggenheim Fund)

212. The Sower *(1888). Oil painting by Vincent van Gogh.* (Rijksmuseum, Kröller-Müller, Otterlo, Netherlands)

213

214

215

216

213–215. *Bas-reliefs of* mithuna, *lovers, and musicians carved on the eleventh-century sun temple at Khajuraho, India.*

216. *A frieze of erotic sculptures on the thirteenth-century sun temple at Konarak, India.*

217. *Kum Kum Mohanti and her companions performing a sun dance on the rampart of the thirteenth-century sun temple at Konarak, India.*

218

**218.** *Yab-Yum, the divine couple, symbolizing the cosmic union of the sun (male) and the moon (female). Eighteenth century. Pemiangtse monastery, Sikkim, India.*

219

220

221

with a sun disc and guarded by the sun god in anthropomorphic or zoomorphic form, or as a closed door of sunset and death, barring the entry of the unqualified. The ancient Egyptians believed that there was no other way to reach the sun door except by climbing the "ladder of Horus," and admission through it was subjected to a psychostasis in which "the heart" must be weighed against the feather of Truth *(maat)*.

G'bilon is the equivalent of the sun door in Hebrew mythology and *Sefer ha-zohar* (The Book of Splendour) tells of the pathway through the sun door which mounts higher and higher until it reaches the Cosmic Throne.

In a Greek myth, when Socrates helps one of the prisoners to escape the darkness of the cave, he climbs out of his ignorance until he finally beholds Truth and Reality in the light of the sun. Turner called one of his works *The Angel Standing in the Sun*, and to it he appended the biblical words: "Light is not only glorious and sacred, it is voracious, carnivorous, unsparing. It devours the whole world impartially, without distinction." It reflects the deep Oriental wisdom symbolized by the sun in the shape of a skull with a flaming golden trident *(trisula)*, called the Lord of Soil, installed on top of Buddhist monasteries perched on the daunting, awe-inspiring dizzy heights of the Himalayan mountain peaks. [**235**]

**219.** *A Chinese Yin-Yang symbol represents the two complementary forces of nature, light and dark, heaven and earth, male and female.*

**220.** *A stylized Yin-Yang motif (1840), in the Valikhanov Museum, Chokhan, Kazakhstan.*

**221.** *Symbolizing the sun and the moon, a* **Mushin-do** *painting of Shamanic spirits is represented by a couple* **(munyô, mudang).** *Nineteenth century.* **(Daea High School, Chinju, Republic of Korea)**

222

The sun-door concept inspired most ancient civilizations to build magnificent gateways of the sun to their shrines, citadels, and fortresses, embellishing them with sun motifs, particularly the lion and the sphinx. [55] The Egyptians, Mesopotamians, Hittites, Greeks, and Romans all built imposing sun gates as did the Buddhists, Hindus, and Muslims in Asia. The glittering sun-door facade of the Taleju Bhawani temple at Bhatgaon in Nepal is a case in point. [234] Like the Japanese *Shinmai-Dorii*, sun doors were also built by Amerindians—for example, the one constructed during the Tiahuanco period (AD 450–850) in the Andean region of South America. The central anthropomorphic figure carved on the gateway, called the Staff God, holds scepters of authority in much the same way as the sun god Sûrya displays a staff in one of his hands in the eighth-century Martand temple in Kashmir.

The universality of the sun door is as intriguing as the identification of a mirror with the sun in different parts of the world. Like the sacred mirror of the sun goddess Amaterasu in Japan, a mirror is also worshipped far south in India in the Suchindram temple, and this sun symbol is widely carved on stone-walls of many medieval temples in South Asia, depicting mirrors held by lovely damsels in a variety of poses. [24] The sun symbol of the Aztecs in Mexico was a sacred bird with a mirror-head which, they believed, reflected auguries such as the several ill-omens prior to the coming of the Spaniards. The magic mirror showed their "Courageous Lord" Moctezuma several ill-luck signs such as hordes of strange armed men, a tongue of fire rising out of the earth and creating new stars, a new comet appearing in the sky, snow falling on their capital Tenochtitlán (modern Mexico City), and one of their temples burnt down mysteriously.

**222.** ***Indian miniature painting on cloth depicting Krishna and his devotees celebrating a festival at a sun temple. Seventeenth century, Rajasthan.*** **(Madanjeet Singh Collection)**

223

224

225

226

227

228

*223. Kum Kum Mohanti's group performing a sun dance at the Konarak sun temple, with four dancers representing the four directions.*

*224. Folk dancers form a circle, representing the sun in the* **Rasleela** *tradition of adoring Krishna. Rajasthan, India.*

*225,226. Mexican dancers wearing hats with mirrors symbolizing the sun.*

*227. A Japanese ceremonial dance, called* **bukabu**, *is performed by four dancers at the Zingu Shicho Kohoka, Ise.*

*228. Four dancers at the Inti-Raymi sun festival, Peru.*

In Europe, the ancient tradition of Etruscan and Greek bronze mirrors representing the sun was carried forward in arts and literature as, for example, Bram Stoker's Gothic horror fiction *Dracula* (1897), in which the mysterious Count Dracula [**397**] avoids the sun by throwing away the mirror used for shaving by his English teacher, whom he had invited in his lonely castle in Transylvania, a region infested with vampires and werewolves.

Likewise, in several mythologies all over the world, the eyes of deities are attributed cosmic significance. The sky god Horus in Egyptian mythology is represented in the shape of a winged sun disc, as well as in human form with the face of a falcon whose two eyes are the sun and the moon. The Japanese sun goddess Amaterasu in the Shinto myth was born from the lustral water falling from Izanagi's one eye while the moon god was born from the other. In the *Râmâyana* of Tulsi Das, Râma manifested himself as Cosmic Man soon after his birth [**237**] In Chinese mythology Pan-gu is the creator deity of Heaven and earth whose two eyes turned into the sun and the moon on his death.

The comparison which some scholars have made between the Amerindian and Greco-Roman pantheons also shows how solar cultures and their mythologies in widely separated parts of the world seem to converge, transcending both time and space, and manifest themselves continually in the global totality of form and content. It is at the heart of the controversy whether or not such similarities are coincidental or resulted from interaction between cultures. Perhaps in this inexplicable phenomenon lies the fundamental character of the prehistoric myth-making age and its cultural universality.

All this and Heaven, too, is reflected in the small round mirror that hangs in the simple wooden shrine at the seashore of Futamigaura in Japan. The sun's pure light is seen in it as the "true heart" of all phenomena. It mirrors the all-embracing light of Aton's *maat* or Truth; the compassion and "avenging justice" of Helios; the wisdom of Odin's one-eyed impartiality and equality; Mithra's custody of treaties and obligations; Sûrya's spiritual enlightenment and healing power; Shamash, Utu and Khvar as controllers of night and day, good and evil; Huitzilopochtli, Inti, and Kinich Ahau, the arbitrators of right and wrong, life and death—in short, the totality of sun gods representing the ultimate cosmogonic universality of different cultures.

**229 a**

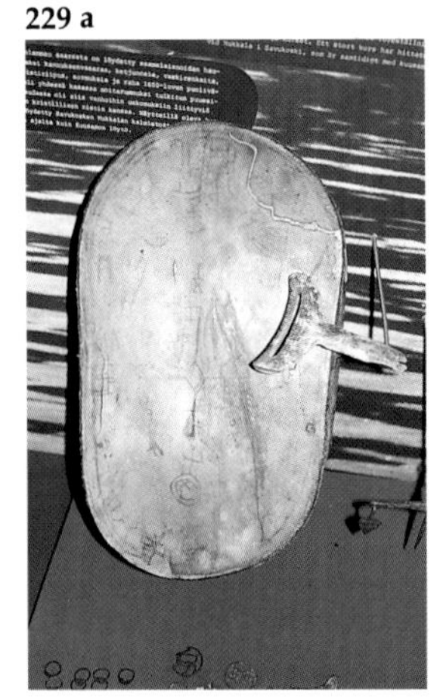

**229 b**

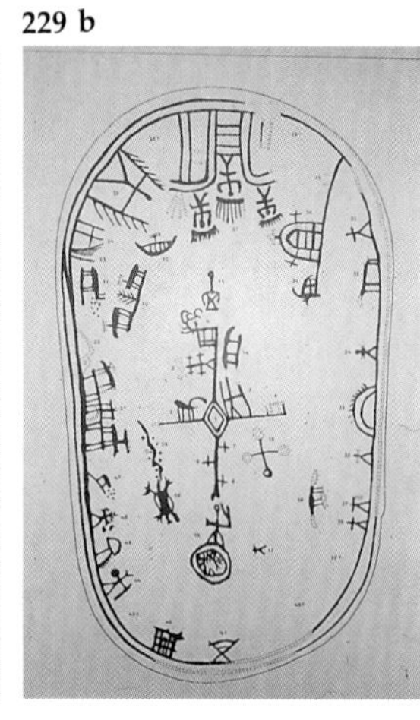

**230 a**

**230 b**

**229 a,b.** *Cosmic symbols on a Shaman drum.*

**230 a,b.** *Solar symbols on a Chinese bronze drum. c. first century* AD. *Guangxi province, China.*

**231.** *A tribal wooden drum in the shape of a woman is a womb symbol, as indicated by the stretched leather across the stomach. Nineteenth century. Central India.* **(Crafts Museum, New Delhi)**

231

232

233

232. *Sarangi, a musical instrument of the Santal tribes. Nineteenth century. Bihar, India.* (National Museum, New Delhi)

233. *Fecundity is symbolized by a woman carrying a drum on her head, as in this wooden sculpture of the Bager tribe, Guinea.* (National Museum of African Art, Smithsonian Institution, Washington, D.C.)

234. *Following pages. The sun door and gilded facade of the Taleju Bhavani temple. Seventeenth century. Bhatgaon, Nepal.*

235

**235.** *The sun in the shape of a skull with a flaming golden trident is the Lord of the Soil, the symbol of life and death. Sixteenth century. Kye monastery, Ladakh, India.*

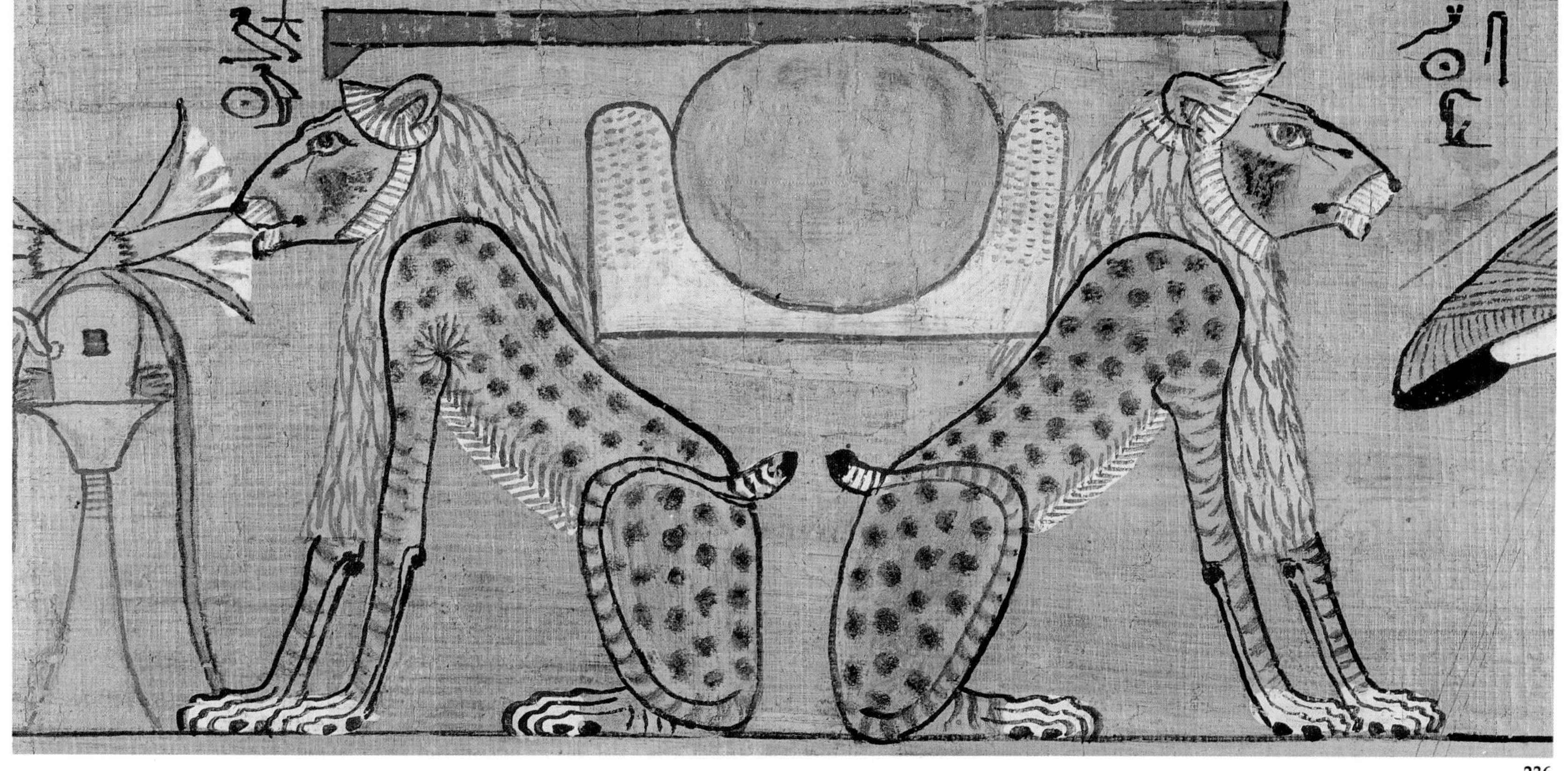

236

Looking through Amaterasu's mirror, the reflection is not one of a vague bygone age of primitive people living in isolated animistic, pagan surroundings, but the eternally unfolding metamorphosis of the ever-evolving, ever-renewing omnipresence of the sun, which is as much a part of our everyday life today as it was in the past. As supreme ruler of both the upper and lower worlds, light and dark, the sun is still very much the "god" who holds in one hand, the deadly mace of fiery destruction about to be hurled through gaping holes in the atmosphere's ozone layer and, in the other, an olive branch of the peaceful dawn of another bright and beautiful day, a reward for our effective utilization of the solar energy, preservation of the natural environment, and respect for animal life.

Personally, I wish this publication to be my passport through the sun door to immortality, and I am much obliged to UNESCO in having invited me to participate in its "Integral Study of the Silk Roads" expeditions, thus enabling me to collect much of the sun-related material for which I have been chasing the sun for years. "Have you any sun-related works of art or literature?" I kept enquiring repeatedly at the numerous museums, institutions, archaeological sites, and libraries we visited during the long and arduous road journey across the Taklamakan Desert from Xi'an to Kashgar in China; the Maritime Route expedition from Venice in Italy to Osaka in Japan which took us to seventeen countries en route; and the Steppe Route expedition from Ashkhabad in Turkmenia to Alma Ata in Kazakhstan.

"Is that all you have?" I asked as the Director of the Museum in Alma Ata showed me a number of sun-related fragments of petroglyphs which I had already seen and photo-

**236.** *Lions of the two horizons guarding the sun door in the middle.* **The Book of the Dead,** *papyrus of the royal scribe Hunefer. Nineteenth Dynasty, c. 1290* BC. **(British Museum, London)**

237

**237.** *As in the mythologies of several cultures, the Hindu god Rama also manifests himself as the Cosmic Man whose two eyes are the sun and the moon. Miniature painting. 1800. Benares School.* **(Bharat Kala Museum, Varanasi, India)**

238

graphed at Tamgaly, some one hundred miles away. She looked at me searchingly, paused, and replied: "Actually, we have one other most beautiful piece of all."

"Won't you show me?" I said eagerly, wondering why she had not mentioned it earlier.

"Of course!" she said and leading me to the patio outside, pointed with a broad smile at the brilliant, shining sun in the deep blue sky.

I looked up and recalling the hymn immortalized in the Heliopolitan texts, "Give me light, that I may see thy beauty," felt like raising my hands in the ancient Egyptian manner of worshipping the sun that we Indians still imitate [**238**] while reciting the *Gayatri* prayer: "Let us meditate on the divine light and splendor of the god *Savitre* [the sun] that he may illuminate and inspire our minds."

**238.** *A morning scene of the River Ganges at Benares, showing the manner of worshipping the sun with raised hands, unlike all other kinds of prayers in India, which are offered with joined hands.*

音霊験記
西國順禮二十三番
摂津國
勝尾寺
千手堂
百済國王后
石亭應賀誌
豊国画
横川彫竹

240

# THE SUN IN JAPANESE ART AND CULTURE

ELIZABETH SCHULTZ AND FUMIKO YAMAMOTO

In the modern world, the image of the sun is instantly identified with Japan. To examine this image, however, as it appears in Japanese culture is to recognize the power of a symbol to reflect and control the values and aspirations of a people as well as to express the changes in these values and aspirations. In European iconography, the sun has often been humanized and familiarized; given a countenance, it may frown or smile; its rays may be long, short, serrated; its color may be white, yellow, orange, variegated. In Japan, however, its image was austere and absolute: round, red, with rays on occasion jutting forth symmetrically from it. The sun was deified for centuries and its only human link was the Emperor himself, ostensibly a lineal descendant of the sun. Its principal symbolic representation was a mirror which would reflect its light directly and brilliantly. In time, the sun came to be part of commonplace Japanese iconography, a sign of material and spiritual prosperity, and of re-

**239.** ***Toyokuni (1786–1864) portrays a Korean queen offering prayer to the sun depicted in the cartouche by Hiroshige (1797–1858).*** **(Elizabeth Schultz Collection)**

**240.** ***Sunrise at the Futamigaura seashore, Ise, Japan.***

newed life. Although the moon has inspired Japanese poets and artists with its lucidity, its beauty, and its emphemerality, the constant sun, seldom the object of lyrical admiration, has more consistently been colored by ideological concepts than has the pale moon. Venerated for its brilliance, its power, its certainty, as was the imperial family, the sun remained the single image that most concretely embodied Japanese political and ethical principles until the end of the Second World War. Although the war, and Japan's subsequent economic success, has resulted in a re-examination of the sun's meanings, it continues to enlighten the lives of Japanese people.

The words and ideographs for the sun in the Japanese language represent a variety of attitudes. The Chinese ideograph for sun is *hi*, which in Japanese denotes both "sun" and "day." Etymology for the abstract contemporary ideograph ( 日 ) shows its direct derivation from a literal picture of the sun. Its pronunciation today is the same as that for the word "fire," suggesting that before they used Chinese ideographs, the Japanese regarded the sun and fire as being kindred aspects of nature. The basic ideograph, *hi*, with its close connection to natural forces, appears more frequently than other ideographs for "sun" in Japan's oldest written record, the *Kojiki* (AD 712). The word for Japan itself is *Ni-hon* ( 日本 ) a compound of a shortened form of *nichi*, which is an alternative reading of *hi*, and *hon*, meaning "source"; the given name for Japan can thus be translated as "The Source of the Sun."

The original settlers of the Japanese archipelago set a sun goddess, Amaterasu ("Heavenly Shining One"), at the center of a mythology which they seem to have adapted from other South Pacific myths. Of this goddess, the scholar and statesman Motoori Norinaga (1730–1801) wrote: "She is without a peer in the whole universe, casting her light to the very ends of heaven and earth and for all time. . . . This goddess is the splendor of all splendors." According to Japan's ancient records, the *Kojiki* and the *Nihonshoki* (AD 720), Amaterasu founded the Japanese nation by sending her grandson Prince Ninigi down from the Plains of Heaven to govern the islands. In the *Kojiki, hi* is used to designate both the names of gods in Amaterasu's line as well as those ancient emperors who were her close descendants. *Hi no miko,* meaning "Prince of the Sun," is a common epithet for royal personages in the *Manyoshu*, the great collection of over four thousand poems compiled between the latter half of the fifth century and the middle of the eighth century. In Murasaki Shikibu's *Tale of Genji* (c. 1002), Prince Genji is known as "the shining one" and his stepmother as "the lady of the radiant sun," both sobriquets reflecting not only their personal beauty and radiance but also their imperial lineage. Thus with their divinity inherited from the sun, the Japanese imperial family became the center of a state religion, Shintoism, and absolute rulers. In them, Heaven and humanity were thought to be one, and it was said that in comparison to the Chinese emperors, who were merely "sons of Heaven," the Japanese emperors were as Heaven itself. Unconditional reverence consequently came to be demanded by this manifestation of the sun goddess on earth.

Also recorded in the *Kojiki* and the *Nihonshoki* are the circumstances of Amaterasu's birth and life, which have become associated with certain precepts fundamental to Shintoism and to the Japanese political and ethical system. At the heart of this system is the fear of pollution, on the one hand, and the reverence for purity, brightness, and directness, on the other. Prior to the birth of Amaterasu, her father, Izanagi,

241

242

had to purify himself of the pollution of death and darkness. In another story, Amaterasu's brother, Susanowo, teased her while she was busy weaving, and in order to put an end to his obstreperous behavior, she hid herself in the darkness of a cave, thereby depriving the world of her brightness. Only when another goddess hung a mirror on a tree outside the cave did Amaterasu, catching a glimmer of her own light, come forth in all her glory. To remind him of herself, Amaterasu presented a similar mirror to Ninigi when he descended to earth to rule.

Because it reflects the sun's pure light, the mirror is said to reflect the true heart of all external phenomena and has been classified as the most important item in the imperial regalia. Of the mirror, it was written in the early fourteenth century, "There is never an instance when the forms of right and wrong, or good and evil, fail to show up [in it]. Its virtue consists in responding to these forms as they come. This is the basic source of correctness and uprightness."

The Imperial Edicts of the seventh and eighth centuries which formed the basis for Japanese political, legal, and ethical thought refer repeatedly to the value of a "bright, pure, and honest and sincere heart." These values are extended into the realm of ancient aesthetics which also honored above all a purity, directness, and brightness whose essence was that of "high noon on a brilliant sunny day."

Shintoism has never encouraged the construction of icons for its deities. The

---

**241.** ***The samurai warrior, Hachiman Taro Minamoto no Yshiie, with a fan emblazoned with the sun. From the woodblock print book* Picture Book of Ancient Stirrups *(1836) by Hokusai.* (Elizabeth Schultz Collection)**

**242.** ***New Year's celebration depicted in a wood-block print by Toyohiro (1773–1828).* (Spencer Museum of Art, University of Kansas, Lawrence)**

reality of the sun itself or its manifestation in the Emperor were sufficient evidence of the Goddess's immanence for the ancient Japanese. Her shining mirrors, placed in many Shinto shrines, are the only embodiment of her spirit; she seldom appears in pictures, and neither she nor the sun appears in statues. On a day-to-day basis traditional Japanese would have expressed their reverence for the sun and the Emperor, not before an icon but through the simple rites of washing their face and hands and then turning toward the rising sun to clap their hands and bow. In certain parts of the country, more elaborate rituals of sun worship, often combining with elements of Buddhism and Taoism, evolved. For example, in Tsushima, on unlucky days, village men gather together in a designated house to wait for the sun to appear; in the Tokyo area, at the vernal and autumnal equinoxes, people dance, chanting a prayer for the rising or the setting sun; whereas in the Kyoto and Hyogo areas, people follow the sun through the course of a day, walking with it from east to west; on New Year's Day, in Mie prefecture, sake is presented to the rising sun; and in Kanagawa prayers and incense are offered.

Except for those myths concerning Amaterasu herself, folktales concerning the sun are few. In one story, a bath attendant informs a kitchen maid that the moon is more important than the sun because it "appears at night when all is dark... . But the sun appears only in the broad daytime when no light is needed." It implies that the sun's presence is so predictable that it may be assumed. Several stories about the sun demonstrate the presumptuousness of human attempts to manipulate it. The *Kojiki* and the *Nihonshoki* record that the first Emperor of Japan, Jimmu (c. seventh century BC), on one occasion chose to fight his enemies facing the sun; consequently he was defeated, for it thus seemed he was trying to attack the sun itself. In several folktales concerning wealthy landowners, the dangers of thwarting the sun's course are made clear. One tale concerns a farmer's son who, becoming disgruntled by the numbers of peasants pestering his father for money, shoots an arrow at the sun in an attempt to keep the borrowers in the dark. Another tale concerns a farmer who demands that the sun shine through the night so that he could complete his rice-planting in a day. Subsequently, the fortunes of both rich men decline drastically. The landowner in the second tale nearly loses his daughter to a dragon and his rice crop at harvest time is changed to rushes. Other stories suggest the sun's power as creator and sustainer of life, source of magic and mercy. In both the Tsushima and Kagoshima regions the story is told of a woman, impregnated by the sun, who gives birth to a son endowed with the wondrous gift of divination.

Amaterasu's splendor and particular promise to the Japanese people seems to become most comprehensible and accessible to them in the image of the rising sun, an image ubiquitous in Japanese culture. Because of its association with the rising sun, the east has been the direction which has been awarded special homage. Ancient tombs were often constructed so that the dead faced east, as were shrines, so that their worshippers could face the rising sun. Political prestige and power also came to be attached to the image of the rising sun and Japan's easterly geographic position vis-à-vis the Asian continent. As early as AD 607, a legend tells of how a Sui emperor in China was so greatly offended by an inquiry from the Yamato court in Japan that "the Emperor of the Land of the Rising Sun" sought to know how "the Emperor of the

243

Land of the Setting Sun" fared. Most schoolchildren in modern Japan are familiar with the associations between the rising sun and the great feudal warlord Toyotomi Hideyoshi (1536–1598). Not only did his mother allegedly have a dream of the rising sun at the time of his birth, but he is also reputed to have evoked outrage from the Chinese emperor when he addressed him in a similar manner.

An examination of the image of the rising sun in popular Japanese culture reveals that, while retaining its associations with the virtues of the sun goddess and the strength of the imperial house, during the almost 250-year period of Japan's isolation

**243. Riogu-Mandara,** *depicting the grand shrine at Ise under the sun and the moon deities. The Japanese worshipped the sun in the open, and the sacred forest, "Himorogi," means a shrine.* **(Ise Museum, Japan)**

from the rest of the world (1635–1868), the image assumed extended connotations. Thus the simple, circular emblem of the sun appears frequently in a militaristic context. A red sun on a white or black background on fans and on conical and disc-shaped hats was a familiar part of the paraphernalia of military processions. The appearance of such a fan in particular originally denoted a samurai's victory in battle. Unlike the moon, which waxes and wanes and which in traditional Japanese iconography is frequently represented in relation to birds, flowers, snow, clouds, or water, the austere sun, which does not change has resisted the Japanese genius for embellishment. Thus among the several hundreds of family crests, there are, according to one source, seventeen depicting the moon, fifty-one the stars, and only seven depicting the sun. Although it appeared on military garb, people never felt that they could be on such intimate terms with the sun that they could incorporate its image into the patterns of their ordinary clothing.

The image that often used to appear on the first page of a book or print-series describing a journey appropriately was that of the rising sun. The journeys designed by masters of the wood-block print, Hiroshige (1797–1858) and Eisen (1790–1848), are off to a good start, as the first print in two of their journey series suggests; in both, the red hemisphere of the sun on the horizon echoes the arcs in the background of the Nihonbashi ( 日本橋 ), the point from which most Tokyo-based journeys began. The beginning of the year and the hopes associated with it, however, prompted the greatest variety in representations of the rising sun. Although the circular red image itself never varies, for the New Year's celebrations it is shown in conjunction with several other conventional Japanese motifs which have auspicious implications, signifying longevity as well as material and spiritual prosperity. In conjunction with the crane, tortoise, and the elderly couple, it conveys hope for a long and happy life; with the pine and the ocean, it conveys hope for the perpetual renewal of life; and with the treasure ship, it conveys hope for material prosperity. Not only does it appear on scrolls and prints at the New Year, it also appears on cake-box covers, toys, and greeting cards; perhaps little boys are especially blessed in being able to raise their own

**244.** *The "Shi Kinen-Sengu" procession at Ise, carrying the soul of the sun goddess Amaterasu from the old to the newly built shrine. Traditionally, the old shrine is demolished every twenty years.* **(Ise Museum, Japan)**

244

rising suns at New Year by flying kites with the emblem printed boldly on them.

In time, the values associated with the rising sun came to embrace a work ethic familiar to Protestant cultures. The ritual of morning sun-worship necessitating early rising became the basis for a code promoting physical well-being, hard work, and material gain. More than a dozen Japanese proverbs, such as "Fortune comes to the family that rises early," "The early riser earns three cents," and "A sleepyhead is a born loser," guarantee profit for the early riser. Calisthenics at six in the morning have been a common part of the day's activities for the Japanese for many years, with instructions nowadays being given by loudspeakers in rural town squares, in school playgrounds everywhere, and, of course, by radio and TV. Children with round red cheeks are said to reflect the healthy influence of the round red sun.

Recent study of the myths surrounding the sun goddess has revealed them to be stories used by the nobility to authenticate the divinity of the Emperor and to ensure undivided support among his people. The power of the image as a unifying device was dramatized in the mid-nineteenth century when it was chosen as the emblem for the flag of the nation newly restored to internal harmony by the Emperor Meiji and by the end of the policy of isolation. The flag would distinguish Japanese ships from foreign vessels encouraged to enter its harbors for the first time and would proclaim the sovereignty of the Japanese people on foreign missions. Following its adoption as the country's official flag in 1870, the *hi-no-maru,* meaning "circle of the sun," was flown from gateways on every political or military occasion, with a separate flag, a sun streaming red rays, developed especially for the navy.

In the early twentieth century, the fledgling Japanese women's movement also appropriated the image of the sun, perhaps seeking to activate their feminist connection with the power and the glory of Amaterasu. Hiratsuka Raicho (1886–1971), founder of this movement, in the Proclamation of Emancipation printed in the first issue of *Seito* (Bluestocking Journal) in 1911, wrote: "I am a new woman. Daily I wish to be and try to become a new woman. What is truly and forever new is the sun. I am the sun." Despite the boldness of this proclamation and the brightness of its imagery,

245

however, Hiratsuka believed that the "genius" of Japanese women resembled the "hidden sun"; the aim of both the magazine and the movement associated with it consequently was to bring this sun out of its cave.

With the outbreak of the Second World War, the image of the rising sun became the most visible symbol for galvanizing the Japanese nation. Soldiers departed for battle wearing flags given to them by loved ones tied diagonally across their chests; they entered battle wearing headbands emblazoned with the rising sun and brave words of old; pilots' planes were marked with the rising sun, and one of their ill-fated kamikaze suicide units was called "The Morning Sun." Children made packets to send to the soldiers which included small *hi-no-maru* flags and took lunches to school which resembled the *hi-no-maru*, that is, a flat box of white rice with a pickled red plum in the center. The emblem of the rising sun was evidence of the soldier's friends' hope that he would triumph in battle and of his country's assurance that his endeavor was conducted in the name of justice and righteousness. When a soldier was killed, the government sent his family a small flag with a sun emblem, signifying that he had not died in vain, for his sacrifice strengthened the nation.

Protesting against the war, Yashima Taro sought to efface the militaristic image of the sun by restoring it to its natural context. In the beginning of *The New Sun*, published in the United States in 1943 using his own words and pictures, he describes "the sunny house" where he, his family, and their small plot of flowers and vegetables were nurtured by the sun; in his drawings, the sun, a small round sphere, shines onto the open veranda where he and his baby stretch to meet its rays. As the power of the military increases, however, and as Yashima is jailed for his opposition, the sun disappears from both his written and his visual text. Only in the conclusion, when he is released from detention and able to return to his family and his new baby, is it possible for him to imagine "the new sun," one which in actuality shines "above [him], big and bright," one which symbolically gives him the hope for global peace. *The New Sun* concludes with a drawing of a sun defined only by a diffusion of rays, the antithesis of the traditional Japanese image, and with a prayer that the traditional virtue of "brightness" would benefit all humankind: "Surely this new sun would increase its brightness over me and over all people everywhere."

Contemporary Japanese continue to acknowledge their culture's special relationship with the sun. They may recall the mesmerizing power of symbols as they contemplate the frequently reproduced 1965 photograph, originally published in the *Asahi* (Morning Sun) newspaper's nationally circulated picture magazine, of the sun setting behind the blasted, skeletal dome of Hiroshima's Industrial Promotion Hall. They may show their respect for the sun and for its particular blessing on them as a people by journeying to Mount Shichimen from which they can contemplate it rising in full splendor over Mount Fuji. They may remember, as Fukushima Roshi, abbot of Tofuku Temple in Kyoto, explains to his disciples, that the best time for meditation is in the moments before sunrise or after sunset, that the day is ordered by the sun's movements. What is certain is that the ideograph for the sun remains an intrinsic part of Japan's name, and its image remains ubiquitous at times of celebration and through the presence of the national flag; for the contemporary Japanese, as for their ancestors, this image remains impervious: round and red, absolute and austere.

---

**245.** ***Sunrise at Shimoda beach. Wood-block print by Fuyo.*** **(Elizabeth Schultz Collection)**

Among the well-known Buddhist monks who elaborated the cosmic philosophy of the *Lotus Sutra* was Dengyo Daishi (767–822), also called Saicho, who studied in China.

Another distinguished scholar, Saicho Kobo-daishi (774–835), popularly known as Kukai, followed to China in 804 and became the disciple of the Chinese guru Hui-kuo (746–805). Kukai systematized the esoteric Shingon "True Word" Buddhism in which the cosmic Buddha Maha-Vairocana, the "Great Illuminator," was regarded as the source of the whole universe. A legend has it that Vairocana transmitted the Yoga doctrine to Vajrasattva, a supernatural personage; it was then introduced from India into China in AD 719 by Vajrabodhi, and later into Japan by Kukai. In Shingon cosmotheism, the universe is regarded as the body of Maha-Vairocana, composed of six elements: earth, fire, water, air, ether, and consciousness—as treated in Chinese and Japanese translations of *Avatamskasutra*, a Sanskrit text no longer extant.

Monk Kukai incorporated several native Shinto beliefs into his syncretized polytheistic teaching of Buddhism, so that Dainichi Nyorai, the "Great Sun," appears in the form of the supreme kami, the sun goddess Amaterasu. Thus by the eighth century, the Shinto kami became the protector of Buddhism and shrines for them were built within the precincts of Buddhist temples. The Buddhist *sutras* (scriptures) were now read in front of the kami, who eventually were elevated as *avatars*, or incarnations, of Buddhist devas (deities), and given the name of bodhisattva. In several Shinto shrines Buddhist statues were placed in inner sanctuaries and Buddhist priests even took charge of their management. This Shinto-Buddhist amalgamation reached its zenith in AD 1192 when the religious theories of Ryobu, known as "Two Aspects" Shinto, were established during the Kamakura Shogunate, making the "Great Sun" the principal source of the whole universe. In commemorative pagodas and stupas as well as in the mandalas (symbolic diagrams) of the Shingon sect, Maha-Vairocana always occupies the central position, with the other four "self-born" Dhyani Buddhas facing the four quarters.

Also prominent among several solar deities is the Healing Buddha Yakushi (Bhaishajyaguru), who became very popular during the Nara period (645–781), when he was worshipped along with Nikko, the Sunlight (Sûryaprabha), and Gakko, the Moonlight (Chandraprabha). Nikko symbolizes nobility, light, and purity while Gakko represents eternity of time and existence.

Another important deity in the Buddhist pantheon is the bodhisattva Ekadasamukhavalokitesvara. He is the direct incarnation of the sun and, as in China, he is said to be the protector of Buddhists who are in trouble. There are a number of magnificent images of solar deities in the six great temples of Nara, especially in the Yakushiji monastery, which was founded by Emperor Tenmu in order to offer prayers for his ailing wife; she recovered from her illness and eventually succeeded her husband to the throne as Empress Jito. The statue of Nikko in the Yakushiji temple is among the most elegant bronzes of seventh-century Japan. Several statues of the Yakushi triad were built during the Hakuho (645–710), Tempyo (710–794), and Heian (794–1185) periods.

Especially after the arrival in Japan of the famous Indian monk Bodhisena and his appointment as the chief priest of the royal monastery of Todaiji in Nara, a great

248

249

**248.** *Sûryaprabha (Nikkô in Japanese) figures among twelve deities on a silk screen; he stands on a lotus holding the orb of the flaming sun on a stemmed lotus in his right hand. 1191. (Tōji Monastery National Treasure, Kyoto)*

**249.** *Among the most elegant seventh-century bronzes is the gigantic Sûryaprabha enshrined in the Golden Hall of the Yakushiji temple at Nara, Japan.*

renaissance of sculpture and painting was ushered in. Founded by Emperor Shomu, the Todaiji temple enshrines one of the largest (fifty-three feet tall) bronze images of Rushana. A lavish and spectacular dedication ceremony was held when this magnificent sculpture of the "Great Illuminator" was completed in the year of Tempyo Shoho (AD 752). Also in the Sangatsu-do, the Third Month Hall of the monastery, there is a beautiful twelve-foot-high painted clay statue of Sûrya. In Kyoto, too, several beautiful sculptures of Sûrya were subsequently made, such as the Nikko in the Koryuji temple. Fashioned in AD 1064, the deity holds in both hands long-stemmed lotuses with orbs of the sun. A beautiful wooden sculpture of Sûrya (Nikko Bosatso), in dry lacquer, from the Kozanji temple at Kyoto is now preserved in the National Museum, Tokyo.

Kukai is said to have produced several "three-dimensional" mandalas as divine sculptures, the most important of which are the twenty-one sculptures systematically arranged in the Lecture Hall of the Toji (Kyoogokokuji) temple in Kyoto. The calm and serene figure of Dainichi Buddha in the center is surrounded by a number of Buddhas and bodhisattvas, the five fierce-looking Great Wisdom Kings as well as the four warlike Heavenly Kings. Sculptures of Hindu gods in the form of Boton (Brahma) and Taishakuten (Indra) are also represented in the hall as multiple manifestations of the "Great Sun."

Sûrya is similarly depicted in some exquisite Japanese paintings. In AD 741, Emperor Shomu established two monasteries in each province of Japan, one for monks and the other for nuns. Known as Kokubunji, several of them produced some remarkable pieces of Buddhist art. In a painting of a mandala preserved in the Kokubunji of Yamaguchi, Sûrya is shown with twelve other devas. It is believed that Kukai was the one first initiated into the transcendental mandala of Mahakaruna by his Chinese guru Hui-kuo, and he brought this cosmic design to Japan. The theme is depicted in a set of eleventh-century mandala woodcuts in which Sûrya is shown along with his consort and disciple Vijaya. So also in an illuminated manuscript of *Goma-rodan-yo*, preserved in the Toji monastery, the *goma* ceremonies (*homa* in Sanskrit) of Sûrya are beautifully delineated, depicting the fire altar, or *homa-kunda*, in which every planet and constellation has a different form of *kunda*. A special Japanese method of illustration (applied also to secular subjects) was the hand-scroll, *emaki* or *emakimono*, in which the pictorial part is not merely a representation integrated into the text, but a full narrative in itself.

The sun inspired much of Japanese art, and its influence is pervasive in haiku poetry, calligraphy, ink-drawn scrolls, the tea ceremony, flower arrangements, garden design, and so on. In social behavior, too, the belief that everything under the sun is equal and integrated perhaps explains the reason a traditional Japanese household has two family altars: one, called *kamidana*, for the Shinto tutelary kami and sun goddess Amaterasu, and another, called *butsudana*, for Buddhist deities and the ancestors. People rarely worship in the Western sense, and they freely mix customs and rituals derived from Buddhism, Shintoism, and even Christianity to mark important events like marriages and funerals. Wedding ceremonies are usually performed in the Shinto style, but funerals are conducted according to Buddhist rites.

250

**250.** *The dry lacquer statue of Sûryaprabha was originally an attendant of Bhaishajyaguru of Kozanji temple in Kyoto. Eighth century.* **(National Museum, Tokyo)**

251

252

# THE SUN IN CHINESE CULTURE

HUA TAO

Reverence for the sun is an ancient Chinese tradition. In the historical remains of the Neolithic Yangshao Culture, in central China (5000–3000 BC), potsherds with images of the sun were discovered. Sun images were also excavated at sites of the Neolithic Da-wen-kou culture (4300–2500 BC), in eastern China, near the coast of the Yellow Sea, including the Shandong Peninsula. A typical example from this culture has an image of the sun with eight horns. Pottery with these interesting sun images was found in many places. Even more interesting was perhaps a picture showing the sun, a portion of cloud, and probably the sea, fire, and mountains. The pottery and some fragments were excavated in two places 60 miles apart. It was natural that the people of that coastal region should create these images when they saw the sun rising from the sea. It is quite apparent that these typical images express the people's feeling for sun worship.

The image of a sun, a portion of cloud, and the sea was regarded by many scholars as a primitive form of Chinese script. It is similar to the oracle-bone inscriptions of the Shang Dynasty (c. 1500–1000 BC). In these early Chinese systematical characters, the sun is illustrated thus. Another meaning of this pictogram was "day," the time when the sun was hanging in the sky. The Chinese pronunciation of this character is "*ri*." In addition, many characters meaning "prosperity and plenty" include the sun's image. It is doubtless true that the inventors of Chinese characters not only displayed their knowledge about the function of the sun in nature, but also showed their reverence for the sun.

Between 1972 and 1974, Chinese archaeologists excavated three tombs at Ma-wang-dui, in Changsha, Hunan Province dating from the Western Han Dynasty (206 BC–AD 24). At that time, a well-preserved body in Tomb 1 aroused worldwide attention—the wife of a marquis, who probably died some time around 175 BC. Many historical relics were found in the tombs, the most interesting of which were two T-shaped silk paintings in Tombs 1 and 3. The painting in Tomb 1 is divided into three sections, depicting, from top to bottom, Heaven, the everyday world, and the underworld. Both Heaven and the underworld are represented using mythological images. Heaven has nine red suns hanging on the mythological "Fusang" mulberry

**251.** ***Ekadasamukhavalokitesvara, the incarnation of the Indian god Sûrya, is painted on the northern wall of Cave Temple 76, Dunhuang. Song Dynasty (960–1279), China.***

**252.** ***A crow is the spirit of the sun in Chinese mythology. Detail from second century-BC T-shaped painting found in Tomb 1, Ma-wang-dui province, China.***

tree, along with a crescent moon, under which there is a woman flying. There are also two dragons, one on each side. In the biggest red sun is a golden crow and, on the moon, a toad and a white rabbit. The figure of a man, with a serpentine tail and long hair, stands at the center of the painting: this is the sun god Fuxi. The other two men at the door of Heaven are most likely summoners of souls. The old woman occupying the central position in the everyday world is the occupant of Tomb 1. This T-shaped painting covered her corpse and is generally similar to the one found in Tomb 3, the main difference being that there, the occupant's image at the center of the picture is a man's. The paintings indicate that the dead hoped to live, after death, in Heaven, which was controlled by the sun god.

Adoration of the sun is also evidenced in many petroglyphs in China. The districts of the Yinshan and Helanshan mountains were important regions in northern China. Here, petroglyphs were chiselled, carved, and engraved on cliffs or huge bare rocks—still quite clear after thousands of years of weathering by wind and rain. Themes are numerous, and involve wild and domestic animals, hunting, herding, and human dancing scenes. There are also many images of celestial bodies, such as the sun, moon, and stars, and the worship of these. But carvings of the sun are more numerous than those of other celestial bodies. This demonstrates the high position of

253

**253.** ***The word "fire" in Chinese oracle-bone inscriptions was illustrated by a blaze, as depicted on the lower part of this pottery painted with the sun, clouds, and the sea. Da-wen-kou culture (3000–2500 BC), a people living near the sea in China.***

the sun and the sun god in the minds of the early carvers and the common people. The carving tradition lasted a long time, from the Neolithic Age through the Early Iron Age and after. The structures and the vistas are scattered and are not in any order.

Conversely, the primitive artists of southwestern China displayed their lives and beliefs mainly through rock paintings. These were numerous in Yunnan and Guangxi Provinces. Also unlike the carvings in northern China, there are many well-arranged scenes, with people dancing in groups to express their homage to the sun. The sun was represented by the figure of a man. It is thus reasonable to assume that this was how they perceived the sun god.

The veneration of the ancient Chinese for the sun and the sun god was recorded in Chinese myths. *Shan-hai-jing* (Treatise on Mountains and Oceans), a work with many illustrations, is the earliest collection of Chinese myths. It was not the work of a single author. The main part was completed in the Spring and Autumn period (770–476 BC) and the period of the Warring States (475–221 BC), while the latest part was written during the Western Han Dynasty. In this work, a sun goddess called Xihe is one of the wives of the Emperor Jun (Dijun), the most important god in the work. She bore this great god ten suns. She and her children lived in Tang-gu (Worm Valley), where there was a mythological mulberry tree. Ordinarily the ten suns slept in the lower part of the mulberry tree. Every morning, the mother bathed one child in the Tang-gu River and then let him fly, on the back of a crow, to the top of the tree, whence he travelled through space. Thus, the ten children did the duty of the sun in turn. Besides the sun goddess, Emperor Jun had another wife, called Chang-yi, who bore him twelve moons, and she also bathed her children every day. Judging by the position of the paragraph on Chang-yi in the chapter on the western areas, it is logical to assume that this moon goddess lived in the west.

Usually, the sun brought light and warmth to humans, who loved and venerated it. But occasionally it brought aridity and thirst. It was said that the ten suns once broke the rules and all went out together in the sky. Because of the intense heat, the whole earth was scorched and many people died of hunger. Yi, a crack archer, went to ask the suns to return home, but with no result. Therefore, Yi shot down the suns one after another. Only one of them escaped with his life. This was a myth reflecting the victory of humans over nature in ancient times.

Although Emperor Jun and his wives were mythological figures in *Shan-hai-jing*, the rulers of the Shang Dynasty deemed this emperor their earliest ancestor and re-

**254.** *Terra-cotta pottery painted with six images of the eight-horned sun. The two parallel white lines are typical of the Neolithic culture of Da-wen-kou. Found at Da-dun-zi, Pixian, East China.*

**255.** *The sun and two birds carved on a Neolithic ivory bowl of Hemudu culture in the Yangzi River valley (c. 4800 BC), later became a "lucky image" in China.*

247

# THE SUN IN JAPANESE BUDDHIST CULTURE

ATSUHIKO YOSHIDA

The date of the introduction of Buddhism in Japan from the Korean Paekche kingdom is traditionally set at either AD 538 or 552, though it is likely that Buddhist beliefs transmitted from China via Korea had already begun spreading among ordinary people much earlier.

However, it was not until the establishment of the idealized government of Prince Shotoku Taishi, toward the end of the sixth century AD, that Dainichi Nyorai ("Great Sun") or Rushana, as the Japanese call Dhyani Buddha Vairocana, came to be worshipped in Japan, along with several other solar deities. The new faith was enthusiastically propagated by Shotoku, a well-known scholar of Buddhism, whose learned commentary on the *Lotus Sutra* (four volumes of which have survived in the original draft written by the Prince himself) is among the oldest written work of known authorship in Japan.

---

**246.** *A huge solar lamp in front of the Todaiji shrine at Nara was installed when the gigantic cosmic Buddha Mahâ-Vairocana was consecrated (AD 752) in the temple during the reign of Tempyo-Shoho.*

**247.** *Among the "National Treasures" of Japan in the famous Tôji shrine at Kyoto, is the mandala of Dainichi Nyorai (Maha-Vairocana), together with several other deities made of wood-core dry lacquer. They are traditionally believed to have been installed by its founder Kukai (744–835) of the Shingon sect.*

vered the sun greatly. There were many records of this in the oracle-bone inscriptions, which tell that a ceremony was held in the morning to await the arrival of the sun and at nightfall to see the sun off; at the ceremony, oxen were sacrificed. The kings and aristocrats of Shang believed that, through these ceremonies, they could live alongside the gods after death.

The people of the Western Zhou Dynasty (c. 1100–771 BC) also venerated the sun. Although they had an abstract concept of Heaven (the largest phenomenon in the universe), the sun was still the main symbol of Heaven in their minds. So in their great Heaven-worshipping ceremony, the sun was the principal object.

The Shang Dynasty and the Zhou Dynasty (the Eastern Zhou, c. 770–221 BC) were prosperous periods for bronzeware production in China. There survive today many kinds from that time. The most important designs are ceremonial sacrificial vessels, which bear symbols of a circle and a whirlpool, at the center of which there is a small circle. In some simpler designs, there is no small circle. This kind of symbol can be seen in oracle-bone and bronzeware inscriptions, where it means *ri* (day) and it was used also in character-building. It is not rational to suppose that the bronzeware bearing these symbols was used only to worship Heaven.

The Eastern Zhou Dynasty was also called the Spring and Autumn period and the period of Warring States. Those were times of political division in China, after which the indigenous culture of the states developed. Different legends and myths about the sun survived in different lands. For example, Qu-yuan, a great poet of the Chu state (in the central valley of the Yangzi River), states in a poem that every day one of the ten suns travelled from the east to the west in a six-dragon-drawn carriage harnessed by their mother, Xihe. He also mentioned another sun god of the Chu state, the Monarch of the East (Dong-jun). This famous monarch started his journey across the sky every morning in the dragon carriage from Fusang (the mythological mulberry tree) in the east, while the people looked at his glorious face, singing and dancing, accompanied by bells and drums.

The culture and art of the Qin (221–207 BC) and Han dynasties (Western Han, 206 BC–AD 24; Eastern Han, AD 25–220) were influenced by earlier legends and myths. Two great emperors of these dynasties, Qin-shi-huang (first emperor of the Qin Dynasty, 246–210 BC), who first united China in 221 BC, and Han-wu-di (Emperor Wu-di of Han, 140–87 BC), who defeated the Hun peoples during his reign, visited Cheng Mountain on the eastern tip of the Shandong Peninsula and held sun-worshipping ceremonies as the orb rose from the sea. Shandong was the eastern cultural area of China, where the Da-wen-kou culture and the sun myths of Emperor Jun flourished. The Western Han Dynasty also held a ceremony to worship the Monarch of the East, the sun god of the former Chu state.

China is a vast country which contains many different cultural environments. Thus, the extant legends and myths of the sun in China were not systematic. Even worse, some of them were missing. Scholars in the Han period noticed this, and did their best to explain and restore the earlier myths. In practice, they added some new mythological systems.

From the early or, at the latest, the middle period of the Western Han Dynasty, there are many paintings and carvings of Fuxi and Nu-wa from various regions of

256 a

256 b

256 c

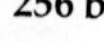

**256 a,b,c.** *A T-shaped painting on a second-century-*BC *shroud found in Tomb 1 at Ma-wang-dui was used to lead the soul (of the woman standing in the middle) to heaven. The "sun door of heaven" is guarded by two leopards and two humans. On the right is the mythical mulberry tree "Fusang" and the nine red suns, the largest of which has a crow, "the spirit of the sun." The sun god Fuxi, with a serpentine tail, is at the central apex, while the woman holding the moon on a dragon is probably Nu-wa.*

257

258

China. Nu-wa was a great mythological goddess in China, said to have created the world. Fuxi was also a creator.

The legends of the pre-Qin-Dynasty period did not refer to their connection with the sun and the moon, but in the Han period, they gradually became the sun god and the moon goddess, and also a married couple. In the picture, they have human heads and bodies but serpentine tails (probably of a dragon). Their tails often intertwine. Fuxi usually holds a sun in his hand and Nu-wa a moon. It should be noted that these were usually paintings and carvings of tombs of the Han period, when people believed in gods and ghosts. They hoped to live, after death, with the gods, especially the sun and moon gods.

In addition to Fuxi and Nu-wa, there were other legends. One of these stated that the sun god was Yandi (Emperor Yan), King of the South, who ruled the summer and whose token was fire; while the token of Fuxi, King of the East, who ruled the spring, was wood; the token of Shaohao, King of the West, who ruled the autumn, was metal; the token of Zhuanxu, King of the North, who ruled the winter, was water; and finally the token of Huangdi, a king of the central area, was earth. The legend was associated with the theory of the five elements (wood, fire, water, earth, and metal). Later, Yandi and Huangdi were regarded by the Chinese as remote ancestors.

The main artistic image of the sun in the Han period was a sun with a crow in it. The origin of the legend is not clear. The "Treatise of Five Elements" in the *History of Han* (Eastern Han) states that in AD 118, the sun was the color of russet, and on it was a black shadow like a magpie, which lasted several months. It is reasonable to assume that this image of the sun was derived from analogous astronomical observations.

The moon is another luminary observed by humans. But the status of the moon god was not high in the minds of the Chinese. It was after the spread of the Yin-Yang concept (the theory of positive and negative forces) in the Western Han period that the moon was worshipped officially.

---

**257.** *Petroglyph, painted with hematite red ores on the vertical cliffs of the Huashan ("flower") Mountains, depicts scenes of hunting, fishing, dancing and sun worship. Second century* BC*-thirteenth century* AD*. Ningming country, Guangxi province, China.*

**258.** *Detail of a Huashan rock painting near the Zuojiang River basin. The sun images are similar to those found on Chinese bronze drums.*

259

The prevailing image of the moon in the Han period was a moon with a toad or a white rabbit or both in it. The image of the moon with a toad in it had been used by the poet Qu-yuan (c. 340–278 BC). *Huai-nan-zi*, a work from the Han period, also mentions a toad in the moon, saying it was the moon's soul. In countries along the silk routes, the toad represented fertility, but there is no satisfactory explanation for moon-and-toad images in China.

As for the myths of the moon and the white rabbit, they can be found in many countries, from South Asia to Latin America. In the past, some scholars thought that the Chinese moon-and-white-rabbit myth came from India through Buddhism. But judging by surviving historical relics from the early Western Han period, the native white rabbit of China had already been associated with the moon before the introduction of Buddhism. Although the myth of the white rabbit in the moon was native Chinese, the culture and art of the sun and other luminaries was indeed influenced by foreign cultures.

During the late period of the Western Han, Buddhism gradually became influential in China. Buddhism came first to the Western Region (Central Asia) and then to the areas of the Yellow and Yangzi rivers. Dunhuang was situated on the important silk routes. The Cave Temples of the Thousand Buddhas near Dunhuang were wonderful achievements of Buddhist culture. There were many mural paintings showing Indian mannerism in the art of the sun.

Cave Temple 249 was built at the time of the Western Wei Dynasty, a dynasty of the To-pa tribe (Jouan-jouan) from the northern steppe. On the western side of its middle sunken panel, there is a picture of Asura holding the sun and moon in his hands. Asura was a demon in India (but Asuras/Ahuras were mighty beneficent gods in Iran), who often fought against Sakra devanam Indra. When he fought against this chief of Trayastrmsa, he could block out the sun and moon with his hand. In this picture, the strong and muscular Asura has, following Indian legend, four eyes and

**259.** ***Stone carvings, belonging to different periods, also depict the sun god of nomadic people who live in the Helan mountains, Ningxia province, northwest China, and also in Lianyung Gang, east China.***

260 a

260 b

four arms, two of which are held high toward the sun and the moon; he stands in the ocean. At his left and right sides, there are a god of thunder and a god of lightning as well as other mythological figures.

Cave Temple 285 was also built during the Western Wei Dynasty. On the eastern side of the sunken panel, there is a picture of Mani, a miraculous pearl in Buddhist legends. It was raised by two vigorous gods, and toward Mani, Fuxi, the Chinese sun god, and Nu-wa, the Chinese moon god, are running. A sun, in which there is a golden crow, hangs round Fuxi's neck and a moon, in which there is a toad, hangs on Nu-wa's. Fuxi and Nu-wa hold in their hands, respectively, a carpenter's square and a pair of compasses. These carpenter's tools were the symbols of the sun and moon gods in Chinese mythology. On the western side of the sunken panel are pictured two gods of thunder. Wang Chong, an author of the Han period, said that the image of thunder was like a string of drums, and that thunder gods were vigorous deities. This Chinese artistic form is pictured here.

It is difficult to suppose that all these figures relating to the sun, moon, and so forth, were worshipped by the cave-builders and the people who lived there, but there were really paintings showing the worship of sun in the Cave Temples of a Thousand Buddhas.

Cave Temple 76 was built during the Tang Dynasty (AD 618–907). On the northern wall of the main hall, there is a painting of Ekadasamukhavalokitesvara, one of the six images of Avalokitesvara, a bodhisattva. Some Buddhist legends have it that Avalokitesvara is the incarnation of Sûrya, the Indian sun god, and the palace of this bodhisattva is in the sun. Legends also proclaim that believers in Buddhism, when

**260 a,b.** *A vessel called "Ding" was decorated with the sun and moon images. The dragons became more prominent during the Ming Dynasty when this bronze was cast (1582) for the temple of Chenghuang, a Chinese town-god of the netherworld.*

261

262

they met with any trouble, could be rescued through chanting the name of Avalokistesvara. The cave builders depicted the image of Ekadasamukhavalokitesvara in the Chinese style. Here the art and culture of the sun of India and China meet.

Besides Buddhism, Zoroastrianism and Manichaeism also spread into China. Zoroastrianism was not influential here, but Manichaeism, called by the Chinese "the Religion of Luminosity," was important. At the time of the Tang Dynasty, Manichaean temples were built in the capital and other cities of China. They were called "Da-yun-guang-ming," or "Temples of Grand Cloud and Luminosity" and some Chinese, though fewer than Buddhist believers, followed this religion and venerated luminosity and the sun. In southeastern China, there stands a statue of Mani in Quanzhou (Zaiton).

There are also many Manichaean paintings and writings in Chinese Turkestan, where the Manichaean Steppe Uighur settled after their defeat by the Qirqiz in AD 840. Later, at the time of the Five Dynasties (907–960) and the Song Dynasty (960–1279), Manichaeism became more popular among the people of eastern China, and leaders of the farmers' uprising even used it in their propaganda. The Religion of the White Lotus and some other popular religions in the (Mongol) Yuan Dynasty (1271–1368), the Ming Dynasty (1368–1644), and the (Nuzhen/Manzhou) Qing Dynasty (1644–1911) inherited the strong traditions of the former Religion of Luminosity. The Ming (luminosity) had its remote origin in the Religion of Luminosity.

After the Qin and Han dynasties, although the abstract concept of Heaven took root among the Chinese, the official ceremony of sun veneration was still held regularly by successive governments until the Qing Dynasty, the last in China. The im-

**261.** *Jade Pi of the Neolithic Liangzhu culture (c. 3300–2200 BC), excavated in Caoxie Shan, Jiangsu province, in 1973. The perforated circular disc symbolizes heaven, and jade, immortality.*

**262.** *Jade Ts'ung represents the earth. It also belongs to Liangzhu culture and was unearthed in Sidun, Jiangsu province, China.*

ages of the sun and moon were often used to symbolize the brightness, righteousness, and divinity of the rulers. It should be noted that some historical Chinese dynasties, such as the Liao, the Jin, the Yuan, and the Qing, were founded by the nomad peoples of the Mongolian steppe. The nomad peoples believed in shamanism and worshipped the sun and other luminaries.

The Xiongnu (Huns) were described by Sima-Qian, a great Chinese historian of the first century BC, in his *Historical Records*. According to his description, the Xiongnu worshipped their ancestors, Heaven and earth, gods and ghosts. Their ruler, the Chan-yu, called himself "the Grand Chan-yu of Xiongnu, supported by Heaven" or "the Grand Chan-yu of Xiongnu, borne by Heaven and the Earth, supported by the Sun and the Moon." But the sun was the most important deity in their pantheon, so the Chan-yu went out of his tent every morning to hold ceremonies for the rising sun. He also went out in the evening to celebrate the rising moon.

The Turkic peoples of the steppe also worshipped the sun. The door of their Khaqan's tents faced the east because they venerated the morning sun. The Khaqans of Uighur, a Turkic-speaking tribe, usually had the title of "Kun ai tangrida. . . Khaqan," of which "*kun*" meant "sun" and "*ai*" "moon."

The Liao Dynasty was founded by the Khitay people who gradually controlled northern China, including the Mongol steppe, after the Tang collapse in 907. They respected Heaven and earth and also worshipped the sun on many occasions, such as the Empress's birthday. There is little evidence of their veneration for the moon. "Treatise on the Military Establishment" in the *History of Liao* even said when raising the army for a battle, the Emperor must lead the officials and the generals in a ceremony for Heaven, the earth, and the sun; but for the moon, black oxen and white horses were sacrificed.

The Mongols, who conquered a vast area of the Eurasian continent and established the Yuan Dynasty in China, believed in primitive shamanism and revered the sun and the moon as well as Heaven and earth, fire and water. John of Plano Carpini, a Franciscan monk, was an envoy of Pope Innocent IV (1243–54) to the Mongol Empire. When he crossed the Eurasian steppe, he saw the Mongolian people making the sun and other things the first offerings of food and drink, especially in the morning before they ate or even drank.

Veneration of the sun and other luminaries is still alive among some minorities of northern China. The people of E-lun-chun Nationality live in the mountainous area of Grand Xing-an-ling, northeastern China. They hold ceremonies for the sun on the first day of the lunar year and worship the moon on the fifteenth and the twenty-fifth days of that month. They swear by the sun in their arguments and pray to the sun when they meet with trouble. The Altai-Uryangqai peoples of the northern district of Xinjiang Province pay their respects to the sun and the moon, venerating the sun every morning. They sprinkle milky tea toward the sun, pray to it three times, and then eat breakfast. This daily ceremony is attended by the whole family or a representative of it. But the moon-worshipping ceremonies are different for men and women (who speak the Tuva language). The men worship the crescent moon while the women revere the full moon.

The minorities of southern China also worship the sun and other luminaries. For

263

example, the people of Yi Nationality in Sichuan, Yunnan, and Guizhou provinces pray to the sun and the moon on many occasions because of their justice to everyone in the world. There is in Yao Nationality, Guangxi Province, a popular verse called "Mi-luo-tuo"; named after a creator goddess who created the sun with her silver necklace, the moon with her silver earrings, and humans out of beeswax (skin), a pear (head), a banana (body), a shoulder pole (legs), and a wooden club (arms and hands).

Pan-gu was a mythological creator of Heaven and earth. His legend did not appear until the time of the Three States (AD 220–265). It states that when this creator died, his eyes became the sun and the moon. Although this mythological figure first came into being in the Yellow River Valley (*Shan-hai-jing* had referred to him), he was not as popular in the Han Nationality as in the area of Minorities of south-western China. Some minorities there even deem him their ancestor.

The homage of minorities to the sun in southwestern China was expressed particularly in bronze drums. More than fifteen thousand pieces of this kind of bronzeware were found in southwestern China, and in some districts of southeastern China about three hundred pieces were found. The drums were recently divided into eight types by Chinese archaeologists. The earliest type was excavated from tombs from the seventh century BC in Chuxiong (near Kunming), Yunnan Province. There were only

**263.** ***Prophet Mani is painted in Cave Temple 285 at Dunhuang together with Fuxi and Nu-wa, the sun and the moon deities. In Chinese mythology Fuxi holds a carpenter's square while Nu-wa a pair of compasses. The painting is dated AD 538/539.***

264

265

simple designs on their surfaces and bodies. This type lasted up to the fifth century BC. Thereafter, the designs became more and more exquisite.

The typical surface design displays a shining sun. Although there is much discussion about the drum's functions and the meanings of the various symbols, the depiction of a shining sun reflects a spirit of veneration. Also included were toad figures squatting on the edge of the drum's surface. This motif did not appear until the first century BC, that is, the later period of the second type of drum. This type originated in Guangxi Province, an autonomous region of Zhuang Nationality. Some scholars have noted that in many districts of Guangxi, the people of Zhuang Nationality keep up the practice of toad worship. They celebrate a toad festival on the first day of the lunar year, praying for a good harvest. It is possible that the shining sun and the squatting toads on the surface of the drum were objects of worship for the ancient people in southeastern China, which was also true of many other peoples of Asia.

**264.** *Chinese and Indian mythologies and painting styles are combined in this sixth-century wall-painting in the Cave Temple of the Thousand Buddhas at Dunhuang (no. 249). An Indian Asura is holding in his hands the sun and the moon as he stands in the sea, while surrounded by Chinese gods, including those of Thunder and Lightning.*

**265.** *Wielding shields with images of the rising sun, ceremonial dancers celebrate the New Year spring festival at the shrine of the "Celestial Empress" at Quanzhou, China.*

266

267

# THE SUN GOD IN SOUTH ASIA

AHMAD HASAN DANI

A concept of the sun god is not attested to in the Indus Valley Civilization, as the religious practices of the time tended to revere plants and animals and their associated divinities. However, planetary ideas were not unknown at this period. The sun might have been represented by the symbol of the circle, as witnessed in the Indus seals. There is little doubt that the rayed circles found on potsherds at Cemetery H at Harappa from the post-Indus period represent the sun. Similar rayed semicircles and full circles have also been found in other places thought to be prehistoric in context but dating from a later period. The first design is to be found in a rock shelter in the Raigarh area at Singhanpur village in Chattisgarh. Two rayed circles are engraved on one of two stone slabs discovered, out of context, at a Late Neolithic level at Burzahom in Kashmir. The slabs depict hunting scenes in the same style as those seen in the upper Indus region from Ladakh, Baltistan, Gilgit, and Chilas. These representations of the sun are purely symbolic and may have other meanings in different contexts. However, solar symbols, even a sun motif held in human hands or even as parts

**266.** ***Sûrya sculpture, as one of the three* pârshva-devatâs, *found in the thirteenth-century Temple of the Sun at Konarak.* (National Museum of India, New Delhi)**

**267.** ***The sun temple at Konarak ("corner of the sun") is constructed in the shape of Sûrya's sun chariot with twelve pairs of massive stone wheels, representing the twelve months, and planets symbolized by seven monolith horses.***

of human limbs, are very common on rock carvings from around Chilas and Hunza, whereas in the Upper Indus Valley context they all belong to the first millennium AD. Culturally and even ethnically they are related to similar sun motifs at Tamgaly in Kazakhstan, Chile-sai, and Saimaly Tash in Kyrgyzstan, as well as at other sites in the Pamirs. Here the sun plays an active role in the shaman way of life of the nomadic peoples spread over a wide area from Mongolia to the western Himalayas.

In Indo-Aryan beliefs and practices the sun assumed great importance, as the Aryans made sacrifices to the forces of nature, the sun being the most prominent. Various aspects of the sun are praised in the Vedic mantras, and it is from several qualities of the sun that other deities, such as Vishnu, are derived. One important conception of the sun implies its eternal movement, riding on a chariot drawn by seven horses, with subsidiary deities driving away the darkness. This is based on the ancient idea of the sun circling the earth. However, the Aryan religion was noniconic, hence, no figurative representation of the sun god is known from this early period. This is the basic difference between the noniconic concept of the sun's movement, implied in the Aryan religion, and the symbolic concept of the sun in rock engravings where humans are seen to derive all their power from the sun, which controls all earthly phenomena; the sun plays an active role in communion with humans and is thus conceived as a symbol. For the Indus Valley Civilization the solar circle was part of the planetary system—an object of scientific experience rather than religious worship.

The figurative representation of the sun god in South Asia was imported from the outside, and its ultimate integration into the theistic religion was developed during the historical period, roughly from the third century BC onward. The first example of the sun god, as discovered at Taxila, has already been described. As the hands of this figure are broken off, the distinctive attributes of the deity are not known. However, this type maintained its identity thereafter.

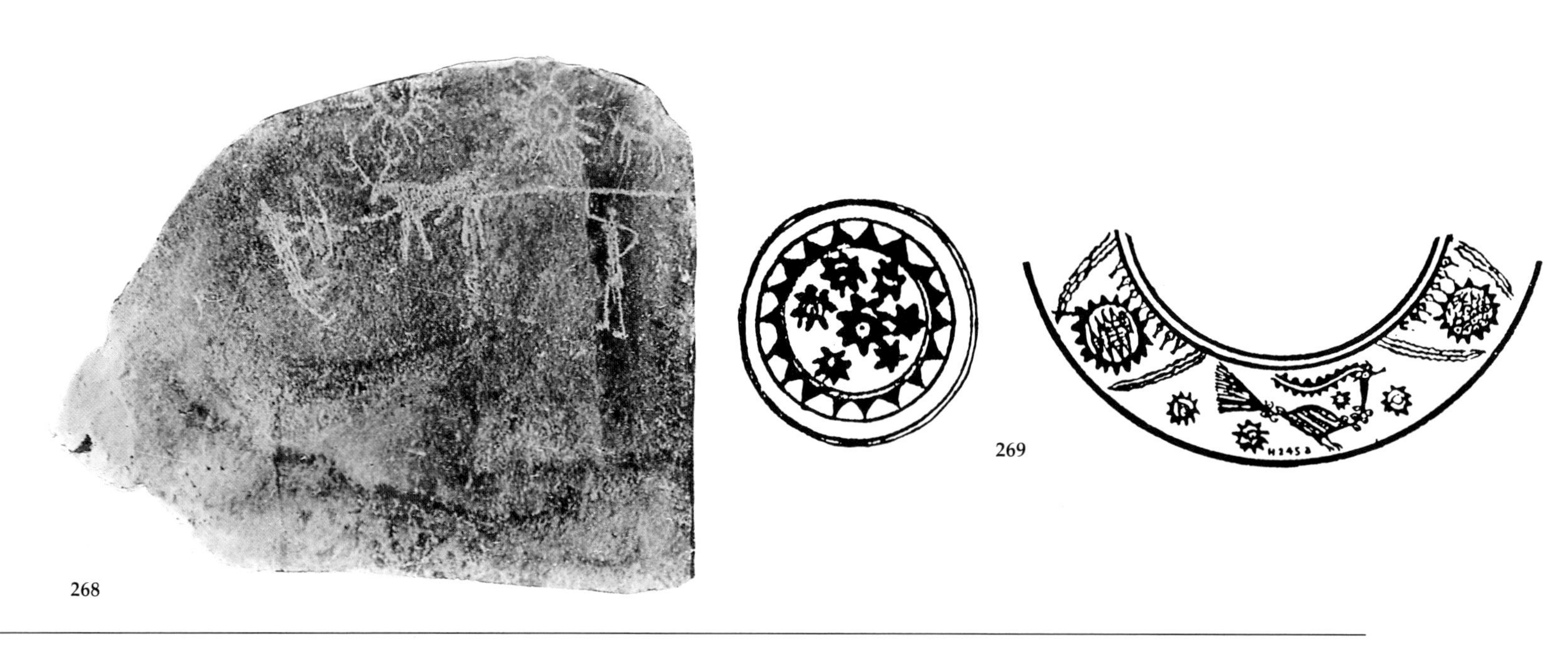


**268.** *A Late Neolithic petroglyph at Burzahom in Kashmir showing two rayed circles, representing the sun.*

One important source for the sun god can be traced back to the Greek deity Helios, represented on the coins of the Indo-Bactrian rulers Plato, Philoxenus, and Telephos. One formulation is seen on the coins of Plato, in which Helios, with radiate head, is riding on a four-horse-drawn chariot. This same type is also seen on the coins of the Scythian ruler Moves.

A second type can be seen on the coins of Philoxenus and Telephos. The first is described by Gardner as: "Sun-god, facing, radiate, clad in chiton, himation and boots; holds in left hand long scepter; right extended." It is this second type of standing sun god that was found at Sirkap, Taxila, but the broken hands suggest different manual attributes. The first type of sun god, riding on a four-horse-drawn chariot, is seen on a railing at Bodhgaya. Here the sun god is more Indianized, as are the subsidiary deities associated with him. Similarly at Bhaja, in the Deccan, the sun god is represented on his chariot, drawn by four horses and accompanied by the goddesses of dawn, who discharge their arrows at the demons of darkness, as described above.

A relationship with the Hellenic Helios is quite clear, though new, Indian, elements have been added to the figure. Whether with two or four horses, this type is also seen in Gandharan art. One example is known from a Corinthian capital at Swat and another from Jamalgarhri. The last example of this type is known from Khair Khaneh in Afghanistan, a work in marble, dating from the fifth century AD, with the sun god seated in a two-horse-drawn chariot, Danda and Pingola on either side, and a charioteer below. The deity wears a highly ornamented, Central Asian costume including high boots.

It is on the coins of the Kushana emperors, Kanishka and Hunishka, that the Greek and Iranian traditions integrate and the sun god stands erect with a scepter in his left hand, his right hand extended holding an object sometimes thought to be noose, sometimes a flame, or a (lotus) flower. On some coins of Kanishka the name is

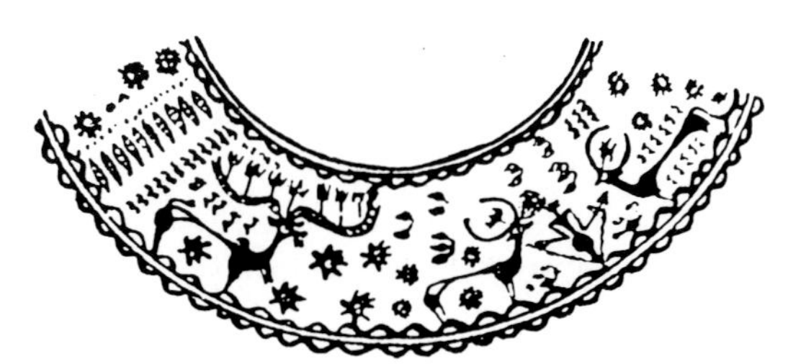

**269.** *A variety of solar motifs are seen on Indus Valley seals, as at Harappa. First millenium* BC.

270

271

written "Helios" and on others "Miiro;" sometimes the name is spelt as "Mioro" or "Miyro." Hunishka's coins give the spelling as "Miiro," "Mioro," or "Miro." This standing type of sun god appears to be Iranian in origin, as the name suggests, but it was most probably made popular by the Kushanas and might have been introduced from Central Asia, as is the case with the Taxila example.

However, most remarkable is the seated bodhisattva type of sun god, for the first time seen at Jamalgarhri and Swat; here, the deity rides in a horse-drawn chariot. In these examples, the right hand is raised, holding what looks like a lotus flower. A similar example, but without the chariot, can be seen on a merlon ornament from Surkh Kotal in Afghanistan. This Gandharan-style sun god from the Kushana period continued here for a long time and is seen in the Martand temple at Anantnag in Kashmir.

This type is rarely seen at Mathura, but one example, a woman's head ornament is known: the sun god is seated on a two-horse chariot. Another example of the sun god standing on a horse-drawn chariot is also found in Mathura.

An entirely different type of sun god, seated on a low stool, but with his knee raised above his waist and his feet placed on a seat, exactly as in the coin portraits of Wima Kadphises and Hurvishka, has been obtained from Mathura. In all these depictions the deity is clad in tight-fitting Indo-Scythian dress and wears high boots. This

**270.** ***First image of the sun god in high boots and wig appears to be a gift of the Scythians as adapted by local craftsmen. c. first century BC. Taxila, Pakistan.***

**271.** ***Sûrya sitting beneath a trefoil arch and holding two sun symbols: a lotus and the staff of authority. Eighth century. Martand temple, Kashmir.***

272

type of dress is also seen with standing sun-god figures. This type became very common in the Gupta period.

It became the basis for the canonical text *Brihat Samhita* by Varaha Mihira, which says: "The Sun God should be dressed in northern style, the body covered from breast to foot. He wears a crown and holds two lotuses by the stalks along his arms. His face is adorned with earrings; he has a long pearl necklace and girdle around his waist [and] his body is clad in armour."

A number of standing or sitting Sûrya figures following this concept from the fifth and sixth centuries AD have been found in Varanabi. In the post-Gupta period, sun temples and images of the sun god became very popular. The sculptures fall into two broad divisions: the South Indian type, for example, the sun god from Alampur in Adhra Pradesh, a standing figure that does not wear high boots or the typical tight-fitting Indo-Scythian dress but rather, has a rayed orb around his head, his body bare but ornamented, wearing only a tight-fitting dhoti below. The second is the North Indian type, for example, the wooden image from Gazan, District Kulu, from the ninth and tenth centuries AD, wherein tight-fitting dress and high boots are clearly seen. Gradually the North Indian figures no longer wore the Indo-Scythian dress but continued to wear boots as is the case with the Sûrya from Khajuraho and from Baijnath in the Almora district.

---

***272.** Ruins of the Martand sun temple. Eighth century. Kashmir.*

273

274

275

Highly interesting is the sun temple at Martand in Kashmir, generally assigned to King Lalitaditya and dating from the middle of the eighth century AD. The main temple stands in the center of a huge courtyard, each side having cellular halls, the main double-hall entrance on the western side. The main temple consists of three distinct chambers: the outermost, the *ardha-mandapa*, resembling the front porch of classical fanes, or temples; the middle one, the *antarala* like the pronaos of the Greeks; and the innermost, the *garbhagriha*, resembling the naos of the Greeks. This structure is the most ornate. On each of the four facades is a pediment supported on fluted, pseudo-Doric pilasters and enclosing a trefoil arch for a deity within. Many elements are derived from the Gandhara school. The seated figure of the sun god within a trefoil arch shows him clad in Indo-Scythian dress and high boots, a scepter in one hand and a lotus in the other, a type well known in Gandhara. However, according to Pran Gopal Paul, "in other Kashmiri Sûrya images... the objects in the two hands of the main figure can be easily recognized as lotuses, the usual attributes of the deity."

Images of the sun god became very popular during the Pala and Sena periods in Bengal. They are most numerous in Bangladesh, next only to those of Vishnu. However, as noted by Dr. Bhattasali, the worship of the sun god has virtually disappeared. Only Hindu women in the villages observe a *Vrata* in honour of Sûrya. A typical example is described thus by Dr. Bhattasali:

**273.** *Sûrya holds full-blown lotuses in both hands and rides a seven-horse chariot driven by charioteer Aruna, flanked on either side by Danda and Pingala as well as the consorts Chhaya and Suvarchasâ, protected by the two arrowshooters Usha and Pratyusha. Eleventh century. Khajuraho.*

**274.** *Sûrya with solar family. Twelfth century. Bengal.* **(Asutosh Museum of Indian Art, Calcutta)**

**275.** *Armed Sûrya with consorts and attendants. Tenth century. Almorah.*

276

277

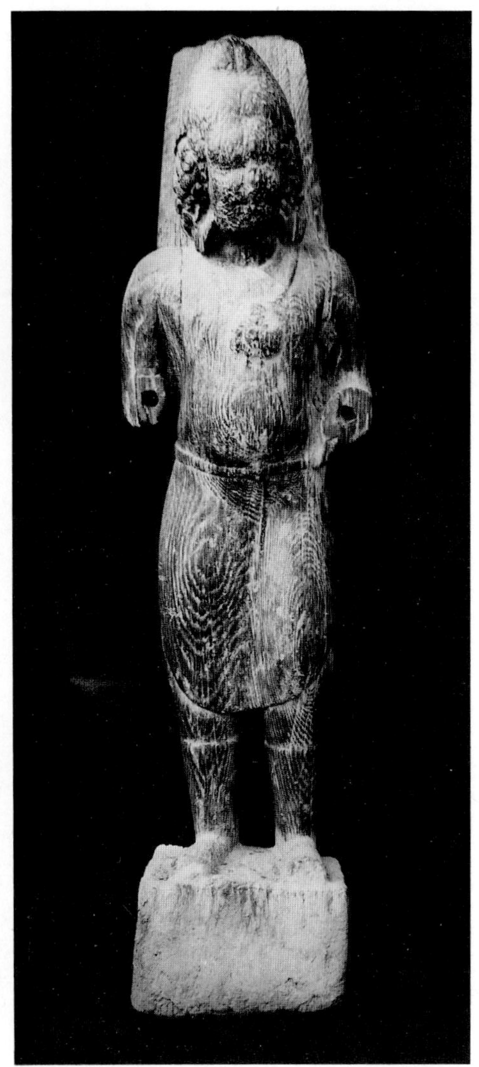

278

The god stands erect on a lotus pedestal, holding in his two hands full-blown lotuses which rise just above the shoulders. He is generally represented as smiling, and his head is surrounded by a halo. His body is covered with armor. His waist is encircled by an ornamental girdle, and a rolled scarf passes over his waist-cloth. His feet and part of the legs are covered by high boots, a feature not met with in the image of any other Indian deity. Directly in front of the god stands a miniature female figure, in front of which is represented the legless Aruna, the Charioteer of the Sun, with a whip in his right hand and the reins of the horses beneath in his left. The horses drawing the car of the god are seven in number and the car moves on a single wheel. To the right of the Sun God, a lady stands with a fly-whisk (sometimes with a lotus) in her right hand and to her right is figured a fat-bellied, bearded man carrying pen and inkstand in his hands. Further to the right, a female figure is represented shooting arrows. To the left of the god are represented three similar figures, but the male one has no beard and holds either a staff or a sword or a *chank-shell* in one of his hands. All these figures, except the two females shooting arrows at the edges, wear boots like the Sun God. Eleven miniature figures, exactly like the Sun God, are sometimes represented near the edges of the slab, generally five on each side of the god and one over his head.

The seven horses of the sun can be traced to the fifth book of the *Rg Veda*. Ushas (i.e., Dawn) is the wife of Sûrya. The Vedic sages put all the poetry and joy of their heart into this. Other wives of the Sun God, such as Saranyu, or Surenu, and Chhaya, are mentioned in the *Rg Veda*, as are Sûrya's children. He is the father of the Asvins,

**276.** *Sun god on chariot. Seventh century.* **(Asutosh Museum of Indian Art, Calcutta)**

**277.** *South Indian style Sûrya with bare feet. Eleventh century. Alampur, Andra Pradesh.*

**278.** *Wooden image of Sûrya. Gazan, Kullu.*

279. *Sûrya. Provincial Pala style. Twelfth century. Bengal.*

280. *Sûrya. Tenth century. Bangladesh.* (Dhaka Museum, Bangladesh)

281. *Sûrya. Eleventh century. Rangpur, Bangladesh.* (Dhaka Museum, Bangladesh)

Yama and Manu. Revanta was one such child, begotten on Surenu in the shape of a horse. The "one-wheel" concept of the sun is found in the Puranas. The Angirasa Brahmins have been associated with solar worship from the earliest times. In the Puranas they are equated with Magas or the Sakadvipi Brahmins, and were instrumental in spreading the worship of the sun god in India. Saka–dvipa is Scythia, the former name of Sind. The Maga Brahmins are thought to have been Iranians, but in fact they appear to have come with the Scythian rulers from Central Asia. This is the principal reason why the Central Asian type of figure became so popular in North India. The image of the sun god has also been discovered at Mrohaung in Arakan, Burma.

Solar worship is as old as the Vedas; but in spite of allusions therein to his chariot, horses, and consorts, it is the divine energy of the dazzling solar power that became the object of devotion rather than his anthropomorphic form. In the time of Kumara Gupta solar worship became very common, and a Mandasor inscription from that time (AD 437) records the erection of a temple to the sun god. The Vardhana emperors of Kanauj were also solar worshippers. Their very names, Aditya-Vardhana, Prabhaka-Vardhana indicate their faith. Emperor Harsh-Vardhana applies the epithet of Parama-adityabhakta and is known to have included sun worship. In Bengal the Varman and Sena rulers, who followed the Palas, called themselves "Saura," that is, worshippers of the sun god. The most famous image of the sun god was in the temple at Multan, which was described by Alberuni. The Arabs did not destroy this temple in the early stages of their conquest and it continued to exist until the seventeenth century. The former name of Multan was Sambapura, where an annual Car Festival was held.

However, the crowning achievement of the Orissan builders was the Temple of the Sun at Konarak, erected during the reign of Narasimhadeva (1238–1264). The design of the temple is conceived as a likeness of the sun god's chariot. Around the base of the temple platform are twelve great stone wheels, and colossal free-standing statues of horses are erected in front of the main entrance. The shrine of Kanaraka originally included a number of reliefs of the sun god. On the chariot with Sûrya are the twin figures of his charioteers and the kneeling maidens of dawn. The sun god himself is framed in a trefoil arch. Below are the horses of the quadriga, the whole group recalling the ancient representation at Bodhgaya. Equally interesting are the large number of erotic figures from the Temple of the Sun at Konarak.

The worship of the sun continued in South Asia right up to the Mughal period, particularly during the reign of Akbar. However, solar worship began to decline with the end of the influence of the foreign, Central Asian conquerors. Thereafter the older form of the Vedic religion merged into the new development of theistic Hinduism and the worship of the sun became integrated with the Hindu gods of the trinity—Brahmā, Vishnu, and Siva—thus losing its individuality and earlier importance.

282

283

# SOLAR UNIVERSALITY OF SOUTH ASIAN CULTURES

MADANJEET SINGH

The solar deity Aiyanâr is worshipped widely in southern India by the Tamil community in the form of a stone set up under a tree on the bank of a river or a pond. "Radiant as a thousand suns," he is the son of the two great Hindu gods Vishnu and Siva. The twin Karuppan is his nocturnal manifestation and hence Aiyanâr has the power both over light and dark, life and death. He is the "hunter deity," as well as the god of fertilizing powers, and, in a ritual similar to the one in which a horse was sacrificed for the Vedic Varuna, Aiyanâr's worshippers customarily offer him two terra-cotta horses—one for Aiyanâr (day sun) and the other for Karuppan (night sun). The devotees who cannot afford to offer terra-cotta horses merely draw on the ground an image of the horse or a circle representing the sun (*dhûli-chitra*) and then dance wildly around the sacred stone, drumming vigorously, creating a booming sound on a large earthenware pitcher.

**282.** **Sûryanamaskar** ***at the tenth century Mukteshwar temple, Bhuvaneshwar, India.***

**283.** ***A father and son worshipping the sun in a pool known as the ancient "River Chandrabhaga," near the thirteenth-century sun temple at Konarak.***

284

285

The worship of Aiyanâr is a remarkable example of the South Asian solar culture in which traditions of so many ancient civilizations are neatly encapsulated. Iranian Avesta texts refer to the sun as "swift-horsed" (*aurvat-aspa*), a notion shared with the Vedas and Greek mythology. The Greek writer Xenophon apparently mistook the Zoroastrian "Ahura Mazda" for "Zeus Helios," as he wrote about white horses being sacrificed at ceremonies performed in Persia during the Achaemenian period. The Seven Virgins associated with Aiyanâr are also very similar to the Greek myth of Helios being the brother and colleague of the Erinyes, or Furies, the terrifying female fiends. Ayanar, the sun god is worshipped along with the tutelary deities of water called the Seven Virgins, the harbingers of sudden death. Apollo's twin sister, Artemis, similarly indulged in wild and lascivious dances accompanied by nymphs (dryads) in mountains, forests, and marshes, and brought sudden death through "gentle darts." The Greeks later identified Apollo with the Egyptian "Horus of two Horizons," a tradition synonymous with Aiyanâr's twin manifestation as Karuppan, representing the day sun and the night sun.

Sun worship was not unknown in South Asia before the nomadic Aryan "sun worshippers" descended from Central Asia around 1500 BC and made their own contribution to South Asian solar mythology and culture. Floor drawing (*dhûli-chitra*) was a pre-Vedic practice, according to the sixth-century Sanskrit treatise on painting *Vishnudharmottara*: "The lotus (as the sun symbol) appears much later, and drawing the flower *on the floor* was not sanctioned by the Vedas." *Shamba Purana* states that "the

**284.** *"Bankura" terra-cotta horses of Bengal belong to a similar tradition as the offering of terra-cotta horses in the Aiyanâr ritual.*

**285. Sûrya Alpana** *drawing by a Bengali housewife, Shikha Sikdar.*

**286.** *The sun (as swastika symbol) was depicted on the Buddha's foot-impressions, before his anthropomorphic image was first created in the first century.* **(Prince of Wales Museum of Western India, Bombay)**

286

sun is represented as an eight-petalled lotus flower, but in early times the sun was worshipped in the shape of a circle called *sunya-mûrti* (cipher-shaped), and this was one of the names of the sun in pre-Vedic times."

Circular sun symbols belonging to the prehistoric period and tribal rock art have been found in several locations in South Asia. The earliest testimonials are the rayed circles engraved on the Neolithic stone slabs found at Burzahom in Kashmir and at other sites in Ladakh, Gilgit, Baltistan, Hunza, and Chilas. Similar sun motifs were found in a rock shelter at Singhanpur in Chatisgarh, among post-Indus-period potsherds at Harappa, and in symbols seen as far south as in the prehistoric rock art of the Vedda tribe in Sri Lanka.

Among the pre-Aryan sun symbols was also the ubiquitous swastika, images of which were found at the Indus Valley sites (c. 2500–1750 BC). Both the right-hand swastika and the left-hand type, called *Sauvastika*, were unearthed at Mohenjo-daro, but there is no evidence to show that the Indus Valley inhabitants attached the same

287

288 a

288 b

289

290

**287.** ***Horned deity. Mohenjo-daro seal. Third millenium*** **BC. (National Museum, New Delhi)**

**288 a,b.** ***Swastika and*** **Sauvastika** ***symbols. Mohenjo-daro.*** **(National Museum, New Delhi)**

**289,290.** ***Mohenjo-daro seal showing an antler emerging out of a bull, and another showing a sun disc on the top of a leonine figure.*** **(National Museum, New Delhi)**

291

292

293

meaning to them as they came to represent in later times; the right-hand swastika is the symbol of light and day (as it rotates along the course taken by the sun) while the left-hand *sauvastika* (like the Nazi emblem) stands for the darkness of night. The swastika's semantics are the sun, procreation, and fecundity and the symbol was popular all over the world, seen on Mesopotamian coinage, ancient Chinese and Japanese ceramics, garments, embroideries, gold and silver vessels, and other objects. In the Christian Gnostic tradition and in Byzantine art it is depicted as the "Cross of Light" or the Gammadion Cross (because its arms resemble the Greek letter gamma). The appearance of swastika motifs is particularly intriguing in Amerindian art. Maya art, the colorful handicrafts of the Navajo Indians of North America, and the embroideries of the natives of Guatemala.

From the objects unearthed in the Indus Valley Civilization sites it is evident that the sun's connection with animals was also a pre-Vedic conception in South Asia. It is reflected in the Mohenjo-daro seal showing six animal heads: the unicorn, the bull, the antlered stag, the leonine figure, and two animals (with broken heads) that fan out like sun rays from the core of a round, sunlike disc. Another Mohenjo-daro seal shows a "deity" with horns and a treelike crown on his head as he sits surrounded by a tiger, a rhinoceros, an elephant, and a bull. The figure is similar to the sun-related, antlered anthropomorphic and theriomorphic images seen on petroglyphs in Central

**291–296.** ***Eight*** **dikpâlas,** ***solar deities representing the four cardinal and four intermediate quarters, were discovered in the twelfth-century Raja-Rani temple, Bhuvaneshwar, India. They include: Kuvera (north) (291), Varuna (west) (292), Agni (southeast) (293), Vayu (northwest) (294), Indra (east) (295), Yama (south) (296).*** **(State Museum of Art and Archaeology, Bhuvaneshwar, India)**

**297.** ***Siva-Nataraja, with phallus erect and several hands, dances within a flaming orb of the sun. This unusual bas-relief of the solar deity in stone is carved above a Sûrya sculpture on a facade of the ninth-century Vaital Duel temple, Bhuvaneshwar, India.***

294

295

296

297

Asia, Europe, and in the prehistoric African rock drawings at Tassilli N'Ajjer in the Sahara. Most deities in the South Asian religions that followed were based on these human-animal composite figures, such as the Hindu solar deity Vishnu in his multiple forms: Narasimha with the head of a lion, the horse-headed Hayagriva, and the boar-headed Varaha.

South Asian solar cultures were boosted following the Aryan arrival because of their contacts with western regions. This is evident from the Indo-European names for the Vedic gods, including Surias, Indas, and Maruttas (Sûrya, Indra, and Marutah in Sanskrit), which can be traced back to about 1760 BC in Mesopotamia where the Kassites bore such names.

Indara, Uruvna, Mitira, and Nasatiya—the four solar deities whom the *Rg Veda* calls Indra, Varuna, Mitra, and Nakshatras—were invoked in a treaty around 1400 BC between the Mittannis and the Hittites of Anatolia. The Hittites, whose empire covered much of Turkey and parts of northern Syria, were themselves foreigners to Anatolia and spoke a dialect which was a branch of the Indo-European language group that includes Sanskrit, Greek, and Latin.

Prominent among the Hittite cult gods was the Storm God of Heaven and the Sun Goddess of Arinna, who were worshipped in the Great Temple at their imperial capital, Hattusa. A tablet from one of the temples states: "The deity has now been made as a statue in silver covered with gold in the shape of a bull on all fours." As the

298

299

**298.** *Crowned with a sun disc and tall feathers enclosed by her two horns, the sacred cow Hathor was found in a temple (c. 1440 BC) of Thutmose III at Dier-el-Bahari.* **(Egyptian Museum, Cairo)**

**299.** *Cow worship at the temple of Suraj Kund, near New Delhi.*

300

301

invaluable statue was never found (evidently stolen) it is not clear whether the bull had a human face, as seen later in Mesopotamia. At one of the gates of the palace at Khorsabad, built for the Assyrian king Sargon II (721–705 BC), stood a pair of human-headed winged bulls as magic guardians against misfortune (they are now in the British Museum). These were the solar equivalent of the human-headed lion sphinx in Egypt, another powerful empire with which the Hittites had a close, love-hate relationship.

Similar human-headed bull sphinxes flank the entrance to the Parsi Boyace temple in Bombay, of which the original models may have been brought by the Maga (Zoroastrian) priests who came to India in the early centuries of the Christian era. They were either Iranian or perhaps came with the Scythian rulers from Central Asia. In any case they were invited to act as priests for the worship of the sun god and were soon elevated to the status of Brahmins. It is believed that Maga Brahmins were also the ones who popularized the Sûrya icon dressed in typical Central Asian attire, as early images of the deity in India show him wearing the Scythian dress of close-fitting coat and high boots. Sûrya is the only deity who is not barefoot in South Asian iconography, though in southern parts of the continent the sun god is depicted without boots, like the other gods. The spread of solar astrology in South Asia is also attributed to the Maga Brahmins, known as Bhojakas in Indian tradition, even though solar astronomy was already well known, due to Hellenistic contacts. The solar calendar of 365 days, which the Egyptians had formulated as early as the fifth millennium BC, is believed to have been introduced by the Greeks, as indicated by fragments of sundials excavated at Ai Khanum in Afghanistan, their markings connected with the winter and summer solstices. The model was also adopted in South Asia and elaborated over the centuries, as seen in the eighteenth-century open-air observatories (Jantar Mantar) of Jaipur.

**300.** *The circular Suraj Kund ("sun lake") temple near New Delhi is designed like a Greco-Roman amphitheatre. Tenth century.*

**301.** *"Jantar-mantar" at Jaipur was inspired by a similar observatory at Ai Khanum (Afghanistan), a colony associated with Alexander the Great.*

302

**302.** *Cows are identified with sun rays in the* **Rg Veda**, *and the solar deity Krishna is their benefactor. Rajasthani silk embroidery in gold and silver thread. Seventeenth century.* **(Sawai Man Singh Museum, Jaipur)**

Solar cultures in South Asia were successively enriched during the Achaemenid era of Persian influence, by Greco-Roman contacts, and following the incursions of the Bactrian Greeks, Shakas, Parthians—and particularly as a result of the brief but artistically very fruitful rule of the Kushans in northwestern India. The Kushans were a nomadic Indo-Scythian people who ruled over most of northwestern India, Afghanistan, and parts of Central Asia. They fostered a mixed culture which combined Greco-Roman, Iranian, and Indian art styles. Actually, the Greek and Hellenistic interactions with South Asia had begun much earlier than Alexander's invasion of India (326 BC), for the Achaemenids had already passed on many ideas which they themselves had absorbed from the Greeks before Darius (the successor of Cyrus the Great of Persia) expanded his empire and annexed eastern Punjab and Sindh in 510 BC. These contacts further multiplied during the reign of the Mauryan Dynasty and the supremacy of the Bactrian kings, known in India as the Indo-Greeks. Testifying to the popularity of sun worship at the time is a memorial stone pillar erected around 100 BC at Besnagar (Vidisha) in Madhya Pradesh. It is located near the temple of Vasudeva (Vishnu) and carries an inscription that this memorial to the solar deity Garuda (*garudadhvaja*) was erected by Heliodoros, an inhabitant of Taxila; Heliodoros was a Bha-

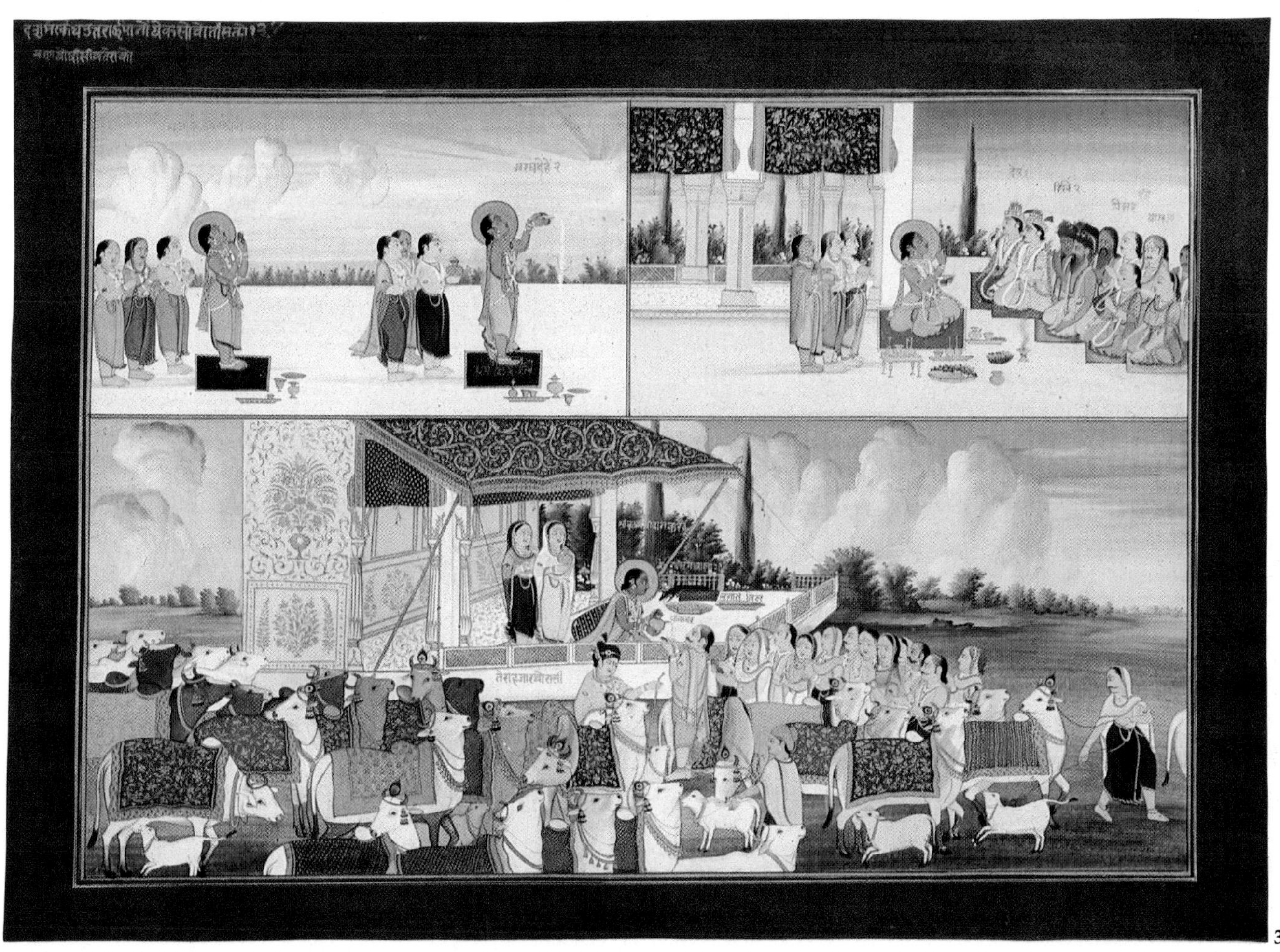

303

**303.** ***It was customary to donate a cow to the poor after worshipping the sun, as shown in a seventeenth-century miniature painting from Rajasthan.*** **(Sawai Man Singh Museum, Jaipur)**

304

gavata and the Indo-Greek ambassador to the Indian king, Kashiputra Bhagabhadra.

A parallel has been drawn between Krishna (Vishnu's incarnation) luring milkmaids with his flute, and Greek legend that describes a procession in which Dionysus, or Bacchus, travelled as far as India while intoxicated Maenads danced to the tune of his flute. In a Pali version of the Krishna legend, Vasudeva and his brothers are said to have assumed sovereignty over Asitanjana (the metropolitan city of Bactria). It is also speculated that perhaps Krishna's *hallisaka* dance was derived from the word "Hellas" (Greece), especially as it resembles the circular dances around the altar of Dionysus. This notion is strengthened by the discovery in Mathura of a stone frieze showing a Bacchanalian group of dancing figures resembling Krishna's milkmaids, in which the drapery of the *yakshis* is carved in the Greek style.

Cows in the *Rg Veda* are identified with the rays of the sun and, contrary to common belief, the adoration of the cow was not peculiar to South Asian culture; this impression persists because the cow is still worshipped in India while the practice has since disappeared in other civilizations. Rock paintings of cattle with discs between their horns can be seen at the Tassili N'Ajjer National Park in the Sahara (7000–4000 BC), which are probably the prefigurations of the Egyptian cow-goddess Hathor, similarly shown with her horns supporting a sun disc. In Egypt the worship of the celestial cow, as goddess of fertility, started in a sanctuary on the rock-strewn arid mountain of Theban necropoli and eventually became associated with the sun god Re of Heliopolis. Temples in her honor were subsequently built near Memphis by six kings of the Fifth Dynasty (c. 2494–2345 BC).

A Mesopotamian legend has it that a cow named Rimat-Ninsun was the mother of Gilgamesh, the Sumerian hero mentioned in the oldest documented epic of the

**304.** ***Sûrya worship at the tenth-century Lingaraja temple, Bhuvaneshwar, India.***

305

**305.** *Sûrya as* **pârshva-devatâ,** *at Lingaraja temple. Tenth century. Bhuvaneshwar, India.*

same name, composed around 2100 BC in the court of the first kings of the Third Dynasty in Ur:

> Offspring of Lugalbanda, Gilgamesh is strong to perfection,
> son of the august cow, Rimat-Ninsun...
> It was he who opened the mountain passes,
> who dug wells on the flank of the mountain.
> It was he who crossed the ocean, the vast seas, to the rising sun,
> who explored the world regions, seeking life.

In Norse (Germano-Scandinavian) mythology, Audumla, the primal fertility cow, was formed from drops of melting rime by the power of the sun and nourished herself by licking salty, rime-covered stones. Four rivers of milk flowed from her udders and thus she fed the giant Ymir. The creation myth of the Mali Fulani herdsmen in Africa expresses a similar tradition. As translated by Ulli Beier in *African Poetry*: "At the beginning there was a huge drop of milk. Then Doondari [the creator deity] came and created the stone. Then stone created iron; and iron created fire; and fire created water; and water created air. Then Doondari descended a second time; and he took the five elements and shaped them into man."

This ancient tradition is still alive in India, as seen in the picture *Cow Worship*, taken at the Suraj Kund temple on the outskirts of New Delhi. The tenth-century "Sun Lake" was constructed by Raja Suraj Pal, a Tomar king, who designed it in the style of a typical Greco-Roman amphitheatre. The shape of the pool curving eastward is circular like the sun, and the effect is enhanced by arched stepped-stone embankments. A similar amphitheatre was excavated at Nagarjunakonda in Andhra Pradesh, showing the widespread diffusion of Greco-Roman sun-culture influences in South Asia.

The Mauryan king Ashoka is believed to have sent Buddhist missions to the lands of Ptolemy Philadelphus of Egypt, Antigonus Gonatus of Macedonia, Alexander of Epirus, and Magas of Cyrene. However, direct contacts between Egypt and South Asia were not common until about the middle of the first century, when Hippalus discovered the monsoon winds across the Arabian Sea. One remarkable result of this interaction appears to be that the ancient Egyptian manner of sun worship, with raised arms, was also adopted in India while all other deities are worshipped with hands joined. This mannerism appears to have reached as far as northern Russia, where Christianity later absorbed the tradition in the form of *dinki* roof-beams in wooden churches, the outer edges of which end in sculptures of human figures with hands uplifted. The tradition can be traced back to hand symbols of the sun on ancient petroglyphs.

How cultures transcend national boundaries is illustrated by the manner in which, like names of individuals, sometimes even identities of geographical locations and rivers are transferred along with myths from one part of the world to another. The great sun temple at Sambapura (modern Multan in Pakistan) was constructed in the early centuries of the Christian era and the legend has it that it was Samba, the son of Krishna, who built the shrine in gratitude for having been cured of leprosy after he propitiated the sun god Sûrya for twelve years in Mitrabana (the forest of

306

Mitra) on the bank of the River Chandrabhaga. The Multan shrine was destroyed, but the Sûrya Deula sun temple at Konarak (Orissa), India, built subsequently in the thirteenth century, is also attributed to Samba, and a shallow pool located in the vicinity of the shrine and the sea is said to be the ancient River Chandrabhaga. Pilgrims from all over South Asia still go there to bathe for purification and to cure themselves of maladies. Curiously, the myth does not stop at Konarak and, in a remarkable blend of mythology, history, and geography, it travelled all the way to Indonesia where the River Chandrabhaga is mentioned in a fifth-century West Javanese inscription, attributing the salvation of the Indonesian king Pûrnavarnam to Vishnu and Pûshan, the two Hindu solar deities. The king of the Târumâ kingdom was a worshipper of the sun god Sûrya.

**306.** *As in ancient Egypt,* **Sûrya-namaskar** *on the banks of the River Ganges in India is generally offered with hands raised and palms facing the rising sun.*

307

308

# THE SUN IN INDONESIAN CULTURE

EDI SEDYAWATI

Among certain indigenous cultures of Indonesia sun worship has existed since prehistoric times; ancient remains are witness to its existence. There is evidence that even today there persists reverence for the sun among some ethnic groups there, as manifested in folk myths. How the peoples of certain regional cultures interpret their universe can be gleaned from myth. In some regions there is a belief that the first human being, the prime ancestor, came down from the sky in a far-off time, lighting onto a mountain of prominence in the region. Such stories can be found in south Sumatra, where it is believed that the first human descended from the sky to Mount Bukit Seguntang. There is also a myth known in south Sulawesi about *to manurung*, the ancestor of all human beings on earth.

This myth is recorded in manuscripts containing the *I La Galigo* cycle of stories. Written versions appear only among the Buginese people, whereas its oral versions are widely known among ethnic groups in south, central, and north Sulawesi. This myth relates that the world of human beings, the middle world, was once empty. There were only supernatural beings, occupying the upper and nether worlds. Then the Great Creator in Heaven decided that one of his sons should be sent down to be the first ruler of the world of humans, and one of the daughters of the ruler of the nether world should become his queen. The story relates that the Great Creator, ruler of the upper world, dwells in the seventh, the highest, stratum of Heaven. If the heavenly beings of the sixth stratum are engaged in directing the stars, and must dwell therefore in the region of the stars, then it can be inferred that the seventh

---

**307.** *Vishnu. Gold repoussé plaque from Gemuruh. Eight century. Central Java.* **(Museum Nasional, Jakarta)**

**308.** *The sun god Sûrya on horseback. Detail from a gold repoussé pendant. Fourteenth century. East Java.* **(Museum Nasional, Jakarta)**

stratum, where the Great Creator dwells, must be the region of the sun. We may then conclude that we have here at least an indirect veneration of the sun, though it is at the same time emphasized in this story that the powers of Heaven are complemented by those of the nether world.

It is further told in this myth that before the first being was sent to earth, the middle world was first endowed with heavenly mountains of gold and iron. It is interesting to note that in a cultural pocket on the island of Java, namely, the region of Bojonegoro, there is still a belief, recently discovered by anthropological researchers, which concerns mountain worship, the believers explaining that the mountain is venerated because the sun "comes from it," that is to say, rises from behind the mountain.

Another illustration is a genealogical myth from East Kalimantan. This myth is found among the *lepo' tau*, or the Tau subtribe of the Kenyah Dayaks. They believed that the first human being came from the roots of a *lurek* plant (the underside of whose leaves is red). When there was a wind, the protruding roots rubbed against each other until they emitted a fluid, which then became a human. The people who related the story were not sure whether the first human being was a man or a woman. But they thought it might be the latter, because the name was Lurek Menek, and Lurek is usually a woman's name. From Lurek came forth many other human beings, who multiplied and then settled on the plateau of Kayu Tau, where there are many *tau* trees. This *tau* is the totem of this Tau subtribe of the Kenyahs. Even now, in their

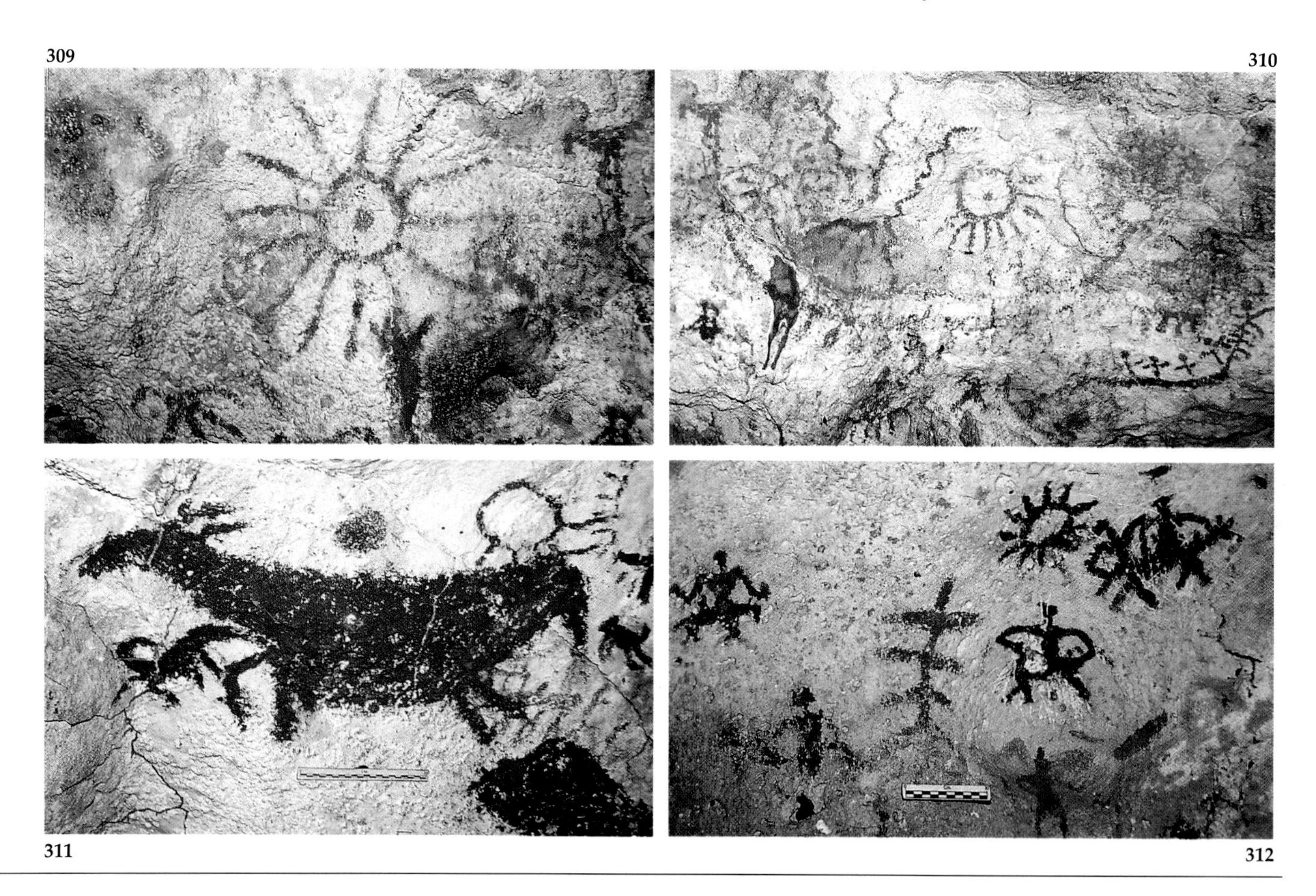


**309.** ***Prehistoric petroglyph representing the sun in Metanduno Cave on the island of Muna.*** **(National Archaeological Research Center of Indonesia)**

**310.** ***Another sun image over a boat in Metanduno rock painting.*** **(National Archaeological Research Center of Indonesia)**

**311.** ***The sun image over a mythical animal in Metanduno petroglyph reflects a similar tradition as Mohenjo-daro seal (290).*** **(National Archaeological Research Center of Indonesia)**

new settlement midway down the Mahakam river, in the village of Long Merah, in front of the head of the clan's house, they erect a symbol of the *tau* in the form of a split wooden trunk with small appendages hanging from its top to represent leaves. It is explained that *tau* means "sun." The split wood symbolizing the *tau* is meant to absorb the sun's heat. As the Tau Kenyahs are a swidden-cultivating people, at certain times they need a hot season so they can burn away forest to produce cultivable land. For this purpose they send an "envoy" (a supernatural power) to the sun to beg for heat. On the other hand, when they need rain for their newly planted seeds, they also ask the sun to produce thick clouds. Here we see another form of sun worship. This might also be present among other tribes in Indonesia carrying out swidden cultivation, and presumably it existed also among the prehistoric forebears of the wet-field cultivators in other ethnic groups.

One type of prehistoric evidence that may give an indication of the existence of sun worship is rock paintings. On the shores of islands in the Banda Sea are cliffside caves or rock shelters, on the walls of which are paintings depicting animate and inanimate objects, among which figure circles which have "rays" radiating from their rims.

A cave site at Dudumahan in the Kei Islands in eastern Indonesia displays a variety of such sunlike images. There are four types to be distinguished: (1) a rayed circle; (2) a circled cross; (3) a concentric circle; and (4) a spoked circle with a smaller circle at the center. Besides these four basic forms, there are also combinations there-

313 314

**312.** *The sun and the five figures dancing around a pole or a tree is perhaps a solstice ritual observed in many countries. This petroglyph was found in Toko Cave on the Muna Island.* **(National Archaeological Research Center of Indonesia)**

**313.** *A variety of prehistoric sun images are painted on the rock walls of the Dudumahan caves on the Kei Islands, Eastern Indonesia.* **(Rearranged after Ballard, 1989)**

**314.** *Rock painting from Risatot on Arguni Island, Irian Jaya.* **(Drawing by C.E. Permana after Holt, 1967)**

315

of, namely, rayed variations on Nos. 2, 3, and 4. The treatment of the rays, moreover, is varied, from simple perpendicular lines emanating from the rim of the circle, to other forms such as slanting lines suggesting movement of the circle, hooked lines, conical lines, and so on. The predominant color of the rock drawings is red, in a wide spectrum ranging from dark russet to light orange.

Another archaeological site on the edge of the Banda Sea lies on Muna Island and comprises a number of caves and rock shelters. Wall paintings depict activities such as hunting, dancing, fighting, and travelling in boats. The objects depicted are human beings and animals, as well as sunlike objects, depicted in brown paint. It is still problematic whether it is correct to interpret all these varieties of circles as representing the sun. An indication that it might be so, however, is the position of the orbs—in the upper part of the scene. One scene with the "sun" in its upper part can be seen on a rock painting from Risatot (Arguni Island, Irian Jaya).

Of course from all these limited extant prehistoric data we cannot as yet be sure whether what we may call sun worship really existed. We can at most confine our interpretation to the affirmation that the sun was, in certain regions, considered as a significant part of the universe as conceptualized in the respective cultures. Aside from the scarce and still insufficiently studied evidence from nonwritten sources pertaining to either prehistoric times or indigenous tribes, there is other evidence related to the more advanced, literate societies of the so-called Indonesian "classical" period and onwards, which includes concepts of sun worship related to India.

Once Indian religions became influential within certain regions of Indonesia, Hindu and Buddhist myths were adopted and adapted. It is indeed remarkable that some aspects of sun worship were also present, to a greater or lesser degree depending upon the era and the region. It could take the form of a whole religious system or exist only peripherally as part of a larger system of worship. The oldest Sanskrit inscriptions (presumably from the earlier part of the fifth century AD) found on Java, the island which later became heavily Hinduized, was interpreted as evidence that the monarch of that time, King Pûrnavarman of Târumâ, was a worshipper of the sun god Sûrya. The basic arguments are as follows.

One of the inscriptions, that of Ciaruteun, consists of imprints of a pair of feet and engravings representing a spider's web, and the text mentions that the pair of footprints *(padadvayam)* of the valiant *(vikranta)* King Pûrnavarman are like those of Vishnu. The qualifying word for king, *vikranta* (which can mean either "valiant" or "stride"), is an allusion to the sun god Vishnu in the *Rg Veda* taking his three cosmic strides. Extant interpretations were that the three steps of Vishnu either represents the rising, zenith, and setting of the sun, or represents the course of the solar deity through the three (vertical) divisions of the universe. Some scholars, however, gave a different interpretation of the three strides, based on the description given in the *Rg Veda*. This Hindu holy scripture mentions that by Vishnu's third stride he passes the *Sûryaloka*, the abode of gods and the place where devoted humans go after death. It means that Vishnu's first step is that from the east rising to the zenith, the second from the zenith down to the west, and the third one, taken during the earthly night, is the most vigorous step from the west surpassing the zenith, through the *Sûryaloka*, back to the east.

**315.** ***A sketched hand, as displayed by this Sûrya figure from Candi Gurah, is a universally recognized sun symbol. Eleventh century. East Java.*** **(Museum Nasional, Jakarta)**

316

**316.** ***Mirror-handle depicting the story of Garuda, as told in the Indian epic*** **Mahabharata** ***and its Old Javanese version,*** **Adiparwa.** ***Tenth century. East Java.*** **(Museum Nasional, Jakarta)**

It has been suggested that the footprints of Ciaruteun were meant as direct evidence of the onset of Pûrnavarman's step to *Sûryaloka*, which, according to the inscription is just like Vishnu's third stride, but of course Pûrnavarman's soul would have stayed in the *loka* for devout souls. The site of the Ciaruteun inscription may have been the place where the ritual of burning the dead was carried out for the Târumâ king. The king's "liberation" followed the way of Vishnu the liberator, and also that of Pûshan, another Vedic sun god, who is known as the dismisser of sins, the preparer of the safe path, and the guide for the soul of the deceased to the heavenly abode of the ancestors. The spider's web engraved around the footprints was interpreted as a symbol of the finely woven night garb of the sun god. The weaver of the garb, the twilight goddess Usas, who leads Sûrya's way, was seen as closely related to the celestial spiders leading Pûrnavarman's soul.

There is another inscription of Pûrnavarman found at Jambu, West Java, also with human footprints chiselled out of the stone. In this inscription the footprints are referred to as *padavimbadvayam*, not just *padadvayam* as found in the Ciaruteun one. This was probably due to a functional difference of the postulated ceremonies related to the making of the inscriptions. The Ciaruteun inscription is assumed to be the earlier one, and created to celebrate the ascent of Pûrnavarman's immaterial self to heaven, whereas the Jambu inscription, which was assumed to be of a later date, with only the *vimba* (likeness) of the king's footprints, was supposedly carved as a com-

317

**317.** ***The sun is symbolized by this bronze hanging lamp with a flying Garuda, holding lotus stalks in both hands (like Sûrya). Ninth century. Central Java.*** **(Museum Nasional, Jakarta)**

memoration for the deceased king. The problem with this interpretation is that later on another inscription of Pûrnavarman, found at Cidanghiang, West Java, is also accompanied by footprints, and the inscription states: "This is the mighty, genuine and powerful stride of Pûrnavarman, the lord of the earth, the illustrious, prospering with the flags of kings."

In any case, the Jambu inscription was likewise seen as giving some clue as to the *saura* (i.e., related to Sûrya worship) character of the belief system of Pûrnavarman's dynasty. The king is here described as having "armor that is impenetrable to the darts of a multitude of foes," and as being "a thorn to his enemies," qualities also attributed to Indra-Sûrya. Other qualities of the Vedic sun gods mentioned in the Pûrnavârman inscriptions have also been stipulated to demonstrate his *saura* character: for example, this king was extolled as the destroyer of hostile towns, just as Indra-Vishnu is always praised as the destroyer of the hundred fortified towns of the Sambaras.

The Chandrabhag, a River mentioned in the West Javanese inscription, was perhaps commemorative of a northwest Indian river of the same name, along which was situated the Mitra forest where the first Sûrya temple was established. It has been proposed that Pûrnavarman's dynasty was somehow related to the Salankâyana dynasty of South India which also worshipped Sûrya. Giving stronger support for this notion that the earliest known king reigning in Java was a *saura*, a ten-inch-tall bronze image found in West Java (no definite provenance) has been identified as a representation of a *saura-rsi* made in the fifth century (however, it could be that the image represents Siva and dates from the eleventh century).

So far the earliest evidence of veneration of the sun in the historical period in Indonesia comes from Vedic sources. Later, however, Hinduism in Indonesia was dominated by Sivaism, glorification of Siva as the greatest god, evidence of which is given by both textual and artifactual data—although Indonesian Sivaism seems not to have been absolutely sectarian. Alongside the greatness of Siva, Vishnu was always present, as the greatest savior of humankind. Vishnu was sometimes even given Siva's epithet, Sadâsiva, and also described as three-eyed, like Siva. The merging of Siva and Vishnu into one god, Harihara, is frequently found in early Southeast Asian iconography. It must be this concept of a unified god that became the underlying basis for further Indonesian-Hindu myth formation. There has even been a coalescence of Hinduism and Buddhism on Java and Bali.

Vishnu retained his solar associations throughout his manifold transformations in Indonesian classical literature and folklore. His most adored incarnations, Rama and Krishna, are often likened to the radiant sun. His carrier is the celestial bird Garuda, and the heroic story of his guarding the *amrita* (the holy water of immortality) and defending his mother has been related in literature and art. Vishnu's weapon, the *cakra* (disc), which since Vedic times has symbolized the sun, frequently appears in Indonesian traditional dramatic puppet-shadow *(wayang)* performances (especially in Java, Bali, and Sunda), but specifically as the weapon of his *avatar* (incarnation), Krishna. This last-mentioned character is also known in *wayang* renderings for demonstrating his terrible *trivikrama* form when his anger is aroused. *Trivikrama* originally meant "three strides," referring to the cosmic strides of Vishnu (as it is supposed to have been referred to by the Târumâ scribe mentioned above); but

**318.** ***A bronze hanging lamp depicting Sûrya riding a fiery horse. He holds the traditional staff in one hand and the empty hand perhaps held a lotus (like the Martand Sûrya in Kashmir, 271). c. fourteenth century. Tenggang, East Java.*** **(Museum Nasional, Jakarta)**

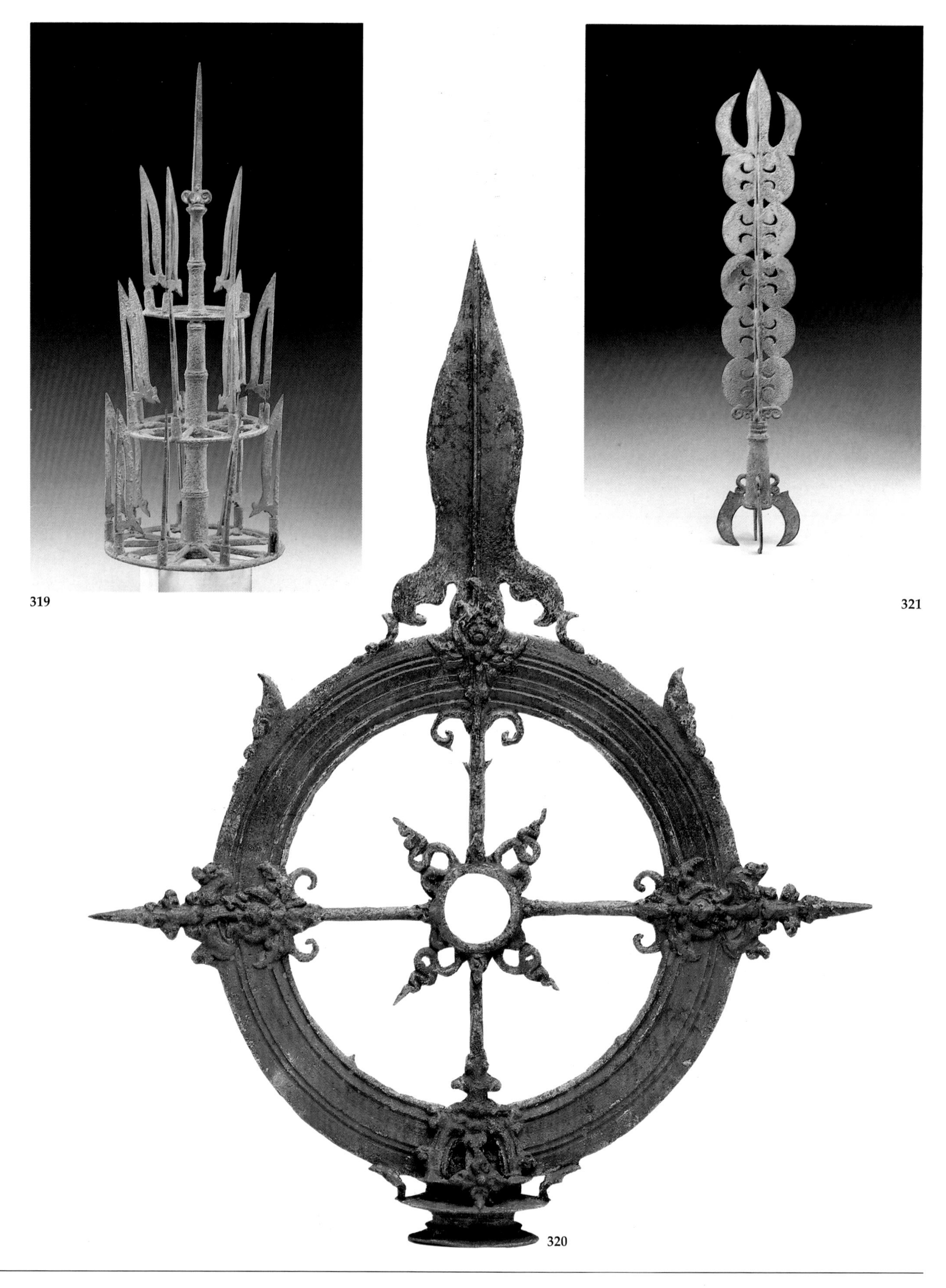

319. *The finial of wheels and blades is inspired by the popular legend of the solar deity's Garuda's search for the Elixir of the God which was protected by the shining sunfire finial. Fourteenth century. Jembrana, Bali.* **(Museum Nasional, Jakarta)**

320. *Wheel-shaped finial. The flat ring crossed with four directions and four flamelike intermediate quarters* **(dikpâlas)**, *rests upon a lotus base topped by a one-eyed* **Kala**, *a nocturnal motif of the sun. Fourteenth century. East Java.* **(Museum Nasional, Jakarta)**

321. *Cloud-and-thunderbolt finial is symbolized by a combination of stylized clouds and* **Vajras**, *lightning. c. fourteenth century. Jembrana, Bali.* **(Museum Nasional, Jakarta)**

later in Indonesia it underwent an extension of meaning. Since its earliest mention in the Old Javanese literature of the twelfth and thirteenth centuries up to the present, this term usually means the terrible and mighty form assumed by either Vishnu or Krishna, as having a body as huge as a mountain, with three heads, each with three eyes glaring like the sun.

Among Indonesian archaeological remains, the god Sûrya is often found depicted, together with Chandra, the Moon God. This coupling can be seen in the largest Hindu-Javanese temple complex, Lara Jonggrang, established in the ninth century. Both Sûrya and Chandra are sitting on lotus cushions, riding in horse-drawn chariots; the number of horses, however, is different. Sûrya has seven while Chandra has ten. The Sûrya-Chandra duo, as a minor complement of a principal deity, is often

322

**322.** *The fifteenth-century temple of Candi Sukuh on the slopes of Mount Lawu in Central Java is embellished with numerous sun symbols.*

323

depicted as a symbolic pair consisting of a full circle (sun) and a sickle (moon).

It is evident in the Lara Jonggrang temple complex that both Sûrya and Chandra as independent figures occupy only a peripheral place within the pantheon. On closer examination, however, the qualities of the sun god might be seen in the central part of the complex, whose main deities are Siva, Vishnu, and Brahmā, each of whom are given separate sanctuaries. Siva's temple is in the center and is much bigger than those for the other two gods. In the central temple of Siva is a row of reliefs depicting the Râma's legend.

In 1928 an analysis was made of the sequence of the Râma reliefs in terms of dramatic plot, and also regarding the number of panels (24) and scenes (60); it was conjectured that the number twenty-four represented the total of *paksa* (half-moons, either the bright or the dark half) within one solar year. The number sixty was a representation of the sixty *nâdî* of the daily sun-time reckoning. The dramatic plot was divided along the four quadrants of the temple, beginning at the eastern point and circling clockwise, consisting of: Râma's birth (the rising sun), up to his victory of winning Sîtâ as his bride; the investiture of Bharata, up to the meeting of Râma with Sûrpanakhâ; the rape of Sîtâ (Râma's—the sun's—light) by Râvana, up to the defeat of Vâlin by Râma; and the seeking of Sîtâ, up to the march on Râvana's kingdom. The ordering of the plot was seen as parallelling the sun's journey through its yearly path, namely, its spring, summer, autumn, and winter points. Râma is a symbol of the sun: in the east and south he is in the upper world, in the west and north he is in the underworld. The fact that early central Javanese temples of the Hindu-Buddhist period face the east may have some significance related to the direction of the sunrise.

This "Sûryaism" is then attached to the worship of Siva, who himself was much worshipped in his *linga* (phallic) form, which is essentially a symbol of the cosmic fire, or of his transposable fiery energy. It is due to these associations that up to the present, on the island of Bali, the principal god invoked in the important ritual of preparing holy water is called Siva-Aditya. In this ritual the Siva-soul is invoked to descend into the priest's body. The preparation of holy water is synonymous with the cult of the sun, and hence the ritual is called *Sûrya-sevana*, or "adoration of the sun."

Between the ninth-century Lara Jonggrang period and its beliefs and those of Balinese Hinduism known up to the present, there came the East Javanese period with its special contribution to the study of sun worship. East Javanese temples normally face the west. Along with this orientation, many typical East Javanese temples have a linear plan: the most sacred part of the sanctuary is at the rear, farthest away from the entrance. The temple, or temple complex, is arranged in successively ascending levels along the west-east line. Thus the progression of a pilgrim within the temple should be from the west ascending toward the east, that is, toward the symbol of the mountaintop and, simultaneously, in the direction of the sunrise. It may then be surmised that the principal worship of Siva or Buddha in ancient East Java was simultaneously accompanied by the age-old Indonesian veneration of the mountain and the sun.

Iconographically, the god Sûrya in the East Javanese period is often depicted on horseback or riding on a unicorn, besides his universal depiction in a horse-drawn

---

**323.** ***Pendant in gold repoussé showing Sûrya on his mount. Below the conch with the two*** **nagas** ***is a symbolic version of Vishnu sleeping on the snake Ananta.*** **(Museum Nasional, Jakarta)**

324

chariot, as was also common in other places (an East Javanese example is Collection 113 in the Archaeological Field Museum at Trowulan). Sometimes the eye of the sun god is depicted as a "one-eyed" monster's head.

Sûrya functions in this period merely as a minor god, appearing in the form of a small statue or only in relief. However, sun symbolism did significantly penetrate into the religious system. Many "keystones," that is, the square blocks of stone fixed at the central and highest point of the conical ceiling of a temple, are decorated with bas-relief figures on their exposed sides facing downwards. These sculpted figures

**324.** ***This winged-sun door of the Sendang Duwar mosque with Hindu solar motifs is a beautiful example of Indonesia's syncretic culture. Mid-sixteenth century. Lamongan, Bojonegoro, East Java.***

vary, but are mostly enclosed within a circle, which is frequently divided into eight sectors with one central part, sometimes clearly depicting the nine aspects of Siva. (One example is a keystone from Candi Rimbi, East Java). With some keystones, the circle is surrounded by rays, which surely refers to the sun. In the Candi Rimbi example the eight figures on the rim are placed within eight petals of a lotus, with intermediate petals in between, thus making a whole of sixteen petals; the central figure is also encircled with sixteen petals. This ever-recurring principle of patterning leads to the suggestion that either the sixteen petals or the rays of the sun represent a single concept, that is, the *sûryamandala* identified in 1966 as one of the secret *cakras* (mystic locus) within the body of a *yogin*, which is symbolized as the sixteen-petalled lotus. It represents the first among the three final steps of the self-soul to united with Paramasiva in the highest *cakra*, the *Sahasrâra*. Paramasiva is often defined as the form of Siva in his nine aspects. If this interpretation is correct, then we see that the structure of the temple was likened to the structure of a yoga process, which aims at the unification of the self-soul with the Supreme Soul.

In areas where Hinduism is the principal religion, such as in Bali, Sûrya the sun god has retained his majesty and has been integrated into the concept of a higher divinity. In other areas, where Islam has become dominant, sun symbolism persists, albeit no longer endowed with supernatural power. It seems, though, to retain the idea of majesty, such as with the outspread wings (of the celestial sun bird Garuda) found in an ancient mosque complex. Sun symbolism becomes descriptive of the physical cosmos, at the summit of which there is still the Highest God. The fixing of the times for prayers and fasting in Islam is done by using positions of the sun as orientation. The sun is then a God-sent means in this immediate world.

326

# SOLAR ROCK ART AND CULTURES OF CENTRAL ASIA

JEANNINE DAVIS-KIMBALL AND ANATOLY IVANOVICH MARTYNOV

The earliest symbolic representations of the sun on petroglyphs in Central Asia are found in present-day Kazakhstan, Kyrgyzstan, and the province of Xinjiang, China. Here ancient artists carved symbolic as well as zoomorphic and anthropomorphic images on cliff faces, and the sun cult is extensively reflected in all the major stone art monuments.

During the second millennium BC, the Indo-European peoples, who came from the grassy steppes of southern Russia, spread throughout Europe and Asia. Some occupied virgin territories while others imposed themselves upon indigenous inhabitants. In each region they introduced their cultic beliefs, which correlated with nature. One of their symbols was the ideograph for the sun, which also signified fire, light, and heat. During this time symbolic and realistic portrayals of the sun, water, and the animals inhabiting the local environment were carved into stone cliffs or boulders. In many cases these locales became cultic sanctuaries enduring for millennia.

The Andronovo people of the Bronze Age (second millennium BC) were sedentary agriculturalists, while the nomadic Saka, as well as the Scythians and Scytho-Siberians, of the Early Iron Age (eighth to third century BC) had mastered horseback riding. The religion and cultic beliefs of these early farmers and cattle breeders were extremely complex, as seen in the rich symbolic representations of the sun god on several petroglyphs. Among the most important of these are at Tamgaly, located in

**325.** *Bronze Age petroglyphs with sun symbols. Saimaly Tash, Kyrgyzstan.*

**326.** *The halo originated from the "visage" of the sun on prehistoric petroglyphs, as at Saimaly Tash, Kyrgyzstan.*

the steppes west of Alma Ata; those in the Eshkiol'mes mountains of Taldy Kurgan oblast north of Alma Ata, near Lake Issyk Kul; and at Saimaly Tash, high in the Kyrgyzstan Tien Mountains.

At these ancient cultic sites, the anthropomorphicized sun god takes on many stylizations. A nimbus may surround the head, rays may emanate from a solid circle, or the head may be composed of concentric circles and multiple dots. In some instances, the god stands on the back of a long-horned bull—thus the bull and antlers become zoomorphicized sun symbols. At Tamgaly, on the highest point above the gods, a solstice symbol appears to have been carved into the slate.

The earliest form of writing began as pictographs, and new signs were added to drawings of the sun. As a result, the connotation of the sun symbol was expanded and it became an ideograph, signifying also fire, light, and heat. Because the sun brought forth the new growth of plants, coinciding with animals giving birth to their young each spring, the sun ideograph also connoted procreation. Included in the semantics of the anthropomorphicized sun god, or found as special individual carvings, are symbols with even more ancient Indo-European roots. In addition to depicting the cosmic attributes, the swastika, for example, symbolized the generative principle of the race, interpreted as a symbol of female fecundity. As the swastika metamorphosed into related forms—spirals, concentric circles, and rosettes—the ideograph, when placed upon an inanimate object, may indicate that object's soul, or it may represent deified fire.

Thus we have the stage set for religious beliefs which later become established

**327 a,b,c.** ***Petroglyphs showing: (a) sun worshipper and solar symbols. Bronze Age; (b) shaman and wild goat. Bronze Age to Early Iron Age; (c) sun chariot and solar bulls. Bronze Age. Saimaly Tash, Kyrgyzstan.***

institutions in cities, states, and empires. The principal solar deities of Zoroastrianism, the dualistic religion of the great Achaemenid Persians, were Anahita and Mithra. The stronghold of the cult of Anahita was in Seistan (eastern Iran). Fire, the main domain of Anahita, was worshipped as divine by the Persians. Animal sacrifices, as well as *haoma*, an intoxicating drink made by crushing a special herb, were offered to the sun god.

Zoroastrianism, Nestorianism, and Buddhism spread through Kazakhstan, Kyrgyzstan, and Xinjiang along the Silk Routes which connected China and the Western world. Here we find that the symbols in ancient petroglyphs have come full circle. Excavated objects from these regions reveal the semantics of the sun god, of deified fire, and of the patroness of the attributes, Anahita.

Several ancient sanctuaries in or near the Tien Mountains in present-day Kazakhstan and Kyrgyzstan reveal an abundance of carved images relating to the sun, indicating that a solar cult was predominant from at least the Bronze Age. The petroglyphic art depicts symbolic, anthropomorphic, and zoomorphic images of the solar deity. It is clear from the iconography that the solar cult was also associated with concepts of fertility and procreation.

A carved image in the Eshkiol'mes mountains northeast of Alma Ata displays a representation with rays radiating from around the head and the accoutrements of a shaman hanging from the waist. Proof of the predominance of a sun cult in those cultures is found in a scene engraved on one of the rocks in the Tamgaly canyon. Human figures are engaged in a circular dance around figures of deities with heads

**328.** *Sketches of Bronze Age petroglyphs at Saimaly Tash, Kyrgyzstan.*

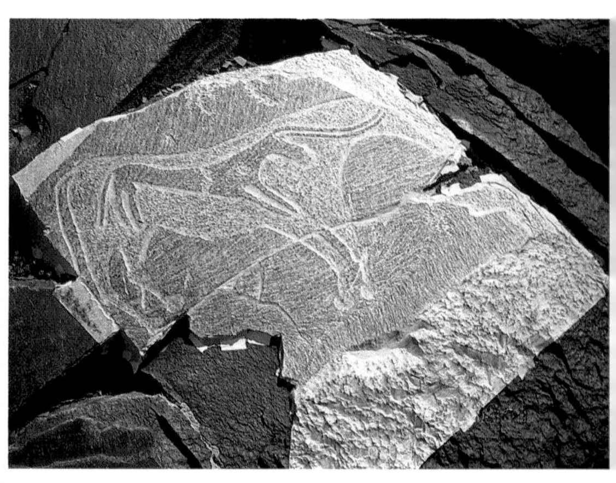

329

shaped like sun discs; at the same time these figures resemble trees, for they tower high above humans and animals. Clearly, the sun cult was closely connected with notions of fertility and the tree of life.

At Tamgaly a sun chariot is depicted as if seen from above. The wheels of the chariot, representing the sun, are gigantic in comparison with the, often unpaired, animals who draw the sun across the sky. Significant anthropomorphic gods are stylized using devices to indicate the solar cult. The heads of various deities are composed of concentric circles, which herald the halo found in later religious art. Others incorporate large dots with rays radiating from a central circle. These sun gods may be either stick figures or more modelled. The total sun iconography of this early

330

331

**329.** *A variety of sun symbols in Bronze Age to first millennium AD petrogyphs are depicted on rocks at Tamgaly, Kazakhstan.*

**330.** *The sun as a coiled motif on the hips of wild goats. Early Iron Age. Lake Issyk-Kul, Kyrgyzstan.*

**331.** *A view of the rocky landscape covered with petroglyphs at Lake Issyk Kul, Kyrgyzstan.*

epoch prepares the scene for the zoomorphic solar representations of subsequent periods.

In fact Tamgaly was witness to the evolution of ancient belief systems. From the portrayal of the sun god as a simple stick figure, the cultic figure was increasingly given attributes of fertility and procreation. It became directly associated with the bull, whose long, curved horns also signified procreation. The solar deity, again given attributes associated with the shaman, engages the bull deity in a procreation act which guarantees the reproduction of the animal. This in turn assures the survival of the human species. These miniature monuments of the late Bronze Age represent concepts about procreation, fertility, and the life-giving powers of the sun and earthly animals.

**332.** *Sketches of Bronze and Early Iron Age petroglyphs at Chankir Kehl, Sakachi-Alian, Aldan, and other highland Altai sites in Siberia.*

To a great extent the increased well-being of these people was dependent upon domesticated animals, a comparatively recent innovation. In addition to sympathetic magic rituals, which involved indigenous animals and were portrayed on cliffs and rocky outcroppings, the sun god was depicted participating in cultic acts with the animal.

At Saimaly Tash in Kyrgyzstan, the open-air sanctuary located more than 9,000 feet above sea level, thousands of images were carved upon the stones. The territory around the "sanctuary" was and still is uninhabited. Only for two months a year did people and cattle visit these highland pastures. The sanctuary was located on the most difficult length of the Great Silk Road, across the Fergana Pass. It is the highest of all the known monuments and extremely difficult to reach. This fact accounts for the transcontinental significance of the sanctuary. Here the wayfarers on the ancient roads connecting East and West stopped to offer their prayers to the sun and the sky and also to mark their routes on the stone maps. Snow around the sanctuary melts only in high summer, during the peak of solar activity. Hence, the distinctly solar and cosmic nature of many representations. Farmers from the valleys and cattle-breeders of the Tien Mountains climbed the peaks in summer to reach the sanctuary and make a wish near the sacred lake. They engraved real or imagined scenes from their lives upon the stones abundantly scattered around the lake. Today these engravings enable us to see the world through the eyes of our ancestors. Surprisingly, many engravings are geniune works of art.

Here the solar symbols range from the swastika and disc to sun-man, sun-bull,

334

335

**333.** *A view of Saimaly Tash, Kyrgyzstan.*

**334.** *A prehistoric petroglyph depicting an antler, symbolizing the sun. Buruna, Kazakhstan.*

**335.** *A scepter with stag as tribute was brought by a nomadic Saka tribe to the Achaemenian court in Persia. Silver. Fifth century* BC. **(British Museum, London)**

336

sun-chariot, and sun-mountain-goat images. The numerous engravings make it possible to trace the evolution of the solar symbol from simple circles to more complex motifs, such as the anthropomorphicized representations composed of a rayed circle given a face and a sticklike body. Some of the Saimaly Tash engravings reflect a unique style of ornamentation going back to the Neolithic Age. The Saimaly Tash petroglyphs are quite remarkable for the abundance of intricate geometric and abstract patterns, specifically the zigzag arrangements reminiscent of the snake cults of some ancient nations, and the so-called "snake arches," designating time cycles. The designs also incorporate triangles, diamonds, spirals, circles with inscribed dots, rosettes and swastikas, and crescent-shaped solar and hieroglyphic symbols. Often these symbols are arranged in elaborate patterns, sometimes in combination with figures that can only be interpreted as reflecting a tradition of worshipping the sun, the sky, the life-giving earth, the mountains, water, and other elements of nature. One can also hypothesize that these symbols constituted a kind of seasonal calendar, or together expressed grandiose and fabulous concepts about the cycles of life, the magnitude of the universe, and the omnipotence of the sun.

Perhaps it can be assumed that fragments of ancient mythology were conserved not only in the Vedic or early Antique texts, but also in the rock engravings of Saimaly Tash. Sometimes solar symbols and anthropomorphic creatures are arranged in more independent compositions. For instance, there is a scene of seven masked men dancing. The postures of the single dancers and pairs of figures are beautifully expressive of their movements and rhythm. Some of the men clearly bear signs of their sex. The scene incorporates two solar symbols, one at the top, the other at the bottom. Occasionally, these scenes include representations of the sun-ox or sun-goat with coiled horns. Remarkable is a solar representation of seven oxen inscribed into a circle.

---

**336.** ***Bronze panel, depicting Imdugud, the lion-headed eagle, with two stags, represents three solar symbols. Al 'Ubaid. c. 2900–2400 BC.*** **(British Museum, London)**

Even now the Saimaly Tash temple is revered by local people as "the holy land." Not long ago pilgrims were still coming every August, bringing a kid or a lamb and seven flat cakes. The animals were slaughtered on the bank of the lake at sunset, then the meat was boiled and eaten, chapters from the Qur'an were read, and prayers were recited in supplication for health and prosperity. Engravings on the stones around the lake were thought to have magical powers. According to one legend, a man took two engraved stones with him back down to the valley. He kept them in a bag, but when he returned home and looked into the bag, he found he had just blank stones. The engravings had vanished.

Petroglyphs near Lake Issyk Kul in Kyrgyzstan combine odd pairs of animals, such as an ox and a horse, an ox and a donkey, or an ox and a camel, with a human driver wearing a horned mask with a long tail attached. The horns and tails of the oxen and other animals bear dots and discs, emphasizing the cosmic origin of these animals. In some instances, the driver is holding a whip. Solar and lunar symbols are abundantly interwoven into these designs: the sun-man, the lunar circles, the sun that walks on feet, and others. Sometimes, the animals' horns are shaped like circles or spirals.

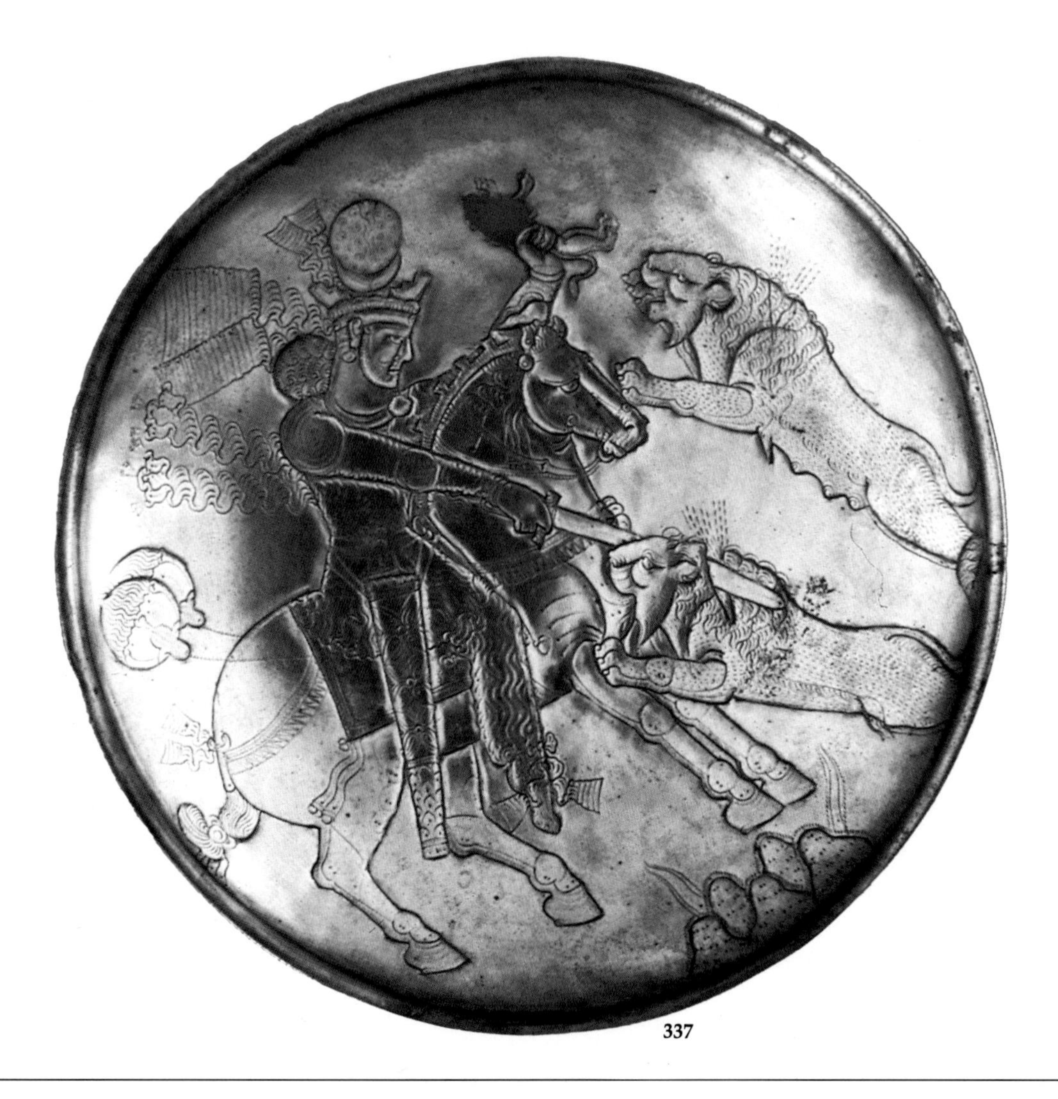

337

**337.** ***Wearing a crown with images of the sun and the moon, the Sassanian Persian King Bahram V holds aloft a lion cub. Silver dish, originally gilded.*** **(British Museum, London)**

Some time after the beginning of the first millennium BC, domestication of the horse allowed the previous sedentary populations to take their herds into pastures higher up in the mountains, as well as out onto the previously uninhabitable steppes. This dramatic change in lifestyle occurred in a region extending from the steppes of southern Russia, east to Mongolia, far north into southern Siberia, and south into western China. Known to their neighbors as the Scythian, Sarmatian, Saka, and Scytho-Siberian tribes, these peoples, because of their habitat and economic lifestyles, shared common modes of life as well as cultic beliefs and world-views.

Monuments from the late Bronze Age and the Early Iron Age no longer bear representations of anthropomorphic figures. The mythology had by that time become far more complex, as can be seen from the rock engravings in the mountainous regions of Central Asia and Kazakhstan. Several cults seem to have been predominant in the Bronze Age. Most reflected the connection between the sun, fertility, and rebirth in nature, between the life-giving powers of the sun and the world of animals and plants.

The well-being of the population was vitally dependent on domesticated animals. Hence, their widespread representation in a variety of media. But these bonds between man, nature, and the cosmos were quite differently reflected during that period of art where a symbolic component noticeably gained in importance. The anthropomorphic representations of the Late Bronze Age gave way to solar symbols—crosses inscribed in circles, and chariots—that reflected the new notions about the sun. Golden horses and sun chariots are symbols of the sun's movement, of the voyage of the sun deity to every corner of the universe. The horse is an integral component of this model of the universe, which also incorporates the sun, fire, the sun deities, and the world tree. These notions were cultivated in both pre- and post-Zoroastrian periods.

The cultic traditions of the Bronze Age were indigenous to the new Iron Age warriors. Now more dependent than ever upon the well-being of their flocks, the nomads executed "animal-style" art. Depending on the region, a zoomorphicized sun god took the form of a ram, mountain goat, deer, or reindeer. Because much of the material that we know from this period has been found in burial sites, we can only imagine the variety of fragile objects that have long since been lost. However, those cast in metal—bronze, silver, or gold—have survived.

The Scythian and Saka epochs were marked by further complications in notions about the sun deity. Also during that period the sun was increasingly represented in images of animals, mainly reindeer, deer, goats, and rams. Some of these representations bear no special signs to indicate a celestial significance. The latter becomes clear only in the context of Scythian mythology incorporating "territorial" symbols, chariots, and color signs: as with the Scythian gold plaques from the Chillik and Issyk burial mounds in Kazakhstan. The golden reindeer and rams, as well as the golden garments of the king, are reflections of color in Indo-Iranian cosmogonic notions.

Curiously, representations of sun-animals are found exclusively in burial mounds and vaults, where they are always located close to other symbolic objects: discs, altars, and snake and bird symbols. These representations are found in the ancient burial mounds of Central Asia, Kazakhstan, and in the Eurasian steppe zone. Images of sky-riding reindeer are related to the widespread eschatological notions of the Indo-

**338.** ***Young Kazakh women at Burana with a modern petroglyph-sun-symbol sign-board.***

МАМЛЕКЕТТИК АРХЕОЛОГИЯ
-АРХИТЕКТУРАЛЫК БУРАНА
МУЗЕЙ - КОРУГУ
ГОСУДАРСТВЕННЫЙ АРХЕОЛОГО
- АРХИТЕКТУРНЫЙ МУЗЕЙ
- ЗАПОВЕДНИК БУРАНА

338

Iranian Zoroastrian religion of the first millennium BC, according to which Ahura Mazda, the god of light, had to fight the god of darkness. After the forces of darkness were defeated, all people were summoned for the judgment and purification of their souls: hence, the presence of zoomorphic solar symbols inside the burial vaults. One of the more traditional images of this period is the golden deer flying through the heavens, its long horns laid low over its back.

Of the earliest Iron Age sun-god symbols, the coiled feline has been recovered from almost all the regions inhabited by nomads, appearing with only minor changes from the Volga River to Inner Asia. One such coiled animal from near the Aral Sea is surrounded by the sun's rays, illustrating its identification with the sun god himself. On many others, the spiral is placed on the coiled animal's shoulder and haunch joints.

Another composition with chariots and a reindeer is also of a solar nature. The reindeer has an elongated trunk, thin neck, graceful legs, and exaggerated antlers. The circular spot on the cross-shaped sign on the animal's croup and the sun disc with inscribed figures at the top of its antlers indicate the solar nature of the reindeer. When worn, these intricate pieces were undoubtedly extremely powerful amulets, protecting their owners and giving them special powers.

339

340

**339.** *Phallic and sun disc symbol. Neolithic period. Kara Koram, Mongolia.*

**340.** *Coiled feline within solar rays. Saka culture bronze button from south of the Aral Sea, Kazakhstan. Seventh-sixth century* BC.

In central Kazakhstan, nearly every cemetery belonging to the Saka, known in this region as the Tasmola culture, had at least one unique kurgan, or burial mound, complex. In this complex, two small kurgans were connected by semicircular rows of stones to a large kurgan containing the body of the chieftain, his horse, and the accoutrements he needed to accompany him to the netherworld; the small kurgans contained only the ashes from a small fire. Because the small kurgans were oriented towards the sunrise, and because fire had been burned within, the complex is considered a manifestation of a solar cult. Fire rituals associated with the solar cult were performed for Iron Age nomadic burials from southern Siberia to south of the Aral Sea.

Solar symbols, widespread in the farming regions of Central Asia during the Persian and Hellenic periods, were connected mainly with the ancient Iranian, and later the Hellenic and Kushan, cultures. These symbols also betray connections with the Buddhist religion as well as with the Hellenic pantheon of pre-Islamic Central Asia. The nations of the region carried on the tradition of using solar symbols to decorate dwellings, burial urns, earthenware, stamps, and metal buckles and other adornments made from metal, bone, or stone. For instance a bronze buckle from the Beshket burial mound (first to second century AD) is decorated with a solar rosette.

341

**341.** *The Asian tradition of depicting frank, erotic couples in shrines was inherited from ancient petroglyph artists, as seen in this rock drawing at Tamgaly, Kazakhstan.*

342

**342.** *Silver dish with biblical scenes. Ninth–tenth century. Central Asia.*
**(Hermitage Museum, St Petersburg)**

Large solar rosettes, circles, and spirals also decorated the walls of the Toprakala palace.

In the history of the steppe lands, the incursion of Turkic-speaking peoples in the middle of the first millennium marks the formation of the modern ethnos. Turkic myths to a large extent were developed on the basis of the ancient mythology. The sun cult continued to be immortalized in bronze plaques and the heavy buckles worn by mounted horsemen, as well as in various handcrafted adornments. However, in general, the solar reindeer or deer of the Indo-Iranians was replaced by the celestial Turkic steed. This is the era of the great epic hero and it is he who rides the golden horse through the heavens. This theme is illustrated on a metal bowl from Siberia: mountains and trees are seen below the great hunter as he rides far above the earth, hunting birds.

The celestial steed is also found in the epic poetry of the period, as illustrated in the Altaic poem "Temire-Sanaa":

> The dark grey steed
> Races along the bottom of the sky,
> Crossing the white cloud,
> Nearing the stars.

In spite of the Turkic incursion, in Siberia the ancient Indo-Iranian mythical sun has survived into this century, as illustrated in a Dolgon fairy tale. A small boy approaches the edge of the world where "the ocean meets the sky," seeking the place where the sun goes for the night. The boy, with magical powers and using elk bones, revives the animal, and they sail across the world ocean to see the sun descend into the sea. In the morning the boy watches as two suns rise. One ascends into the heavens and the other glides across the water. As the boy watches the second sun he realizes that it is an elk whose antlers blaze like the sun.

Even today, Russian festivals in Siberia retain their pagan roots. Springtime carnivals are related to the cult of the sun and the Lord of the Heavens. During the festival, stuffed effigies of the fire god are burned and flat, round pancakes symbolizing the sun are eaten.

344

# THE KHVAR SUN CULT OF CENTRAL ASIA

BORIS I. MARSHAK

Although the Khorasmian, Sogdian, and Bactrian of Eastern Iranian origin were written languages of Central Asia as early as in the first millennium BC, they produced few texts that have actually survived. Therefore our knowledge about local religions, and specifically about the worship of the sun, is very fragmentary.

The main sources of information about the ancient beliefs of the region are ethnographic and archaeological studies. Paradoxically, twentieth-century ethnographic materials from the Pamir and the contiguous territories of Tadjikistan, contain references to ideas more archaic than ancient texts contain. It turned out that the Muslims of the Pamir and the inhabitants of Nuristan, who were converted to Islam only in the nineteenth century, had similar solar calendars.

The inhabitants of Nuristan were descendants of the ancient Aryans. They lived in isolation from the neighboring peoples, and therefore maintained and cultivated their Aryan paganism, whereas the Iranians of Central Asia originally professed the Zoroastrian faith and in the early Middle Ages were converted to Islam as a result of the Arab invasion. The calendar of the highlanders goes back to the ancient Indo-Iranian culture. Meanwhile, the Zoroastrian calendar had already gained wide currency in Khorasmia (the lower reaches of the river Amu Darya) and Sogdia (the Zeravshan valley) in the first millennium BC. Therefore, the names of days in the Khorasmian and Sogdian languages are traceable to archaic Iranian forms.

The principal distinction between the Zoroastrian calendar and that of the pagan highlanders was that the Zoroastrians assumed that a year lasted exactly 365 days (previously, 360 days), whereas the inhabitants of the mountain regions established the coming of a new year by observing the sun. Every month of the Zoroastrian calendar consisted of 30 days, each named after a particular god who had to be wor-

---

343. *Goddess Nanaya holds the sun and the moon in two of her four hands. Silver dish framed in Khorasmian inscription. Seventh century. Khorasmia.* **(Hermitage Museum, St. Petersburg)**

344. *Helios, wearing his radiant crown, drives the celestial chariot. Third century BC. Greek.* **(Hermitage Museum, St. Petersburg)**

345 a

345 b

345 c

346 a

**345 a,b,c.** *Nanaya murals in a private house, Pendjiken. Eighth century. Sogdia.* **(Hermitage Museum, St. Petersburg)**

**346 a.** *A reconstruction of the second Pendjiken temple's eastern facade. Seventh-eighth century.* **(Hermitage Museum, St. Petersburg)**

shipped on that day. Thus, the eleventh day of each month was dedicated to Khvar, the sun god, and on the twelfth day the highlanders prayed to Makh, the Moon God. Those who observed these daily rituals were able effectively to keep track of time.

The year consisting of 365 days is shorter than the astronomical year by approximately six hours. For this reason every 120 years the Zoroastrian year would be out of sync by a whole month, which created confusion when, for instance, a vernal feast shifted first to winter, then to summer and finally to autumn. Usually, these difficulties were resolved by intercalating additional months to the ritualistic year. However, in Khorasmia these intercalations ended many centuries before Islamization, and as regards Sogdia no evidence has been found to suggest the existence of such practices.

There was no time shift in the calendars of the highlanders, because they calculated time on the basis of astronomical observations. For instance, in the valley of the Hoof River the vernal equinox and the New Year came when the shadow cast by Mount Chirog (meaning "luminary") reached certain points. In springtime, when the rays of the sun reached a house of a peasant, a ritual feast was held there, the guests treated to a special dish called *bodj,* made of wheat and peas (in wealthy homes the head, legs, and stomach of an animal specially slaughtered for the occasion were also served). And in autumn, when the sun was "leaving," farewell feasts were held, during which a special milk dish, called *shir-rugan,* was served.

In the mountainous regions days were calculated according to the movement of shadow along the body of a prostrate man. It was believed that forty days after the winter solstice, the sun "entered" the man's toes and stayed there for three days. Then for another three days it dwelt in the instep, then in the ankle and so on, until reaching the eyes, the brows, and the brain. Definite types of weather corresponded to each three-day period: when the sun "stayed" in the eyes, it was supposed to rain,

**346 b.** *Reconstruction of a painted wall in the sanctuary of the second Pendjiken temple. Goddess Nanaya is shown as superior to an armor-clad god, possibly the Zoroastrian god Srosh. Early eighth century.* **(Hermitage Museum, St. Petersburg)**

and over the nine days that it "traveled" through the man's intestines, the weather would be mild and warm. The passing of the sun through the body covered a period of one hundred days, whereafter the movement backward from brain to toes would commence.

Various phenomena linked to the sun indicated the time of day. In the Hoof valley it was believed that small patches of light appeared on the slopes of the hills precisely at midday.

---

347. *Detail of a wooden frieze from Pendjiken, charred by fire. The sun is represented as an archer riding in a chariot. Eighth century. Sogdia.* **(Hermitage Museum, St. Petersburg)**

Highlanders not only observed the shadows and patches of light, but also built small "observatories" that looked like miniature replicas of Britain's famous Stonehenge. Many inhabitants of the mountain region turned their dwellings into observatories, marking the spots where during the winter and summer solstice or vernal and autumnal equinox the rays of the sun, coming through a special opening in the ceiling, would touch walls and columns.

Al-Biruni, a Khorasmian scholar, wrote in the eleventh century that the moment of summer solstice had been registered when the shadows were the shortest.

The calendar systems of the Central Asian highlanders were based not only on primitive, yet reasonably effective, astronomy, but also on mythology. The periods between spring and autumn were thought to be the time when the sun went to the desert to visit his two wives: the old and ugly one in winter, and the young and pretty one in summer.

Traces of the Zoroastrian (Iranian) calendar were found in the Fergana Valley, but not in the Pamirs, except in the Persian-based names of the months. The valley people believed there were 360 wells, lined along the horizon, and that the sun entered each of them in turn. Only for six days, around the summer solstice, did the sun stay in one and the same well. These beliefs clearly echo the Zoroastrian calendar with its year consisting of 360 days plus an extra 5 days in summer.

The only known sun temple in Central Asia was located in the Fergana Valley. It was called Kavusan, after a certain King Kavus who probably built the temple. "It was a unique edifice, dedicated to the sun, in the capital of Fergana. Later it was ruined by Caliph Mutasim [833 and 842]" (Al-Shahrastani). Presumably, Kavus was the ruler

348

**348.** *Ceramic window in a Pendjiken dwelling. Eighth century. Sogdia.*
**(Hermitage Museum, St. Petersburg)**

of Ustrashana, a province to the west of Fergana. During the reign of Mutasim the power of the caliph no longer extended to the eastern outskirts of his huge empire. He did not interfere in the affairs of his vice-regents who eventually turned into hereditary vassals. The only act of "tough policy" committed by Mutasim was the execution in 841 of the ruler of Ustrashana, Heidar, the son of Kavus and an outstanding military commander, on charges of conspiracy against the caliph and apostasy from Islam. There are reasons to believe that the sun god was supposed to patronize the Ustrashana dynasty.

Before the advent of Islam in the eighth and ninth centuries, every family in the countries belonging to the Sogdian culture had a patron god. The walls opposite the entrances of houses, palaces, and ceremonial chambers, excavated by archaeologists, bear representations of various deities. Usually, the god is depicted bestride an animal or sitting on a throne on the backs of two winged animals. For instance, the ceremonial chamber of the seventh to ninth-century palace of the Ustrashana rulers in the Shakhristan settlement has a representation of the god under a painted arch, his throne posed on the backs of two horses.

On both sides of the arch were three tiers of paintings, reflecting the motifs depicting the struggle between Good and Evil. A fully armed god rides in a chariot pulled by two winged horses, toward a lion upon whom the four-handed goddess Nanaya is sitting, her hands holding up the sun and the moon. The face of the goddess is turned toward the chariot. She has no armor or weapons, but her serenity in the midst of battle proves that she is in full control of the situation. A similar scene

349 a

349 b

349 c

**349 a,b,c.** *Silver jar with solar motifs has Arabic (Kufic) inscription with the name of the owner, "Abu Ali Ahmed," identified as a minister who lived in Balkh.* AD *1050.*

350

was found on the wall of an eighth-century private house at Pendjiken. The chariot pulled by winged horses is always an attribute of the sun god. In Iran it was Mithra who was depicted as riding in such chariots. But in the Sogdian lands, including Ustrashana, it could not be he, for Mithra was a great god, whereas the chariot-riding personage in the Shakhristan and Pendjiken paintings is evidently inferior to the goddess Nanaya; in Shakhristan he is even depicted as kneeling before her.

Possibly, the paintings depict Khvar, the natural god of the sun. The eleventh day of each month was dedicated to him and in Avesta, where the supreme deities were always associated with the sun, a special hymn was sung in his honor. In the Avesta texts the supreme gods were Akhur-Mazda and Mithra, the god of observance of treaties. In Sogdia, Khorasmia, and, probably, Parthia, it was the goddess Nanaya, whose cult originally emerged in Mesopotamia. In Sogdia, Nanaya had the title of Mistress. Clearly, the Zoroastrians, whose existence vitally depended on farming, could not afford to let the sun be represented by just one second-rate god, Khvar. In Avesta the sun was believed to be the eye of Akhur-Mazda, and among some eastern Iranian nations the name of this god became synonymous with the sun.

In Avesta texts, Mithra arrives in the sky at sunrise, his chariot following the sun, while he defeats hordes of demons. Many Iranian nations identified Mithra with the sun, yet he was always ranked above Khvar.

Khorasmian and Sogdian Zoroastrianism were not very orthodox, therefore it is not clear to what extent the Zoroastrian texts are characteristic of the Central Asian

**350.** ***A lion attacking an ox is an old Achaemenian symbol related to the vernal equinox of the solar year, because the coronation of the king fell on New Year's day. Silver dish. Seventh century. Iran.*** **(Hermitage Museum, St. Petersburg)**

religion. Scholars have to rely on Sogdian and Khorasmian representations, comparing them against Iranian ones.

The most widespread solar representation is of Nanaya sitting on her throne or mounting a lion. Her image uses motifs from the Middle East and India (e.g., the four hands). It also shows strong affinity with the iconography of Durga, the wife of Siva, and other Indian goddesses. However, the sun and the moon that she holds reflect a non-Indian concept.

Apparently, the meaning of these two symbols, the sun and the moon, is to stress that the Mistress administers her power daily and nightly. This desire to embrace the entire time cycle is characteristic of fifth- to eighth-century Iranian culture. Thus, in Sassanidic Iran (third to eighth century) the king's crown initially contained just the sun ball, but in the fifth century began to incorporate the crescent moon too. Toward the end of the Sassanidic period the sun and moon became indispensable components in very popular hunting scenes. A famous eighth-century Iranian dish bears representations of a hunting scene with the moon god Makh riding in a chariot pulled by oxen. But the painter also depicted the sun as the figure of an archer inside a palace with columns where he waits for the morning to come. The charred wooden frame of an eighth-century house in Pendjiken bears a representation of the sun chariot pulled by horses. This composition was once incorporated into a frieze under the ceiling, consisting of arches, each housing a deity. The sun god was depicted with a bow in his hand. Since not all the components of the frieze have survived, it is not clear whether one arch depicted the moon god. However, the ceramic "window" in the center of the ceiling, through which the light of the sun came in, was decorated with representations of crescents and stars.

The equinox, as a major moment in the solar year, also attracted ancient artists. The old symbol of the equinox, a lion preying on an ox, is depicted on a seventh-century silver dish from Iran. The artist clearly intended to convey the universal significance of this natural phenomenon by incorporating in the scene the mythical world ocean and the sky-high tree. A late-eighth-century Sogdian dish shows a lion preying on an antlerless reindeer, thus bringing in the motif of spring, which is the season when reindeers shed their antlers.

The architecture of two Sogdian temples that date from the fifth to eighth century vividly reflects a ritual of sun worship. The entrance to the rectangular site of each temple was from the east, while prayers were said facing the west. Worshippers entered a first courtyard through a portico with two rows of columns and then proceeded into the next courtyard through another portico. There they stood before the raised facade of the main building, accessible through yet another portico, whereafter they entered a square chamber with a bay on either side of an entrance door. The bays accommodated statues. The porticos and chambers had painted walls. The eastern wall of the chamber was open, so that the rays of the rising sun could light up the bays and the statues. Worshippers must have gathered at the first portico long before sunrise. In Pendjiken, as in all highland regions, there is a long interval between the beginning of dawn and the moment when the sun appears from behind the mountains. The Pendjiken temples were used for morning prayers. The minutes before the arrival of the sun could also have had ritualistic meaning: the earliest rays of the sun

351

**351.** *Mesopotamian bas-relief showing a Babylonian king before the sun god Shamash. Twentieth–nineteenth century* BC. *Susa.* **(Musée du Louvre, Paris)**

352

were embodied in the image of Verethranga, the god of Victory, who was depicted as a ferocious wild boar running ahead of Mithra. According to certain scholars, the Armenian word *mehean*, meaning "temple," goes back to the Parthian notion of "Mithra's place", which could mean the place for divine services that were always held between sunrise and midday, the time of Mithra's special benevolence.

With the advent of Islam, the old symbols lost their original meanings but did not disappear. A unique late-eleventh-century silver jar, in addition to Arabic inscriptions detailing the name and title of the owner (dignitary Abu-Ali Ahmad ben Muhammed be Shazan from Balkh), is decorated with two large medallions, each bearing a small circle inscribed inside a larger one. The representations have a benevolent meaning. The small circle is light, while the large one is dark and filled with ornamentation, incorporating the figures of two lions and two dragons; the artist thus depicted the sun and its orbit. According to Al-Biruni, the Sassanidic shahs wore crowns that bore representations of both the sun and the orbit in which it moved. Thirteenth-century artists represented the ecliptic in the form of a dragon, and the image of a lion had been connected with the sun as far back as the times of the worshipping of the goddess Nanaya. Three small medallions decorating the jar show two solar (?) lions and a lunar (?) hare.

In the thirteenth century the lion-and-sun motifs acquired the canonical form of a sun rising from behind the lion's back. Such compositions occur widely on coins from Asia Minor and on tiles from northern Iran. The facade of a seventeenth-century Shirdor *madrasah* in Samarkand bears a more intricate representation of a lion preying on

**352.** ***Kazakh horsemen display their shields at a Lugovoye festival, an armor which is especially identified with the sun.***

353

a gazelle, which echoes a lion-and-ox motif. However, there is no evidence that the connection between this motif and the vernal equinox survived till the seventeenth century, especially as, starting in the eleventh century, the vernal equinox became the first day of the solar New Year.

The image of the sun represented as a beautiful face, clearly under the influence of Persian love poetry, gained wide currency in Iran, starting in the eleventh century.

In the northwestern territories of Central Asia, Islamization began in the late ninth century. From the eighth to the tenth century these lands were ruled by the Karluk nomads who, in the late eighth century, were converted to Christianity. Scenes on Karluk dishes of that period reflect biblical motifs and sometimes incorporate representations of the sun. One such dish with illustrations from the Book of Joshua is in the Hermitage in St. Petersburg. One of the representations incorporates several episodes: troops approaching Jericho; Rahab the Whore looking out from a window in the fortress wall; the carrying out of the Ark of the Covenant and the seven priests blowing horns; the taking of the Canaanite city; and Joshua, with a raised hand, ordering the sun and the moon above to stop. Another dish bearing a similar portrayal is in Novosibirsk (Russia). Both dishes testify to the existence of ties between Central Asia and the far-away Christian civilizations of the Mediterranean.

The religious, scientific, and poetic notions about the sun that spread throughout the settled nations of Central Asia, were very distinctive and reflected the ties between this vast region and neighboring civilizations, first and foremost of which was Iran.

---

**353.** ***The sun deities in pre-Islamic Iran were gods, not goddesses; a female sun-face was an Islamic innovation. A beloved's face in Persian mystic poetry is compared to the sun. Early nineteenth century. Iran.*** **(Hermitage Museum, St. Petersburg)**

354

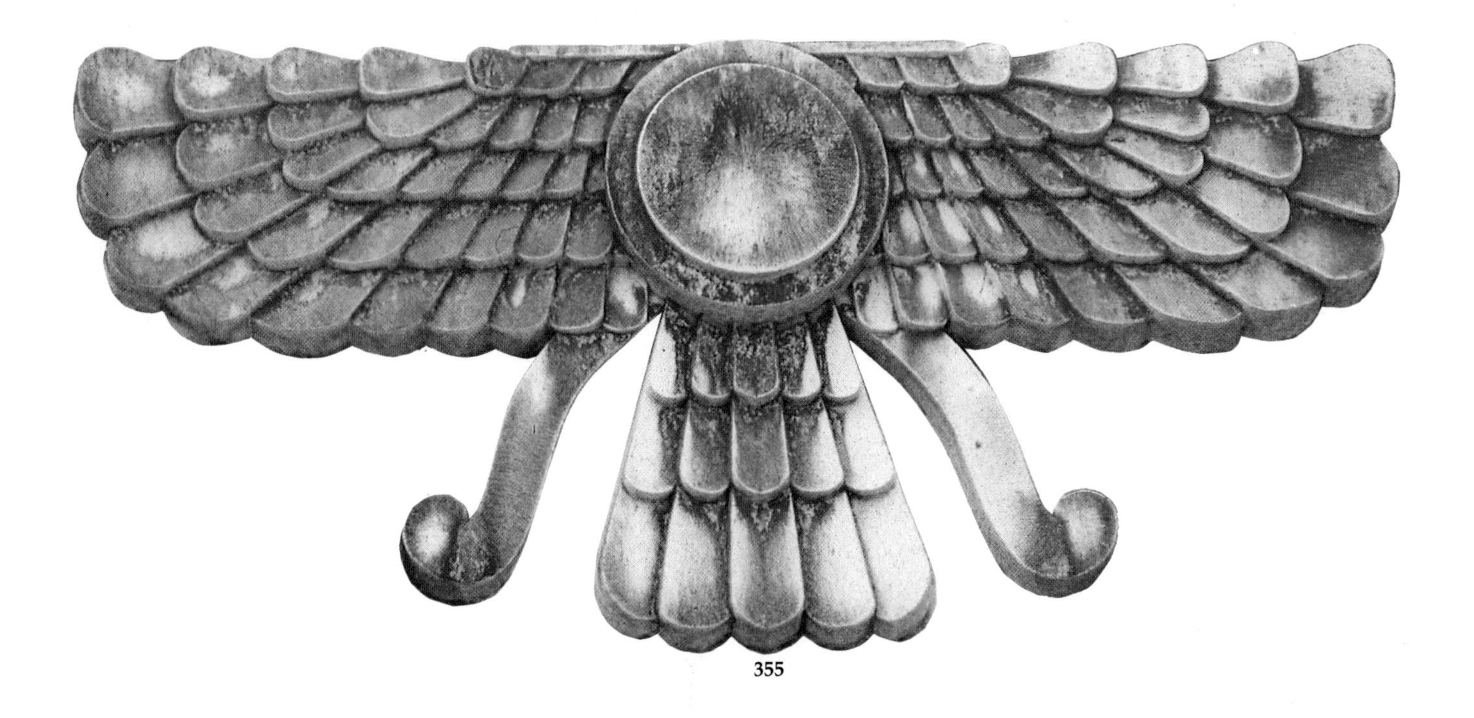

355

# THE SUN IN ZOROASTRIAN CULTURE

JAMES R. RUSSELL

Zoroastrianism was one of the great faiths of the ancient Mediterranean world. The three pre-Islamic Iranian empires, Achaemenian, Parthian, and Sassanian, were for nearly thirteen centuries the sole powers to remain free of Hellenistic or Roman domination; and they were Zoroastrian. At a time when most people in the cradle of Western civilization worshipped idols and were incapable of conceiving of a common human denominator, the Zoroastrians proclaimed that there was only one Creator God, Ahura Mazda, who reigned over all his material and spiritual children. This deity was opposed by a wholly evil and reprobate demon, Angra Mainyu (Ahriman), who was independent of Ahura Mazda and inimical to him. Zoroastrianism was unique in that it was the only major religion that was thoroughly dualistic.

Zoroastrians believed in the intrinsic and inalienable dignity of the human being, in equality under law (*data*, the word which later became the Hebrew *dath*, "religion"), in the right of every individual to pursue a just and happy life in this world, and in the duty of human beings to exercise responsible stewardship over the other sacred creations of this world. Zoroastrians first promulgated the doctrines of Heaven and Hell, of final judgment, of a linear course of history, and of messianic redemption. The Hebrew prophet Isaiah hailed the Zoroastrian king Cyrus the Great as the Messiah—the anointed one of God; and in Greece, Zoroaster was believed to be the first world philosopher before Plato. Neither the Greeks nor the Jews accepted

---

354. *A Zoroastrian priest tending the fire at* navjote *(child's initiation) ceremony, Bombay.*

355. *The winged-disc sun symbol* farohar *at the Boyace fire temple, Bombay.*

356

357

the cosmic dualism of Zoroaster's vision in its entirety. But the Zoroastrian explanation of evil as an independent force did affect Christian conceptions of Satan (Dante's *Divine Comedy* has its ultimate source in the Zoroastrian *Book of the Righteous Viraz*); and a heresy of Zoroastrianism, Manichaeism, was for many centuries a significant intellectual force in the lands of Christendom, numbering among its adherents in the fourth century the man later to be known as St. Augustine, a doctor of the Church. The influence Zoroastrianism exerted upon the religions of Israel and Greece—and, thereby, upon Christianity, Islam, and all civilized humankind in subsequent generations—is incalculable. Yet, after the Arab invasion of Iran in the seventh century AD, Zoroastrianism, never a proselytizing religion, was largely eclipsed from the scene of history. In the tenth century, numbers of Zoroastrians, seeking religious freedom, fled their homeland and settled in western India, where their descendants, the Parsis, still live. There are only about 100,000 Zoroastrians left, a number that is steadily diminishing.

The historical background of Zarathustra (in English, Zoroaster, from a Greek form of the name) is unknown, and there are still fundamental disagreements among scholars as to the time and place—and even the content—of his prophetic mission. But certain reasonable hypotheses can be advanced on the internal evidence of the sacred texts of the Zoroastrians, the *Avesta*, and from comparative and archaeological data. The earliest parts of the former are composed in an Eastern Iranian language of great antiquity, related to Vedic, the oldest known form of Sanskrit, from the early

**356.** *Façade of Anjuman Atashbehram fire temple, Bombay.*

**357.** *The winged-disc sun symbol* farohar *at Anjuman fire temple, Bombay.*

358

359

second millennium BC. They do not mention any recognizable place-names; but subsequent texts list Iranian settlements in a line roughly from the northeast to the southwest. It has been suggested, therefore, that the early Iranian tribe to which Zarathustra belonged lived somewhere in northeastern Central Asia in the mid-second millennium BC, centuries before Iranian-speaking migrants settled in present-day Iran. The semilegendary Iranian homeland, Aryana Vaijah (the Iranian Expanse), was a wintry place, where the longest night of the year was equivalent to two of the shortest days. Zarathustra's name means something like "venerable camel," and his father's and mother's names, Pourushaspa and Dughdhova, mean "possessor of many horses" and "milkmaid," respectively; his was a seminomadic, pastoral people, worshippers of the forces of nature. It made sense that in the harsh conditions of the country they deified fire and the light of the sun, seeing in darkness the embodiment of all evil. To this day, white is the color of Zoroastrians, who are forbidden to wear black, that hue emblematic of evil and the absence of light. The ancient Central Asian Andronovo culture may provide the material remains of Zarathustran society; and it has been suggested that around the time he lived, bands of young mounted marauders, like the Scythians of later centuries, were terrorizing his people and disrupting their ancient patterns of life. His tradition contained the elements of dualism in the symbolic opposition of light and darkness, then; and at Zarathustra's time the theological questions of divine justice, and of the nature of the battle between the two moral forces, was particularly acute.

---

**358.** *Fire temple of the Parsi community at Surat, India.*

**359.** *Karani Agiary fire temple's tower in Bombay, shaped like a flame.*

Zarathustra seems to have been trained in childhood as a priest, his tasks including the composition of sacred verse; but it seems that the worship of certain violent divinities, the *daevas*, repelled him. At twenty years of age, vexed by inner spiritual searchings and dismayed at the distress wrought by evil men, he left his clan and wandered for ten years in the wilderness. At the age of thirty he had a vision in which a luminous being, Vohu Manah (the Good Mind), led him into the presence of Ahura Mazda, the Lord of Wisdom. In his hymns, the *Gathas* (the word is cognate to Sanskrit *gita*), Zarathustra proclaimed his message of cosmic dualism: there is only one God, Ahura Mazda (later, Ohrmazd, in Pahlavi), but he has an independent, eternal, and wholly evil adversary, Angra Mainyu (Ahreman, in Pahlavi), the Destructive or Frightful Spirit, who is responsible for all the wickedness, suffering, and death in the world. The *daevas* are Angra Mainyu's creations: one of them, Aeshma (Wrath), entered Judeo-Christianity as Asmodeus (Ashmedai, in Hebrew, that is, Aeshma *daeva*). Seven holy beings embodying at once moral qualities and pure creations, the Amesha Spentas (Immortal Bountiful Ones), emanated from Ahura Mazda "like torches lit from a torch." These include, for example, Asha Vahishta (the Best Righteousness or Truth), who is inherent in fire. Every human being possesses a *daena* (insight, or conscience), which empowers him or her to make free moral choices—to determine, in fact, whether the world will cast in its lot with good or evil. The *daena* of the just person appears to them after death as a luminous young girl of surpassing beau-

360

361

**360.** *Parsi fire altar in an eighteenth-century manuscript of the* **Videvdat** *in Avestan, Gujarat.* **(James R. Russell Collection)**

**361.** *The Parsi* **Jashan** *ceremony is performed to propitiate fire as one of the seven creations, along with water, plants, animals, humans, the earth and sky.*

**362.** *The sphinx guarding the Parsi Boyace fire-temple, Bombay, India.*

362

ty. This term became the general word for religion among Zoroastrians; it was later adopted by Arabic as *din*, the word for religion in Islam.

According to the developed Zoroastrian cosmology of the *Bundahishn* (*Creation*, a Pahlavi work of late Antiquity, based largely on a lost Avestan source), the sky, water, earth, plants, animals, and humans were fashioned; then Ahura Mazda made fire, which in visible and invisible forms animated them all. At the dawn of the world, the sun stood in midheaven, at its noon position, in an eternal spring. Ahreman's assault shook the universe, and the celestial and earthly equators were at an angle to each other, hence the change of seasons. But Zoroastrian eschatological doctrine holds that at the end of time eternal spring will ensue once more. In anticipation of that fulfilment, Zoroastrians instituted the vernal New Year, the Persian *No Ruz* (from old Iranian *nava raochah*, new light), which the Safavid dynasty restored as the official New Year of Shi'ite Iran.

The light of fire makes all things visible, hence its association with truth. All things live and move through the energy of fire; so *asha*, which means literally "the way things move" (cognate to Sanskrit *rta*), that is, cosmic order, is also fire. Thirty-three lesser divinities in the Zoroastrian pantheon are *hamkaran* (associates) of the Amesha Spentas: thus, Atar (fire) and Khvar (sun; modern Persian *khurshid* comes from the older Iranian term with its epithet *khshaeta*, shining) are associates of Asha Vahishta. Because of its power to warm and light the world and to repel victoriously (*verethragan-*, in Avestan) the forces of evil and death, fire became and has remained the living icon of the Zoroastrian faith. Although the Persian Muslim poet Ferdousi sought to exonerate the Zoroastrians of the charge of being *atashparastan* (fire worshippers), orthodox Zoroastrian practice does enjoin the service and worship of fire, particularly of sacred fires enthroned in temples over the last centuries. Some of the holiest "victorious fires" (*atash-i bahram*, in Persian) are believed to have souls, and to display the anthropomorphic features of Vohu Manah or Atar to the pious.

Avestan texts customarily refer to the sun as *aurvat-aspa* (swift-horsed), an image shared with the Vedas and with the Greek conception of Helios. In the Persian Empire of the Achaemenian Dynasty (sixth to fourth centuries BC), which was Zoroastrian, white horses were sacrificed, according to the Greek writer Xenophon, to Zeus Helios (that is, most likely, to Ahura Mazda as the sun). The Achaemenians celebrated with great splendor the yearly feast of the sun god Mithra, Mithrakana (Mihragan, in Pahlavi; Mehekan, in Armenian), at their capital, Persepolis. The Zoroastrian day is divided into five watches: during each of the three daylight ones, it is obligatory to recite the *khwarshed niyayishn* (litany to the sun) to Mithra and the sun together.

As the world is still under the attack of the forces of Ahreman, who defile it in diverse ways, Zoroastrians are enjoined to purify their surroundings in various ways, and this includes not exposing the sun and fire to pollution. Thus it is customary not to cut one's hair or nails (once separated from the living body, these parts are regarded as corpse matter) at noon, when the sun is at the zenith of its glory. But the worst defilement is moral. Since Zarathustra saw righteous rule as the best way to promote *asha* (order) in the world, tyranny is perhaps Angra Mainyu's most pernicious assault against human society. Zoroastrian mythology and subsequent Iranian epics preserve the tale of Yima, the radiant (*khshaeta*, in Avestan; *Jam-shid*, in Persian), the primal king who fell through hubris; he demanded that his subjects worship him as God. His punishment was banishment to the underworld, where he rules still, but, as the Pahlavi *Denkard* notes, without seeing the light of the sun. The same figure exists in Hindu mythology as Yama, the king of the dead. Yima's fate in Iranian folklore may be a reflection of another aspect of the legend of Yima: the deprivation of sunlike *khvarenah*. On a coin of the Kushana dynasty, *khvarenah* leaves Yima in the shape of a bird.

*Khvarenah*, an Avestan word which probably contains *khvar* (sun), is a radiant glory bestowed by Ahura Mazda—in this case, upon righteous kings. In Persian it is called *farr* (from the form *farnah* in Old Persian) or *khoreh* (from the Pahlavi reflex of the Avestan), and is frequently mentioned in Ferdousi's *Shah-nameh* (Book of Kings) as the *farr* of the legendary Kayanian dynasty. In the Pahlavi *Karnamag i Ardashir i Papakan*, a text which describes in wholly epic and legendary terms the accession to power of Ardashir I in the third century AD, the *khwarrah* runs alongside the galloping steed of the king-to-be and eventually leaps onto its back, confirming God's election. On the bas-relief of Naqsh-e Rustam in southern Iran, Ohrmazd is shown as a warrior on horseback extending the glory to the mounted Ardeshir in the form of a sunlike ring. This symbol seems to derive from an older Near Eastern prototype which had been employed by the Achaemenian dynasty nearly half a millennium earlier. A number of Achaemenian monuments, from great bas-reliefs at Persepolis to

363

**363.** ***The panel of the Assyrian king Assurnasirpal II (883–859 BC) in his palace at Nimrud, Iraq.*** **(British Museum, London)**

minuscule cylinder seals, depict a winged solar disc, either alone or surmounted by the upper half of a man. The prototype of this figure is the symbol of the Egyptian sun god, Re; and the addition of a human figure may be traced to Assyria, where it was most likely an icon of the god Asshur. The Iranian symbol has been variously interpreted as Ahura Mazda, the *fravashi* (i.e., the immortal protecting spirit of an individual), or *khvarenah,* with most recent research favoring the latter. The symbol was not used by successive Iranian dynasties, but was rediscovered by archaeologists and then adopted anew by the modern descendants of the ancient Zoroastrians, the Parsis of India. At the present time this ancient solar symbol adorns fire temples in Bombay and is worn by the faithful much as today Christians wear the cross. "But unto you that fear my name shall the Sun of Righteousness arise with healing in his wings," wrote the Hebrew prophet Malachi (4.2)—perhaps with the Iranian symbol in mind.

Achaemenian art also makes abundant use of the rosette—a single one adorns the gateway of the tomb of Cyrus the Great at Pasargadae—and it has been suggested that the spreading red petals of the rose were seen as homological to the burning fire of the sun. In Armenia, a Christian land steeped in older Zoroastrian traditions, the play of sound and symbol between rose *(vard)* and burning *(varr)* sun was used to advantage by medieval poets. In India yet another emblem, probably employed long before the resurrected winged sun, can be seen in the Zoroastrian villages of Gujarat: the sun rising over the waves of the sea, symbolizing, undoubtedly, the warmth and moisture (*garm-khwed,* in Pahlavi) which are together essential to life and to the repulsion of the cold and dryness of Ahriman's assaults on the world. The same symbol appears to be used for the Hindu sun god Sûrya, whose worship was unusually prominent in northwestern India in the first millennium of the Christian era. This may not be entirely fortuitous for Zoroastrian priests from Bactria in Eastern Iran, called in Sanskrit *magavans,* were settled in the Punjab, Sindh, and Rajasthan; the two former regions are described with the veracity of an eyewitness account in the later *Avesta,* and the Punjab was for many centuries an Iranian province. The Zoroastrians, who were respected as members of the Brahmin caste, quite naturally revered the sun, and their Hindu neighbors seem to have responded with approbation and emulation.

The dual typology of sun and sea, again, finds attestation in Armenian culture: in a hymn on the Nativity of Christ, the tenth-century poet Grigor Narekatsi writes that the eyes of the Blessed Virgin Mary were *"tsov i tsov tsitsaghakhit tsavalanayr harravotun yerku paylakadzev aregakan nman"* ("sea into laughing sea dilating in the dawn like two suns shining"). At the time of Narekatsi's writing, and for some centuries thereafter, there survived a number of Armenians who seem to have adhered firmly to the Zoroastrian faith. They were called *Arevortik* (Children of the Sun), and probably resembled—and in time many merged with—the Kurdish *Shamsiyya* (sun-worshippers), in the south of the country. St. Nerses Shnorhali, a patriarch of the Armenian Church in the twelfth century, was concerned with the mass conversion of a group of Arevordis. Once he heard his own guards, at his mountain fortress in Cilicia, chanting a—presumably pagan—hymn to the rising sun. He thereupon composed a Christian hymn for the Sunrise Office:

364

**364.** *For Zoroastrians the moon stores the seed of the Primal Bull, released when Evil first assaulted the universe with death. Silver dish representing the moon god. Seventh century. Iran.* **(Hermitage Museum, St. Petersburg)**

365

366

Light! Creator of light,
Primal light, Who residest in unapproachable light:
Heavenly Father, blessed by the ranks
Of the ones adorned in light.
At the dawning of this morning light,
Make the rays burst forth in our souls
Of Thy wisdom's light.

Armenians, like other Christians, regard Christ as the Sun of Righteousness foretold by Malachi; but their perception is further enriched by the power of the solar worship of their ancestors, and on many Armenian crosses the body of Christ is represented by an intricately worked disc fusing the shapes of sun and rose, of light and the gently radiant homologous flower of light.

Visions of the sun god asleep or in a meditative trance are frequent in Antiquity. Parmenides, early in the fifth century BC, had a vision in which he beheld a goddess of light who explained to him the difference between being and nonbeing. In the seventh century, the Armenian scientist Anania Shirakatsi dozed off in the chapel of St. Eugenius at Trebizond, a holy place frequented by pilgrims in search of miraculous divine intercession. The sun, in the form of a radiant youth, descended from the sky and explained to him that there were no human beings (!) in the Antipodes. Such experiences have Iranian parallels which remain consistent through the ages: a Greek magical papyrus of the Hellenistic period instructs the adept on achieving a detailed

**365.** *A terra-cotta lamp with sun and moon symbols, perhaps used for Zoroastrian rituals such as the* **Mâh Niyâyisha** *prayer, when the moon is invoked. About eighth century from Barkan citadel.* **(Djambul Museum of Regional Historical Studies, Kazakhstan)**

**366.** *Zoroastrian terra-cotta ossuary, depicting the Tree of Life and sun symbols (spirals).* **c.** *seventh century. Found in the Chu River Valley, Kyrgyzstan.* **(Historical Museum, Tashkent, Uzbekistan)**

trance-vision of the sun god Mithra and his bull (to be considered below); and in seventeenth-century Kerman, an Iranian Zoroastrian *dastur*, or high priest, Anushirvan Marzban, recorded in Persian verse a dream in which Mihrized (i.e., the god Mithra) came to him as a shining youth and told him hidden secrets. In the *Rivayat* of Darab Hormazyar, the sun's light is that of wisdom, with Mithra as the illuminator.

In the Roman Empire, the Iranian sun god Mithra was the focus of a secret society which imparted knowledge of the secrets of life, death, and resurrection to its male initiates. If there were any books of the Mithraic religion, none has survived. All that is known comes from abundant cult sculpture, literary references by pagan and Christian authors, and a handful of inscriptions. The central icon of the faith shows Mithra, a handsome young man in Iranian trousers and felt cap (the latter was to become the "Liberty Cap" of the American and French revolutions), killing a bull. The ring of the Zodiac arches over the sacrifice; and smaller scenes on the side often show

**367.** ***An unusual terra-cotta figure with the sun and moon depicted on its head. Possibly it is a dog, an animal revered by Zoroastrians. Fifth century.*** **(Historical Museum, Tashkent, Uzbekistan)**

Mithra shaking hands with Helios and riding into the sky with him in his chariot. His cap is sometimes surrounded by a rayed nimbus. This particular detail of the depiction of the god seems to have been standard within Zoroastrianism to a degree unparalleled by almost any other symbol. For Mithra is shown thus on Kushana coins in the East, on the rockrelief of Taq-i Bostan in Iran proper, and in Commagene in Anatolia—just west of the Iranian frontier on the Euphrates. On the feast of Mihragan, the kings of the Iranian Sassanian dynasty (third to seventh centuries AD) donned a special headdress of this shape, as though becoming the god for one day. Mithra is often called in Latin Sol Invictus (the invincible sun), and his initiates are "[re]born to light."

In one Zoroastrian Pahlavi text, Mithra is to impart certain secrets, probably concerning the apocalyptic war with the forces of evil, to a man at the seashore near the end of time, at the foot of the mountains of Padashkhwargar (the shore of the Caspian and the Demavand range seem to be meant). One way Ahriman will be defeated is the rendering of humankind immortal through the sacrifice of the bull Hudayos and the ritual consumption of its flesh. Some of Mithra secrets perhaps concern this sacrifice; and the bull-slaying scene of the Mithraists of the West may conflate it and the

368 a

368 b

**368 a,b.** *A stone mortar for sacrificial* **haoma,** *engraved with solar symbols borrowed from different cultures. A stylized swastika represents the sun and fire, and the bird-and-cross symbol is perhaps reinterpreted from Eastern Christian art.* c. *eighth century.* **(Museum of Regional Studies, Chimkent, Kazakhstan)**

369

**369.** ***Virtues of a pious Zoroastrian are symbolized by a beautiful girl held by an eaglelike bird flying to paradise, while the two boys holding a bow and a battle-axe represent the sun and the moon. Silver dish. Sixth–seventh century. Iran.*** **(Hermitage Museum, St. Petersburg)**

370

**370.** *Mithra killing the bull is alluded to in a Zoroastrian Pahlavi text, which states that one way the evil Ahriman will be defeated is through the sacrifice of the bull Hudayos and the ritual consumption of its flesh—the blood being the fire. Marble. Second century.* **(Hermitage Museum, St. Petersburg)**

death (at Ahriman's hands) of the primal bull at the beginning of time, from whom flowed the cornucopia of all good creatures.

Many Mithraic initiates seem to have been Roman soldiers: the Latin *miles* (soldier) is the name of one of the seven grades of initiation, and it would seem that the militant aspect of Mithra, the mace-bearing enemy of evil in Iranian Zoroastrianism, was still part of his personality as a Western, Romanized god. Another figure in the Mithraic cult is a malevolent-looking lion-headed god. One statue of this being has an open mouth with signs of scorching around the edges, and there are various iconographic and literary indications that the initiate had to pass through the lion's fiery breath. Dedications hail this being as the *deus areimanius*: though the latter word can mean merely "hostile," there are other Persian words deliberately employed in Mithraic inscriptions, so it would require special pleading to assume the Iranian Ahriman was wholly ignored here. The name should therefore be something like "the Ahrimanian god," though such a concept would be to any orthodox Zoroastrian wholly blasphemous. It seems the lion and his fiery exhalations represented the destructive aspect of the sun's rays, by which the initiate was purged and brought to rebirth. A similar lion-headed figure is mentioned in modern tales from Kurdistan and is actually shown on an early medieval Iranian medal.

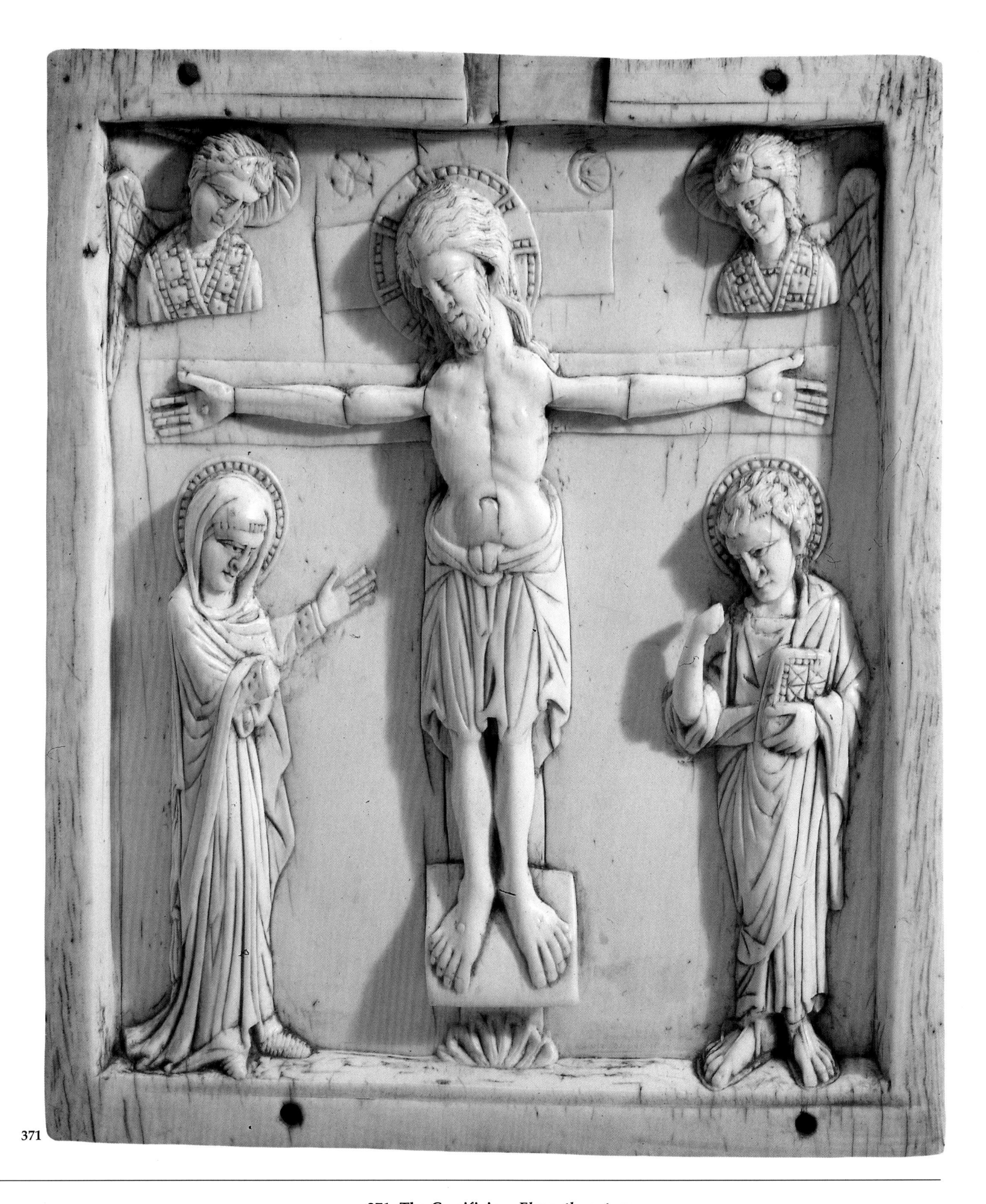

371

**371. The Crucifixion.** ***Eleventh century. Byzantium.*** **(Hermitage Museum, St. Petersburg)**

372

# THE SUN IN BYZANTINE AND RUSSIAN ART

VERA N. ZALESSKAYA AND YURI A. PIATNITSKY

In Byzantium, as in the rest of eastern Christendom, idolization and worship of the sun were incompatible with fundamental Christian dogma. No entity could rank with the Almighty, and everything was His creation. However, varying iconographic representations of the sun emerged in the arts of the Orthodox countries. The sun and its invariable companion, the moon, occurred in two basic settings: the triumph cycle, glorifying the Byzantine emperors, and the passion scenes, first and foremost the Crucifixion and the Bemoaning of Christ, from the Gospels. Furthermore, in the early Byzantine period (from the fourth to the seventh century) there widely occurred such special symbols as hands uplifted toward the sun, which echoed the Roman monuments to Sol Invictus, as well as astral signs, like the eight-pointed star. The medieval notions also reflected a degree of kinship between the cult of the sun and the fiery ascent of the Prophet Elijah, or the image of St. Mamantes mounting a lion and holding the horn of plenty (a fresco in the Manglisi temple in Georgia).

Representations of the celestial lights, as well as their invariable appearance in the triumphal and Passion scenes, to some extent functioned as illustrations of the

**372.** ***The crowning of Emperor Constantine (AD 324–337) at the first ecumenical council in Nicaea (AD 325). The gold medallion shows the sun with the face of a woman, while Constantine himself is the sun. Sixth century.*** **(Hermitage Museum, St. Petersburg)**

373

373. *The presence of the sun and the moon in the* **Assembly of the Virgin Mother with Her Infant** *was a new interpretation of ancient beliefs. Eighteenth century. Russian icon.* **(Hermitage Museum, St. Petersburg)**

374. **Emperor Constantine and His Mother Find the Cross.** *The ecumenical symbolism of the sun disc is portrayed by its human face. c. twelfth century. Byzantium.* **(Hermitage Museum, St. Petersburg)**

374

375

Scriptures. In the Bible the sun and its dazzling, life-giving light is used in three basic contexts: literal, symbolic (to designate the cosmic element), and metaphoric (i.e., as epithets applied to the divine personages). The sun and the moon as conventional designations of the parts of the universe are mentioned in the Book of Genesis, when God divides the day from the night and makes "two great lights; the greater light to rule the day, and the lesser light to rule the night." (Gen. 1.16). In the meantime both lights remain completely subordinate to the Creator. When the Day of Judgment

---

**375.** ***A fifth-century Byzantine philosopher Prokl Diodoh wrote that "gold belongs to the sun, and silver to the moon," as seen in this silk shroud of Christ. c. sixteenth century. Palestine.*** **(Hermitage Museum, St. Petersburg)**

376

**376.** ***The Transfiguration recreates the vision of the gospel that "His face did shine as the sun and His raiment was white as the light" (Matt. 17,2). c. twelfth century. Byzantium.***
**(Hermitage Museum, St. Petersburg)**

comes, by God's will "the sun shall be turned into darkness, and the moon into blood" (Joel 2.31). And in St. John the Evangelist's Revelation of the Second Coming of Christ the sun is a metaphor, expressing the grandeur and magnitude of God lighting up the renewed world: "And his countenance was as the sun shineth in his strength" (Rev. 1.16). Also, the Gospel according to St. Matthew reads: "Then shall the righteous shine forth as the sun in the kingdom of their father" (Matt. 13.43).

Apart from the influence of Christianity, the pictorial style of Byzantine art reflects the powerful impact of Antique culture. The sun and the moon as signs of the universe, flanking the central representation in some icons, reveal the merging of biblical tradition with the Roman interpretations of the emblems of the Palmyra deities and of the Iranian god Mithra, who in Rome was known as Sol Invictus.

The Antique personification of the sun as a female figure, haloed by luminous light and holding a lighted torch in one hand, appears on early Byzantine phylacteries and amulets. One of the most characteristic examples of this art is a sixth-century golden medallion (Hermitage Museum, St. Petersburg) from Mersina (ancient Zephyrion, Turkey), showing the emperor Constantine the Great flanked by figures personifying the sun and the moon. Above the radiant headdress of the sun, who hands a crown to the emperor, there is a solar sign, the eight-pointed star. This emphasizes the cosmic implication of the triumph of the destroyer of paganism, whose power now extends to the east (the sun) and to the west (the moon). Curiously, the flames of the torches held by the sun and the moon seem to be diminishing, as though dimming against the light radiated by the divine emperor. The court poet Flavius Cresconius compared the enthronement of Justin II (565–578) to the rise of two celestial lights, and according to the *Book of Ceremonies of Constantine* (913–959), it was customary to liken the emperor to the sun, which all sorts of panegyrists eagerly did. On the Mersina medallion the emperor is even bigger in size than the sun, who is in fact rendering homage to him.

In some versions, the sun and the moon, flanking the emperor, stand in a chariot, corresponding to the canonical representation of almighty deities. With the advent of Christianity these luminaries, as symbols of cosmic power, became attributes no longer of the emperor, but solely of Christ or the Cross. For instance, on the column of Arcadius (395–408) in Constantinople, the chariots carrying the sun and moon flank the Cross as a token of victory. This style of symbolic expression of the cosmic significance of an event continued through the entire middle period of the Byzantine empire (from the ninth to the twelfth century). Noteworthily, during that period, representations of the sun and moon no longer occur on cult objects and also lose their anthropomorphic dimension. In essence, they became purely decorative signs as, for instance, on an ivory icon with the Crucifixion scene. Meanwhile, miniature painting and the design of Byzantine manuscripts continued to reflect Antique traditions. Illustrations in nonliturgic manuscripts often feature representations of the sun portrayed as an enthroned figure, flanked by seven planets. Furthermore, the texts of some liturgic books, like the *Homily* of Gregory Nazianzus or the *Church Calendar*, opened a vast field for the choice of styles and techniques in representing the change of seasons as well as of various scenes from the lives and trials of the patron saints of farmers.

The emphatic spiritualism of classical Byzantine art, enriched by the ideas of the

**377. The Descent of the Holy Spirit** *is associated with the fiery red rays of the sun that give light and warmth and awaken life in all living beings. Twelfth century. Byzantine icon.* **(Hermitage Museum, St. Petersburg)**

377

outstanding theologist and mystic Simeon the New Evangelist (949–1022), was most eloquently expressed in the festive scenes representing The Divine Light, The Transfiguration, The Descent of the Holy Spirit, The Taking Down from the Cross, and The Entombment of Jesus Christ.

The last scene was traditionally embroidered in polychromatic silk, gold, or silver threads on church shrouds. Usually the embroidery was done by women, but initially the pattern of the "sign" would be drawn on by male icon-painters. The embroidered composition of The Entombment is more symbolic in nature than is the actual Evangelic text. It expresses the triumph of Christ, who defied death itself. Iconographic treatments of this scene invaribly feature profile, bust, or full-face representations of the sun and the moon. Fully conscious of the symbolic nature of the representation, the designer also imparted to it the theme of the Day of Judgment, when "the sun shall be turned into darkness and the moon into blood." Accordingly, the embroiderers rendered the face of the moon red. Following the traditional color symbolism of Byzantium, they used golden threads for the sun and silver ones for the moon. As the philosopher Procles Diadochus wrote in the fifth century, "Gold belongs to the sun and silver to the moon." This coloration of the heavenly luminaries became canonical in Byzantine and early Russian art.

In the Transfiguration Christ appears before his disciples in all His divine glory. recounting this phenomenal vision of the divine light, the Gospels use the sun as a metaphor: "And His face did shine as the sun, and His raiment was white as light" (Matt. 17.2). According to Christian interpretation, the light on the face of Christ is the light of the glory of God Himself. The figure of Christ is often portrayed as the true sun, shining from Heaven. He is the source of all light, and the rays of this light touch the faces of the Apostles and Prophets. In Byzantium color always conveyed important religious meaning. Thus, red is the color of purifying fire, the source of life-giving heat, the symbol of life, and the token of the future salvation of humankind. It is contrasted against white, symbolizing the divine light, the purity and exaltation of the spirit. Dark and light blue are symbols of the transcendental world. Curiously, in their treatment of the Transfiguration, Byzantine writers and philosophers were trying to resist the temptation to draw parallels between the divine light and the sun that were too literal, wherefore they never failed to accentuate the divine essence of the light. Thus, a Byzantine writer of the late twelfth and early thirteenth century, Nicholas Mesarites, wrote: "There is a cloud of light, floating in space, and it carries Jesus, who shines more brightly than the sun, the source of this radiance being the light of the Father, brightening both the clouds and the human race."

Associations with the resuscitating rays of the sun are eloquently expressed in the scene of the Descent of the Holy Spirit. According to the Evangelical Acts, at the Pentecost the Apostles gathered together "and suddenly there came a sound from heaven as of a rushing mighty wind, and it filled all the house where they were sitting. . . . And there appeared unto them cloven tongues like as of fire, and it set upon each of them" (Acts 2.2–3). In representing The Descent of the Holy Spirit as a heavenly segment, with red-and-white and red-and-gold lights radiating from it, the medieval artist must have been inspired by Psalm 84.11: "For the Lord God is a sun and shield: the Lord will give grace and glory."

---

378

**378. The Fiery Ascension of Prophet Elijah to Heaven.** *The bright red wheels are among the universal symbols of the sun. c. sixteenth century. Greek icon.* **(Hermitage Museum, St. Petersburg)**

While prohibiting the worship of heavenly bodies, the Christian Church tried to time religious feasts with the dates of the solar calendar. Thus, Christmas (December 25) concurs with the winter solstice and the related agricultural ritual of the "sun birth." Closely related to the solar cult is the feast of St. John the Baptist (June 24). It is not accidental that this saint is often provided with such epithets as "radiant," "light-giving," and even "St. John the Solstice." In rural areas, especially in Russia, peasants believed that at Easter the sun danced in the sky, and the custom of painting eggs red on this day points to solar symbolism.

Kinship with a sun cult is also reflected in the veneration of the Prophet Elijah. On the day of this saint (July 20) Byzantines climbed the high hills and lit fires on their summits. A sacrifice of a red rooster, as a symbol of the sun, was made for St. Elijah. The image of St. Elijah became closely related with the ancient Greek god Helios, owing to the consonance of their names. This link with Antiquity is clearly expressed in the icon *The Fiery Ascent of Prophet Elijah*. According to the Bible, God wanted to take Elijah to Heaven alive, and so he sent him a huge chariot pulled by fiery horses. For this scene the icon-painter borrowed the Antique motif of the sun god driving a fiery quadriga. But instead of Helios, it is Elijah in the chariot. No less eloquent of this association are illustrations in the ninth-century *Book of Psalms* (State Historical Museum, Moscow) where the Fiery Ascent and a personification of the rising sun (the illustration to Psalm 49) coincide down to the smallest detail. Compositions with Antique quadrigas occur widely in post-Byzantine art from the fifteenth to the nineteenth century, as exemplified in a 1655 icon in the Musée d'Art et d'Histoire in Geneva, or a 1593 silver basin from Boboshovo Village now housed in the Hermitage. In the design of the basin, ties with the cult of Helios are expressed in

379

380

**379. The Adoration of the Cross,** ***in this drawing of a unique icon with ancient Syrian roots, interprets the biblical Day of Judgment "when the sun shall be turned into darkness and moon into blood." c. twelfth century. Old Russian Novgorod.*** **(Tretyakov State Gallery, Moscow)**

**380.** ***The sun at the center of the universe is a sketch of a ceramic plate derived from Persian and Syrian pottery. Byzantium. c. fourteenth century.*** **(Hersoneski Museum, Sevastopol)**

381

**381.** ***The throne on which Jesus Christ sits on the Day of Judgment is also an ancient sun symbol. c. sixteenth century.*** **(Hermitage Museum, St. Petersburg)**

the gilding of the chariot and horses: in Antiquity people believed that gold nuggets were the frozen rays of the sun.

In the meantime, there occurred compositions done in a more naturalistic style. The Hermitage holds a late-sixteenth-century Greek icon in which the chariot is pulled by brown horses; only the red wheels (solar symbols) call up the image of the fiery celestial quadriga. The distinctive qualities of the representations of the sun in old Russian art reflect the pre-Christian beliefs of the eastern Slavs.

In the second half of the ninth century, the Slavic tribes inhabiting the vast territories of Eastern Europe became united within the Kievan state. The cults of the sky and heavenly luminaries, and the idolization of the natural elements, were central to the religious experiences of the ancient Russians. In the Slavic religion, the sun god appeared under the names of Choros, Dajbog, and Yarola. The Supreme God was Perun, the Thunderer. These cults were manifested in various symbols and ornamental motifs, some of them surviving into the present. The emblem of the solar deity and the purifying symbol of resurrection and immortality was the cross. Solar emblems also included the swastika, the cross inscribed into a circle, the wheel, and so on. Worship of the moon was reflected in the widespread Slavic "moon pendants."

In 988 Russia adopted Christianity, which became the official religion and edged out the local pagan cults. Christianity brought Russia within the orbit of Byzantine culture with its intricate symbolism, including its solar and lunar symbols. In time the original pagan meanings of the ancient symbols were revised so that the latter either became associated with the cross, or were reduced to performing purely decorative functions.

Nonetheless, some ancient notions about the forces of nature persisted in folk consciousness and culture. Quite often elements of paganism were interwoven with the cults of the Christian saints. Perun the Thunderer was replaced by St. Elijah the Prophet, believed to travel over the sky in a fiery chariot. On various Russian art objects the figure of Elijah is often depicted haloed in a round cloud that reiterates the fiery disc of the sun. The wheels of his chariot are decorated with such solar signs as a cross inscribed into a circle, or a rosette. Elijah was one of the most popular saints in Russia, and the agricultural component of his cult was particularly strong in the northern regions. The ancient Russian icon-painters created numerous icons of St. Elijah for country churches and chapels, drawing inspiration predominantly from the realities of their world and from traditional notions about the forces of nature. Therefore in Russia, representations of the Fiery Ascent always had a strong narrative component and largely incorporated solar symbolism.

However, Russian painters did not always follow the primitive style. A unique twelfth-century Novgorodian icon depicting *The Adoration of the Cross* (Tretyakov Gallery, Moscow) clearly betrays kinship with ancient Syrian sources. Specifically, a sixth-century stamped silver dish from Syria (in the Hermitage) bears a representation of the Cross erected upon a star-patterned globe. On both sides of the Cross stand two angels, and above it are engraved representations of the sun and moon. In the Novgorodian icon a Cross towers above the Cave of Adam and is decorated with the Crown of Thorns. Angels hold a stick and a spear, the symbols of the Martyrdom of Christ. Profile representations of human heads are inscribed into round shields,

382

**382. Fiery Ascent of Prophet Elijah.**
*An ancient Byzantine ritual is still observed in parts of Central Asia when on the Day of the Prophet Elijah (July 20) people light fires on hill tops and sacrifice a rooster (a sun symbol). Sixteenth-century. Russian icon.*
**(Hermitage Museum, St. Petersburg)**

haloed by rays. One of these heads, with fluffy hair, represents the moon and clearly repeats an Antique prototype. The entire composition is enclosed in a dark-green frame decorated with red and yellow stars. *The Adoration of the Cross* reflects intricate Christian symbolism deeply rooted in biblical texts. For example, this scene echoes the motif of the Day of Judgment which will take place on Mount Golgotha, where the Cross will be erected.

Therefore all the celestial symbols on the Novgorodian icon are taken from biblical sources. The Gospels describe the Second Coming of Christ thus: "Immediately after the tribulation of those days shall the sun be darkened, and the moon shall not give her light, and the stars shall fall from heaven and the powers of the heavens shall be shaken" (Matt. 24.29; Mark 13.24–25). The Apocalypse offers a similar treatment of the heavenly signs theme: "and the sun became black as sackcloth of hair, and the moon became as blood; and the stars of heaven departed as a scroll when it is rolled together" (Rev. 6.12–14).

The texts of the Gospels and the Apocalypse are clearly reflected in an icon representing The Day of Judgment. The icon-painter provided detailed representation of all the events, from the malicious signs appearing in Heaven to the tortures of sinners in Inferno. In accordance with the text cited above, the icon shows the angels weaving together the sky and the stars, the sun and the reddened moon. Illustrative is a sixteenth-century *Day of Judgment* from a church near Archangel (Hermitage). Like most of the old Russian icons, this one stands out in its strong narrative component and also in its faithfulness to the Evangelical texts. Nonetheless, the images of the moon and the sun are represented in a distinctly Antique style, as faces in profile inscribed into circles.

In Byzantium the sun and the moon are even included in Crucifixion scenes. However, although ancient Russia could be regarded as peripheral to Byzantine culture, representations of the sun and moon occurred very rarely in Russian Crucifixion scenes until the sixteenth century. To some extent, this can be ascribed to the fact that idolization of the sun was still widespread in Russia, especially among peasants. In the late seventeenth century Deacon Feodor Ivanov testified that in some villages peasants, and even priests, worshipped the sun. And in the 1860s an old believer, Vasili Zheltovsky, refused to go to church, arguing that "God is in Heaven and on earth there is no God."

Solar and lunar representations gained currency in Russia in the sixteenth century. Wide-ranging symbolic and allegoric compositions were incorporated into the traditional scenes of the Crucifixion, the Taking Down from the Cross, the Entombment, the Day of Judgment; they reflected the themes of the Psalms. Such icons as *The Soul Glorifies the Lord God, The Liturgy, The Fatherland, The Purity of Soul, The Son of God,* and *The Cathedral of Our Lady* contain representations of the firmament including the sun and the moon. As a rule, these were profile, bust, or full-face renderings haloed by rays.

In these complicated symbolic compositions the sun and the moon either directly illustrated Evangelical texts or were depicted as servants of Yahveh, ruling the day and the night. They are no longer idolized, that is, the radiance of the sun, the beauty of the moon, and the glitter of the stars speak only of the glory of God and symbolize an earthly reality that reflects Providence and Sophia, the Wisdom of God. The latter betrays a connection with pre-Christian dualist concepts of the female deity of fertility, the emanation of the heavenly energies, described in the gnostico-Christian Gospels not only as the mother of everything, but also as the Truth and the Primordial Thought, named Maria and Sophia. On the one hand, this is related to the image of Our Lady, and, on the other, to that of Mother Church. The moon was the symbol of Sophia in the gnostico-Christian treatises.

During the Palaeologus Renaissance from the thirteenth to the fifteenth century, two traditions took shape in the way the sun was represented: the Renaissance tradition, based on Antique values, and the Oriental tradition, which came to the Mediterranean from Iran and was most vividly expressed in thirteenth- to fourteenth-century ceramics, that branch of applied arts that reflects the strongest influence of Islam. These ceramic vessels and large dishes bear representations of a human face haloed by seven rays and lily petals. These representations, with a strong affinity with the style of Persian luster ceramics of the twelfth and thirteenth centuries, reflected the predominant medieval astrological concept of the sun as the center of the universe.

383

**383. Fiery Ascension of Elijah,** ***also called Prophet Boboshov as it was a silver engraver from that town who first replaced the ancient sun god Gelyos with Elijah. Gold plate dated 1593. Bulgarian Macedonia.***
**(Hermitage Museum, St. Petersburg)**

**384.** ***A Hutsul stove tile depicting saints Caterine and Barbara by ceramic artist Oleksa Bakhmatuk (1820–1882). Ukraine.***

385

# THE SUN IN SLAVIC CULTURES

JAN L. PERKOWSKI

In Bulgaria during the month of August, when the days are brightest and the sun is warmest, there occurs an annual migration to the Black Sea coast. The young come to frolic in the surf and to "worship the sun" with their boon companions, while a large portion of the middle-aged and elderly visitors seek out a more serious and structured regime of "re-creation." They take the cure at some of the many health spas that dot the shoreline from Romania in the north to Turkey in the south. Today these cures are viewed as a medically valid series of therapeutic sessions and they may well have a sound scientific basis. Unknown to these patients, however, is the fact that they are actually performing an ancient ritual in celebration of the only pre-Christian cosmogonic myth known to survive in the Balkans, the cosmogonic dive.

According to one folk-tale version of this myth, in the primordial past there was only an endless sea upon which God and Satan walked. One day God set about to create the earth. He bade Satan dive to the bottom of the sea and, in God's name, fetch some earth-seed to be found there. Satan dived twice, but gathered the seed in his own name. As he ascended it slipped through his fingers. On the third dive he took seed in both his name and God's. When he surfaced, the amount of seed taken in God's name remained with him, under his fingernails. The rest was lost, as before. God took what had been retrieved in His name, made a mound, and lay down upon it to rest. Satan, believing that God was asleep, tried to push him into the water and

**385.** ***Silver commemorative medal struck by Peter the Great of Russia to celebrate the capture of Azov from the Turks (1696).***

drown him so that he alone would be master of the earth. Yet the farther Satan rolled God, the further the earth spread, until there was no longer any room for the sea.

The cure ritual, as observed by this author, is repeated daily, once a day, for two weeks. It begins each morning with a half-hour of sunbathing on the shore of the Black Sea. Then toward noon the patient crosses a thousand-foot strip of sand to a saline lake, where he disrobes and coats himself with a layer of sediment taken from the bottom of the lake. The entire body must be covered, from head to toe. The patient next stands naked facing the sun, in silence, arms extended, until the mud is baked dry and small cracks appear. He then joins others at the same stage in the warm lake, where he becomes animated and his spirits rise as the water melts the mud away and the midday sun shines directly overhead. Next he emerges from the lake and stands in the sun and breeze to dry. The final acts entail rinsing the mouth and feet with fresh water.

Clearly involved in this ritual is a magical manipulation of the four elements: fire (= sun), earth (= mud), water (= lake), air (= wind), with the aim of metaphoric rebirth and renewal, in which the patient becomes one with the earth/mud retrieved from the lake bed, shedding it in the lake/primordial sea, and emerging from it reborn to bask in the rays of the life-giving sun in a manner imitating the way the earth was first created, according to the myth of the cosmogonic dive.

There are two related and compelling themes found in this myth and the cure-ritual based on it: heliolatry and dualism. Let us first discuss heliolatry and then take up dualism.

Another heliolatry ritual practised in contemporary Bulgaria, and also until quite recently in Russia and Serbia, is the St. John the Baptist Day rites, which clearly combine Christian and pre-Christian elements. This holiday falls on June 24 and is in origin a calendrical cycle celebration of the summer solstice, when the sun was be-

**386.** *Pre-Christian painted eggs from a tenth-century site in Kiev.*

**387.** *Colorful eggs called* **pysanki**, *painted with ancient symbols of the sun, still play a key role in Ukrainian Easter rituals.*

lieved to hesitate and waver in the sky and then to begin to "die," since each subsequent day is shorter as the darkness and chill of winter slowly encroach. Traditionally on this day young girls sing the following incantation to the sun:

Hail Marina, St. Marina!
Queen Domna says to the sun,
"O sun, sun bright and high,
As you shine bright and high,
Bright, high, and all around,
Don't you know of a herb for childbearing,
A herb for childbearing, for a sad heart?"
"I know about one, I know, Queen Domna,
But it is said to be very far,
Very far and very costly. . . ."

The song goes on to say that Queen Domna, in order to convince the sun to give her a childbearing herb, promised that if she bore a daughter she would give her to him. When she had the beautiful Marina, she hid her until she was grown. One

388

**388.** ***Jeweled coronation Fabergé egg presented to Alexandra Feodorovna by Nicholas II of Russia in 1897.*** **(Messrs. Wartski Collection)**

Sunday the girl went out to fetch some water, and the sun caught sight of her, lowered a swing (i.e., the sun's rays), and hoisted her away.

According to Bulgarian folk beliefs the sun is anthropomorphicized as a male who has a mother, stars for sisters, and the moon for a brother (or sister). He can fall in love with a beautiful girl and want to marry her. In the case of this incantation it should be borne in mind that St. Marina (celebrated July 17) is popularly held to be a "fiery" martyr.

The whole ritual of which this incantation is but a small part, serves, on the one hand, to assist the sun at the weakest point in its cycle—for which purpose fires were once lit and jumped over—and, on the other, to request that the sun grant fertility to both human beings and plant life. A sun symbol, the circle, appears throughout the festivities: in large and small wreaths, a tight circle dance, ritual bread.

Sun symbols such as the rosette, swastika, and wheel are to be found throughout Slavdom, ranging from Polish decorative paper cutouts called *wycinanki*, to patterns in Slovak embroidery, to carved wooden designs on northern Russian churches. Two other sun symbols, which emanate from pre-Christian times but are now solidly incorporated in Slavic Christian ritual, are the Easter egg and the halo on icons. The egg symbolizes the whole universe with the sun (the yolk) at its core. The halo came to the Slavs via Byzantium, but originated with the Sassanian Persians, who were sun worshippers and depicted their kings' heads as surrounded by the sun's corona. In general the Slavs have been affected by several waves of ancient Iranian religious influence, primarily solarist and dualist.

For the purpose of this chapter it is convenient to divide Slavic history into three eras: the prehistoric period, the medieval Christian period, and the secular modern age. The first extends from approximately 2000 BC, when the Proto-Slavs settled in the Pripet Marshes between the Vistula and Dnieper rivers north of the Carpathian Mountains. Their immediate Indo-European neighbors were the Balts to the northwest, the Germanic peoples to the west, the Iranians to the east, the Illyrians to the southwest, and the Thracians (and Dacians) to the southeast; the latter two groups have since died out. In the period from the fifth to the ninth century AD the Proto-Slavs migrated into the regions they now inhabit—Russia, Belarus, Ukraine, Poland, the Czech lands, Slovakia, Bulgaria, and former Yugoslavia—and by the middle of the ninth century began to accept Christianity. This inaugurated the medieval Christian period, which lasted in rural areas until the nineteenth century. The nineteenth and especially the twentieth century constitute the secular modern period.

Although precious little data from the prehistoric period have come down to us, we do know from the tenth-century Arab traveler Al Masudi that the Proto-Slavs worshipped the sun. He even provides us with a description of one of their temples, which had a hole in the roof to allow the sun's rays to be traced on the temple floor. From other sources we know that the Slavic pre-Christian pantheon included the god Svarog (from the Indic *svargas*, radiant sky) who was believed to be the forger of the sun. In old Russian sources both celestial and earthly fire are said to be Svarog's son Xŭrsŭ Dažibogŭ, the first part of whose name is an Iranian term (*Xŭrsīd* in Persian) for the personified radiant sun. Another direct borrowing is the Slavic word *ray* (paradise) from the Iranian *ray*, meaning beatitude and heavenly radiance. These are

389

**389.** ***Girl with a sunflower. Painting from the Croatian Naïve School by Ivan Rabuzin. 1962.*** **(Galerije Grada, Zagreb, Croatia)**

390. *Polish folk paper-cut sun symbols in different colors, called* wycinanki, *created over the past 20 years by countrywomen from Kurpie, Puszcza, and Zielona.* (Muzeum Etnograficzne, Toruń, Poland).

391. *Ceiling woodcarving from the 1807 Daskalov House in Tryavna, Bulgaria.*

392

**392.** ***Russian wooden tub with straw appliqué sun design, by Alexander Slivetsov. 1980.***

among the oldest vestiges of Iranian influence on the pre-Christian belief structure of the Slavs.

It is impossible to trace with accuracy the very earliest Iranian religious influences. The Slavs and Iranians, as closely related branches of the Indo-European family, doubtless share a core of ancient religious concepts and vocabulary. However, beginning with the Scythians (750–200 BC) and the Sarmatians (200 BC–AD 400) direct borrowings of the *Xŭrsīd* and *ray* type begin to occur. Receptivity to Iranian religious influences continued up to the fifteenth century AD.

Throughout the Scythian and Sarmatian periods the ancient Slavs continued to occupy their original European homeland in what is now Ukraine. By the ninth century their subsequent migratory expansion had come to an end and they soon became absorbed into the Eastern and Western Christian communities. Although several Slavic states officially adopted Christianity (Great Moravian Empire, 863; Bulgarian Empire, 865; Poland, 966; and Kievan Russia, 988), for a rather long period, especially among the East and Balkan Slavs, there existed a state of "dual faith" in which Christianity existed side by side with the older Slavic religion, whose gods were now either perceived as devils or transformed into saints.

The period of Slavic settlement in the Balkan peninsula lasted from the beginning of the sixth to the middle of the seventh century. Immediately preceding their arrival, two world religions had spread throughout the Roman Empire: Christianity and Mithraism, the latter a sect of Iranian origin. Our knowledge of ancient Iranian religious beliefs is somewhat more complete than that of the Slavs. Texts from the Zoroastrian religion date from the sixth century BC. There are two aspects of this religion that are of interest to us here: its dualism, and its use of sun symbolism in its cosmogonic scheme, since these two elements reappear to a greater or lesser degree in each of the subsequent Iranian sects that reached Europe and influenced the Slavs.

Despite the fact that Mithraism gained sufficient strength to oust Christianity, however briefly, as the official religion of the Roman Empire, little is known of its beliefs and cult practices. Tradition has it that Christianity was brought to the Balkans by St. Paul during Apostolic times. This new religion quickly prospered in the cities, but eventually suffered setbacks during Diocletian's persecutions (303–313). Although Christianity was established as the official religion of the Roman Empire in 312, subsequently, during the reign of Julian the Apostate (361–363), the Mithraic Mysteries held sway. Julian, who worshipped the bright god Mithra, even wrote a discourse on the heavenly Sun King. Before accepting Christianity Constantine himself had worshipped Sol Invictus (the invincible sun), or Mithra.

Mithraism, which was first introduced to Roman soldiers stationed in the Middle East beginning in 67 BC, was later carried to the Danube frontier by the Fifteenth Legion in AD 71–72. In AD 107 Trajan repopulated Dacia (present-day Romania) *ex toto orbe Romano* (from the whole Roman world) and Mithraism soon flourished. A glance at European archaeological maps marking surviving Mithraic temple sites shows that the cult spread as far north as the Carpathian Mountains, as far east as the Black Sea, and as far west as the Rhine. Although no definite proof exists that the Mithraic cult was dualistic in nature, there is no doubt of its Iranian origin and heliolatrous nature.

Although Mithraism had become a world religion, there is no indication that it was uniform in cosmology, theology, or rites.

The next Iranian cult to penetrate the Balkans was that of the Persian prophet Mani, who died in AD 274. During the fourth century his dualistic cult spread throughout the Roman Empire, supplanting the Mithraic Mysteries and challenging official Christianity. This first wave of Manichaeism, which spread throughout the whole Mediterranean world, including both Rome and Constantinople, flourished until the seventh century. Then came a second wave from the ninth to the fourteenth century, which spread throughout southern and central Europe from the Black Sea to the Atlantic. It took especially strong hold in Bulgaria, Greece, Serbia, and Bosnia, not to disappear until the coming of the Turks in the fourteenth and fifteenth centuries. It is at this time and in this context that the vampire cult arose among the Slavs.

By the time the Slavs had completed their colonization of the Balkans during the middle of the ninth century they had already been recipients of at least two waves of Iranian influence: from the Scythians and the Sarmatians. Upon arrival in the Balkans they once again came into contact with Iranian religious beliefs: the Mithraic Mysteries and Manichaeism that existed among the indigenous Romans, Greeks, Dacians, Thracians, and Illyrians.

The second wave of Manichaeism swept through the Balkans at a time when the Slavs were already present. It came not as a purely Iranian sect, but in the form of a Christian heresy, whose basis was the persistent Iranian notion of dualism, which holds that Evil has the same positive and ultimate quality as Good. There are, therefore, two separate forces in the world: God versus Satan, Good versus Evil, Spirit

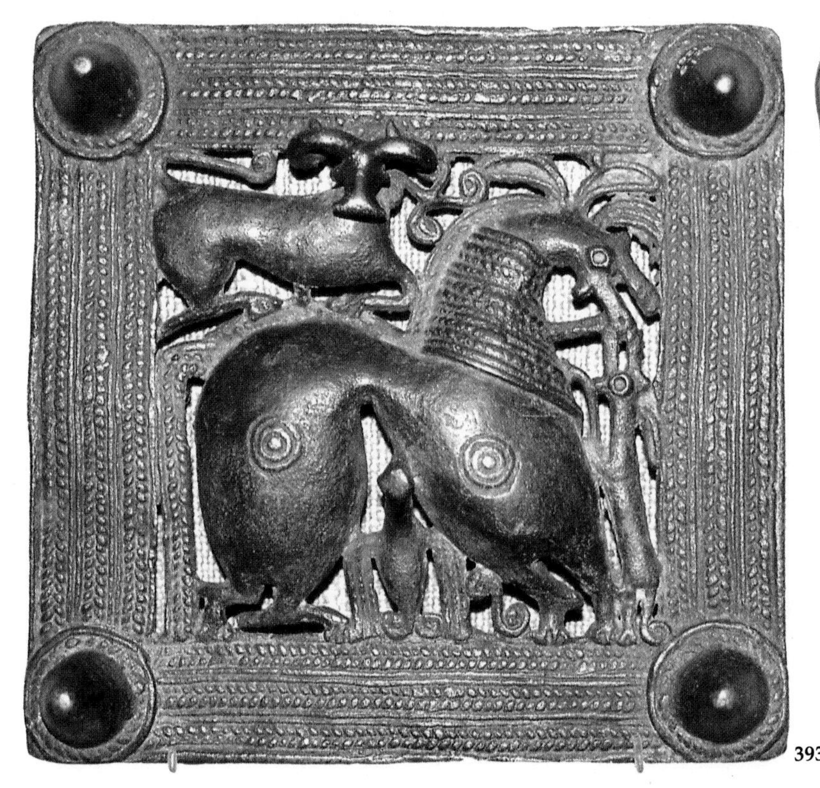
393

394

**393,394.** ***Bronze open-work belt-clasps with animal designs are only found in the Caucasus, Georgia. 200 BC-AD 200.*** **(British Museum, London)**

versus Matter, Light versus Darkness. In this system humans are dual; their souls are divine and their bodies evil. The body serves as the tomb of the soul. Satan seeks to imprison light in the darkness of matter and to prevent the soul from returning to Heaven. Redemption is the release of the soul at death. According to the teaching of Mani, humans are a microcosmic mixture of Light (good) and Darkness (evil). Just as Light and Darkness separate at death, so too will there be a total and final macrocosmic separation of Light and Darkness at the end of the world. Manichaeism was a non-Christian dualist religion which adapted to Christianity. In seventh-century Armenia there arose a Christian heretical sect, the Paulicians, who attempted to adapt Christianity to dualism. These heretics were persistent in their beliefs, and many were condemned to the stake by the Byzantine emperors. Records show that in 869 the Paulicians were planning to send missionaries from Armenia to Bulgaria. It is by such means that the second wave of Manichaeism reached the Balkans and beyond. In Bulgaria this belief came to be called Bogomilism after its leader Bogomil, who lived in Bulgaria during the reign of Tsar Peter (927–969).

No complete picture of the doctrines and rituals of the Bogomils has come down to us, but their existence for four hundred years during the first and second Bulgarian empires is well documented. They are known to have survived a century longer among the Serbs in Bosnia under the name "Patarene."

The cradle of Bogomilism was that region of the Bulgarian Empire which is now the Macedonian republic. This is also the region from which the Slavic term *vampir* originated. None of the standard Slavic etymological dictionaries offers a satisfactory origin for this word. A plausible one is the name of the Manichaean god Bā̊m (Bă̄n in Syriac), which appears in a thousand-year-old Sogdian (Iranian) manuscript found in the Turfan Oasis of Chinese Turkistan at the turn of the century. This manuscript is especially pertinent, since it is one of the few sacred Manichaean tracts extant. Bam is described as the great builder who, at the end of the world, will carve a tomb of stone to serve as the grave of Darkness. Evidence of the penetration of this name into the Balkans is found in a letter of Bishop Theophylactus, Patriarch of Constantinople (933–956), where a certain heretic is listed as Βααvηs *[Vānēs]*. The name might have appeared in Slavic as **van-*. This plus the form (Old Church Slavonic) *pirŭ* meaning "revelry, drinking bout" (cf., the Slavic verbal root *pij*, "to drink") could well produce **vanĭ pirŭ* (Van's Festival) > **vanpir*< *vampir*. Originally the term would have referred to a ritual libation in honor of the god Van. Such rituals of sacrifice, called *kurban*, survived in Bulgaria until the nineteenth century, the last vestiges of the dualist Bogomils and Paulicians.

It is not in name only that Iranian dualism has left its mark on Slavic vampirism. This cult practice is surely a result of the conflict between Orthodox Christianity and the dualist heresy. In his *Chronicle of the Slavs* (1164–68) Helmold describes the following pre-Christian practices of the Western Slavs:

> After the victim is felled the priest drinks of its blood in order to render himself more potent in the receiving of oracles. For it is the opinion of many that demons are very easily conjured with blood... The Slavs too, have a strange delusion. At their feasts and carousals they pass round a bowl over which they utter words... in the name of the gods... of the good one, as well as the bad one—professing that all propitious fortune is arranged by the good god, adversity by the bad god.

395

396

From this account we know that dualism, whatever its immediate source may have been, was practised by Slavs as far from the Balkans as the Baltic Sea.

The Slavic vampire of folklore is considered a creature of darkness, frequently a heretic, who is either immobilized or destroyed by the sun's light. (Bogomils believed that all things in the world were created by Satan except the sun and the human soul.) Surely these are expressions of dualism. In Russia the chief means of coping with the deadly force of vampires was to drive a sharpened aspen stake into the chest or between the shoulder blades of a corpse, or sometimes into the burial mound; but when a corpse persisted in attacking the populace, it would then be necessary to cremate it. Was it not a custom of Byzantine emperors to impale heretics? For Orthodox Christians it was anathema to cremate the dead; even heretics were buried. But for the dualist, cremation meant liberation of the soul from the body, allowing the soul to travel up to the source of all light, Sol Invictus.

This, however, was not the last migration of these ancient Iranian beliefs. Toward the end of the seventeenth century, as the Habsburgs slowly forced the Ottomans to

**395.** ***Christ with the type of halo borrowed from the sun symbols of Sassanid Persians.*** *AD 1259* ***fresco in the Boyana Church, Sofia, Bulgaria.***

**396.** ***Prophet Elijah in his fiery chariot with solar wheels. Nineteenth-century Bulgarian icon from a church in Malko, Turnovo.***

397

**397. The Vampire** *by Edvard Munch. 1893.* **(Göteborgs Konstmuseum, Gothenburg, Sweden)**

398

relinquish their hold on the Balkans, customs strange to Western Europe were discovered among the newly liberated Serbs, the most notorious of which was vampirism. First there was an imperial inquest commissioned to look into the matter. Then, by the middle of the eighteenth century, learned treatises on the subject were published. Finally, in the nineteenth century, the Slavic folkloric vampire entered Western fiction. Few in the English-speaking world are unfamiliar with the final scene in Bram Stoker's novel *Dracula,* involving a race against the sun. At the fatal moment Dracula's pursuers appear to have lost: "As I looked [Dracula's] eyes saw the sinking sun, and the look of hate in them turned to triumph." But his hope of triumph is premature; he is impaled—pinned to the earth to which he belongs—and the creature of Darkness is no more.

**398.** ***Traditional Bulgarian Easter bread is decorated with sun symbols and ritually eaten at home, presented to neighbors and relatives, and taken to the graves of ancestors.***

400

# THE SUN IN GREEK ART AND CULTURE

GREGORY NAGY AND PANOS D. VALAVANIS

Early evidence for Greek conceptualization of the sun comes from the Greek language itself, especially as used in the oldest surviving Greek poetry, Homer's *Iliad* and *Odyssey*. In these epics, the sun is visualized as rising from and setting into a cosmic fresh-water river called the "Okeanos," which surrounded a flat and circular world and thus in effect contained the earth and its seas. Only with the advances of scientific inquiry in the fifth century BC, and with ever-expanding knowledge about the "outer limits" of the earth and its seas, did the ancient concept of the Okeanos begin slowly to become equated with the modern concept of "ocean" (a word derived from ancient Greek).

In the mythical world view of early Greece, the sun sets into the Okeanos in the far west every evening, only to rise again in the far east each new morning from the same world-encircling river. As we learn from the Greek poet Hesiod, the abode of ancient Greek heroes who are immortalized after death is located precisely in this realm in the far east, on the banks of the Okeanos where the sun rises. Different

**399.** *Marble head of Helios found in Rhodes, possibly part of a statue or quadriga. Hellenistic period.* **(Museum of Rhodes, Greece)**

**400.** *Relief of Helios on his chariot, excavated at Troy in 1872. c. 300 BC.* **(Staatliche Museen zu Berlin)**

401

402

**401,402.** ***Representing fertility rituals of the Mycenaean religion, the two rings from Tiryns (401) and Mycenae (402) symbolize the sun in forms of a wheel, a circle with rays, or a rosette. 1500 BC.*** **(National Archaeological Museum, Athens)**

Greek myths have different names for this realm, the most celebrated of which is Elysium. A related concept is the mythical realm of Ethiopia, situated at both ends of the world, both the far west and the far east, according to the *Odyssey*. The King of the Ethiopians is Memnon, the son of Eos, the Dawn Goddess; this hero is conventionally represented as a black man in early Greek traditions, as are also his people, the Ethiopians.

The vertically circular course of the sun and the horizontally circular flow of the Okeanos combine to symbolize the cycle of life and death through light and darkness, wakefulness and sleep, even consciousness and unconsciousness. In the Greek language, the cyclical movement from darkness to light and from death to life is conceived as a *nostos* (return home). This ancient Greek word is related to *noos*, meaning "consciousness" or "mind" in the language of Homer (the word recurs as *nous* in Classical Greek, as used by Plato). When Odysseus finally returns home to his long-awaited Ithaca after so many adventures and sufferings, the *Odyssey* captures the precise moment of his homecoming with a poetic description that embraces both *noos* and *nostos*. The hero is described as sailing in the middle of the night (an extraordinary event for any Greek sailor), and he is in a deep sleep, which seems like death itself, says the poet. At the exact moment that the ship carrying Odysseus reaches the shores of Ithaca, the sun rises, and the hero wakes up.

The poem thus synchronizes the hero's return home and his regaining consciousness with the actual arrival of the sun's light, which is the driving symbol of the epic. In Greek mythology, the hero's return home is the return to light and life.

It is one thing for Helios, the anthropomorphic sun god, to drive his solar chariot along its circular course, day in and day out. If a mortal attempts the same feat, however, it is no longer a cosmic process but an event that can happen only once. So goes the myth of the hero Phaethon, as retold by Euripides and later, in the Roman era, by Ovid. Phaethon's father was none other than the divine sun himself, and the

**403.** *Reconstruction of an "acroterion" solar symbol which crowned the pediment of the Archaic temple of Hera in Olympia in seventh century* BC.

**404.** *Attic black figure skyphos showing the first anthropomorphic representation of the sun with a solar disc over his head. Eighth century* BC. *Taranto (ancient Taras).* **(Museo Nazionale, Taranto)**

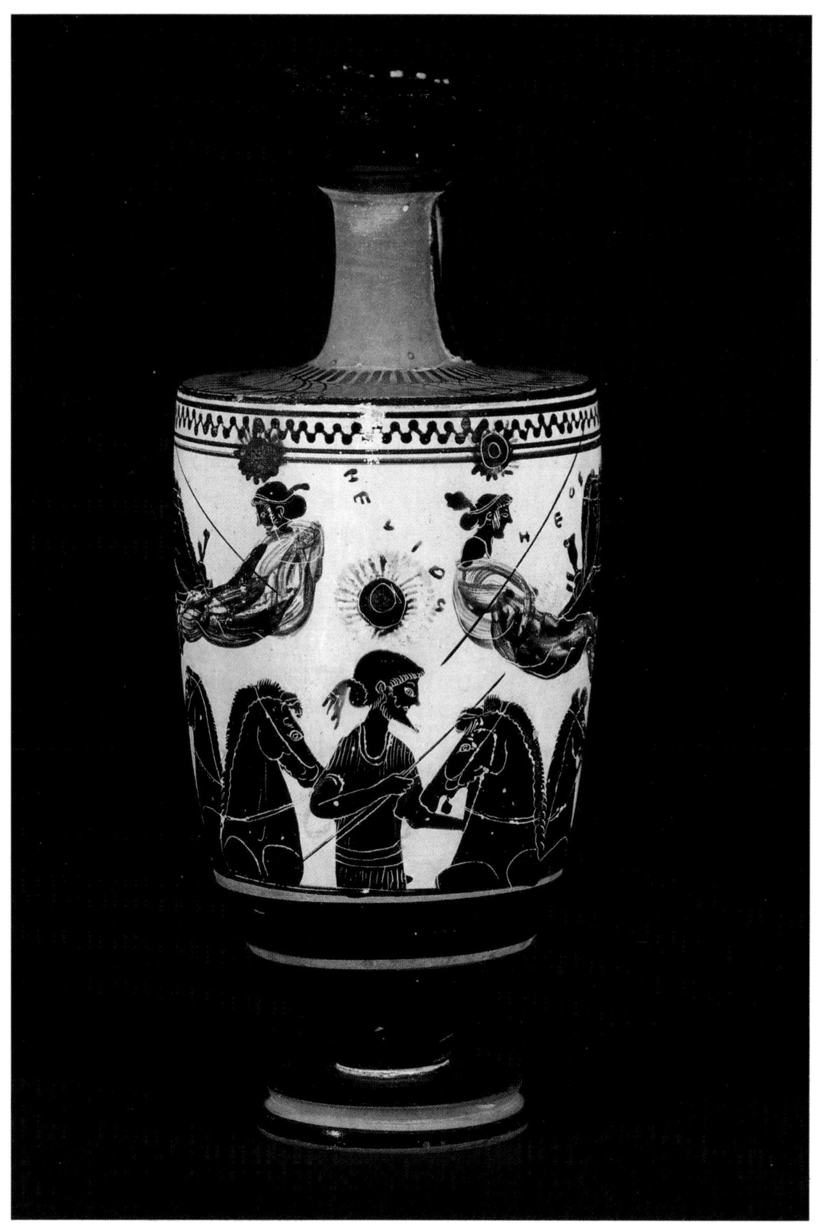

405

406

hero's very name means "radiant like the sun." The problem was that Phaethon's mother was a mortal. In Greek myth, mortal "genes" are dominant, and Phaethon is destined for the ultimate disappointment of death. He can prove that he had been sired by the sun if the god lets him drive the divine solar chariot, but this affirmation of the hero's deeply felt affinity with the divine is simultaneously an affirmation of his human condition. Once Phaethon reaches the triumphant apogee of his solar chariot course, he is blasted out of the skies, hurled back down to earth in the utter failure of death.

Still, a ceaseless yearning for the sun is a subject of hope as well as disappointment in Greek mythology. In Greek poetic expressions of death wishes, the spirit or psyche (to use the Greek word) of the deceased can be pictured as traveling into the far west, plunging ultimately into the earth-encircling waters of the Okeanos. The implicit hope is that, just as Helios plunges into the Okeanos in the evening only to emerge restored from the same waters the morning after, so also the human

**405.** *Greek terra-cotta vase showing Helios rising from the sea as Nyx and Eos disappear on either side. Attributed to Sappho painter. 500–490 BC.* **(Metropolitan Museum of Art, New York. Rogers Fund)**

**406.** *Greek terra-cotta called "the Queen of Vases" represents the solar theology of Pythagorean and Orphean doctrines. Fourth century BC. Hydra.* **(Hermitage Museum, St. Petersburg)**

407

spirit can find a way to prove its own intuitive affinity with the light of the sun.

The representation of the sun in Greek art can be traced with some certainty back to the Minoan and Mycenaean period (third to second millennium BC). Several depictions of solar symbols have been preserved in ritual scenes from those times. Among the most typical are examples to be seen on two gold rings, one from Grave Circle A at Mycenae and one from Tiryns, both dated to around 1500 BC. Here, according to the most widely accepted interpretation, a seated goddess of fertility is shown in the first instance accepting offers from two women and a girl and in the second from disguised deities. In the upper part of both compositions, the sun is visible in the sky in the form of a circle of rays, and next to it stands the moon. It is believed that these representations depict rituals associated with vegetation which took place on certain days of the year when the two celestial bodies were visible simultaneously in the sky.

This "naturalist" manner of representing the sun as a round shape, a circle, a wheel, or a rosette is found in older works of art, for instance on seal rings or impres-

**407.** *The theme of "the Queen of Vases," in black and gold (symbolizing darkness and light), represents the gods of Eleusinian mysteries in which the goddesses of the earth and the underworld invoke the sacred fire, flaming from the water.* **(Hermitage Museum, St. Petersburg)**

sions from the mid-Minoan period (early third millennium), and it persisted through the Bronze Age period and early historical times (tenth to eighth century BC) in many forms of art, especially on seal rings and in vase paintings. It is true that it is not always easy to distinguish cases in which these images have a purely decorative function from those in which they are used as symbols. The same way of representing the sun is frequently found in later times, the most impressive examples being the monumental representations of the symbol of the sun on the huge disc-shaped clay acroteria which decorated the apex of the pediments of a few temples of the early Archaic period (seventh century BC). The most beautiful example comes from the Heraion at Olympia. It measures seven feet across, consists of concentric zones filled with ray- or flame-shaped decorations, and is surrounded by tiny rays around the edge.

In Homer's and Hesiod's poetry and in the slightly later Homeric hymns, the sun had already acquired an anthropomorphic character, since "he" is described, in beautiful verse, setting out each morning from the land of the Ethiopians, which for the ancient Greeks was the easternmost part of the world, in his chariot, pulled by one, two, or four horses, to spread his light over the whole earth. In the lyric poetry of Archaic times the picture is completed with the description of the nightly return of the sun from the land of the Hesperides, the western limit of the world, asleep in his chariot or floating in a vase on the waters of the Okeanos. These poetic images of both the daily and nightly excursions of Helios the sun were so successful that they put their seal on the entirety of Greek literature and art from that early period up to the end of Antiquity. The conception of the sun in human form is not unusual in Greece; it fits into the framework of one of the most typical expressions of Greek thought and imagination, which loved to give human form to everything from

natural phenomena to social institutions, even to complicated abstract concepts.

The Archaic period (from the seventh to the sixth century BC) saw the ripening of the Greek spirit, which manifested itself in an explosion of spiritual and artistic expression, and the birth of an interest in cosmic questions, explored by the first philosophers (Thales, Anaximander, Anaximenes). These developments were accompanied by anthropomorphic representations of the sun and other celestial bodies in Greek art. The first such representations come exclusively from vase paintings, which form the wealthiest source of information on the art of the period.

Some researchers consider a painting on a Theban amphora found on the island

408

409

**408.** *A horse head from the sculpture of Helios driving his chariot out of the sea at dawn, which was originally on the east corner of the Parthenon. Acropolis, Athens. 447–432 BC.* **(British Museum, London)**

**409.** *The triumph of light over darkness, represented by Helios and Selene, is the theme of a wedding scene depicted on the lid of a marble sarcophagus. Third-century Roman copy of the Greek original.* **(Hermitage Museum, St. Petersburg)**

of Kythera and dated around 670–660 BC (now in the British Museum) as the earliest representation of Helios in human form. It depicts a bust, a male with short hair and a beard, holding the reins of a horse that runs facing the right. The identification of this figure with Helios is clearly based on descriptions in slightly older poetic texts. However, this interpretation has not been unanimously accepted by scholars, because, as we shall see, this work does not include any of the typical characteristics of Helios.

Images of the sun are easily identifiable from the end of the sixth century onward, especially on Attic black-and-red-figure vases. Helios always appears dressed in the long chiton of a charioteer standing in an oncoming chariot drawn by two or four winged horses. In early paintings he has a beard, and in his hand he holds reins and sometimes a scepter and a long pointed stick to spur on the horses. The features that lend certainty to the identification of this figure with Helios are, on the one hand, the depiction of a solar disc over his head and, on the other, the occasional presence of an inscription with his name.

The vast majority of such representations are found on black-figure lekythoi and on white-ground vases dated between 510 and 480 BC. When only the upper part of the figure is shown, the rising of the sun is being depicted, while the appearance of the sea at the bottom of the picture suggests his long journey over the ocean. One of the most characteristic paintings is one on a black-figure skyphos, or drinking vessel, in the Museo Nazionale of Taranto, while on a white-ground black-figure lekythos in The Metropolitan Museum of Art in New York, the best-known vase of its kind, Helios appears between Eos (Dawn) and Nyx (Night), who are setting out in opposite directions, ceding to him the reign of Day. Here, all three figures are accompanied by inscriptions bearing their names.

From the beginning of the fifth century BC, in particular from 480 onwards, when the identification of Apollo with Helios, already existing in embryo in Archaic times, is solidified, the god appears beardless, that is, in the form of a young and beautiful man. A characteristic example is a painting on a white-ground clay bobbin found in the Agora of Athens. At the same time, the luminous disc disappears from over the head of the god; instead, it surrounds his head as a circle of rays or a diadem. This is

**410.** *The transition from the old to a new solar religion was symbolized by the killing of Niobe's children by Apollo and Artemis. Fifth century. Roman copy of the Greek original.* **(Hermitage Museum, St. Petersburg)**

how he appears in many paintings on red-figure Attic and southern Italian vases of the fifth and fourth centuries BC.

Another important iconographical change is that by the middle of the fifth century BC both Helios and his chariot have begun to be pictured in profile, a position that gives artists the opportunity to develop the subject extensively in both depth and width, which they achieve through diagonal axes and partially concealing the horses' bodies with each other. This way Helios is portrayed facing sometimes right and sometimes left. While it is not a simple matter to give a definite interpretation to these directions, it would seem that Helios looking left denotes the sunrise, while his looking to the right denotes the sunset. One of the most delightful examples of this new iconographic convention is a painting on the neck of a red-figure Apulian krater in the Munich Museum, dated around 330 BC. Here the god's head is surrounded by a triple halo or nimbus. The sun's chariot is preceded by that of Eos: one of the horses of the latter is reined in by a star in the form of a winged child. Schematic stars can be seen over the horses' heads. This vase manifests another aspect of solar symbolism, which is witnessed only in southern Italian art. On vases of this type, Helios is depicted only on the vase's neck, while the body depicts a funeral scene. This suggests that the signification of Helios here is metaphysical. His position over the funeral

411

**411.** ***The legend of the Fall of Phaethon depicted on this marble sarcophagus symbolizes life as a circular motion of the sun. Third-century Roman copy of the Greek original.*** **(Hermitage Museum, St. Petersburg)**

scene could suggest the hope of another world filled with light. It should be pointed out that the Greeks held the belief that their nobler dead, heroes for instance, lived in the Elysian Fields, in eternal light.

The oldest known sculpted representation of Helios is on the eastern pediment of the Parthenon (c. 432 BC). In the center is shown the birth of Athena from the head of Zeus, while around them the Olympian gods watch ecstatically. Helios is shown rising with his chariot at the left end of the pediment, while Selene (the moon) is setting at the right end, thus delimiting the miracle of the goddess's birth within one day. The artist Pheidias' genius managed not only to incorporate the two gods harmoniously into the composition, but also to solve the problem of the outermost pediment figures, which had to be squeezed into the awkward acute angles on the triangle. Of the surviving parts of this sculpture, the headless body of Helios and two of the horses' heads are in the British Museum, while the two other horses' heads remain in their original position on the monument. Helios has also been identified on some of the east and north metopes of the same temple, which however have not been very well preserved.

Helios and Selene here play much the same role as they do in the representation of many other myths, such as the Birth of Aphrodite, the Judgment of Paris, and the Gigantomachy (battle of the giants). These scenes are frequently depicted on vases, sarcophagus reliefs, and other ancient Greek art objects. Helios and Selene are placed at the outer edges to delimit these events temporally. They play precisely this role in two compositions of great importance which served to decorate secondary parts of famous gold and ivory cult statues by Pheidias, known to us only through the descriptions of ancient writers. The first was a composition in relief of the Birth of Aphrodite on the base of the throne of the statue of Zeus at Olympia. It was visited and described by the AD second-century traveller Pausanias (5.11.8). The second was the painting of the Gigantomachy on the inside of the shield of Athena Parthenos in the Parthenon, described by Pausanias (1.24.5) and the AD-first-century Latin writer Pliny (*HN* 36.18). It is possible to get an idea of what Helios looked like in these compositions from Attic red-figure vases of the late fifth century BC with similar subjects—for example the red-figure krater with a representation of the Gigantomachy in the Museum of Naples. Here, the young Helios, dressed in short chiton, thorax, and chlamys, rises, barely visible in his quadriga in the sky, denoted by a decorated curved line, while the solar disc shines over his head.

One of the most beautiful relief compositions preserved with Helios directly present in the mythical battle between the gods and the giants, and with a much

**412 a,b.** *Rhodian gold coin showing on the obverse side the head of Stelios (taken from the Colossus of Rhodes); the rose on the reverse symbolizes Rhodos, which is the Greek word for rose. c. 85 BC.* **(British Museum, London)**

**413.** ***Painted tombstone with solar symbols which go back to prehistoric times. Fourth century*** BC. ***Hersoness, a Greek colony on the Black Sea coast.***
**(Hermitage Museum, St. Petersburg)**

more active role to play, is on the great Altar of Zeus from Pergamon (now in Berlin) dating from 180–160 BC. The god is battling from his chariot, while his horses, rearing backward, are attacking the giants. His radiance is more readily obvious on a metope from the temple of Athena at Ilion (Troy), also in Berlin, dating from around 300 BC. On the first level we have the horses, one behind the other, with the radiant head of the god rising behind them, crowned with a multirayed diadem.

Rhodes was the island of Helios and probably the most important center of his worship in Antiquity. In one of Pindar's odes a beautiful myth is told: When the gods were sharing out the earth among themselves, Helios was out on his daily trip, so they forgot to put something aside for him. When he returned, Zeus, not wanting to be unfair, was about to start the process anew. Helios, however, stopped him; he had already made his choice: he had seen Rhodes rising out of the waves. Zeus let the god of light have the beautiful island unveiled by the salt water. It follows that many important works of art associated with Helios should come from Rhodes. Among them two sculptures of great significance are to be found. The older is a bronze composition by the great fourth-century-BC sculptor Lysippos, showing Helios standing on his four-horse-drawn chariot. The composition was either intended for Rhodes, or was dedicated by the Rhodians to Apollo in Delphi and stood in front of the temple. Its fate was, at any rate, identical to that of most bronze and marble sculptures decorating Greek cities and sanctuaries, which were carried off to Rome by generals and emperors who conquered or visited Greece, and later to be taken to Constantinople. This particular sculpture, of widespread fame in Antiquity, is known to us solely from written descriptions, (Pliny *HN* 34, 63) and also through its influence on other representations, especially reliefs and on coins, as well as on marble copies of Helios heads of the Roman period. The identification with Helios of a fairly large group of such heads is based on the existence of a row of holes around the hairline which were used to hold inlaid metal rays. The connection with the original is established through comparisons with known works by Lysippos. Certain scholars have maintained that the four horses that nowadays decorate the facade of the San Marco Basilica in Venice once possibly formed part of the original bronze composition by Lysippos.

Another famous Rhodian work of art was the Colossus of Rhodes, known to us both through written sources (Pliny *HN* 34.41; Strabo 14.2.5; Polybius 5.88; and so on) and through representations of its head in other works of art. It was a gigantic bronze statue by the Lindian sculptor Chares which took twelve years to build, from 304 to 292 BC, attaining a height of nearly a hundred feet. It stood in the city of Rhodes, probably in the sanctuary of Helios. This is the first time that a statue of the god alone, without his chariot, makes its appearance. This enormous creation stood upright for only a few years, until 227–26 BC, when it was brought down by a tremendous earthquake, which also destroyed a large part of the city. The Rhodians, following the advice of the oracle of Delphi, did not re-erect it, and it was left lying there until AD 653, when the Arabs conquered the island and sold the statue as scrap to a Jewish merchant. According to Byzantine texts, the latter had to use nine hundred camels for its transportation. The Colossus was represented by Renaissance artists and their followers as standing astride the entrance to the harbor; this does not correspond with reality, but it does give us an idea of the size and the grandeur of the statue, which had impressed the ancient Greeks so much that they included it among the Seven Wonders of the ancient world. The head of the statue is known to us through its depiction on the coins of Rhodes, and there are also several works of sculpture from the Hellenistic and Roman periods which represent the head of the Colossus or other Helios statues among the many that were to be found on the island.

Apart from Rhodes, which always placed the head of Helios on the obverse of its coins, in the manner of a national symbol, depictions of the god's head are to be found on the coins of many other cities, especially in Asia Minor and Sicily, during the late Hellenistic and Roman period (the second century BC to the third century AD).

Of interest is the marked similarity between certain portraits of Alexander the Great and statues of Helios from the Hellenistic era (third to fifth century BC). It must be due to the tendency of the Macedonian king to identify himself with the sun, analogous to the Egyptian Pharaohs, who identified themselves with Amun-Re. After Alexander, several kings of the Hellenistic and Roman periods, as well as many Roman emperors, adopted iconography associated with Helios, and they are depicted rising in the sky in their chariot of *apotheosis*, which resembles that of Helios.

The iconographic portrayal of Helios as a beautiful youth with a radiant crown of rays survives in Roman art, which has bequeathed several depictions of Sol (the sun) in wall paintings, reliefs, mosaics, and on coins and vases. One of the most striking is a fresco from Pompeii, where the god is shown alone, young and exquisitely beautiful, holding a horsewhip, as a reminder of the (absent) chariot, and a globe of the world with the zodiacal circle, a symbol of his eternal cosmic rule.

414

**414.** ***Black basanite disc with a bust of the god Helios-Serapis. Late second century.*** **(British Museum, London)**

416

# THE SUN GODS OF ANCIENT EUROPE

MIRANDA GREEN

The evidence for the sun cult manifests itself in Europe from as long ago as the fourth millennium BC, when Neolithic farmers recognized the divine power of the solar disc. The main theme of this chapter is the dominance of the sun as a supernatural force in the perceptions of human beings living in temperate (i.e., non-Mediterranean) Europe during the period 3000 BC to AD 400. From the Neolithic until the official end of paganism and even later, European communities drew symbols of the sun, built sanctuaries, and fashioned images that acknowledged the daily and seasonal behavior of the sun, its essential heat- and light-giving properties, and its multifarious functions and associations.

Throughout the period under discussion the divine sun was recognized as a force with many differing roles and concerns, a force that needed to be controlled by religious and magical means. Solar religion manifested itself not only in acknowledgment of the overt functions of the sun—as a provider of heat and light—but also in recognition of influences that were more wide-ranging. The sun was perceived to possess a dualistic character, a dimension associated with both light and dark, day and night, life and death, which runs as a thread through the different phases of prehistoric and Romano-Celtic Europe.

To early communities, the sun was an enigma, with its nightly disappearance from the sky and the withdrawal of its heat for half the year. The sun's value as a life-force was revered; its capriciousness and its ability to destroy (by means of extreme heat or the lack of it) were feared. The control of the sun could be achieved in various ways: by making images of the solar disc or of a sun god; by building temples in its honor; by prayers, ceremonies, and festivals; and by sacrifice. There is evidence for all these activities in European prehistory.

The behavior of the sun was especially important for farming communities. People needed to be able to measure time: so the movement of the sun across the sky, the

---

**415.** ***Lighting fires and jumping over them during summer solstice was performed to "energize" the sun when it became "tired and weak" at the turn of seasons. A Christian message is now associated with this ancient ritual as seen in this picture taken in Finland.***

**416.** ***Sheet-gold "sun disc" from Ireland worn as button-caps. Beaker period, c. 2000 BC.*** **(National Museum of Ireland, Dublin)**

417

times of its rising and setting, and its positions were plotted and used as a calendrical device, for farmers to judge the best time for plowing, sowing, and reaping their crops, for putting livestock out to pasture, for mating them, and for every other farming activity based upon the seasons. Moreover, the sun was acknowledged as a fertilizing force, which stimulated the germination, growth, and ripening of the crops. The visual imagery of the sun reflected this fertility role: the penetration of the solar rays into the ground could be likened to the entry of the phallus into the female; the rising and setting of the sun paralleled the erection and subsidence of the phallus.

As early as the fourth millennium BC, circles constructed of upright stones or wooden posts were oriented toward the rising or setting sun. The Later Neolithic Woodhenge in Wiltshire altered its earlier alignment and became an ellipse oriented to the midsummer sunrise. The first Neolithic monument at Stonehenge was positioned at the precise latitude where the directions of the midsummer rising sun and the midsummer rising moon at its extreme southerly point are at right angles.

Stonehenge is frequently claimed to be a solar temple. It is a unique monument whose active use spanned a period from the end of the fourth millennium to the close of the second millennium BC. About seven hundred years after the original Neolithic bank-and-ditch "henge" was constructed, Stonehenge underwent a radical reconstruction, in the first metal-using, "Beaker" phase. Eighty bluestones from the Preseli

**417.** *The "sun temple" at Stonehenge is a unique monument which was in active use from the end of the fourth to the close of the second millennium BC.*

418

Hills in West Wales (some 150 miles from Stonehenge) were set up to form two concentric circles, their entrance pointing toward the rising sun at its northerly position at midsummer. At the same time, the original entrance to the earthwork was widened to match the new axis. During the Bronze Age, Stonehenge was further modified: the first bluestone setting was replaced by a larger-scale sarsen structure consisting of a lintelled circle and an inner horseshoe, again pointing to the midsummer sunrise. Additions and changes continued; the final major reconstruction of the monument included the erection of a concentric circle and horseshoe of bluestones inside the existing sarsen structures (the pattern thus being: sarsen circle, bluestone circle, sarsen horseshoe, bluestone horseshoe). The last modification, which took place in about 1100 BC, consisted of the extension of the sunrise-oriented avenue (originally constructed during the first stone phase of the monument) to the River Avon.

Was Stonehenge a solar temple? There is no doubt that the axis of the Early Bronze Age bluestone and sarsen settings deliberately pointed to a position where an observer standing at the center of the monument would see the sunrise on the longest day of the year—the summer solstice. The builders of stone circles like Stonehenge may well have had precise knowledge of the way the directions of the sun's and moon's rising and setting vary through time. But to postulate exact scientific astronomic observations is unnecessary and speculative. All that may have concerned ancient

**418.** *A modern Druid ceremony at Stonehenge. Antiquarians in the seventeenth century associated the Druids with Stonehenge, and a society called the Ancient Order of Druids was established in 1781. They observed Midsummer Day ceremonies at Stonehenge until the 1960s.*

419

420

solar observers was the ability to see the positions of the rising and setting sun on the horizon, particularly at midsummer and midwinter. A "sun watcher" standing at the center of Stonehenge would thus be able to calculate the correct time for solar festivals and to instruct farmers on the seasonal rhythm of their work. Was the sun actually venerated at Stonehenge, or was it merely a useful calendrical device? In a sense the question is invalid, since in most pagan societies it is spurious to separate sacred from secular activities. But it is difficult to look upon the magnificence of Stonehenge and not to imagine some kind of propitiation or reverence for the forces of the supernatural.

Neolithic communities in many parts of Europe erected megalithic tombs in honor of their dead. Sometimes the stones of these graves were decorated with symbols, notably what appear to be solar motifs in the form of radiative or concentric circles or images which resemble spoked wheels (albeit long before spoked wheels were used in these areas). It is fairly certain that megalithic tomb art was religious in function. As pure art, the motifs do not conform to a particularly high standard and, more significantly, the stones were sometimes carved with symbols before they were placed in position, the designs being thus rendered invisible.

Passage graves in Ireland, Brittany, Iberia, and Denmark are particularly rich in "solar" art. The interpretation of these motifs as sun symbols must necessarily be speculative, but such images do closely resemble the sun, and on some Spanish tombstones, at Antelas and Granja de Toninuelo, for instance, sun and moon symbols are associated. Breton tombs, especially in the Morbihan region, depict large wheel-like or radiative designs. The great Irish group of passage graves in County Meath, including Knowth, Dowth, and Loughcrew, possess a bewildering variety of solar symbols, including daisy-like motifs and radiative circles. Many scholars believe that these Boyne tombs are marked with symbols that could well represent the gods worshipped and the natural world they had created. In my opinion, solar motifs could

**419.** *Rock carving from Ekenberg, Sweden, showing ships, horses, swords, and concentric circles, interpreted as sun discs. Early Bronze Age, 1500–1000* BC.
**(Riksantikvarieambetet, Stockholm)**

**420.** *Rock carving from Engelstrup, Scaland, showing ships and people, with sun motifs. The two persons beneath the ship appear to be worshipping the sun. Bronze Age.*
**(Nationalmuseet, Copenhagen)**

have been placed in the graves in order to comfort and illuminate the dead and as a pledge of rebirth in the next world.

The importance of the sun and light in Neolithic cults of the dead manifests itself not simply in tomb art but also in the use of light itself. Sometimes the design of chamber plans within the grave was such as to create specific and contrasting zones of light and darkness: the side chambers with their resting dead were in shadow, while the entrance and the passage were lit by the sun. The most striking example of the use of light in a megalithic tomb is observed at Newgrange, County Meath, in Ireland, which was built so that at the time of the winter solstice (December 21) the rays of the rising sun would penetrate to the end chamber of the tomb. The central line of the passage was purposely aligned so that on the shortest day the sun rising over the horizon shone its rays straight through the doorway. The uphill gradient of the passage, which caused a problem in this respect, was brilliantly resolved by the construction of a "roof-box" directly above the entrance. This tiny opening channelled the beams of the rising midwinter sun and caused them to strike the end recess as an intense beam of light, flooding the grave with light. A similar construction is present at the great tomb of Maes Howe, far away in Orkney, where an aperture was left in the entrance to allow the rays of the midwinter *setting* sun to enter and wash over the dead.

Was this megalithic sun ritual for the living or the dead? The provision of light

**421.** *Wheel-shaped whirls are the earliest sun motifs seen on picture stones. Stone from an Iron Age cemetery at Havoz, Gotland, Sweden.* *AD 400–600.* **(Riksantikvarieambetet, Stockholm)**

**422.** *Rock carving from Ekenberg, depicting an ithyphallic man with a sword who holds a huge sun disc above his head. Bronze Age.* **(Riksantikvarieambetet, Stockholm)**

and warmth for the dead may have been perceived as important, especially in winter. Perhaps the rituals were part of propitiatory ceremonies which magically persuaded the sun to become stronger and regain its life-force in spring, after the "death" of earth in winter and, in parallel, caused the dead to reawaken and be renewed in the other world.

The beginning of the Bronze Age and the first use of metals (gold, copper, and bronze) around the beginning of the second millennium BC coincided with the florescence of solar imagery. Both gold and new bronze are bright and sunlike, and their appearance may have been a factor in their use as media for sun symbolism. During the Middle and Later Bronze Age, the climate in temperate Europe became colder and wetter, and some farmland became nonviable. One of the causative factors in this deterioration may have been the volcanic eruption of Mount Hekla in Iceland in 1150 BC, which had a devastating effect upon the climate over a vast area, obscuring the sun by dust and cloud. It may have been this catastrophe which was a partial cause of the great upsurge of solar veneration during the second millennium BC.

Gold is the sun's metal: its rarity, ease of working, its untarnishable, incorruptible properties and, above all, its color, rendered it an appropriate medium for solar imagery. In the very earliest Bronze Age, about 2000 BC, Irish gold was used to make small sheet-gold "sun discs," decorated with cruciform or radiative designs closely

423

424

**423.** ***Bronze statuette of the Celtic wheel-god with his solar wheel, thunderbolt, and lightning flashes, from Le Châtelet, France. Roman Period.*** **(Musée des Antiquités Nationales, Saint-Germain-en-Laye, France)**

**424.** ***Celtic silver coin shows the head of the antlered god Cernunnos, with a solar-wheel sign between antlers worn as part of a headdress.*** **c.** ***AD 20. Petersfield, Hampshire.*** **(National Museum of Wales, Cardiff, England)**

425

426

resembling the sun. At Mere in Wiltshire, a small Beaker round barrow, raised over a chalk-cut grave, contained the bodies of a man and woman embracing: with them were various grave goods, including a pair of gold sun discs.

Other Bronze Age goldwork may well have been used in solar ceremonies. Gold vessels, like those from Boslunde and Mariesminde in Denmark, consist of a cup or bowl decorated with solar motifs, with long handles terminating in horse's heads. Curious gold objects, which must have had a ceremonial function, consist of tall cones resembling hats, decorated with sun symbols. One from Etzelsdorf in Bavaria is 38 inches high. Carried in processions or worn by priests, these cones would form a dazzling display in the sunlight, and they were perhaps used in festivals at specific periods of the year to invoke the sun at special times—midwinter or early spring perhaps—to encourage the sun to fertilize the crops, or at midsummer to secure a good harvest.

Spoked wheels were adopted for vehicles in temperate Europe by the middle of the second millennium BC. This new tradition stimulated the use of the image of the wheel to represent the sun. The wheel was perceived to resemble the radiating sun and, in addition, the element of movement is common to both.

From about 1500 BC miniature wheels were buried in graves, and this tradition continued until the Celtic Iron Age. Wheel-shaped pendants were worn and buried

**425.** *Sheet-bronze vessel-stand decorated in repoussé, with solar wheels and water birds. Seventh century* BC. *Cemetery at Hallstatt, Austria.* **(Naturhistorisches Museum, Vienna)**

**426.** *Sheet-bronze vessel with sun motifs, together with gold bowls with solar decorations and horse-head handles, which were found in the vessel on which a bird-ship with a large sun is also depicted. Early Bronze Age. Mariesmindo, Funen.* **(Nationalmuseet, Copenhagen)**

**427.** *Romano-Celtic bronze swastika-brooch with an incised diagonal cross in the center from Cologne. Roman period.* **(Römisch-Germanisches Museum, Cologne, Germany)**

**428.** *Amber sun disc in a bronze frame with handle. Perhaps an amulet, it is similar to the sun discs seen on Swedish rock carvings. Early Bronze Age.* **(Nationalmuseet, Copenhagen)**

**429.** *Gold-plated belt buckle in the shape of a human mask surrounded by stylized sun rays.* c. *third century. Found in a southeast Zealand grave near the medieval church of Uggelose, Denmark.* **(Nationalmuseet, Copenhagen)**

432

with the dead, perhaps to light their way in the next world. Solar amulets were attached to armor, to ward off harm and protect the wearer. At the same time, sheet-bronze vessels were made in northern and central Europe, decorated with the curious composite imagery of the sun wheel flanked by water birds, which sometimes form a boat carrying the solar disc. The Later Bronze Age vessel at Mariesminde (in fact the container of a hoard of gold horse-head–handled bowls alluded to above) is a good example. That the tradition of sun and bird-boat symbolism was retained over a long period is demonstrated, for instance, by the sheet-bronze vessel-stand dating from the early Iron Age at the Hallstatt cemetery in Austria; the wheel-and-bird pendant at Charroux (Allier, France); and the group of bronze torcs ornamented with wheels flanked by ducks in the Marne region of eastern France. In the Urnfield Bronze Age and later, this composite motif was prominent on both sides of the Alps, occurring among the north Italian Villanovans as well as in central and northern Europe.

The symbolism of the sun and bird-boat is interesting but enigmatic: the carriage of the sun disc on a boat may reflect the journey of the solar orb to the underworld at night, a theme found in Egyptian solar imagery. The water bird may have been chosen as a motif because of its ability both to fly and to swim, thus perhaps being perceived as a link between the upper and lower worlds.

If the sun travelled in a boat by night, during the daytime it was conveyed across the sky by means of a horse-drawn chariot or cart. This image is not peculiar to prehistoric Europe but is common to many Indo-European societies, including Greece and Persia. In Sparta and Rhodes, sacred horses and their chariots were sacrificed to the sun god. The horse was perceived as a suitably swift and noble animal to pull the sun's vehicle, and thus the creature was a recurrent associate of solar deities. One of the most spectacular cult objects associated with the veneration of the sun in prehistoric Europe is the Trundholm bronze "sun chariot," which dates from about 1300 BC and was discovered deliberately broken and buried in a peat bog. The object consists of a six-wheeled wagon, about 24 inches long, pulled by a horse and carrying a large, vertically mounted bronze sun disc, gilded on one side. The cart was perhaps a miniature replica of a larger carriage driven in cult processions and ceremonies. The bright gilt surface represents the diurnal sun, the plain side the nocturnal aspect of the sun,

**430.** *A Middle Age bronze belt-pendent in the form of a ring enclosing a swastika sun-symbol with bird-head terminals, found in the cemetery of Tabariane at Teillet, Ariege, France.* **(Musée Saint-Raymond, Toulouse, France)**

**431.** *Clay antefix as gable-end roofing tile, showing a severed human head, stars, and a Celtic sun-wheel, from the Roman legionary fortress at Caerleon, South Wales. Roman Period.* **(National Museum of Wales, Cardiff)**

**432.** *Detail of bronze torc decorated with suns and water birds, from Somme-Taube, Marne, France. Iron Age.* **(Musée des Antiquités Nationales, Saint-Germain-en-Laye, France)**

hidden from earth dwellers as it journeyed to the underworld. The cart may have formed part of a religious rite whereby the carriage of the sun disc imitated the movement of the sun across the sky, a magical device to persuade the sun to return, perhaps after a cold, wet winter. Celebrants may have faced south to the meridian in daytime ceremonies, so that they would see the golden image of the sun moving east to west. If the carriage were turned round at sunset, the bronze face of the solar disc imitated the invisible nighttime return passage of the sun.

The rock carvings of Scandinavia and the Camonica Valley in northern Italy are important in the present context because of the prominence of solar symbols. The petroglyphs of northern Europe are concentrated particularly in Denmark and on the Swedish and Norwegian sides of Oslo Fjord. An interesting piece of modern folklore concerns a Danish stone at Venslev, which was carved with three pairs of sun symbols: farmers attempted to blast the rock, as it was in their way, but it flew up into the air and descended facedown but undamaged, protected, apparently, by the solar force. The sun is just one of a vast range of symbols that were carved on the rocks between about 1300 and 800 BC. The sun disc is constantly associated with boats and horses, just as it is in metalwork. A curious group of images consist of "sun men," ithyphallic warriors whose bodies take the form of solar discs. They may represent imaginary figures associated with the cult of the sun or perhaps living worshippers wearing the insignia of the solar force. Some images show people carrying sun discs

**433.** *Bronze statuette of the Norse thunder deity, Thor, with his hammer Mjollnir on his knees, found in northern Iceland. Viking Age.* **c.** *AD 1000.* **(National Museum of Iceland, Reykjavik)**

**434.** *Bronze statuette of Freyr, the solar deity of sunshine, rain, and fertility in Norse mythology, who was especially worshipped in Sweden, Norway, and Iceland. Viking Age, c. AD 1100. Rallinge, Sweden.* **(Statens Historiska Museum, Stockholm)**

**435.** *Bronze scepter terminal with figure of the sun god. Roman Period. Willingham Fen, Cambridgeshire, England.* **(University Museum of Archaeology and Anthropology, Cambridge)**

436

on stands, as if participating in solar ceremonies. If northern European rock art is symbolic in a religious sense, then the solar images may represent a combination of depictions of sun deities and cult ceremonies, related perhaps to fertility ritual and the importance of the heat and light of the sun as life-giving powers.

Italian rock art occurs in the remote Camonica Valley, deep in the mountains around Brescia. The Camunians carved rocks with images of everyday life and the gods from the Neolithic until the end of the Iron Age. In this landlocked area, boat images are entirely absent; the most important symbols are the sun and the stag, which seem to have been linked in a powerful hunting and fertility cult. The Camunians were apparently preoccupied by the behavior of the sun: its journey through the sky after its morning arrival and its disappearance at night were central to their cults and beliefs.

The European sun cult attained its full development as a formalized and anthropomorphic religion during the Romano-Celtic phase, from the first century AD. Now, for the first time, sun gods were repeatedly depicted in human form, accompanied by solar emblems or attributes. By this time, the concept of the sun as a supernatural entity had been transformed from a simple visual symbol to the status of a recognizable divinity. One of the first possible anthropomorphic manifestations of the sun god occurs on the great Danish silver cult-cauldron, found in a Jutland peat bog, and dating from about the second century BC. The vessel consists of a number of plates,

**436.** ***Inner plate from a gilded silver cauldron with the solar wheel-god in the middle; its Celtic imagery has several sun motifs. The vessel was probably brought to Denmark from southeastern Europe in the third–second century BC. Gundestrup in Jutland.*** **(Nationalmuseet, Copenhagen)**

highly decorated in repoussé with mythological scenes and deities. One of the inner plates depicts the solar-wheel god.

During the Romano-Celtic period, the Celtic solar god is identified by means of his spoked-wheel emblem, which, as described above, was a potent prehistoric sun symbol. Romano-Celtic tradition merged the identities of the native sun god and the Roman Jupiter, epigraphic dedications to the Roman sky god being accompanied by Celtic solar motifs. One bronze figurine, from Landouzy in France, depicting a naked wheel-god, has a basal dedication to Jupiter. The unequivocal link between the wheel and sky symbolism depicted by the iconography of the Celtic Jupiter proves beyond question that the wheel was itself a celestial motif. All over Gaul, the Rhineland, and Britain, altars dedicated to the Roman god bear Celtic sun wheels. In the Pyrenees, small shrines were furnished with altars bearing motifs of wheels and swastikas, the latter being another common solar design among Indo-European peoples.

The Celtic sky god was associated with both the sun and thunder. The Roman poet Lucan comments on a great Celtic god called Taranis, "the Thunderer," and dedications to him are recorded all over the Celtic world. A later glossator on Lucan's text links the cult of Taranis with a barbaric ritual that involved the sacrificial burning alive of humans and animals in a gigantic wicker image. The fire festival of the Wicker Man is also chronicled by Caesar and Strabo. In much later fire festivals, Christian Germans burned wicker effigies at Easter, calling them "Judas Men." In the pagan period of Romano-Celtic Europe, thunder and sun were linked on altars that were carved with wheels and thunderbolts. The Celtic sun god himself is frequently portrayed holding his solar wheel in one hand and a thunderbolt in the other.

At such widely separated localities as Provence and Corbridge in Northumberland, the sun god appears as a soldier, in full military regalia. Linked to this iconography is a group of monuments known as Jupiter Giant columns, which occurred especially in eastern Gaul and the Rhineland during the Roman period: these consisted of tall pillars dedicated to Jupiter, decorated to simulate a tree, on top of which was a sculptured group comprising the sky god on horseback trampling down a snake-legged monster. The horseman bears a thunderbolt as a weapon and a solar wheel as a shield. The symbolism of this imagery appears to be the conquest of evil, darkness, and death by the glittering forces of light.

We have seen that the sun was closely linked with fertility in European prehistory. This association is clearly manifested in Celtic sun cults. A solar fertility goddess was venerated, her clay images covered with sun motifs. Figurines of this deity were mass-produced in the workshops of central Gaul and Brittany and were set up in shrines and buried with the dead. One Breton example, from Caudebec-les-Elbœuf, has wheel symbols on her breasts, belly, and thighs. Sometimes the wheel-god himself was associated with fertility symbolism: at Naix (Meuse) he was depicted with his sun emblem and two horns of plenty.

The great Celtic healer-goddess who presided over the important curative sanctuary at Bath was called Sulis, a name philologically linked with the sun. A powerful association between the sun and the solar force was perceived and manifested itself in different ways. Many healing spring shrines received votive objects in the form of miniature suns: this happened, for instance, at Bourbonne-les-Bains. At the sacred

**437.** ***A marble head of the sun god Mithra, found in the center of London at Walbrook Mithraeum. Its typical Roman style shows that the sculpture must have been carried from Italy in the late second century AD.*** **(Museum of London)**

437

438

spring of Essarois in Burgundy, the healer god was called Apollo Vindonnus, his Celtic surname meaning "clear light," and his image was that of a radiate sun god. The link between water and the sun was retained in post-pagan Wales, where it was a Christian tradition to walk "sun-wise" around a holy shrine three times, to ensure fertility and conception.

The association between water and the sun may be related to purification and cleansing. Another great purifier is fire, and this element was perceived to possess a strong affinity with the sun in pagan Celtic tradition. Fire is the terrestrial element that corresponds to the sun in the sky and is an earthly source of heat and light. The many fire festivals of Europe demonstrated a magical association between the sun and fire. At the Insular Celtic festival of Beltene on May 1, animals were driven between two bonfires in a symbolic purification ceremony. Fire festivals took place at specific times in the solar year: at the beginning of summer (Beltene); at Lughnasad on August 1, which celebrated the harvest; and at the onset of winter, at Samhain on November 1.

A great fire festival which originated in pagan Celtic times and was recorded as late as the nineteenth century consists of wheel-rolling. In the fourth century AD, the Christian St. Vincent observed a solar rite in Aquitaine, which involved rolling a flaming wheel downhill to a river. A virtually identical ceremony occurred at mid-

**438.** *Gold bowl decorated with images of deer, suns, and moons from Alstetten, Zurich, Switzerland. Sixth century BC.* **(Schweizerisches Landesmuseum, Zurich)**

summer, ostensibly to celebrate the birth of St. John the Baptist, but in reality it was an enactment of an ancient pagan fertility ritual. At the village of Basse Kontz (Moselle), the festival was last witnessed in 1822: a huge wooden wheel covered in straw was carried to the top of the Stromberg mountain, where it was set on fire by torches, at a signal from the local mayor, and rolled violently downhill to the Moselle River. If the wheel reached the water without mishap, this was seen as a blessing for the village and perceived as particularly propitious for the wine harvest.

British observers chronicled the wheel-rolling solar fire festival from the twelfth to the sixteenth centuries: it took place at night when the great flaming sun-wheel would be at its most dramatic:

> Some others get a rotten wheel, all worne and cast aside,
> Wich covered round about with strawe and tow they closely hide:
> And caryed to some mountaines top, being all with fire light,
> They hurle it down with violence, when darke appears the night:
> Resembling much the Sunne, that from the heavens downe should fal.

(R. C. Hope, *The Popish Kingdome or Reigne of Antichrist written in Latin verses by Thomas Naogeorgus and englyshed by Barnabe Googe, 1570*, London, 1880).

439

**439.** ***Metal plaque showing a rayed sun and the policy number beneath the sun motif. It was the emblem of the Sun Fire Insurance Office established in London in 1708 following the Great Fire in 1666.*** **(Museum of London)**

**440.** *The month of June (summer solstice), from* **Les Très Riches Heures du Duc de Berry** *(1413–16) by the Limbourg brothers.* **(Museé Condé, Chantilly, France)**

441

# THE SUN IN TRADITIONAL FRENCH CULTURE

JACQUES LACARRIÈRE

In the religious and scholarly traditions of the Mediterranean region, the sun is a sovereign god, moving high in the sky in a chariot harnessed to flaming horses, and having well-defined functions—to illuminate, to warm, to reign, and to purify. In French popular and peasant beliefs, which derive primarily from Celtic traditions, the sun tends to be a god or personage close to the earth and to humans, so much so that beliefs about it sometimes merge with an old animist substratum that attributes human behavior, thought, and speech to celestial phenomena (stars, winds, rainbows, and clouds). In the popular tales that Paul Sébillot, scholar of folk traditions, painstakingly gathered from all over France at the beginning of this century, the material universe, the land, and human beings live in perfect symbiosis, if not perfect harmony.

The vault of Heaven (the word "vault" is itself significant) is seen as an immense bell covering the earth and touching it at its edges. This peripheral region is a mysterious and inaccessible place reached only by a few heroes who have gone through a great many ordeals, and who then attain the privilege of being able to touch the foundations and roots of the sky.

The space between the earth and the sky is traversed by the sun and moon, who are of course husband and wife, and whose children are the stars. But as they can

**441.** ***Mask of the sun, carried in processions during the festival of the Immaculate Conception. Eighteenth century. Geispolsheim, Alsace.***

only see—or rather meet—each other during eclipses, the life of the couple is not an easy one, and their constant quarreling causes the frequent clouds, rains, and storms!

The sun appears as an anthropomorphic being whose face is sometimes bright, sometimes crimson, rather attractive and friendly toward humans but, like them, subject to changing moods. When annoyed, it begins to sulk and hides behind clouds; and when angry, it causes storms and scorches the earth with drought. Like all celestial or sovereign beings, the sun likes to be respected, honored, and even feared. It likes to be gazed at and admired; in short, it does not want to shine for nothing! It therefore has a dual nature and dual aspect as a companion who is, at one and the same time, bright and gloomy, warm and remote. As a result, humans treat it with a respect tinged with familiarity and give it different nicknames in different parts of France: Red John (Jean le Roux) in the Jura Mountains, Pol in the Manche, the Burguadian in Poitou and in Vendée (a probable reference to his ruddy face at sunset), or, again, the clog-maker in Morbihan in Brittany.

In a large number of popular legends, particularly in Brittany, the sun, tired of continually searching for the moon and not finding her, sometimes comes down to earth to look for and carry off a pretty girl.

"He" then settles her in his palace, which is usually in the west, where the sky touches the earth. It is a palace with a great many gleaming rooms made of crystal and

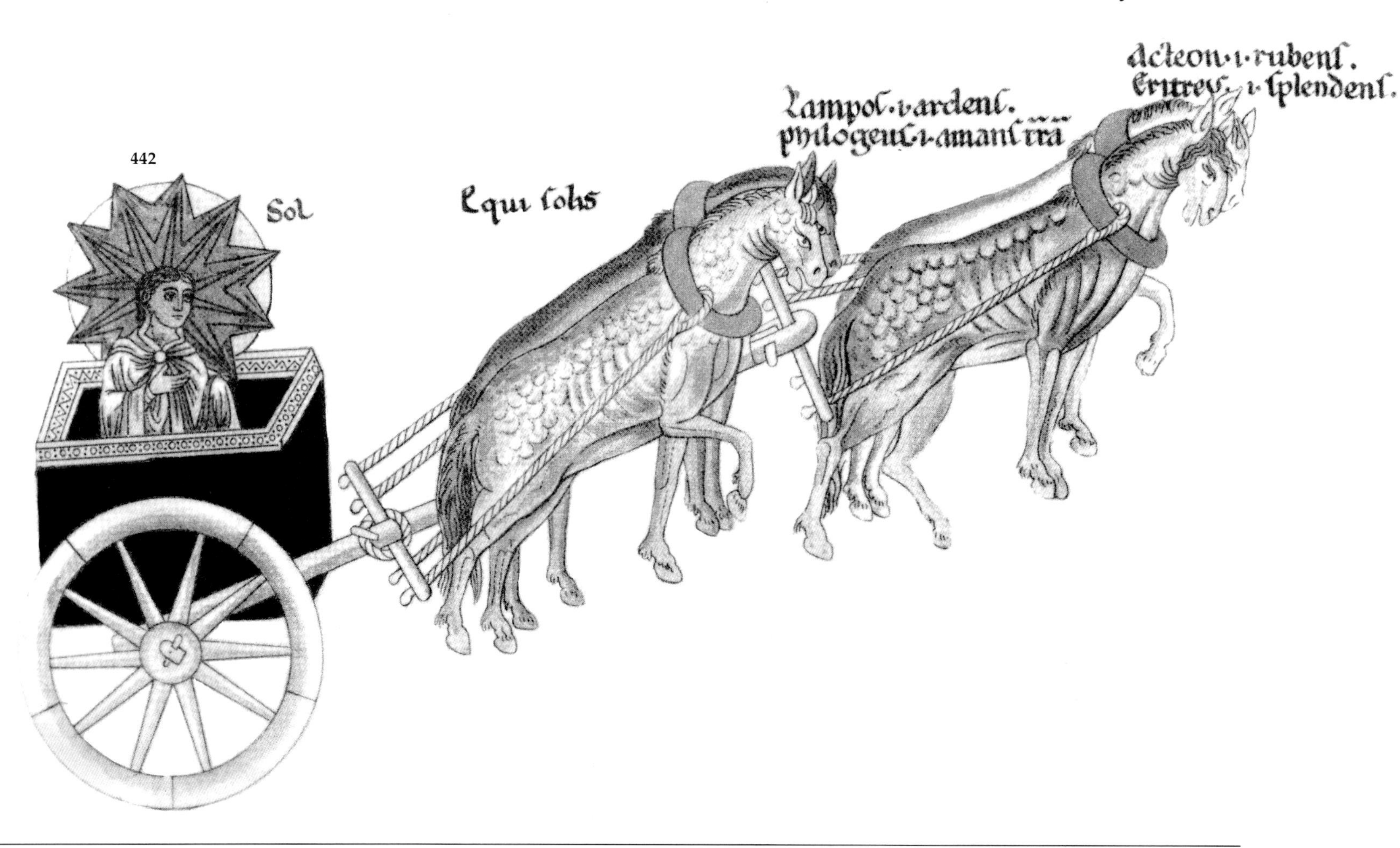


**442.** ***Chariot of the sun. A twelfth-century miniature painting in the manuscript* Hortus Deliciarum *by Herrad of Landsberg.* (Bibliothèque Nationale, Paris)**

precious stones which change color according to the time of day. Pink in the morning, they become a dazzling white at midday and, finally, red and gold at nightfall. Sometimes the parents or brothers of the young wife eventually search her out to discover what has happened to her. She generally tells them that she has everything she wants, but that she is bored because she is alone all day, her husband leaving her at dawn and not returning until night.

In other versions, the sun, upon setting, goes to light the land of the dead or to rest in his mother's house, having to regain his strength each night, as he is exhausted by his day-long journey. Accordingly, in her large house in the west, his mother prepares a large and revitalizing meal for him which, in the oldest versions, may even include human flesh. In the past, the sun was regarded as an ogre, as recounted in a legend from Upper Brittany in which he was a giant known as Grand Sourcil (Great Eyebrow) who lived in an immense cave where he went to rest each evening, feeding on human blood.

Not only did the sun weaken in the evening after its journey but it also cooled. This is logical as the inhabitants of the Atlantic coast thought it plunged into the sea. In the last century, the sailors of St. Malo, Brittany, would still tell you that some evenings, if you listened hard enough, you could hear a loud hiss like red-hot iron being plunged in cold water when the sun touched the sea!

443

**443.** ***Jumping over fire during the festival of St. Jean, Alsace. A nineteenth-century engraving by Thiophile Schuler.*** **(Cabinet des Estampes, Strasbourg)**

The sun does not confine itself to shining, heating, or withdrawing behind clouds when there is a coolness between it and humans. It also sees, observes, and watches over the earth. Its eyes miss nothing, at least not during the day, and it is the alert and supreme witness of our actions and even our thoughts. In a strange medieval text from the fifteenth century called *Les Evangiles des Quenouilles* (The Distaff Gospels), which I translated, for the first time, four years ago, the sun is again portrayed as a familiar character, but one who is sensitive to and appreciative of honors. Among all the adages, proverbs, and wise folk sayings contained in this collection, there is one that states, for example, that if a man urinates into the sun, you are sure to get a stye in your eye or suffer from gravel. On the other hand, the person who often blesses the sun will see his or her wealth increase during the year. In an equally strange work, published later, in 1679, the *Traité des Superstitions* (Treatise on Superstitions), the author, Father Theirs, draws attention to and condemns a practice that was still common at that time in the countryside, that of exposing oneself completely naked to the rising sun and saying numerous Our Fathers and Hail Marys as a cure for fever. To this the good father adds: "There are women and girls who carry out this practice, being more mindful of their health than their integrity, modesty, and salvation."

Another very old popular saying still in use—my mother used it time and again during my childhood—states that there is never a Saturday without sunshine. Why? Because this is the day on which the Virgin washes the shirt that the infant Jesus has to wear on Sunday and she needs the sun to dry it!

In addition to the privilege of illuminating and warming the earth, the sun has many different powers, such as curing fevers, bestowing wealth and fertility—as well as drying the shirt of the infant Jesus. Farmers nevertheless still ask it for other blessings, such as helping hens to lay large eggs or husbands to discover who their wives' lovers are! Of course, the biggest problem facing farmers is the weather, and certain prayers and songs were thought to influence the sun, helping it to appear when the weather was dull or to make a very late spring come. Thus, when the weather was poor the farmers of Finistère in the last century would sing:

Little sun of God,
Rise up quickly over the world,
Put on your violet hat
And come on your rounds.

In addition to a fascination with day and night, the popular imagination was, of course, intrigued by the passage of the seasons. This led to the belief that at certain times of year—for example, during the winter and summer solstices—the sun took on special and marvelous characteristics. In Franche-Comté it was believed that whoever climbed Mount Dôle on Trinity Sunday would see three suns rise. In Normandy and the Auvergne, it was thought that the same thing could be seen at dawn on Midsummer Day. That same morning, one might also see the sun fighting the moon, and, in the Creuse and Limousin, one might see something even rarer—the sun dancing in honor of St. John! If the sky was clear, the sunrise would be full of marvelous colors, which were the robes of the angels, dancing to express their joy.

---

**444.** ***The "sun king" of France, Louis XIV, dances the part of Apollo at Versailles on 23rd February 1653, for the* Le Ballet royal de la nuit. (Cabinet des Estampes, Bibliothèque Nationale, Paris)**

444

This passage of the seasons, which runs from the longest night (December 22) to the shortest (June 21), produced a great number of rites in the countryside. Their purpose was to maintain the energy of the sun in its journey round the earth and, above all, to help it overcome the joint forces of cold and night. It is strange to see to what extent the sun is thought to need humans to maintain its fire and light. This is, of course, a purely subconscious idea and concept, but one which is at variance with all official religions, pagan or Christian. In Roman Mithraism which long dominated the countryside of southern France (the Romance and French word for "sun" comes from the Latin *sol*), Phoebus was an entirely independent god who drew his energy exclusively from his own divine nature. The Romans gave the name Sol Invictus (the invincible sun) to the crucial time in the winter solstice (the equivalent of the week of December 21 to 26 in our present calendar) when the sun is at the lowest and coldest point of its journey. This clearly shows that the sun god was seen as immortal and that it was primarily in himself that he found the force to begin his round all over again.

These solstice rites—which might be called rites to help the endangered sun—were thus widespread throughout the countryside until the end of the last century, and, in some areas, even until the end of the First World War, notwithstanding the virulent opposition of the Church, which rightly saw them as pagan relics. Their purpose was to give renewed strength to the sun when it needed it, and to receive its energy when it was at its height. The word "solstice" indeed comes from *sol stare* (the stopping of the sun). It signifies the time when the sun pauses before continuing or reversing its passage. During this pause it is at its weakest and most vulnerable and, as a result, most receptive to external intervention.

During the second half of this century, the rural world has undergone such changes that this highly sensitive and pagan view of the sun (as a divine but vulnerable friend and relative), and the rites that give it expression, have completely disappeared. As long ago as 1905, in his monumental book *Folklore de France*, Sébillot wrote: "It is probable that ceremonies relating to an old form of sun worship were carried out in the past on high ground. About one hundred years ago, traces of them were to be found in the mountainous part of Provence. Several of them took place during the summer solstice which, in many countries, is still celebrated with fires that a number of mythologists see as the remains of ancient sun worship."

These ceremonies include the festival of torches. This festival still exists today in many villages in France but clearly has lost much of its original significance. It was held on the first Sunday in Lent, in order to revive the energy of the weakening sun. Torches of straw (known by a variety of names, depending on the region) were lit. These were carried in procession through village streets, country lanes, and, more especially, into orchards, where they were thought to protect fruit trees from pests. It was also an opportunity for making an immense bonfire—sometimes several—in the village square, using brambles, thorns, and brushwood from pruned hedges. A sapling, with the top turbaned and the branches removed, was stuck in the middle of the bonfire and when it fell, half-burned, into the flames, dancing round the fire began. When the fire died down and was reduced to embers, young people, especially those who were to be married during the year, started to leap over it.

In other places, especially in some villages in the High Alps, in Franche-Comté, Lorraine, and Aquitaine, large wheels of straw were plaited, set ablaze, and rolled from the top of a hill down to the nearest river. One can hardly find a brighter and more dazzling (in all senses of the term) image of the blazing sun. Today, these village processions, country rounds, firebrands, bonfires, dances, and leaps have as their avowed aim the fertility of orchards, the land, and of couples. Their older, deeper, and, in the past, vital purpose was nevertheless to give renewed strength to the weak winter sun through these rites, these burning wheels and fires that are "sympathetic," in the magical sense of the term.

The great many fires which are still lit today on Midsummer Eve on the summer solstice have a different meaning. June 21 is the longest day in the year and is, therefore, the day on which the power of the sun is at its strongest. As a result, everything alive on earth—from plants to people—is thought to be imbued with and uplifted by this vital energy.

Medicinal herbs gathered at dawn on June 21, for example, were supposed to have special powers, sometimes miraculous ones, provided that they were gathered before the sun rose and in accordance with rites that varied from village to village: for

445

446

**445,446.** *The tower as it is put on fire during the festival of St. Jean at Urbes, Vallée de Thann, Alsace, France.*

example, collected on an empty stomach, while walking backwards, while reciting this or that prayer or this or that formula. According to a tradition in Picardy still prevalent at the beginning of the century, an infusion made of walnut leaves gathered on Midsummer morning would arouse in the person who drank it an unfailing love for the person who prepared it. Similarly, dew gathered at dawn that day had purifying powers. For a long time, therefore, boys and girls took Midsummer dew-baths, rolling naked in the grass in meadows and on hills before sunrise. The Church, as was to be expected, had the greatest difficulty in preventing and prohibiting these very special baths!

However, the most important part of the Midsummer rites are in the many fires lit that night. These rites and customs vary from region to region and sometimes from village to village, and the tradition has continued almost to the present day. The charming ceremony in a cluster of villages near Munster in Alsace is thus described in *La Paille et le Feu, Traditions Vivantes d'Alsace* (Straw and Fire: Living Traditions of Alsace): "Sitting in a circle in the middle of a river of red roses, women and girls are busy sewing the flowers onto broad-brimmed hats in the small village courtyard. After pinching the stems, they fix the roses in little bunches of four or five until the whole of the hat is covered them. The mothers keep an eye on what the girls are doing because these strange hats are to be worn by their sons that same evening when they jump over the fire. It is, in fact, the moisture in the middle of the roses that provides a cool area round the head and protects the boys from the flames and the intense heat of the bonfire."

Afterward, at nightfall, a procession forms to a musical accompaniment and the whole village goes to the bonfire, which has been set up on a nearby hill. First, torches made of bundles of wooden sticks stuffed with shavings are lit; boys and girls then whirl them round as they run down the hill. "This takes a few minutes and is just a simplified version of the complete circuit of the hill which was still being made ten years or so ago, an imitation of the movement of the sun round the earth. The mad dash of the young people whirling their lighted torches seems to be a physiological and even a psychological preparation for facing the fire."

On their return from this dash, they use the torches to set the huge bonfire alight. This particular bonfire is made of dry vine shoots some 20 feet long. A distance away, in some of the villages of the Thurn and Thann valleys, real towers of fire up to 100 feet high are built, called *chavandes* in the Vosges dialect and *Fackel* in Alsace.

As soon as the flames of the bonfire of vine shoots, which the girls have just set ablaze, dies down and the embers have begun to spread, the boys put on their magnificent hats of roses, cover their faces with scarfs, and jump over the fire, while the girls remain as near as possible to the embers, at the starting point of the downhill dash. The presence of these girls so near the bonfire is reminiscent of a touching practice from the past. It was the custom in the area for engaged and young married couples to jump hand in hand over the solstice fire. The success of the jump, a token of love and proof of mutual fidelity, was seen as a good omen which would influence the couple's future.

"At the end of the ceremony, with the piles of embers still giving off smoke, the young people, full of enthusiasm, go back down to the village with shouts of victory rising to the starry sky. For a long time still, the night will be filled with their laughter, songs, and dances."

447

In the square in front of the town hall, the young people then begin another dance, a round of a very particular kind. "To the sound of an accordion, the boys and girls join hands and dance cheerfully round in a circle. This dance turns in a clockwise direction like the sun, imitating the sun's movement. Although now danced to decadent music, it must be considered as having descended from a genuine sacred dance formerly executed in honor of the sun. It is the one and only calendar-based dance extant in Alsace."

This account dates from 1980, so one would be justified in thinking that there still exists in France, in this cluster of villages, one last relic—a dance—of the most ancient forms of sun worship.

We are grateful to these hamlets and to the young people, the fires, and this round dance, for having managed to keep alive, right up to the present, the vital splendor and light of the sun!

**447.** ***The sun, in a traditional French bed-canopy.***

448

449

# SOLAR CULTURE IN ANCIENT EGYPT

JAMES F. ROMANO

In the polytheistic world of the ancient Egyptians, the sun had many names and many forms. In its most elemental aspect, the source of light and warmth in the daytime sky, the sun was the god Re. He could exist both independently or merged with other deities. For example, by the Old Kingdom (Dynasty III–VII; c. 2675–2130 BC) Egyptian priests had combined Re with Horakhty (Horus of the Horizon), an early sky god. The resulting figure of Re-Horakhty appears as the majestic falcon of Horus wearing a sun disc on his head. Khepri, the morning sun, is seen as a scarab beetle pushing the sun disc across the skies much as a beetle rolls a ball of dung across the desert floor. To the Egyptians, the sun that set over the western horizon and travelled through the netherworld at night was the ram-headed Atum. Aton (Disc), the physical form of the sun, was acknowledged in religious texts throughout Egyptian history. It enjoyed divine status, however, only during the latter part of the Eighteenth Dynasty, primarily under king Akhenaton.

The Egyptian sun cult rose from obscure beginnings to a position of supremacy in Egyptian religion. The absence of writing in the predynastic period, the era preceding the establishment of a unified state around 3100 BC, restricts our understanding of the earliest solar beliefs. Yet we can see that the predynastic Egyptians paid homage to the sun in their funerary practices. For much of the predynastic period, the dead were buried with their heads oriented toward the west where the sun "died" each evening. Re-neb (Re Is My Lord), the name of one of the kings of the Second Dynasty (c. 2800–2675 BC), provides a hint of the sun cult's growing importance. In the Fourth Dynasty (c. 2625–2500 BC) kings proclaimed themselves "the son of Re"; and one of them, Khafre, erected a temple for sun worship at the base of the Sphinx at

**448.** *Re-Horakhty (a combination of the sun god Re and the falcon-headed sky-god Horakhty) in a scene from the tomb of Nofretari, wife of King Ramesses II (c. 1279–1213 BC), accompanied by the goddess Hathor, the awesome "Eye of Re".* **(Ägyptologisches Seminar der Universität Basel)**

**449.** *Gold pectoral of Khepri in which the scarab beetle is combined with the sun disc to form one of the King's names, Neb-Kheperu-Re. It was found in the tomb of Tutankhamun. c. 1332–1322 BC.* **(Egyptian Museum, Cairo)**

450

Giza. By the Fifth Dynasty (c. 2500–2350 BC) Re had become Egypt's main official god. The *Westcar Papyrus*, a document from the Second Intermediate Period (Dynasty XIV–XVII; *c.* 1630–1539 BC) describing events in Egypt's long-distant past, identifies the first three kings of the Fifth Dynasty (c. 2500–2350 BC)—Userkaf, Sahure, and Keku—as the product of sexual union between Re and the Lady Rededjet.

The solar theology of the Old Kingdom taught that the sun brought into being the entire universe—including gods, the earth, and all living things—at the moment of Creation. The priesthood of Re, centered at Heliopolis (now a suburb northeast of Cairo), devised a cosmology recognizing the sun, in the form of Atum, as the Creator. Before the appearance of an ordered cosmos, all existence lay in a potential state inherent in the Nun, a boundless ocean of dark, motionless, inert water. At the beginning of time, Atum, Lord of Heliopolis, arose out of the watery nothingness of Nun. Standing on a primeval mound called the Benben, Atum radiated light that penetrated Nun's darkness, heralding the beginning of universal existence. A passage from a later text describes the event:

> There comes into being a speech by me, Atum. I was alone; I was Re at his first appearance, when he rose from the horizon, I am the Great One, the self-created one, who created his names... who will not be repelled from the gods. Yesterday is mine, I know tomorrow.

451

**450.** ***Alabaster relief depicting the pharaoh Akhenaton, his wife Nefertiti, and one of their daughters worshipping the Aton sun disc and its light as a manifestation of universal principle.*** **(Egyptian Museum, Cairo)**

**451. The Pyramid Texts** ***are the most ancient body of religious texts carved in the vestibules and sarcophagus chambers of the pyramids. Sixth Dynasty, 2320–2170 BC.*** **(Egyptian Museum, Cairo)**

Just as the sun's emergence from the watery abyss of Nun had determined all universal existence, so did the daily cycle of the sun confirm the eternal renewal of Creation. Each morning, the sun repeated the drama of the "First Time" as it rose over the eastern horizon, flooding the Nile Valley with light that vanquished darkness and brought forth the promise of new life.

The universal forces Atum created were personified by three generations of deities, collectively called the Ennead. First Atum made the god Shu (Air) and his sister Tefnut (Moisture). Accounts of their birth differ. In one version Atum produced the pair by masturbation; in another he "spluttered out Shu and spat up Tefnut." Shu impregnated Tefnut, who eventually bore the earth god Geb and the sky goddess Nut. They in turn produced the gods Osiris and Seth and the goddesses Isis and Nephthys.

These youngest deities of the Ennead provided the paradigm for Egyptian royal succession. Osiris had reigned on earth as a wise and benevolent monarch. His brother Seth, jealous of his popularity and power, lured him into an ornate wooden chest, sealed it, and cast it into the Nile, drowning the god-king. Claiming his right to succeed Osiris, Seth assumed the Egyptian throne. When he learned that Isis, Osiris's widow, had recovered her husband's corpse, Seth cut it into fourteen parts, scattering them throughout Egypt. Isis and Nephthys set out to find the pieces of Osiris's dismembered body. Eventually they located all but the god's penis. The goddesses fashioned a new phallus for Osiris and, using Isis's magic, restored Osiris to life. Osiris impregnated Isis with the child who would grow up to be the sky god Horus. After he was born, Isis hid the infant Horus from Seth's murderous agents until the god was old enough to avenge his father's murder. Eventually Horus and Seth fought

452

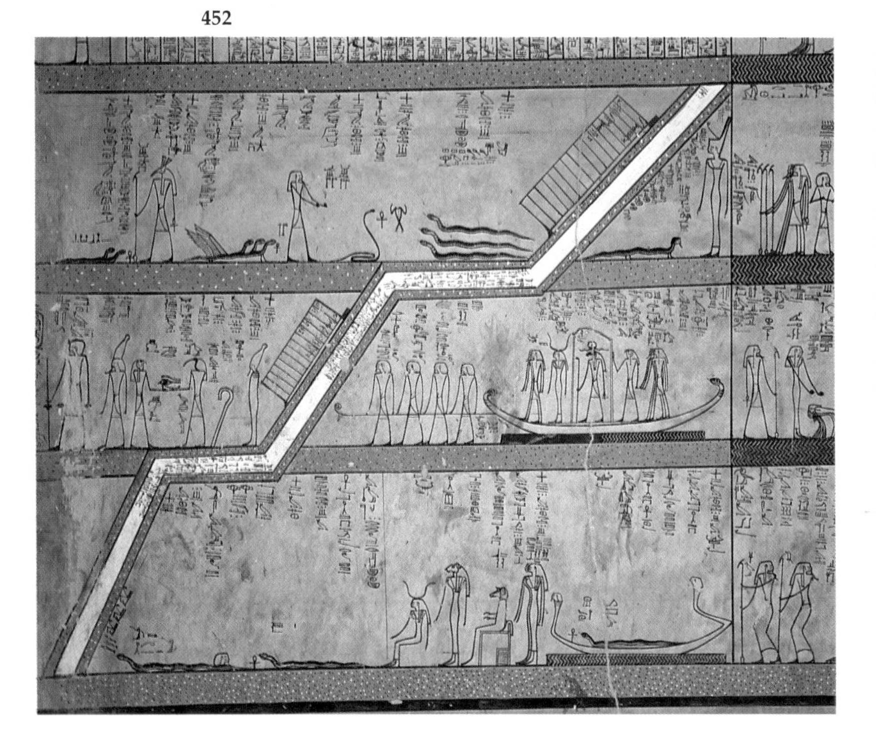

453

**452,453.** *The* **Book of Am-duat** *recounts the sun god's night voyage through the underworld, represented in the tomb of the Eighteenth Dynasty pharoah Thutmose III (c. 1479–1425* BC*) in the Valley of the Kings.* **(Ägyptologisches Seminar der Universität Basel)**

a violent battle so disruptive to universal order that the other Egyptian gods demanded that they stop. Geb summoned a divine tribunal to hear the rival claims. Horus was declared Osiris's rightful heir; he would rule on earth as king of Egypt. Osiris, too, would rule, albeit in his own domain; since he had died he would dwell eternally in the underworld as the god of the dead. For most of Egyptian history, living kings were recognized as the earthly embodiment of Horus, and all deceased monarchs became the immortal Osiris.

As the center of the solar cult, Heliopolis was the home of the major sanctuary dedicated to Atum, the sun as the god of creation. This sanctuary, known to us only through inscriptions, was called the Hewet-Benben (House of the Benben) and contained a pyramidal-shaped stone fetish believed to be the mound that emerged from Nun at the "First Moment." Although no trace of the original Old Kingdom Hewet-Benben at Heliopolis survives, it probably resembled the two imposing open-air sun sanctuaries built for Kings Userkaf and Nyuserre of the Fifth Dynasty at Abu Gurob.

Old Kingdom solar religion taught that when the king died he ascended into Heaven, joining Re in the god's divine bark as it travelled forever across the sky. This belief reflected the Egyptians' cyclical view of eternity. The Egyptians had two views of time: linear time provided the means of ordering historical events, such as wars and coronations; in contrast, cyclical time grew out of the Egyptians' understanding of nature. Their world was dominated by a series of predictable, recurring natural events such as the Nile's annual rise and fall and the return of migratory birds. Of all these cycles, the most conspicuous and potent was the daily circuit of the sun. It was "born" each day at dawn, ascended dramatically and voyaged across the sky, grew "feeble" at dusk, and inevitably "died," only to be "reborn" the next morning. The

454

455

**454,455.** *A detail from the* **Book of Am-duat** *in which the sun travels through the underworld during the night, and his appearance next day heralds the glorious outcome of the journey.*

456

**456.** *Tapéret worshipping the sun god Aton. The circumference of the stele represents the goddess Nut giving birth to the sun. Wood with polychrome decoration on both sides. Ninth century* BC. **(Musée du Louvre, Paris)**

solar cycle thus served as an exemplar for rebirth. Nature was both repetitive and eternal. If a king (and in later times a commoner) could merge with one of the natural cycles, especially the circuit of the sun, death could be overcome and rebirth as an immortal aspect of nature would be guaranteed.

To guide the king on his solar journey, the Egyptians inscribed a series of obscure spells, utterances, and myths on the inner walls of royal pyramids. First seen in the pyramid of King Unis, ultimate ruler of the Fifth Dynasty, these so-called *Pyramid Texts* are the oldest written corpus of religious beliefs from Ancient Egypt. Many describe the king's place in the solar cycle. Thus we read:

> O Re-Atum, this king comes to you, an imperishable spirit, lord of the affairs of the place of the four pillars [the cardinal points of the compass]; your son comes to you, this king comes to you. May you traverse the sky, being united in the darkness; may you rise in the horizon, in the place where all is well with you.

Throughout the Old Kingdom the solar cult had been linked to the Egyptian kings' quest for immortality. By the Middle Kingdom (Dynasty XI; c. 2000–1786 BC), the hope for immortality in the company of the sun had spread to the common people as well. But this belief was not the only means of achieving eternal life. Along with traditional solar creeds we now encounter the notion that by invoking Osiris, god of the dead, an individual might be reborn after death. Both concepts were codified in the so-called *Coffin Texts*, a series of inscriptions painted onto the interiors of large rectangular coffins. Although many of these texts were edited renditions of spells from the *Pyramid Texts*, they differ in one fundamental point. In the *Coffin Texts* the netherworld is at once celestial (the realm of Re) and chthonic (the Osirian underworld). This duality represents the coming together of the older solar traditions and

457

458

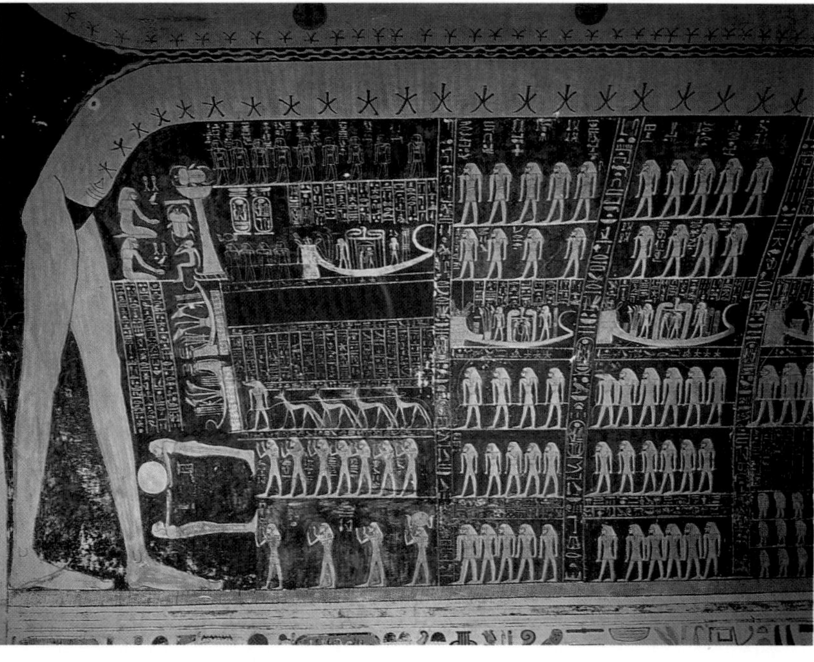

**457,458.** ***The sky goddess Nut giving birth to the sun, as described in*** **The Book of Day** ***and the corresponding*** **Book of Night.** ***Vaulted ceiling in the tomb of King Ramesses VI. c. 1145–1137 BC.*** **(Ägyptologisches Seminar der Universität Basel)**

the increasingly important cult of Osiris, which achieved widespread popularity, especially in the Twelfth Dynasty. Re and Osiris were now interpreted as different expressions of the same theme: the "reborn" god.

Most of the trends we have traced—the sun as creator of the universe, cyclical rebirth, the king's association with Re, the merging of the Osirian and solar afterlife—coalesced in the New Kingdom (Dynasty XVIII–XXI; c. 1539–1075 BC) in the most dramatic testament of Egyptian solar religion: the paintings and reliefs in the royal tombs of the Valley of the Kings. These painted scenes and explanatory texts, conventionally called *Books,* recount the devitalized sun's descent into the underworld, or Duat, the realm of Osiris. They describe the dangers the sun must overcome during the perilous nighttime hours before re-emerging at dawn as a glorious reborn deity.

In the earliest of these *Books,* the *Am-duat,* the sun passes through twelve stages, or hours, toward eventual rebirth. He enters the underworld in the form of a ram-headed god, identified simply as "the Flesh." He stands in a shrine on the deck of a simple bark, accompanied by his divine entourage. As the journey unfolds, the sun god finds the sealed gateway to each hour guarded by fearsome serpents who must be propitiated before he can proceed. Eventually he reaches the nadir of his journey in the Fifth Hour, when he finds the Cave of Sokar, god of death. Only after confronting the ultimate expression of physical death can the sun god begin his ascent towards rebirth. Yet the remainder of the sojourn is not without danger. In the Seventh Hour, for example, he must overcome his greatest foe, the enemy of all creation, the serpent Apophis. Selket, the scorpion goddess, pierces Apophis's body with knives, temporarily disabling him so the sun bark can continue toward the Twelfth Hour. Here the sun bark enters the tail of a huge snake, where the god is transformed into the rising sun, Khepri, and emerges from the snake's mouth.

Other *Books* present variations on the sun god's journey. These include *The Book of Day* and its companion, *The Book of Night, The Book of Caves, The Book of Gates, The Book of Nut, The Book of the Earth,* and *The Book of the Celestial Cow.* But perhaps the most unusual of the underworld compositions is *The Litany of Re.* An explanatory text provides the most explicit statement of the king's identification with the sun god. Here the Pharaoh makes a threefold claim: he *is* the sun; his soul *(ba) is* the sun's soul; and his journey through the netherworld is the sun's journey. The god's ubiquity is stressed by the presentation of seventy-five different names and images of the sun, each charged with protecting the dead king. We encounter the sun in forms such as "He Who Comes Out of His Own Members," "He Whose Brilliant Eye Speaks," and "The Ever-Becoming One."

Although most of the underworld *Books* describe a sun god devoid of individuality or emotion, *The Book of the Celestial Cow,* however, presents him as capable of both vengeance and compassion. The text relates that in most remote Antiquity an aged, weary Re learned that humanity was "devising evil plans" against him. He summoned a council of Egypt's eldest gods and was advised by Nun to unleash the invincible "Eye of Re," in the form of the cow goddess Hathor, to slay the conspirators. Although the human race learned of its impending destruction and fled to the Egyptian desert, Hathor transformed herself into the leonine goddess Sekhmet and slaughtered all she could find. The goddess waded in her victims' blood, revelling in

**459.** ***Limestone stela of Queen Cleopatra offering two vases to the seated goddess Isis nursing Harpocrates.*** *AD 51 (in a Greek text).* **(Musée du Louvre, Paris)**

459

460

the carnage she had wrought. Eventually the insatiable bloodlust overcame her, and she collapsed from exhaustion.

Despite humanity's disloyalty to him, Re was disturbed by Hathor's butchery and decided to spare those who had eluded Hathor's initial attack. First, however, he had to incapacitate the goddess, whose rapacity, once loose, could not be checked. While Hathor slept, Re's agents gathered huge quantities of red ocher that the High Priest of Heliopolis mixed with potent Egyptian beer, producing seven thousand jars of intoxicating liquid resembling blood. The drink was then poured on the ground near the sleeping goddess. Upon awakening she greedily lapped it up and immediately lapsed into an inebriated stupor. Although humanity was allowed to escape annihilation, the episode left Re disillusioned and dispirited; he abandoned his earthly "children" and rose up to Heaven to live forever on the back of the Great Celestial Cow.

While each of the underworld *Books* sought to guarantee the spiritual resurrection of the king, the powerful religious theme of the sun as a source of rebirth found expression among New Kingdom commoners as well. Beginning in the Twentieth Dynasty (c. 1190–1075 BC) many private burials included so-called *Am-duat* (That

**460.** ***Funeral sledge of Khonsu. Two lions support the sun disc nestled in the horizon, from which hangs the sign for life. New Kingdom, reign of Ramesses II (1279–1213 BC).*** **(Egyptian Museum, Cairo)**

461

Which Is in the Underworld) papyri. These documents provided private persons with abbreviated versions of the texts and illustrations of the royal *Book of Am-duat*. They differ from their royal prototypes in the substitution of the commoner's name for that of the dead king.

Even more common were a series of 190 funerary spells known collectively as *The Chapters of Coming Forth by Day* or, simply, *The Book of the Dead*. These illustrated texts frequently appear on papyrus rolls left in the tomb or painted on coffins or funerary sledges. *The Book of the Dead* enabled the deceased to overcome the inevitable dangers encountered in the underworld by providing spells to ward off evil. In addition, the texts sought to secure the protection of major deities, such as Osiris and Re. Spell 15, for example, contains a lengthy prayer to Re, beginning:

> Hail to you, O Re, at your rising, O Atum-Horakhty! Your beauty is worshipped in my eyes when the sunshine comes into being over my breast. You proceed at your pleasure in the Night bark, your heart is joyful with a fair wind in the Day bark, being happy at crossing the sky with the blessed ones. All your foes are overthrown, the Unwearying Stars acclaim you, the Imperishable Stars worship you when you set in the horizon. . ., being happy at all times, and living and enduring as my lord.

**461.** ***Funeral sledge of Khonsu, showing the adoration of the celestial cow Mehet-weret.*** **(Egyptian Museum, Cairo)**

Egyptian kings and commoners alike associated the behavior of certain animals with solar worship. Because the first sound they heard each dawn was the croaking of frogs, they came to view frogs as harbingers of the sun's appearance and worshipped Heket, a goddess in frog form, as a birth deity. Similarly, because the Egyptian baboon warms its belly by facing the rising sun while placing its forepaws on its knees, the Egyptians thought that the baboon was "greeting Re as he rises," in a solemn gesture of obeisance and incorporated representations of the animal in the decoration of temples dedicated to the sun.

In the Eighteenth Dynasty (c. 1539–1292 BC) Re merged, or syncretized, with Amun, the god of Thebes, who had achieved the status of state deity. Coincidental with the appearance of Amun-Re (King of the Gods), Egyptian theologians devised a series of solar hymns praising the god's omnipotence. Some are lengthy compositions, others are concise expressions of personal devotion to a benevolent divinity:

> Amun-Re who was first to be king,
> The god of the primeval time,
> The vizier of the poor.
> He takes not rewards [bribes] from the guilty,
> And speaks not to him who brings testimony,
> Nor does he look at him who promises,
> Amun judges the earth with his fingers,
> And speaks to the heart
> He judges the guilty,
> And assigns him to the East,
> And the just to the West.

The cult of Amun-Re experienced a dramatic and unprecedented change around the middle of the fourteenth century BC. Until then, Egypt had been the most powerful nation in the ancient Near East. Trade and tribute had enriched the royal treasury, and Egyptian military influence had spread from Western Asia to sub-Saharan Africa. The Egyptians attributed their success to divine intervention, particularly to the intercession of Amun-Re. They erected great temples honoring him, and his priesthood's wealth and prestige rivalled the power of the Pharaoh.

Few, if any, Egyptians could have anticipated the religious upheaval that would occur after the Egyptian throne fell around 1353 BC to an enigmatic ruler called Amunhotep IV. The king's representations conformed to Egyptian convention, showing him as a perfect being slaying Egypt's traditional enemies, and several decorated blocks picture him worshipping Re-Horakhty.

In the second year of his kingship, however, Amunhotep IV began erecting unusual sandstone sanctuaries in the precinct of Amun-Re at Karnak. These shrines celebrated the cult of the sun as manifest in the solar disc, or Aton. The Aton appears as an icon: a disc with radiating beams of light ending in tiny hands. As for Amunhotep IV, his images do not show him in the traditional representation of a king as an idealized perfect being. Rather, royal artisans showed him with many striking physical distortions.

In the fifth or sixth year of his rule, Amunhotep IV transferred the Egyptian capital from the royal residence near Karnak to a virgin site some 190 miles north at El

Amarna. This move, heralding the beginning of the so-called Amarna Period, was accompanied by the change of the king's name from Amunhotep (Amun is Content) to Akhenaton (The One Who is Effective for the Aton). Eventually, Akhenaton proclaimed the exclusivity of the Aton, declaring that "there is no other except him." In defiance of sixteen centuries of tradition, the king closed the temples of many ancient gods, seized temple holdings, and ordered most divine names, particularly that of Amun, expunged from temple and tomb inscriptions.

Akhenaton's philosophy was so intimately tied to the king's own personality that shortly after his death Egypt rapidly returned to orthodoxy. His successors reopened the neglected temples and undertook massive building campaigns to restore the grandeur of traditional gods. The ease with which old religious beliefs were restored should hardly surprise us. Excavations indicate that the Amarna religion never percolated down to the level of the common Egyptian. Even at El Amarna itself, amulets of proscribed deities including Amun, Isis, and Hathor have been found in workmen's houses. Akhenaton's unique version of solar religion offered none of the compassion of earlier beliefs; the Aton gave life but offered neither help nor comfort to the needy. Similarly Akhenaton's version of the afterlife was indistinct, in marked contrast to the concrete reality of the solar Osirian tradition. In a culture as firmly rooted in reality as that of Ancient Egypt, Akhenaton's abstract beliefs could not endure.

462

**462.** *Funeral sledge of Khonsu. While the deceased plays the game of "senet," his wife observed his success; the rich bouquets behind her are symbolic of vital, regenerative forces.* **(Egyptian Museum, Cairo)**

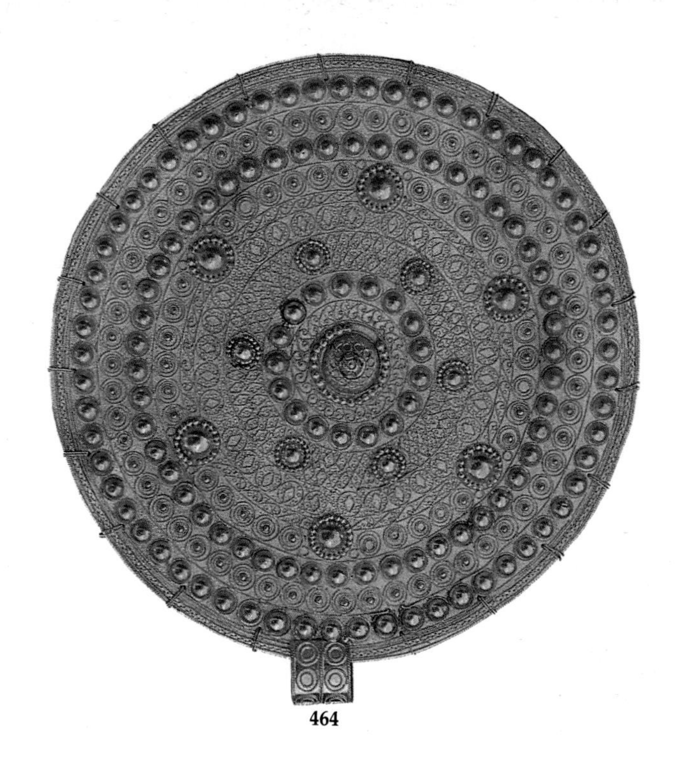

464

# THE AMBIVALENT SUN OF SUB-SAHARAN AFRICA

ALLEN F. ROBERTS AND CHRISTOPHER ROY

The anthropomorphic sun is rarely represented in African art. This is because the sun is considered ambivalent. Although the sun's light and warmth are necessary to fecundity, growth, and fruition, the sun also desiccates, sterilizes, and kills. Instead, the sun's transformative power is often implicit in ideas and relationships represented in sculpture, architecture, body arts, drama, and other expressive forms.

In much of Africa, the year is divided into two major seasons in constant alternation, one rainy and life-promoting, the other marked by the sun's scorching, deathly power. In African cosmology, each season has its hero. For the Luba people of Zaire, for instance, a primordial solar king is the avatar of all excess, kept in check by a lunar hero's assertion of periodicity, dark coolness, rain, and reason. The dialectic of the seasons is often a model of and for social relations in African societies. Among the peoples of Burkina Faso, sacred kings share the unyielding powers of the sun. Opposed to these solar rulers are earth-shrine priests, whose powers, derived from water and fertility, allow them to prophesy and heal. The "contrapuntal" interplay of solar and earthly powers, prerogatives, and loyalties provides the cohesive vitality of these peoples.

As demonstrated by three brief studies, the sun's ambivalent powers are felt and made instrumental in the transformative circumstances of everyday life in Africa through narrative, art, and magic. Contemplation of solar qualities and events assists people in understanding their own lives, for in the sun they see a metaphor for perplexity, choice, and decision making.

In 1947, a sage named Ogotemmêli began one of the most remarkable intellectual

**463.** ***Tabwa mask of glass beads, feathers, pelts, leather, thongs, and vegetable fiber. The central solar motif is encompassed by a triangular "rising of a new moon" symbol*** **(balam wez). (University of Iowa Museum of Art, Iowa City. Stanley Collection of African Art)**

**464.** ***African gold jewelry from Senegal. Probably seventeenth century.*** **(Museum of IFAN, Dakar, Senegal)**

dialogues in the history of anthropology in which he explained to French anthropologist Marcel Griaule the origin of the universe as seen by the Dogon people of Mali. Ogotemmêli described both the transformative powers of the sun and the profound ambivalence with which the Dogon understand such powers.

In Ogotemmêli's story, Amma, the Dogon Supreme Being, lived in the heavens with beings called Nommo. Nommo were humanoid in form, but were hermaphroditic and had lithe, snakelike arms, legs, and bodies. Wishing to establish order in the universe and create human existence on earth, Amma built a celestial ark in the form of a granary or silo. This granary-ark contained all creatures, objects, and phenomena and was to be sent to earth to introduce them to both physical and social life as the Dogon would come to know the universe.

When Amma's "miraculous granary" was ready for its descent to earth, one Nommo realized that no provision had been made to introduce fire to earth. The Nommo entered the workshop of Amma and stole a piece of the sun used to forge Amma's creations, employing the open mouth of an object the Dogon now call a *yo domolo*, or "robber's crook." As it did so, the Nommo became so agitated that it could no longer find the entrance to the granary-ark and climbed on to the roof of the vehicle. As the granary began to move, the Nommo triumphantly shouted *"Guyo!"* (stolen), a word still used to mean "granary," for without fire, Dogon blacksmiths would not be able to forge the iron tools necessary for farming and there would be no crops to store in Dogon granaries. The Nommo guided the granary along the rainbow in its descent to earth.

Knowing that Amma would seek to punish it, the Nommo took a defensive stance on top of the granary, with a blacksmith's hammer in its hand and an iron anvil in a sack on its back. Amma hurled lightning bolts at the granary, which increased its velocity so that it crashed to earth, scattering its contents of creatures, objects, and phenomena into their present distribution. The impact was such that the hammer and anvil broke the Nommo's snakelike arms and legs at the wrists, elbows, shoulders, hips, knees, and ankles. The being "thus acquired the joints proper to the new human form, which was to spread over the earth and devote itself to toil."

The Nommo's act marks a disjunction of humanity from divinity and is the origin of human culture based upon the transformative power of fire derived from the sun. But the Nommo's Promethean defiance, while positive in its creativity, also introduced the ironies of the difficult life the Dogon must lead in the ever-harsh environment of their part of Africa. Ogotemmêli's story, then, tells with sophisticated economy the most profound truths about the ambivalence of an act which is at once creative and fraught with pain, which begins culture as well as backbreaking toil, and which produces both sublime joy in the fruits of labor and abject grief in poor harvests, malnutrition, and famine. The sun and fire *transform*, an act that the Dogon consider paradoxical by definition, for that which creates can also and does destroy.

Today, the Dogon contemplate and portray these dilemmas in rituals, wearing masks and dancing with accessories such as the *yo domolo*. Each Dogon clan possesses a *yo domolo*. The object's animal head may be that of a hyena, a "thief" among beasts, while the ears sometimes take the form of the first human couple. The zig-zag "mane" of the *yo domolo* symbolizes the descent of the ark and the transmission of its

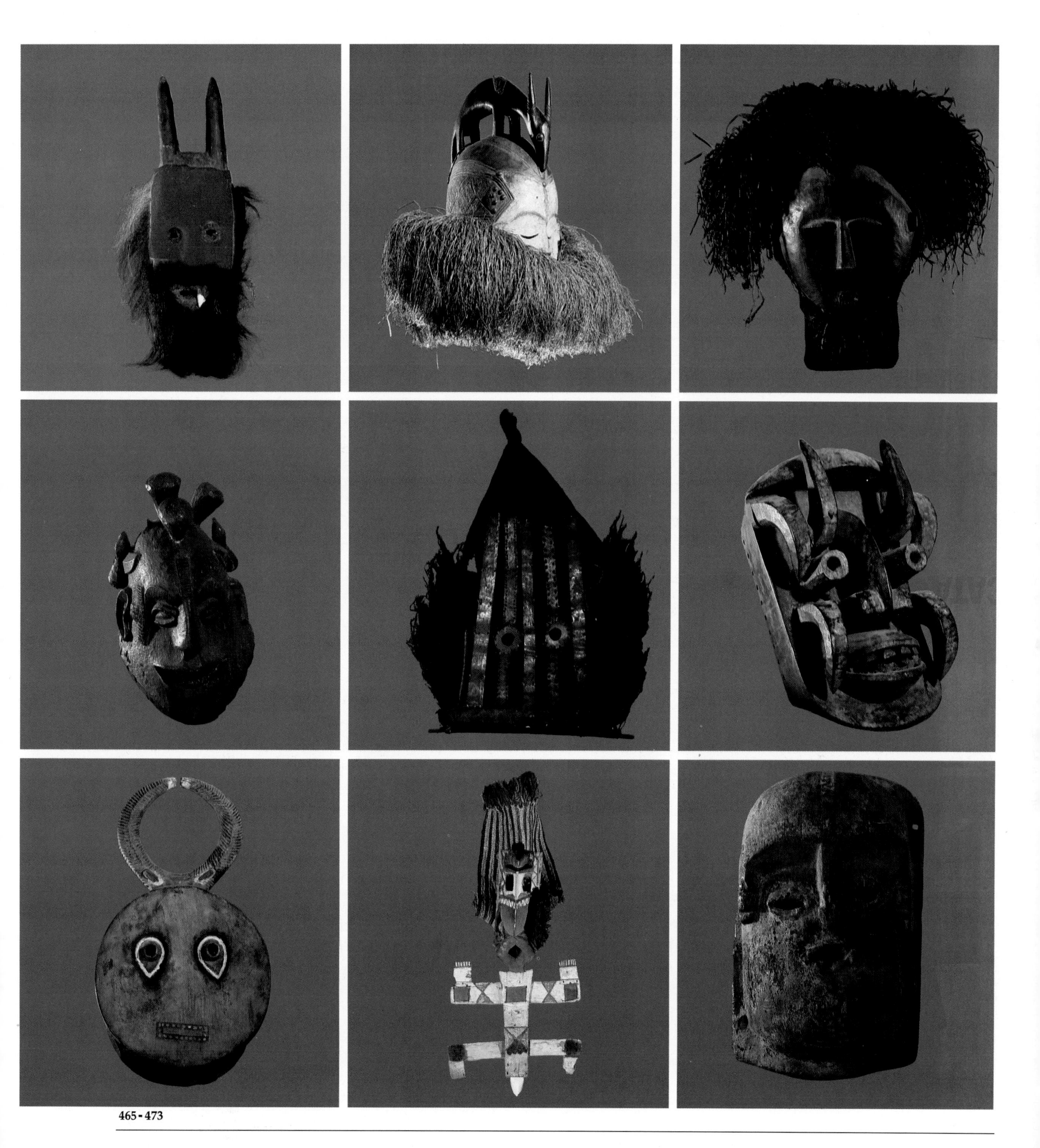

465–473

**465–473.** *In sub-Saharan Africa, the sun rarely appears in anthropomorphic form, but makes its power felt through a variety of fantastic masks: Guerze boundary mask, Guinea (465) Suku circumcision mask, Congo (466) Pende initiation mask, Congo (467) Ibibio helmet mask, Nigeria (468) Sousson divination mask, Guinea (469) Guere social-function mask, Burkina Faso (470) Baoule mask of buffalo spirit, Burkina Faso (471) Dogon incantation mask, Mali (472) Dogon ancestor mask, Mali (473).*

474

475

elemental knowledge and power to humans. During the funeral of an elder responsible for the powerful information the *yo domolo* embodies, the elder's successor holds the *yo domolo* as he steals and slaughters any livestock he can find. In so doing, the successor reaffirms the ultimate separation of humanity from divinity as caused by the Nommo's theft of a piece of the sun, and so makes sense of, and even celebrates, the loss of the beloved elder who has just passed away. Ironically, the socially disruptive ritual theft also provides an opportunity for the community to reflect upon the order and expectations that cement their everyday relations. For the Dogon, *this* is the ultimate ambivalence of the seasons of the sun, which give life but then take it away, so that life may begin anew as the seasons turn, once again, from rainy to dry to rainy.

In about AD 1500, bands of horsemen rode northward from the kingdom of Dagomba in what is now northern Ghana. The men were well organized militarily, and they soon established themselves as rulers over many small groups of farmers who had lived in the upper basin of the Volta rivers for centuries. The warriors used their horses and massed cavalry to overwhelm the farmers, who had little ability to resist. The invaders rode first to the area of the modern town of Tenkodogo, in east-central Burkina Faso, then westward to found the Ouagadougou kingdom, and finally northward to create the state of Ouahigouya. They established one of their own as

474. *The Bwa people of western Burkina Faso dance with spectacular masks at the start of the rainy season, in annual renewal rituals.* **(University of Iowa Museum of Art, Iowa City. Stanley Collection of African Art)**

475. *Wood carvers in Sudan traditionally make a variety of discs depicting lunar and solar motifs.* **(University of Iowa Museum of Art, Iowa City. Stanley Collection of African Art)**

476. *The Yoruba people of Benin believe that by sacrificing a chicken, they assert their sunlight perception because roosters stir and crow with the first light of dawn. A rooster is also a sun symbol in an ancient Byzantine ritual in Central Asia: see 382.*

**(University of Iowa Museum of Art, Iowa City. Stanley Collection of African Art)**

hereditary ruler, or *naba*, in each community they conquered, and surrounded him with a court. The original farming families were permitted to keep their land, possessions, and their own traditions, but were required to swear allegiance to the *naba*, provide conscripts for the army, pay the first fruits of their fields as taxes, and adopt the language of the invaders. The sons of the rulers married the daughters of the conquered farmers, and a new society was formed which is today called Mossi (sing., Moaga), a name referring to this intermarriage. The Mossi name for their nobles, *burkina*, has been adopted in the name of the modern state of Burkina Faso.

By right of their original identification with the land, the descendants of the original farmers are called *nioniosse* (the ancient ones). Prior to conquest, they recognized earth-shrine priests as responsible for apportioning land and making sacrifices to the spirits of the earth, *tenga*, who assured fertility and bounty. Such priests, known as *tengsoba*, still stand in counterpoint to the rulers of the Mossi states of Tenkodogo, Ouahigouya, and Ouagadougou. Of these latter, the Moro Naba, or king, of Ouagadougou has assumed the status of *primus inter pares* in what has often been called the Mossi Empire.

The annual cycles of ceremonies, appointments, sacrifices, and observances at the courts of Mossi rulers are determined by the movements of the celestial bodies, especially the sun and the moon. The Moro Naba himself has been compared to the sun by early court historians. Each morning the king rises and greets his subjects in a ceremony called *Wend pus yan* (the sun rises). Mossi court historian Dim Delobsom stated that the Moro Naba's subjects consider him as radiant as the sun. When he

***477. A variety of African jewelry with cosmic motifs from Senegal with a headdress (in the middle) for initiation. Senoufo, Ivory Coast.***

478

479

emerges from his palace to greet his subjects, the Moro Naba wears a great red robe and a cap with silver streamers representing the rising sun. The king's palace is also a virtual solar calendar, with royal seats in various quarters representing the solstitial course.

The king's appearance is marked by a drummer drawing a finger across the membrane of his drum to imitate the roar of a lion, with which the king is also associated. For the Mossi, the sun, horse, and lion have become ubiquitous symbols of political power. A visitor to any Mossi community—even to Ouagadougou, capital of the modern state—can recognize the house of the king by the horse always tethered outside the palace door. Indeed, it may be suggested that the horse itself, with its marvelously complex and beautiful trappings in leather, brass, and silver, has become the major political art form of the Mossi ruling elite.

While the invaders succeeded in welding people in the basin of the Volta rivers into new Mossi states, many on the periphery resisted and remained independent. These include the Winiama, Nuna, Nunuma, Bwa, Samo, Zaose, and others who have retained their political decentralization to the present day. The vast majority of the art produced in Burkina Faso both today and in the recent past has not been produced by the Mossi rulers, or in the context of their political power, but by the descendants of the conquered Voltaic farmers originally identified with the land. Masks made by the *nioniosse* are not used by chiefs or nobility descended from the invading cavalry. Similarly, beyond the frontiers of the Mossi states, the Bwa, Winiama, Nuna, Lela,

**478,479.** ***The wooden granary door-panels are painted by Dogon people of Mali and Burkina Faso with motifs taken from myths such as that of the Nommo who stole a peice of the sun, thus introducing fire and human culture on earth.*** **(University of Iowa Museum of Art, Iowa City. Stanley Collection of African Art)**

480

**480.** ***Nuna sun mask made for the western tourist trade by the Konate family of wood-carvers, well-known throughout western. Burkina Faso for their artisty and ability.*** **(Allen F. Roberts Collection)**

and many other peoples continue to make great quantities of art objects to celebrate their ties to the land and to the spirits of nature disturbed when the wilderness is cleared for farming.

Among the Mossi themselves, knowledge of masks is kept secret from the ruling class. Chiefs and their relatives never attend performances at funerals or other events at which masks of the *nioniosse* perform. Nor do the *nioniosse* masks ever appear in public at festivals associated with the modern rulers of Burkina Faso.

*Nioniosse* masks make many symbolic references to the spirits of the wilderness, the fertility of the earth, the moon, and the rules for the moral conduct of life established by the ancestors. Among the Bwa, a large white crescent moon surmounts each of their great plank masks worn at funerals and other significant events. Symbols associated with the secular powers of Mossi kings, especially the sun, horse, and lion, are never seen. These sources of power are kept separate from those of the *nioniosse*—in contrapuntal balance, perhaps, but separate all the same.

Peoples of the Bantu linguistic family inhabit most of central, eastern, and southern Africa. Their closely related cultures and histories are underlain by a common logic from which metaphors, art, and other expressive modes are generated. The sun is not directly represented in Bantu art, but its ambiguity is implicit in symbolic use of the color red.

Bantu-speaking peoples recognize a primary triad of red, white, and black. Red signifies indeterminacy, unpredictability, desire, alienation, aggression, violence, transition, and transformation. Red pigment made from camwood (*Pterocarpus* spp.) bark or ferruginous minerals has long been used by the Bantu peoples in contexts where, as a Tabwa man said, a person wishes to show that "he is fierce, he has no friendship with anyone, now he is someone else, another person. He is like a policeman. He has no father or mother or mother's brother. He is blood!" Shamanistic healers wear red face-paint and feathers as homicides did in the past, marking their willingness to engage in bloody conflict with the sorcerers and vengeful ghosts who bring dire affliction to the living. Rituals such as male initiation often include red masks and other paraphernalia to denote the violent transition as neophytes are torn from their previous immaturity to be symbolically reborn into adult prerogatives and responsibilities.

Red and white pigments are often juxtaposed. Of the Bantu color triad, white is the most consistent in the symbolic sense, representing that which is enlightened, auspicious, beneficent, pure, and good, no matter what its context. Red lies at a conceptual cusp that can be represented schematically as a basal point of the red-white-black isoceles triangle. From such a position, red may lead to a white state of grace at the apex of the triangle, or to black at the opposite basal point. Black is *insight,* in its most literal sense: a looking inward at that which is not apparent but which is nonetheless the essence of being—something like the "natural suchness" of Zen Buddhism.

Black is also the artfully indirect suggestion of *insinuation*—the gnawing suspicion that there is meaning to an act or event beyond what is seen. Magic is the Bantu concept "black" made instrumental, often by unleashing the transformative power of "red." The activating agents of magic employed by Bantu-speaking peoples are not iconic: even if one sees them, they are ground up, mixed together, burned, or otherwise reduced to a state that no one can identify—no one, that is, except those few who know the secrets of the particular elements chosen. It is not necessarily what is in magic, but what *might* be in it that frightens people, sometimes literally, to death.

Bantu-speaking people contemplate solar ambiguities through a genre of cultural heroes who sometimes take the form of gigantic serpents that breathe forth rainbows. These appear opposite the sun as a result of the refraction of solar light by raindrops. Because rainbows are most frequently seen once a rain shower has passed, Bantu peoples perceive that there is a causal relationship between the sun and the rainbow. They say that the rainbow-breath of the solar serpent has "burned" the rain and "eaten" the storm, bringing it to an end. Anything a rainbow falls upon will be reddened, desiccated, and will soon perish. The solar serpent and life-giving rains are thus opposed in what may prove a deadly contest.

The best known of these solar serpents is Nkongolo Mwamba, personified as a primordial king whom the Luba people of south-central Zaire believe began consolidation of their precolonial state. Nkongolo was known for his "red" skin and is the avatar of all excess in Luba myth: drunkenness, incest, murder, and destruction. Nkongolo finds his nemesis in Mbidi Kiluwe, who comes from the east to establish social order and royal culture as recognized by the late precolonial Luba. The Luba epic explains how Nkongolo was eventually defeated and beheaded by Mbidi Kiluwe and his son Kalala Ilunga, who then founded the perfected, refined, and principled sacred kingship the Luba still revere.

Mbidi is a member of a central African genre of calm, cool, refined lunar cultural heroes associated with rain and fertility who are divided down the midline of their bodies and are often represented as half-human, half-wax. As such, Mbidi and his fellows personify dichotomous representation, paradoxes, and indeterminacy as represented in the ambiguous powers of blackness and the auspiciousness of "white" enlightenment. The opposition of the genres of which Nkongolo (the "red" sun) and Mbidi (the "black-and-white" moon) are members is a pivot of Bantu dualistic philosophy.

Other Bantu-speaking peoples such as the Tabwa of southeastern Zaire and the Fipa of southwestern Tanzania did not develop highly organized precolonial states as did their Luba neighbors, but they did and still do recognize the transformative powers of the solar serpent that the Luba call Nkongolo. The serpent's rainbow-breath is associated with epidemics and with such latter-day phenomena as mining accidents from toxic gases. It is said that in the past, the solar serpent might be captured or at least tricked into giving up some of its flesh or blood, which could then be used in the most powerful magic. Such magic might assure the success of iron-smelting, healing, and other transformations crucial to human life, but it could also be used to attack one's enemies. The Tabwa still speak of how those possessing such magic can "make the sun stand still" and cause an adversary's crops to wither and die. In this way, the sun's ambivalence can be directed to the advantage of one person and to the peril of the other.

481. *Wooden figure of a chief of the Chokwe peoples of Angola, Zaire, and Zambia, holding* **hampa** *spirits that are intermediaries between people and the forces of nature.* **(University of Iowa Museum of Art, Iowa City. Stanley Collection of African Art)**

482. *The Luba wooden stool, like the throne, is a symbol of authority and bears many references to cosmology. The cowry-shell shapes along the seat and support symbolize the duality of the chief's vision.* **(University of Iowa Museum of Art, Iowa City. Stanley Collection of African Art)**

484

# THE SUN IN THE MAYA WORLD

MARY ELLEN MILLER

All across Guatemala, Belize, Honduras, and the Mexican states of Yucatán, Campeche, Quintana Roo, Tabasco, and Chiapas, the Maya recognized the power of the brilliant tropical sun and worshipped it. By the first millennium BC, the Maya had inhabited the region, first in villages, then in towns; by about 100 BC, in both the highlands and the lowlands of Guatemala, the Maya began to construct large architectural complexes and erect sophisticated monuments inscribed with hieroglyphic writing to commemorate human rulership. Some of the earliest Maya monumental sculpture focuses on the sun, and from this point on, the Maya have left us records in both art and architecture of their perceptions of the sun and other heavenly bodies. Classical Maya civilization, the most sophisticated civilization of the New World, thrived in the first millennium of our era (AD 100–900) in the tropical lowlands, at such diverse places as Tikal, Palenque, Copan, Yaxchilán, and Caracol, and around the year 1000, the Maya city of Chichén Itzá, in northern Yucatán, may have been the largest and most powerful city in Meso-America. At the time of the Spanish Conquest, the era of great Maya cities had passed, but there was no higher

**483.** *Blowgunner pot, the death of Vucub Caquix. To destroy the pompous parrot reigning falsely as the sun, a Hero Twin uses a blowgun to shoot out the radiant pyrite in his mouth. Having brought down the false sun, the Hero Twins set the stage for civilization. Probably El Peten, Guatemala, Early Classic,* AD *300–500.*

**484.** *Black mirror disc with turquoise. Fire serpents, or* xiuhcoatls, *often were associated with the bearing of the sun through the heavens, and their configuration on mirror backs that were worn at the back of the waist may have been to show the wearer as the sun, carried through the heavens. Chichén Itzá, Yucatán, Mexico. Tenth century.* **(Museo Nacional de Antropologia, Mexico City)**

485

485. *Jaguar God of the Underworld incensario. In the 1950s, archaeologists discovered large, ornate cylinders featuring the face of the Jaguar God of the Underworld stacked on stepped tiers of the Temple of the Foliated Cross at Palenque, a building commemorating maize agriculture and abundance. Temple of the Foliated Cross, Palenque. c.* AD *690.* **(Museo Nacional de Antropologia, Mexico City)**

486

title of office than *ahau kin*, or "sun lord." Because Maya civilization depended on no single central site of administration, surviving accounts, both sixteenth-century narrative and works of art created in the Classical era, reveal subtle variations and overlaps in gods and religious practice. Modern understanding of the ancient Maya sun, then, is not without some confusion.

All Meso-American peoples were keen observers of the sun and kept track of the solar year, but the Maya, particularly during the Classical era, surely kept the most sophisticated records and designed the most meticulous calendars. Most students of Meso-American calendars have commented on the problems inherent in keeping

**486.** ***The early Maya decorated this facade with the image of a young man from whose headdress issues abundant and copious maize: he may be a Hero Twin, in his apotheosis as the sun, bringing his father, the Maize God, back from the underworld. Probably southern Campeche, Mexico. AD 50–200.*** **(Museo Nacional de Antropologia, Mexico City)**

track of only a 365-day year that fails to include leap years from time to time, and it has long been assumed that even the sophisticated Maya could not manage such a count. Although normal Maya record-keeping as it has come down to us inscribed on monumental stelae kept track only of solar years of 365 days, the pattern of celebrating anniversaries at Piedras Negras, for example, reveals that the true tropical year of roughly 365.24 days was charted for hundreds of years. And tracking the accurate lunar calendar, the Maya predicted both solar and lunar eclipses. In Yucatec Maya, eclipses were called *chi'bil kin*, or the "biting of the sun," and solar eclipses were considered far more dangerous than lunar ones. The Maya also knew exactly when Venus would guide the sun into or out of the underworld as the evening or morning star. The Maya followed the sun and its movements with more attention than any other people in Meso-America.

The Maya had no knowledge of gold through most of Classical times. Their first experience with the material came during the eighth century, when Central American gold objects occasionally reached Maya lands, and the first dated objects come from sealed eighth-century caches. Knowledge of metallurgy was slowly working its way north from the Andes, but Meso-Americans did not begin manipulating metals successfully until at least AD 900 or perhaps 1000. Throughout history, of course, precious

487. *Kinich Ahau and Jaguar God of the Underworld. Kinich Ahau, the squint-eyed Maya Sun God, can be distinguished by the distinctive flower-like* kin *signs that mark his body and face. The Jaguar God of the Underworld, the nocturnal Maya sun god, has jaguar ears. A "cruller" runs under his eyes, twisting on his nose.* **(Drawings by Linda Schele)**

488 a

488 b

**488 a,b.** *San Agustin Acasaguastlán pot. In this rich and convoluted scene, a seated sun god in a skeletal headdress sits crosslegged and arms folded in front of his chest, holding two undulating serpents whose mouths gape open, revealing a human head and the head of the sun god himself. San Agustin Acasaguastlán, Guatemala Highlands. Early Classic, sixth century.* **(Museum of the American Indian. Smithsonian Institution, Washington D.C.)**

489

*489. Probably in the tenth century, the Maya lords of Chichén Itzá rebuilt the structure known today as the Castillo, encompassing an earlier building within a nine-level, radial pyramid of the sort that often bears associations with the completion of periods of time or the movements of the heavens. Toward sunset, on the two annual equinoxes, the nine levels of the pyramid cast a shadow that reveals a segmented serpent along the northern balustrade. The flight of stairs on that side has 92 steps, if one counts the serpent heads at the base; each of the other three staircases has 91, for a total of 365, emphasizing the solar cult at Chichén Itzá.*

490

491

gold and the sun have been identified with each other. So the question is asked: Without gold, how does a culture represent the sun? What material can substitute for the brilliance of gold? And does it change the conception of the sun itself? The ancient Maya seem to have solved the problem by focusing on the preciousness and importance of the sun. As a result, they used their most precious material, jade, to symbolize the sun when they wished to adorn themselves with the solar image. When representing the sun in a larger format, they often used red terra-cotta or paint. When they conceived of the nocturnal, underworld sun, they saw it as a jaguar with shimmering yellow fur and black rosettes.

The sun has always guided the lives of peoples around the world, throughout time, but the Maya depended on the ever-moving sun for their sustenance, for they recognized that maize, native to the New World, needed many long, sun-filled days to yield a substantial crop. In this, the Maya linked the green jade (maize foliage) and the precious yellow jade (sun). Maize was fundamental to the Maya: according to most sources, they believed that the gods had made several unsuccessful attempts to form a race of humans, succeeding only when they fashioned people from the soft, ground-corn mash that has always been the staple Maya diet. This creation took place just before the dawning of a new era, or New Sun, as Meso-American peoples termed their eras (the Aztecs, for example, believed that they were living in the Fifth Sun). In Maya accounts, maize agriculture, the creation of humans, and the rising of the sun occurred in close sequence. The Maya deified not only the powerful sun of the current era but also the "false" sun of the past.

According to the *Popol Vuh*, a sixteenth-century epic that relates the story of the Quiche Maya of highland Guatemala from the beginning of time up until the period of the transcription of the text into European letters, there was a monster bird, Vucub Caquix, or Seven Parrot, who set himself up as a false sun in the darkness before the

**490,491.** ***Huge faces of Maya gods adorn the facades of Structure 5 and other buildings at Cerros, Belize, giving evidence of a solar cult. The lower masks represent Kinich Ahau, the sun god, in one of his earliest representations.***

492

dawning of the current era and the rising of the real sun. In order for that dawning to take place, the Hero Twins, divine offspring of an underworld goddess and a man later revealed in the story to be the Maize God, must slay this Vucub Caquix, this false sun. His radiance, the Twins discover, comes from his mouth aglitter with pyrite, or what we call fool's gold today. So the Twins, brilliant with the blowpipe and wily strategists, take their blowpipes and shoot out the glittering teeth of Vucub Caquix, who is embarrassed, humiliated, and defeated.

The Maya elite emulated the Hero Twins. Young, clever, and particularly gifted at wordplay, the Twins outsmarted, rather than overpowered, their opponents. They descended into Xibalba, the Maya underworld, in search of their forebears, and overcame the nightly trials by which the underworld gods tried to trick them: eventually they turned the tables and tricked these gods into becoming sacrificial victims themselves. According to the *Popol Vuh,* once the Twins resurrected their father, they ascended to the heavens to reign as the sun and moon. Once the tale of the Hero Twins is completed, the *Popol Vuh* narrator relates the pilgrimage of ancestral lineages to a sacred mountain to await the dawning of the true sun, which at long last is led by Venus out of the underworld to begin its diurnal journey.

The ancient Maya called the daytime sun Kinich Ahau, or "squint-eyed" or "sun-faced Lord," probably from the way the brilliant tropical sun dazzles the eyes, but

493

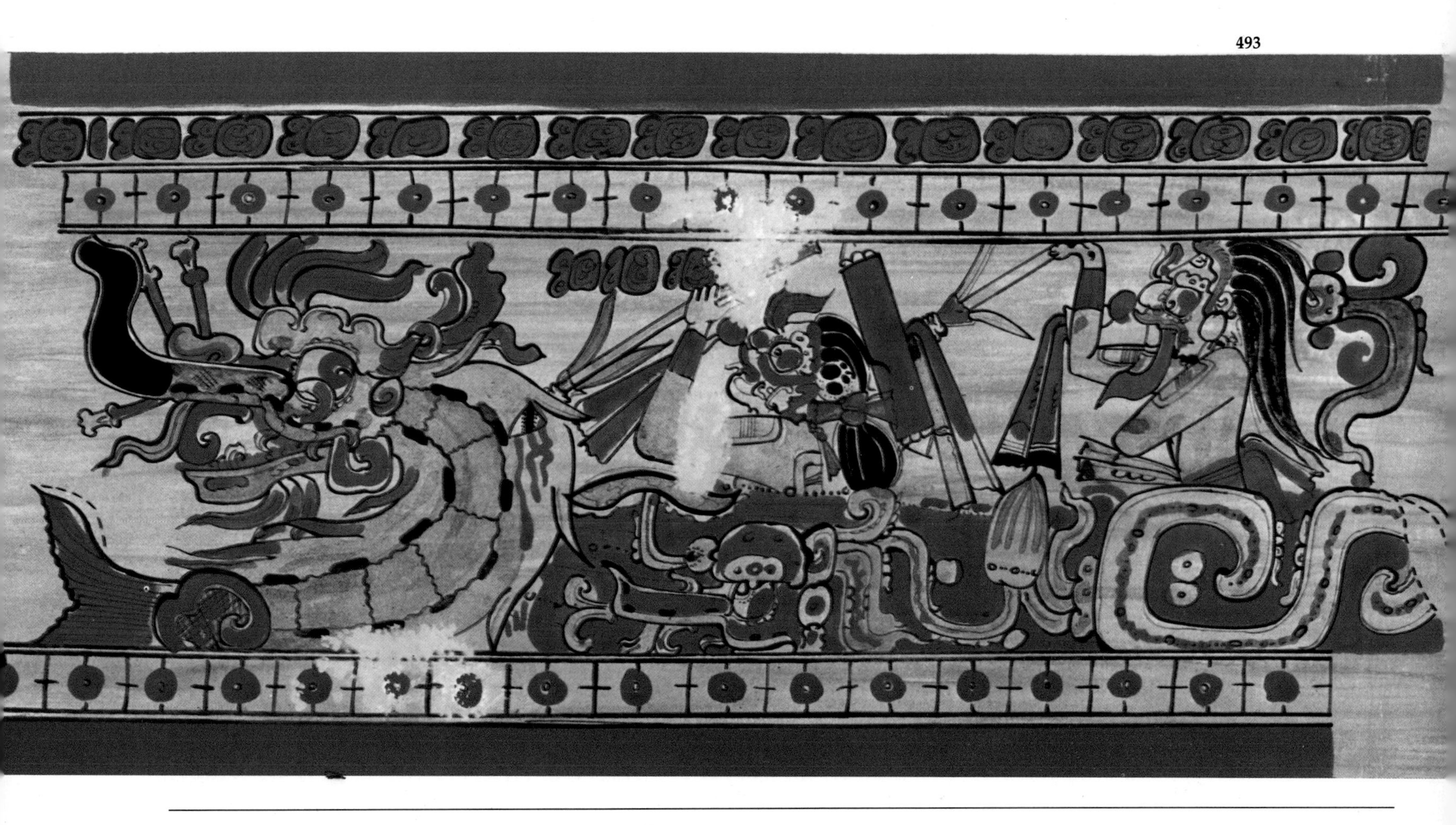

**492.** ***Lintel 24, Yaxchilán, Mexico. In a ritual probably carried out at night, King Shield Jaguar holds a burning torch over the head of his wife, Lady Xoc, who draws blood from her tongue with a rope imbedded with thorns. Shield Jaguar wears the face of Kinich Ahau on his chest.***

**493.** ***Polychrome pot with Jaguar God of the Underworld and Patron of Pax. The Patron of Pax, right, joins the Jaguar God of the Underworld in stabbing a feathered serpent in a sea of blood. The Patron of Pax is probably another aspect of the nocturnal sun, but one particularly associated with sacrifice. Late Classic, probably eighth century.*** **(Dumbarton Oaks, Trustees for Harvard University)**

494

**494.** *Jaguar God of the Underworld, Jaina figurine. At dusk, when it sank into the west, the sun took on the characteristics of the jaguar, the most powerful nocturnal creature of the Maya world. On his nightly journey, the Jaguar God of the Underworld travels on a caiman through the underworld. Probably Jaina Island, Late Classic, seventh-eighth century.* **(Australian National Museum)**

when they represented him in Classical art, they also often showed him as a great squint-eyed lord, with his front teeth filed to a T-shape, as if his entire face were puckered from looking at the sun itself. The ancient Maya believed that at night the sun took on the qualities of a jaguar and journeyed underneath the earth through the underworld, coursing from west to east, from dusk to dawn. This Jaguar God of the Underworld, as he is called today, was a vital part of the sun, the most widely represented aspect in Classical Maya art. The sun god is usually neither aged nor young, but mature in his appearance, whether in his diurnal or nocturnal aspect. In Maya hieroglyphic writing, the diurnal sun is the god of the number four and the month Yaxkin; the Jaguar God of the Underworld is the god of seven and the Month Uo. Both aspects of the sun may be marked by the four-petaled *kin*, or sun sign, although this is more commonly borne by the diurnal sun. *Kin* means not only "sun" but also "day" and in Maya hieroglyphic writing, particularly in the count of time, the head of the sun god may substitute for the *kin* glyph.

Many Maya kings of the Classical period proudly called themselves "Ahau Kin" or "Kinich Ahau," both equivalent to Lord Sun. In this way they became living embodiments of the deity. In the period 100 BC to the beginning of our era the early Maya kings at Cerros and El Mirador and elsewhere commissioned the first great gods, including the Maize God and Sun God. At Palenque, the great king Pacal was known as Kinich Ahau all his life; Kinich Ahau was recognized as one of the three patron deities of Palenque, and, according to the Palenque version of Maya history, his birth had taken place at the dawn of this era, in the third millennium BC. When Pacal died, his heirs and successors carried his body down into the chamber at the base of the Temple of Inscriptions, where a jade mosaic mask was assembled directly on his face. Although the great king was over eighty years old, the jade mask gave him an image of permanent, ideal youth, like the Maize God, but with the very distinctive, filed T-teeth of the daytime sun. In death, Pacal joined with the deities he had personified all his life. The Temple of Inscriptions itself is not a shrine to particular deities, but rather is dedicated to the cult of the powerful ancestor, united with those deities.

At Piedras Negras, the Late Classical (AD 600–900) rulers called themselves Ahau

495

**495.** ***Codex-style pot with Water Lily Jaguar. The Water Lily Jaguar god leads this procession of supernaturals. In this unusual depiction, the Water Lily Jaguar wears a*** **kin*****, or sun sign, on his belly. Late Classic, probably eighth century.*** **(Brooklyn Museum, N.Y. Guennol Collection)**

Kins, but what is perhaps more surprising is that a young woman, daughter of the powerful Lady Ahau Katun and Third Ruler, was also known by this title, even when little more than a child. Was she a special priestess to the sun? At Yaxchilán, King Shield Jaguar wore the sun god as a pectoral when he held a torch over the head of his wife, Lady Xoc, while she drew a rope with thorns through her tongue. In this way, he, too, proclaimed that he was a Kinich Ahau. Recent research into the dates of Yaxchilán has demonstrated that the buildings of Yaxchilán were oriented toward the rising sun on the days of summer solstice, and in these buildings lintels commemorate a solstice ritual in which "flapstaffs" (as scholars have dubbed them) were exchanged.

King Shield Jaguar initiated this solar ritual of the flapstaff at Yaxchilán. After his death, once his son had become king, Bird Jaguar erected a series of monuments to celebrate his own kingship, including the exchange of flapstaffs. On these monuments, Bird Jaguar paid homage to his dead parents by portraying them within symbols for the sun and moon at the upper margins of his monuments. Shield Jaguar appears inside a solar cartouche, confirming the late king's unity with the sun in death, while the mother is rendered inside the symbol for the moon. Images of both the sun god and the Jaguar God of the Underworld accompany them. When Shield Jaguar died, he achieved union with the sun itself. Many Classical Maya kings were apotheosized as the sun, but Shield Jaguar's transformation is particularly explicit.

At dusk, when the sun sank into the west, it took on the characteristics of the jaguar, the most powerful nocturnal creature of the Maya world. Although imbued with the same T-shaped teeth of the diurnal sun, this night sun has jaguar ears and a twisted "cruller" (named after the twisted pastry!) that runs under the eyes and twists over the nose. On his nightly journey, the jaguar god travels through the underworld on a caiman.

The Jaguar God of the Underworld is frequently associated with a star or Venus symbol, perhaps because the planet, in its periodic appearance as morning and evening star, leads the sun both into and out of the underworld. But unlike the Venus of the Old World, the Meso-American Venus is not associated with erotic love or beauty: the Meso-American morning and evening star were the forces of danger and malevolence, of stabbing, sacrifice, and warfare. In both central Mexico and among the Maya, battles took place on the days of Venus's first appearance as either evening or morning star, when its penetrating rays were thought to abet the slaying of enemies. The frontally rendered face of the Jaguar God of the Underworld is the most common motif on shields carried by Maya warriors, and the jaguar god himself can appear as a victorious warrior. The jaguar god, then, is both the sun at night and the patron of warfare. Maya kings at Yaxchilán, Tikal, Caracol, Naranjo, and elsewhere adorned themselves from time to time as the Jaguar God of the Underworld when they presided over preparations for human sacrifice. This association of jaguar, sun, and warfare may relate to the later central Mexican warrior cults, whose patrons, the jaguar and eagle, were born out of the solar pyre at Teotihuacan.

The Maya sun is represented in a few other Maya contexts. The Water Lily Jaguar occasionally wears the *kin*, or sun sign, on his underbelly. The Patron of Pax, a frequent companion of the Jaguar God of the Underworld and, like him, a jaguar god associated with war and sacrifice, may be an aspect of the sun at night. The Bicephalic Monster, literally a two-headed monster, describes the arc of the heavens and the movement of the daily sun. While the front head of the Bicephalic Monster usually bears either a Venus sign or crossed bands in the eye, its upside-down skeletal rear head carries the sun inside a closed cache vessel. Most commonly, the Bicephalic Monster frames scenes of accession or rulership for the Maya, but its intrinsic meaning may be to represent the arc of the heavens, with the front head identified with Venus, pulling behind it the fleshless head of the sun in the underworld.

All across Meso-America, by around the year 1000, skilled craft workers had begun to manipulate metals, particularly gold. Perhaps it was this shift in materials that led to a new conception of the sun in art, for from that moment on until the Spanish Conquest, as had already taken place in the rest of the world, the raw material gold began to be identified with the radiance of the sun. At the time of the Spanish Conquest, the Aztecs called gold *teocultlatl*, or godly excrement. The Maya called it *tahkin*,

496

**496.** ***Bicephalic Monster. Literally a two-headed monster, it describes the arc of the heavens and the movement of the daily sun. Most commonly, the Bicephalic Monster frames scenes of accession or rulership for the Maya. Doorway, Structure 22, Copán, Honduras. Late Classic, eighth century.*** **(Drawing after A.P. Maudslay, 1899–1901)**

497

or excrement of the sun, and from the highland Tzotzil to the lowland Yucatec, the word survives today to refer to money in general, a survival from the time when it meant only gold and, by extension, gold coins.

From the year 1000 on, the Maya and other Meso-American peoples used gold, and specifically gold configured in the form of the rayed solar disc, to represent the brilliant, radiating sun. At Chichén Itzá, in scenes of war and conflagration, deified ancestors reigned from these discs, just as earlier kings had been commemorated within solar cartouches at Yaxchilán. Over a period of several centuries, the Maya at Chichén Itzá hurled quantities of valuable offerings into the Sacred Cenote there, including gold, copper, and tin objects. Discs of gold were beaten thin and smooth, then worked with repoussé images, and some of the discs were configured as the sun. Fire serpents, or *xluhcoalts*, were often associated with the bearing of the sun through the heavens, and their configuration on mirror-backs that were worn round the waist

***497. The Black Background Vase. Perhaps among the most striking and elegant paintings to survive from Classic times, the Black Background Vase shows two aspects of the nocturnal sun, the Jaguar God of the Underworld, left, and the Patron of Pax, right, with Xbalanque, one of the Hero Twins, between them. Late Classic, probably eighth century.*** **(Boston Museum of Fine Arts)**

at the back may have been to show the wearer as the sun carried through the heavens.

In the wake of the Spanish Conquest and the assault on indigenous religion, Maya beliefs and practices took new forms. Early in the twentieth century, the sun was often identified with Jesus Christ, son of the Virgin Mary, who in turn was identified with the moon. The sun and moon have also been considered to be quarrelling spouses, with the sun having plucked out one of the moon's eyes in a fight. Many accounts are still told today of the life that the sun and moon shared on earth before their transformation into celestial bodies, and this idea, that the sun and moon once dwelt on earth, takes us back to the *Popol Vuh*, where the Hero Twins become the sun and moon, and from there far back into ancient times, when Maya religious ideology was forged.

498

**498.** *Jade pectoral. Small representations of the sun god are often of jade, and it is just such a pectoral as this one that Shield Jaguar wears. Late Classic, seventh-eighth century.* **(Museo Nacional de Antropologia, Mexico City)**

500

# THE AZTECS: PEOPLE OF THE SUN

EDUARDO MATOS MOCTEZUMA

Throughout history there have been many examples of a special bond between agrarian societies and the sun. This is no mere coincidence. Observation of the motion of the heavenly bodies, the alternating seasons of rain and drought in the tropics, plant life, and all the other knowledge people have acquired about nature have led them to forge mythical and religious associations with the sun, moon, and stars as fundamental features of their world view, in which a given order is seen as governing the origins of humankind and the universe.

The Aztecs of Mexico were no exception. They were essentially farmers and warriors; this duality was reflected in many aspects of everyday life and is crucial to an understanding of all the institutional arrangements within their complex society, which was to hold sway over a substantial part of Meso-America until the beginning of the sixteenth century. The Aztecs settled in the Valley of Mexico, where they founded the city of Tenochtitlán in the middle of Lake Texcoco about AD 1325. For nearly a century they lived as vassals of other peoples, such as the Tepanecas of Azcapotzalco, to whom they paid tribute. However, by about 1428 they had gained their independence, throwing off the yoke of the ruler of Azcapotzalco. The roles were then reversed, and the peoples of Azcapotzalco were in turn subordinated by the Aztecs and their allies, who set about expanding their territory on an unprecedented scale, conquering first the neighboring peoples and then pushing on as far as the Meso-American coastal regions, 250 miles from the city of Tenochtitlán. All these conquests were to be associated with the god of war, Huitzilopochtli—also god of the sun—who vanquished his enemies for the glory of Tenochtitlán.

Myths reflect different peoples' peculiar conceptions of their origins and the be-

---

**499.** ***Headdress of the Aztec chief Moctezuma, which Bernad Díaz de Castillo of Spain described as a "wonderful sight" when he entered the great Mexican city of Tenochtitlán in November 1519.*** **(Museo Nacional de Antropologia, Mexico City)**

**500.** ***The sun god Tonatiuh and twenty names of days encircling it. The Aztec calendar is filled with symbols of previous world epochs, heaven, and color.*** **(Museo Nacional de Antropologia, Mexico City)**

ginning of the world. The ancient Nahua peoples of Central Mexico (among them the Aztecs) have left us detailed accounts of their relationship with the sun through their myths and legends. An interesting source is a document written in the Nahuatl language in 1558, known as the *Leyenda de los Soles* (Legend of the Suns), which recounts ancestral lore about how four Eras or Suns had been created and how each in turn had been destroyed at the hands of the gods and through their struggles:

This is the oral account of what is known about how the earth was created a long time ago. Here, one by one, are its several stages [eras]. In what form it began, in what manner each Sun came into being, 2,513 years ago: this we know, counting from this day of May 22, 1558. This Sun—Four-Tiger—lasted 676 years. Those who lived in this first Sun were devoured by jaguars [tigers] at the time of the Sun, Four-Tiger. And what they ate was our lifeblood—seven-grass—and they lived for 676 years.

501

**501.** ***A cosmic infinity and a finite statement of the Aztec universe. The massive Aztec stone calendar weighs twenty-four tons and has a diameter of thirteen feet.*** **(Museo Nacional de Antropologia, Mexico City)**

502

**502.** ***Tlaltecuhtli, the Lord of the Earth, 1500. Aztec culture.*** **(Museo Nacional de Antropologia, Mexico City)**

503

504

And the time when they were eaten was the year 13. Whereupon they perished and the end [of everything] came and it was when the Sun was destroyed. And its year was one-reed; they began to be devoured in one day—Four-Tiger—and in a single day it was over and all perished. This Sun is called Four-Wind. Those who in the second place lived in this second [Sun] were borne away by the wind at the time of the Sun Four-Wind and perished. They were snatched away [by the wind] and changed into monkeys; their houses, their trees, everything was snatched away by the wind, and this Sun was also carried away by the wind. And what they ate was our lifeblood. Twelve-serpent, the time in which they were alive, was 364 years. And so they perished in a single day, borne away by the wind, and in the sign Four-Wind they perished. Its year was one-flint.

This Sun Four-Rain was the third. Those who lived in the third [era], at the time of the Sun Four-Rain, also perished, fire rained down on them and they turned into turkeys and the Sun was also consumed by fire, all their houses burned down, and now they had lived for 312 years. Thus they perished, fire rained down for a whole day. And what they ate was our lifeblood. Seven-Flint; its year was one-flint and the day Four-Rain. Those who perished were the turkeys and that is why the young of turkeys are called *pipil-pipil* today.

This Sun is named Four-Water, and the water lasted for 52 years. And those who lived in this fourth era were at the time of the Sun Four-Water. The time it lasted was 676 years. And this is how they perished: they were submerged by the water and turned into fishes. The sky came down in a single day and they perished. And what they ate was our lifeblood. Four-flower; the year was one-house and the sign Four-Water. They perished and all mountains perished, the water lasted for 52 years, whereupon its years ended.

**503.** ***The Aztecs also believed in the universal concept of three worlds, as depicted in this modern painting.*** **(Museo Nacional de Antropologia, Mexico City)**

**504.** ***The sun god of the underworld (AD 750). Teotihuacán culture (200 BC–AD 900).*** **(Museo Nacional de Antropologia, Mexico City)**

505 a

505 b

As can be seen from the above account, humankind passed through four Suns or Eras without its existence becoming firmly established. It had to wait for the emergence of a new Sun—the Fifth Sun—for this to become a reality. How did it happen? There is a significant myth which tells us that it was in Teotihuacan, the ancient Central Mexican city which flourished from the beginning of our era until AD 750, that the event occurred. Why Teotihuacan? When they founded the city of Tenochtitlán in AD 1325, the Aztecs knew that there had been a great city at Teotihuacan, as witnessed by the large number of mounds under which vestiges of the older city lay buried. But as they did not know who had built it, it entered their mythology, and the work of humans was mythically transformed into the work of the gods. Hence, many centuries after its destruction, Teotihuacan retained its significance through myth.

It was the monk Father Bernadino de Sahagún, a sixteenth-century chronicler, who recorded the series of accounts from indigenous sources about the creation of the Fifth Sun. According to this version, there were two gods who wished to be changed into the sun. One of them, Tecuciztécatl by name, was arrogant, while the other, Nanahuatzin, was modest and ailing:

At midnight, all the gods positioned themselves around the hearth... . In that place the fire had burned for four days... and they said to Tecuciztécatl: "Now, then, Tecuciztécatl, cast yourself into the

**505 a,b.** ***Aztecs at work under the sun, in which a serpent is coiled. The temple of Quetzalcoatl was also a rounded structure entwined with serpents. The base of their society was a*** **macehualli,** ***a peasant who was at the same time a part of the agrarian militia. Modern wall paintings.*** **(Museo Nacional de Antropologia, Mexico City)**

fire!" And he then rushed up to throw himself into the flames, but as the fire was great and was burning fiercely, he felt the great heat and became afraid and dared not cast himself into it and turned back... . The gods then spoke to Nanahuatzin, saying to him: "Now, Nanahuatzin, you try!" And as the gods had told him to do, he plucked up courage and, closing his eyes, rushed up and cast himself into the flames and then he began to burn... . When Tecuciztécatl saw that [Nanahuatzin] had thrown himself into the flames and was burning, he, too, rushed up and cast himself into the hearth... . After both of them had flung themselves into the fire and had burned away, the gods sat down to wait and see where Nanahuatzin would reappear. They waited a long time, and then the sky began to glow red and the first light of dawn could be seen all around. They say that after this the gods fell to their knees to wait and see from which side Nanahuatzin-turned-sun would appear. Some thought that he would appear in the north... others toward the south... others started to look toward the east and said that it was there that the sun was to come up, and it was they who spoke the truth; they say that those who looked east were Quetzalcóatl... and that the other is called Tótec... and when the sun did appear, it was brilliant red... and no one could look at it... it blazed forth and shed great rays which were cast out in all directions.

This is how the new Era, the new Sun, was created. But still there was no movement. The sun stood still and, once again, the mediation of the gods was needed. They discussed the matter and decided that in order for there to be movement and hence life, there must be a sacrifice. They spoke thus:

---

**506.** ***Like the Buddhist Wheel of Existence, the Cuauhxicalli sun-stone depicts the gods and warriors in the ever-moving wheel of the Aztec universe. 1500.*** **(Museo Nacional de Antropologia, Mexico City)**

507

How are we to live?
The Sun is not moving!
How in truth shall we make people live?
Let the Sun gain strength by our mediation,
Let us sacrifice ourselves, let us all die!

Life-giving movement derived thus from the sacrifice and death of the gods. This conception of the pre-Hispanic world is crucial to an understanding of many things, since the future existence of the world was believed to hinge on a duel between the gods and the victory of one of them. We know that the confrontation between Tezcatlipoca and Quetzalcóatl was necessary for each Sun to emerge. The Fifth Sun is associated with the latter of the two, whose mission was, moreover, to create humankind. Again, it is the old Nahua myths that tell us how humanity was created. Quetzalcóatl had to descend into Mictlan, the abode of the dead, the underworld, to seek the bones of the ancestors. The privilege of going to the place of the dead was bestowed upon certain persons only. Here is a passage from my book *El Rosro de la Muerte* (The Face of Death):

We are going to embark on a journey to Mictlan, the world of the dead. Such journeys are the

**507.** ***As in many other parts of the world, the eagle is also a sun symbol in Aztec culture, as can be seen in this massive stone. 1500.*** **(Museo Nacional de Antropologia, Mexico City)**

preserve of a privileged few... . It will be recalled that, after the Trojan War, Odysseus set sail and, after the many adventures that occurred on his return voyage, reached the shadowy realm of Hades, the land of the dead. Dante made his poetic journey to the Christian Inferno, accompanied by Virgil. Christ descended into Hell and rose from the dead, as we are told in the Creed, and Quetzalcóatl, too, had the privilege of going to the place of the dead in the pre-Hispanic world. Only those regarded as cultural or religious heroes... were able to cross the tenuous boundary separating the living from the dead, and no one else.

Having secured the bones, the god returned and went to the sacred place of Tamoanchan. There he ground up the bones and placed them in the precious bowl of the goddess Quilaztli, into which he poured blood which flowed from his penis, in self-sacrifice. The sexual act expressed in this form was once again an occasion for sacrifice and penance performed by the gods. Only thus could the act of creation be sanctioned, and humankind was born, its right to existence earned through penance.

So, out of these recurring cycles of creation and destruction, this universal dialectic of conflict, death, and divine sacrifice, human beings came into the world. It is therefore necessary for humans to repeat the sacrifice ritual constantly so as to preserve the cosmic order. Just as the gods died so that there could be life, so today humankind must offer the gods its most precious possession—life itself. If this is done, the sun will not halt its course and the harmony of the universe will be maintained. This is the concept of how life is achieved—through death.

In the case of the Aztecs, we have a legend that tells us about the birth of their god Huitzilopochtli, the god of the sun and of war. It relates how the mother of the gods, Coatlicue, "she of the snake-skirt," lived on the hill of Coatepec, "hill of the snake," and was doing penance there. One day as she was sweeping, a white feather floated down; the goddess picked it up and placed it in her bosom, whereupon she immediately became pregnant. Her daughter Coyolxauhqui, "she with bells in her cheeks," a moon-goddess, learned that her mother was with child and incited her brothers, the 400 (innumerable) Huitznahua, to avenge this outrage by killing their mother on the hill of Coatepec. This they decided to do, and they marched on the hill with the intention of killing her. The goddess was distressed and greatly saddened, but she heard the voice of the child in her belly telling her not to be troubled. Meanwhile, the Huitznahua led by Coyolxauhqui, in full battle array, were advancing resolutely on the sacred hill. The god of war, Huitzilopochtli—for it was he who was in Coatlicue's belly—asked to be told whence his half brothers were advancing. When they came up the hillside, the god was born and in a fierce battle destroyed his enemies.

There are several interpretations of this myth which tells of the fratricidal battle on the hill of Coatepec. First, we know that some myths are derived from actual historical facts or events but, because of their importance to the people concerned, they become mythicized over the ages; thus a battle waged by humans becomes a battle between the gods. This seems to be true of this myth, since, according to various historical sources, before the Aztecs founded their city of Tenochtitlán, problems had arisen among the various *calpulli* ("wards," or groups of households) making up the major group. One of these *calpulli* was in fact that of the Huitznahua, and from this it may be concluded that there was internal strife between the followers of Huit-

**508.** *The Aztecs symbolized the sun with their Eagle Knights, as in this terra-cotta piece (1480). Such motifs were also carved in stone and on wooden drums, and jaguar motifs appear also at the Maya center of Chichén Itzá.* **(Templo Mayor Museum, Mexico City)**

509

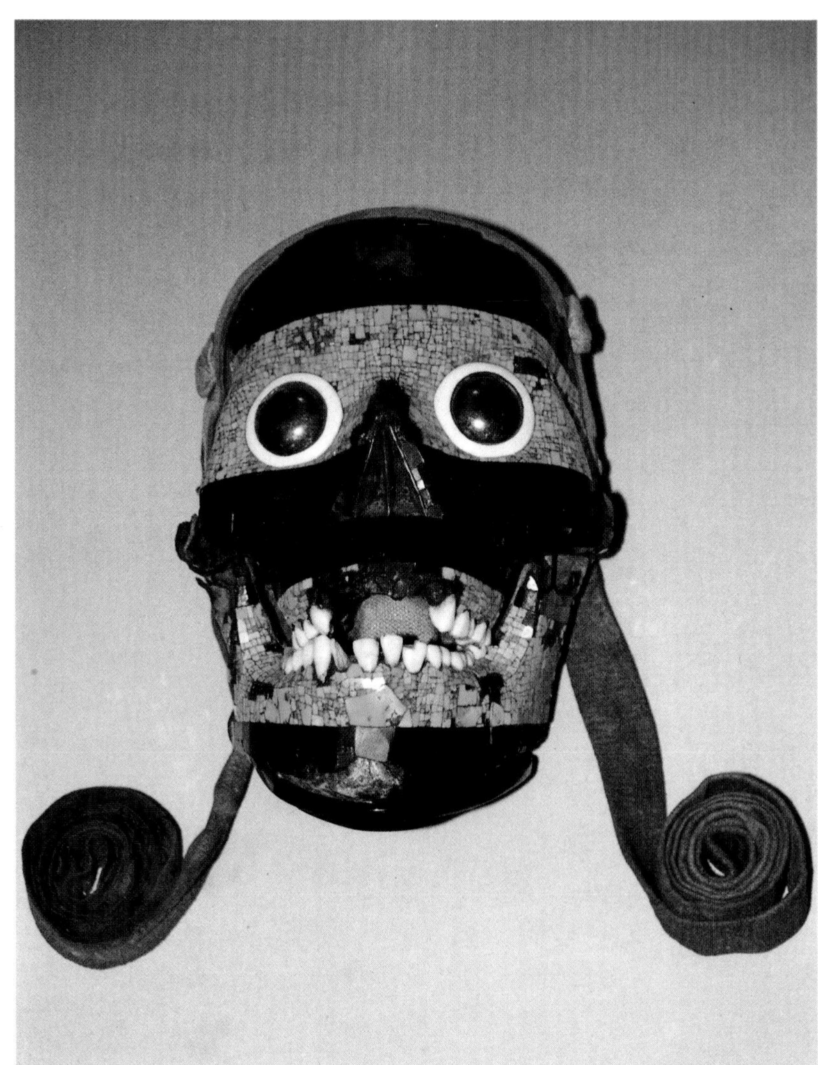

510

zilopochtli, who appears to have been the ruler and leader of the group, and the people of the *calpulli* of Huitznahua under the command of Coyolxauhqui. The former emerged as victors. But, down through the ages, this event which consolidated their power was to be commuted into one of the principal Aztec myths. It has a number of implications. For one thing, it marks the birth of their war and sun god, whose fate was determined from the moment of his birth: he was born to fight. The destiny of the Aztecs was thus to follow in the footsteps of the god Huitzilopochtli, and that was how war became the fundamental incentive for expansion and change, since, as we have seen, gods joined battle in a world of dualities in which everything is born and dies. The Aztecs thus justified their expansionist wars through ancestral myths which sanctioned conquest and the imposition of tributes so badly needed to sustain Tenochtitlán.

But the same myth has been interpreted another way—as the daily struggle waged by the sun, Huitzilopochtli, against the powers of night led by the moon (Coyolxauhqui) and the 400 southerners (Huitznahuas) thought to represent the stars. And so, day after day, they engage in a battle, from which the sun, giver of life, emerges victorious. The weapon with which Huitzilopochtli defeated Coyolxauhqui, called the Xiuhcóatl, the fire-serpent, has been interpreted as the rays of the sun,

**509.** *The Aztec mask decorated with mosaic of turquoise represents a Tonatiuh, Lord of the Daytime Sky, who threw himself into a great fire and arose out of it as the sun (with boil-marks on his face). Fifteenth century.* **(Museum of Mankind, London)**

**510.** *The lord of the underworld and night sky was Tezcatlipoca ("smoking mirror"). The powerful god was the patron of warriors, highway men, and diviners. Fifteenth century. It was a magical bird with the head of a mirror, which foretold the arrival of Spaniards to the Aztec chief Moctezuma.* **(Museum of Mankind, London).**

which rises every day and dispels darkness. The triumph of the sun will occur every day for a people for whom the sun is the source of life and also a cause of death through constant warfare. Again, this life-death duality recurs throughout nature and the universe.

All these beliefs were exemplified in the great temple of the Aztecs, the Templo Mayor. It was built facing west, where the sun goes down, and was flanked by two monumental stairways leading to an upper level. The stairways gave access to two sanctuaries situated at the top of the temple—one dedicated to Huitzilopochtli, god of the sun and war, and the other to Tláloc, god of water and fertility. They symbolized the Aztecs' basic needs—on the one hand, war, a means of subordinating other regions and exacting tributes from them as a vital input into the Aztec economy; and, on the other, the essential requirements for agriculture—water and earth—so important to a farming people like the Aztecs. But this was not all. The Templo Mayor was the place where some of the major legends were symbolically represented through sacred rites. Thus, for instance, the sanctuary dedicated to Huitzilopochtli represented the sacred hill of Coatepec, the place where the battle was fought. It was here that the feast of Panquetzaliztli was celebrated every year in honor of the god of war, with a re-enactment of the battle in which the people of the *calpulli* of Huitznahua fought against those of Huitzilopochtli, the feast culminating in the sacrifice of warriors captured in the empire's most recent wars of expansion. The sanctuary consecrated to the rain god also represented a sacred mountain, Tonacatépetl, or "mountain of sustenance," the repository of the primordial nourishment that the god Quetzalcóatl had to go and fetch to dispense to mortals. As we can see, myth and ritual find expression in the main Aztec temple, the center of the Aztec conception of the universe, from which it was possible to ascend to the heavens and descend into the underworld. From the temple extended the four quadrants, representing the universe, and it thus lay at the heart of a cosmological conception in which observation of nature's changing cycles and of the movement of the heavenly bodies was perceived as part of a dialectical construct in which everything is born and dies, only to be born again in a constant cycle kept moving by ritual sacrifice. The sun in its daily round sets in the west, descending into the world of the dead, only to be reborn through combat. Perhaps this is the reason the Aztecs are known as the People of the Sun.

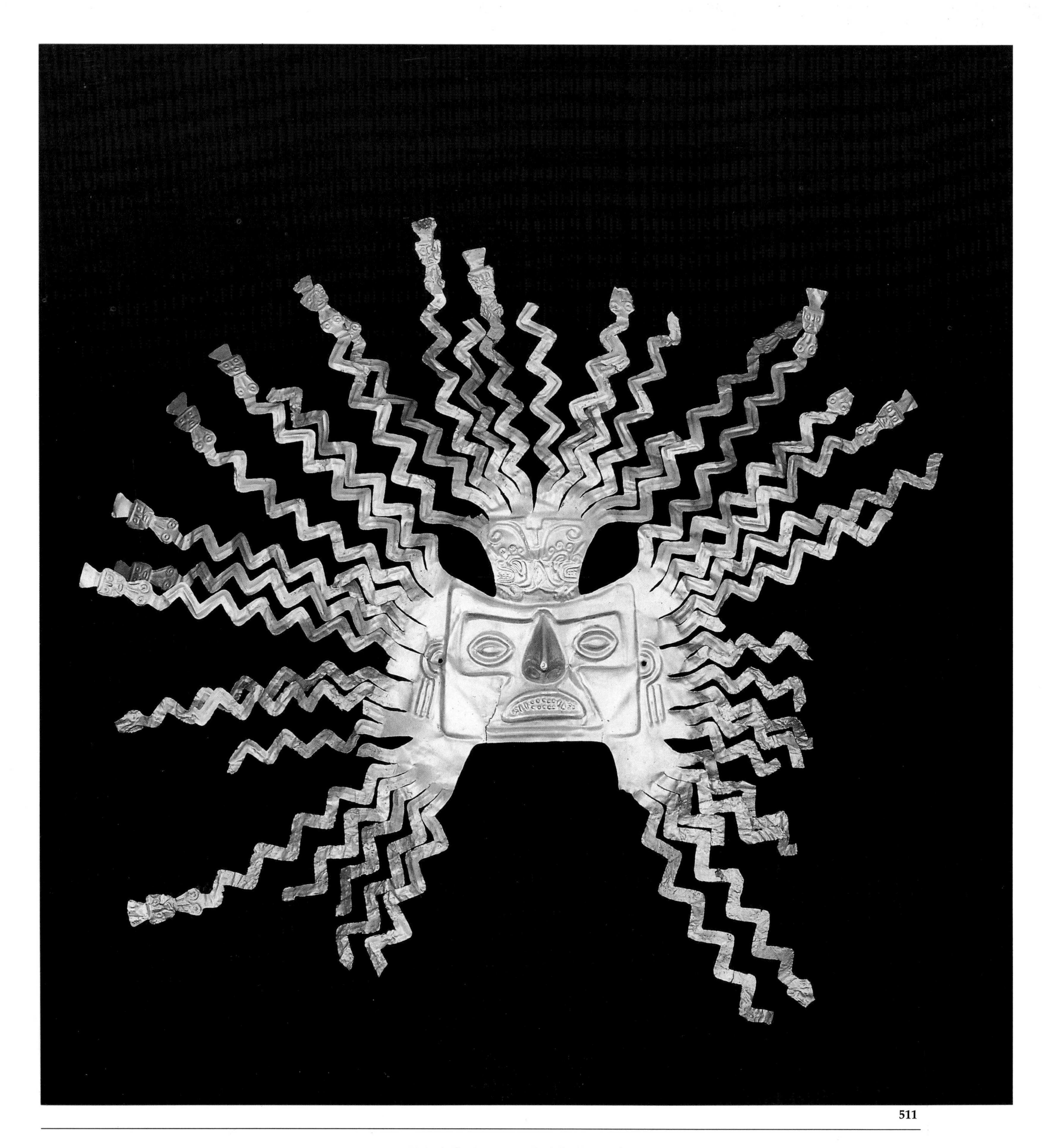

511

**511.** ***Inti, the sun god of the Incas, is also called Apu-Punchau. He is usually represented as a human-faced gold mask, from which sun-rays and flames flare out. His sister and consort is the moon, Mama-Kilya, portrayed as a silver disc.*** **(Museo Arqueologico y Galerias de Arte del Banco Central, Quito)**

512

# INTI, THE ANDEAN SUN GOD

RAMIRO MATOS MENDIETA

In Andean theology the sun made its first tentative appearance as an object of worship during the formative period, in the first millennium BC. That early cult was associated with temples, whereas the Chavín iconography consisted of figures of cats, falcons, and snakes. In the Moche culture during the second to the fifth century AD, the cult of the dead seems to have grown in importance. Recent discoveries in Sipan, El Brujo, Cerro la Mina, and Huaca de la Luna are examples of this funerary cult.

After Tiahuanaco IV or the Classical Tiahuanaco period (AD 450–850) and with the iconography of the Gateway of the Sun, the sun began to play a leading role in Andean religion. Stylistic analysis suggests that the central deity of the Gateway of the Sun of Tiahuanaco was the same as the deity in the Chavín culture known as the Staff God. The same is said of the so-called "angels" on the gateway of Tiahuanaco and the "falconines" on the Gateway of Chavín.

In the Central Andes of Peru, the decoration of the urns of Conchopata (Huari) is similar to the figures on the Gateway of the Sun. The central figure is anthropomorphic with a quadrangular head, wearing a headdress with sunray appendages and a tuft of feathers ending in felines and falconines in profile. It has a staff in either hand, its fangs and eyes divided vertically. Tiahuanaco art was taken up in Huari iconography, naturally with some modifications, and spread throughout the Andes.

During the following period (from the ninth to the fourteenth century), the image

**512.** ***Viracocha, the creator of the sun and the moon in the Inca pantheon, is depicted on the gateway of the sun, holding a staff of authority in each of his hands.***

513

of the sun again took second place. In Chimú, the moon, called Shi, Si, or Chinan in the Yunga language, was considered to rank higher than the sun. Eclipses were celebrated as conquests by the moon of the sun's space. The temple of the moon was called Sian-in. Among the Chincha, however, the sea or ocean *(jatun-mama-cocha)* took precedence and had a cult of its own, and the *wamani* and the *jirka*, divinities connected with the mountains, were the major deities among the Wanka and Chanka peoples.

**513.** *The universal belief in the sun door of immortality is represented by this monolithic Gateway of the Sun from the Tiahuanaco culture (AD 500–800), to the east of Lake Titicaca, on the Collao High Plateau, Bolivia.*

During the final period of the Andean cultural process (fifteenth century), the image of the sun, Inti, became dominant as the official divinity instituted by the Inca state. As that period was closely followed by the Spanish Conquest, it was possible for some colonial writers to provide firsthand accounts.

They describe complex hierarchies involving "greater gods" and "lesser gods." There was a variety of personages in the Andean pantheon, some gods coexisting in harmony and others in conflict. For example, there were two major deities, Ticsi-Virakocha and Inti, in the Inca cosmos. Ticsi-Virakocha is thought to predate Inti and is perhaps the same personage as the central figure on the Gateway of the Sun at Tiahuanaco, while Inti would be the Inca version of Ticsi. According to other accounts, they are two distinct persons forming a single divinity, as in Christianity.

Inti became the ideological symbol of the Inca state, while Ticsi-Virakocha was presented as a legendary and mythical personage. On some occasions the two divinities were superimposed on each other, for example, at the Apu-Inti celebrations at the summer solstice. Inti could sometimes be opposed to Ticsi-Virakocha, especially in the context of matters of state.

Lake Titicaca and Mount Tamputocco, both to the south of Cuzco, were identified as the place of origin *(pacarina)* of the Incas in their mythical history. The Incas would thus have come from the Collao region, but archaeologists have not been able to confirm this version. The style immediately prior to that of the Incas belongs to the Killke culture and is of local origin. It is the Ayarmaca who are recognized in ethnohistory as the immediate ancestors of the Incas.

It is thought that the Inca dynasty was founded around AD 1400. The chronicle by Miguel Cabello de Valboa (1586) has helped to establish the chronology of the thirteen rulers from Manco Capac to Atahualpa. The task of government was carried out by a dual structure, the administration being diarchical, which meant that two Incas held power at the same time. Some resided at Hanan Cuzco. The latter occupied the Sun Temple (Inticancha or Coricancha) and so were of higher rank.

As a direct descendant of Inti, the Inca was thought to have the same sacred characteristics as those attributed to the sun. Furthermore, the Inca was the sun-made man on earth *(caypacha)*, his representative *(Intip-rantin)*. The process of identification with the sun started with Viracocha. Some peoples meekly accepted this view, while others had it forced upon them politically or militarily. The sun was considered "creator of the world," but each ethnic group had a different conception of the sun god. The Inti of the coastal fishermen was not the same as the Inti of the shepherds on the high plateaux or that of the farmers in the valleys, and this enabled the Incas to manipulate the sun symbol according to circumstances and their own interests.

In the Inca cosmogony, there were at least three personages, namely, Ticsi-Virakocha (ancestral divinity), Inti (divinity and symbol of the state), and Illapa (thunderbolt, the fury of the heavens) in the sky or firmament (*hanan-pacha*). Together with these divinities, six other "major gods," Tunupa, Pachacamac, Pariaca-ca, Guari, Catequil, and Chicopae, are recognized by ethnohistory.

Ticsi-Virakocha was the divinity ranked highest by colonial chroniclers, to the point of outshining Inti. They knew full well, from Atahualpa himself, the last Inca of Tahuantinsuyo, that Inti was the universal and official divinity of the state; but they

514

did their best to belittle him—perhaps to salve their consciences after the great damage done to his temples or perhaps hoping that by undermining the Andean divinity they could assist the cause of Christian evangelization.

Illapa's characteristics, and even his name, varied from region to region. He was called Catequil in the north, Libiac in the central mountain ranges, and Catuilla in the south.

In some provinces of the empire, a distinction was drawn between Inti and Punchao, the former being the star and the latter the "solar day." Punchao regulated time and everything contributing to the life cycle on earth.

The imposition of one major deity over other existing deities not only implied the subjugation of the conquered ethnic groups but also brought the different peoples together under the same ideology. As worship signifies human submission to a supernatural power, so the Incas imposed Inti as superior to all the other Andean divinities, and as the Incas considered themselves to be Inti in human form, they endowed material things with supernatural significance during their time on earth.

In the hierarchy of the gods, Inti and Killa stood at the top of the constellation and were incorporated into regional beliefs without coming into conflict with local

**514.** *Most spectacular of all Inca sites is the* **Machu Picchu** *fortress where a stone* **Intihuatana**, *or "hitching place of the sun" sundial, was used to determine the solstices by the shadow cast by the sun.*

515

"gods." The cult of Inti, which started in the mists of the mythological origins of the Incas, made a deep impression within a very short time and became the most widely practised in the whole of pre-Columbian America.

Ethnohistorical sources suggest that Inti could be split into sub-deities. The best known of these are Apu-Inti (the sun as lord, or great sun), Churi-Inti or Punchao (the sun as son, or solar day), and Guauqui-Inti (the sun as brother). The astronomical axis based on the summer and winter solstices was the dividing line between Apu-Inti and Punchao.

Sun rites were performed during the day at sunrise (*Inti-ccespimuy*), midday, or the sun's zenith (*Chawpi-punchao*), and sunset (*Inti-seccaycuy*). Lunar rites were performed at night. The four stages of the monthly cycle, namely the new moon (*Musocc-Killa*), full moon (*Huntun-huntay-Killa*) and the intermediary quarters of the moon (*Chawpi-Killa*) were also distinguished. Santa Cruz Pachachuti Salcamayhua's diagram sets the Inca cosmogony in a universal perspective, showing the sky gods (*hanan-pacha*) and the earth gods (*cay-pacha*), with Inti and Killa at the top, the former to the left and the latter to the right, with nature at the bottom.

An interesting episode in the history of the Incas occurred during the reign of

**515.** ***An important sun temple was located at P'saq, another gigantic fortress, which guarded the upper reaches of Uzubamba River as well as the pass which led east to Pancartambo.***

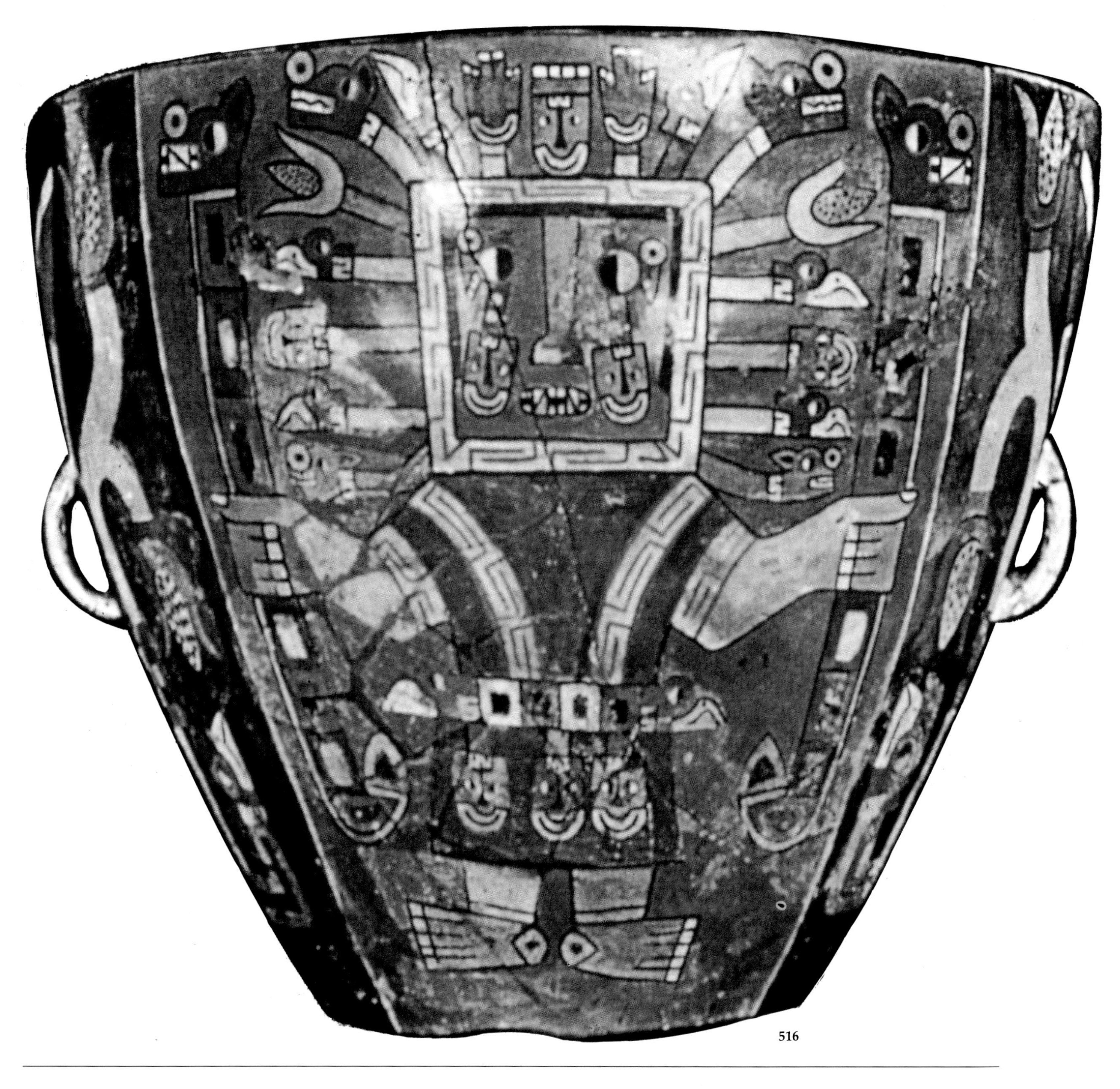

516

**516.** *Close iconographic links are indicated between Conchopata and Tiahuanco cultures in the similarity between the design on the Conchopata vessel and the one seen on the Tiahuanco Gateway of the Sun.*

Virakocha Inca, around 1438, when the Chankas besieged Cuzco. The Inca fled and the defense of the city was left to his son Cusi Inca Yupanqui, who succeeded in reorganizing his army. At that moment, a mysterious supernatural being appeared before him and told him that he would win the war and become a great ruler. Cusi routed the Chankas and assumed power under the name Pachacutec Inca, or "great transformer of the universe." The mysterious apparition might have been Inti or Ticsi-Virakocha. In any event, the images of Inti and Pachacutec came to express the power of a revitalized state.

Killa (the moon) was a female divinity, the stereotype of the Andean woman. She was Inti's consort and performed domestic tasks. She was connected with reproductive and fertility rites. Eclipses of the moon were considered to be encounters between the moon and the sea (*hatun-cocha*).

The most important of the temples built for the worship of Inti was in Cuzco. It was called *Inti-cancha* or Coricancha and was later converted by the Spaniards for use as a Catholic church dedicated to St. Dominic. Richly adorned with gold and silver, it was regarded as the center of the city and of the empire. Forty-one imaginary lines (*ceques*), joining together some 328 *wakas*, radiated from this holy precinct. Each *waka* was connected with an event in the history of the Incas.

During the early colonial period, an imposing idol with dazzling rays representing the sun is said to have been worshipped in the Coricancha. An effigy of the moon was housed in another room. Next came the Inca pantheon, where the mummified rulers of the empire were preserved. The anthropomorphic effigy of the sun was made of solid gold. In 1564, Friar Bernabe Cobo wrote: "This golden statue had a hollowed stomach which was filled with crushed gold mixed with the ashes or dust of the hearts of Inca kings." The association of the mummies of the Incas with the image of Inti is thus made clear.

In addition to Cuzco, there were temples in every province. Some, like the ones at Titicaca and Pachacama, were major sanctuaries, while others, like the *usnu* of Vilcashuaman, Huànuco Pampa, Pumpu, and so on, were merely sacred precincts where offerings could be made. The priest would stand on a platform performing the rites and making offerings, generally a libation of blood and some maize liquor (*chicha*), to the sun and *mama-pacha* together. Some reproductions of these scenes are to be found on the wooden vases of the colonial period (*kero*).

Ritual sacrifices took many different forms. Sacrifices of camelids and guinea pigs are mentioned in colonial documents. Some chroniclers insinuate that there were human sacrifices, especially of children, among the Incas, as among the Maya and Aztecs, but there is no evidence of this. Animals, especially guinea pigs, are still sacrificed today.

Like any centralized and hierarchical state, the Inca empire was tightly organized. The sector responsible for religious administration was made up of a highly respected priestly class. At the head of the structure was the High Priest (*Willak-Umu*), who was always a close relative of the Inca and therefore of the royal family (*panaca*). He resided in Cuzco and headed the church from the Coricancha, attended by a council of priests.

The "sun virgins" (*acllas*) formed a substantial part of the cult. These "maidens,"

517

assigned to the service of the Inca and the religion, discharged important state and religious functions.

Sundials (*Intihuatana*) were invented in order to measure time. They were generally carved of stone and placed in prominent positions; the best known of these is the one at Machu Picchu.

In his comments on indigenous rites, the chronicler Cristobal de Molina reported that there were many rites, including the *aymoray*, connected with the maize harvest, and the *Inti-raymi*, the sun festival held at the summer solstice. The *Goya-raymi*, or *Capac-Situa*, was celebrated in September, and in December there was the *Capac-raymi*, which coincided with the male initiatory rite, called *huarachicuy*, and the winter solstice.

One of the accounts transcribed by Molina contains the following:

> O Creator, who told the Sun to come into being and then said "Let there be night and let there be day, dawn and light," go in peace, keep the peace to enlighten the men whom you have created, O Creator. O Sun, who are at peace and safe, shed light on these persons whom you nourish, do not let them fall ill. Keep them safe.

**517.** *Cosmic beliefs of the Chimú culture (AD 1100–1400) are depicted in the Temple of Dragons, as seen in the rainbow motifs in this frieze. Between the two mythological figures in the center of the rainbow is the* **tumi**, *a Chimú solar symbol.*

518

519

Another account comes from Friar José de Acosta and reads as follows:

> They do the greatest honor to the Sun, and then to thunder; they call the sun Punchao and the thunder Illapu; they also honor the keel which is the moon and Cuillo, the stars; the earth which they call Pachamama and the sea Mamacocha... and then their kings, men of great renown to whom they attribute divinity; whom they adore and whose bodies they have to this day kept intact and lifelike... so much that they could compete in ingenuity with the Greeks.

Although Ticsi-Virakocha is referred to in colonial documents as the "creator and maker of the universe," Inti continued to appear in the accounts and confessions of Andean people after the Spanish conquest as the creator and as the basis of human life. He continued to be worshipped secretly and his shrines and temples were preserved for several centuries. Many of the priests appointed to serve him continued to discharge their functions in secrecy.

Faced with the colonial administration's campaign to eradicate indigenous customs and its imposition of new ones, the Indians began to reflect on the beliefs that were being forced upon them. They compared the Spanish symbols with their own and questioned the divine power of Christian images. The answers were obvious. There was no alternative. The indigenous peoples identified with their own "gods."

**518.** ***Felipe Guaman Poma de Ayala was an Amerindian chronicler, and his sensitive drawings accurately depict social customs, as in this worship of local divinities.***

**519.** ***Another sketch by Ayala depicts Hatun Inti-Raymi, the festival of the sun, during the solstice on June 21.***

Andean priests remarked that "the Spaniards adored pieces of painted and gilded wood, whereas the Indians adored their *Camaquenes* who would respond to all their requests." They also stressed that "the Christians' gods were good for the Spaniards, but not for the Indians... the *wakas* were their gods, because they gave them food to eat." When the Andean temples were destroyed and traditional beliefs denounced, Andean ideology seemed to have lost its force. But indigenous practices such as those connected with Apu-Inti continued for several centuries.

The official sun image of Cuzco was broken up and buried at Cajamarca, next to the last Inca. But belief in the *wakas,* the local divinities, was never eliminated and has continued until modern times. The *wamani, auqui,* and *apachetas* are still alive in peasant ideology to this day.

In Canta and Cajatambo in the seventeenth century, Indians accused of idolatry confessed to performing rites to the sun in secrecy as a people who wished to keep their identity struggling desperately against others who were trying to suppress it. They themselves described the idol of the sun that they knew as "having human form, being made of black stone, and as tall as a man standing upright." The description calls to mind the idol in the Coricancha and also the resemblance between the sun and Molina's Inca Yupanqui.

The *Inti-raymi* celebrations are held each year in June to coincide with the summer solstice. The best known is held in Cuzco, ancient capital of the Inca empire and archaeological capital of the Americas today.

The *Capac-raymi* festival, albeit weakened, has retained its Andean character among the peasants in the central-southern mountain range. The *hatun-pocoy,* the rainy season when crops are sown, is also marked by a festival.

The *Inti-raymi* in Cuzco has become a popular pageant. Atahualpa's death at the hands of the Spanish is evoked and the ritual is intended for Inti. As part of the action, the Inca enters the square on his throne accompanied by his *goyas, acllas, sinchis,* and the *Willak-Umu.* They sacrifice a white alpaca and its blood is offered by the Inca to Inti, requesting better times for his people. The ceremony is held to coincide with the sun's disappearance behind the mountains, with dances and songs performed by the *acllas* (sun virgins) and *sinchis* (warriors).

As the climax of the ritual, the Inca is arrested and killed, and his death is mourned by the people. The staging of the Inca's death on the day of *Inti-raymi* perhaps constitutes the social explanation for the disappearance of the cult and symbol of Inti in Andean ideology.

The territory controlled by the Incas extended as far as present-day Colombia, and the cult of Inti, as a religious symbol, extended even farther.

There was a long-established tradition of sun worship among the Chibchas to the north of Tahuantinsuyo. They called the sun Zuhé and the moon Chía. Their rituals were accompanied by animal and human sacrifices. Sacrificial blood was mixed with maize and yucca liquor and sprinkled over the mountains as an offering to the sun.

The sun was the supreme divinity for the Chibchas and the Muiscas. The shamans also invoked the power of the sun to ward off evil spirits.

Female divinities were of greater significance than male divinities along the coast of Ecuador and on the grassy plains of Venezuela and, as the sun was a male symbol, its presence in these cultures did not have the same force as in the central Andes.

In the Central and Middle American cultures, on the other hand, the sun god had a long and varied tradition. Although the sun symbol was universal, the concepts connected with it varied locally and regionally. The sun worshipped by the Maya was not the same as that of the Aztecs and the sun god worshipped by the Cunas in Panama was different again.

In conclusion, the sun was worshipped by all the peoples and cultures of pre-Columbian America, although in a few cases the moon ranked higher than the sun. The characteristics of the sun god varied from one locality or region to another and it was only as the symbol of the Inca state that the cult extended to cover a very large area.

520

**520.** *Conquerors often absorbed cultures of the people they vanquished, as symbolized by the sun emblem which a Spaniard installed in his* casa del sol *at Cáceres on his return to Spain from Peru in the sixteenth century.*

# GLOSSARY

**Abhaya-mudrā:** the "fear-dispelling" mudra, or symbolic gesture, made by raising the right hand, the palm facing outward.

**Acroteria:** sculpted ornaments, especially at the apex or outer angle of a pediment on a Greek temple.

**Agni:** Hindu deity of fire, who appears as the sun in heaven, lightning in the atmosphere, and fire on earth.

**Ahau kin:** Maya sun lord.

**Aja-ekapad:** ("swift-one-foot") the Hindu sun deity Pûshan's goat, representing the power of solar movements. It precedes Sûrya's sun horse en route to heaven.

**Akhenaton:** Egyptian king (c. 1353–1337 BC) of the Eighteenth Dynasty. Originally called Amunhotep IV, he erected several sanctuaries of the Aton at Karnak. Eventually, he changed his name to Akhenaton ("The One Who Is Effective for the Aton") and proscribed worship of the traditional gods of Egypt.

**Am-duat:** ("The Book of That Which Is in the Netherworld") the earliest of a series of painted scenes and texts found on the walls of the royal tombs of the Egyptian New Kingdom. It describes the sun god's descent into the Underworld during the night hours and his eventual rebirth at dawn.

**Amaterasu:** ("Heavenly Shining One") Japanese sun goddess.

**Anathema:** a person or object subject to intense dislike, having been cursed or banned by the Church.

**Aphrodite:** Greek goddess of sexuality and regeneration; lover and immortalized by Phaethon, according to the Hesiodic tradition.

**Apollo:** Greek god of speech, poetry, song, and music whose luminous essence qualified him to be the sun deity.

**Apophis:** a great serpent who dwelt in the Egyptian Underworld; the archenemy of the sun god Atum, who fought Apophis during his nightly descent into the Underworld.

***Asahi:*** ("morning sun") name of a leading Japanese newspaper.

**Aton:** ("disk") the physical form of the Egyptian sun. The Aton became an object of worship during the reign of Akhenaton (fourteenth century BC).

**Attic black-and-red figure vases:** ceramics produced especially in Attic, the broader area around Athens, from the sixth to the fourth century BC.

**Atum:** one version of the Egyptian creator god. According to the Heliopolitan creation myth, Atum rose out of the waters of chaos at the moment of creation, bringing about existence. Depicted as a ram-headed man or a human-headed cobra, Atum personifies the sun which sets over the western horizon and travels through the Underworld.

**Benben:** the primordial mound which arose with the waters of chaos. The Egyptian creator god stood upon the Benben when he brought the universe into being.

**Bhaishajyaguru:** (*Yakushi* in Japanese) a benevolent, curative bodhisattva, usually depicted in a triad along with the sunlight deity, Sûryaprabha, and the moonlight deity, Chandraprabha.

**Bhûmisparsa-mudrā:** an earth-touching mudra, or symbolic gesture, in which the middle finger of the right hand touches the ground and the left hand rests in the lap, palm upwards. This gesture was used by Sākyamuni Buddha to call upon the earth goddess to witness his resistance to the temptations of Māra, the evil one.

**Book of the Dead:** a compilation of 190 Egyptian funerary spells, also known as the "Chapters of Coming Forth by Day." The spells helped the deceased to overcome any dangers that they might encounter in the Underworld.

**Brahmanda:** a polished stone found in flowing water and identified by Hindus as the golden egg of Brahma, *Hiranya-Garbha.*

**Candi:** commemorative shrine; also, other Indonesian monuments.

**Candraséngkala:** rebus-like Javanese method of indicating the year. Four words or images are assigned numerical values; the four digits together form a year, usually of the *saka* era.

**Candi Bêntar:** (literally, "split *candi*") a gateway consisting of two separate, symmetrical parts flanking the entrance to a temple. If placed together, these two parts would form the outline of a *candi.*

**Chandraprabha:** (*Gakkô* in Japanese) counterpart of the sun deity Sûryaprabha in the Yakushi triad (*see* Bhaishajyaguru).

**Chi'bil kin:** among the Maya, an eclipse, or the "biting of the sun."

**Coffin Texts:** Egyptian inscriptions painted on the interior walls of royal and private coffins beginning just before the Middle Kingdom. They are related to the *Pyramid Texts* of the Old Kingdom but reflect the growth in the cult of Osiris.

**Cosmology:** the study of the universe as an orderly system.

**Danda:** staff or mace.

**Da-wen-kou culture:** a late Neolithic people of eastern China.

**Dharmacakra-mudra:** mudra, or symbolic gesture, representing "Turning the Wheel of the Law," a reference to the first sermon delivered by the Buddha at Deer Park, Benares, India. The two hands are raised before the chest, making the shape of a wheel, the fingertips touching.

**Dhûli-chitra:** ritualistic and decorative floor-drawing technique, traditionally practiced throughout South Asia under different names, such as *alpana, rangola, aripan, kolam,* and *sanjhi.*

**Dhyāni-Buddha:** ("Victorious") the Five Cosmic Buddhas. Vajrayâna Buddhism introduced the Five Cosmic Buddhas and their "families" of associated deities, which are evoked mystically through mantras, yantras, mudras, and mandalas.

**Dualism:** a theological concept, probably Iranian in origin, in which the universe is ruled by two opposing forces, one good and one evil.

**Dvarapāla:** door guardian.

**El Armana:** the modern name for the site of Akhenaton's Egyptian capital ("the Horizon of the Aton"); also known as Amarna or Tel el-Armana.

**Elysian Fields:** in Greek mythology, a paradise-like place on the banks of the Okeanos, where the sun rises; heroes abide here after they are immortalized.

**Ennead:** a group of nine beings. In Egyptian religions, an association of nine deities. The Heliopolitan Ennead comprises the creator god Atum and the three generations of gods descended from him.

**Eos:** the Greek goddess of dawn.

**Five elements:** wood, fire, earth, metal, and water; according to traditional Chinese theory, the five forces of nature of which the universe is composed. In rotation, each element is believed to cause the next; when united properly, they create peace and prosperity, when incorrectly joined, they bring suffering and calamity.

**Four elements:** a scientific theory, first propounded by the fifth-century-BC Greek philosopher Empedocles, that the universe is composed exclusively of fire, air, water, and earth.

**Fusang:** the mulberry tree of Chinese mythology.

**Garuda:** the mount of Vishnu in Hindu mythology, a mythical half-human, half-bird whose lustre was so brilliant that he was mistaken for Agni, the god of fire, and was worshipped as the sun.

**Gayatri:** sacred verse in the *Rg Veda* devoted to the worship of Savitre (the sun).

**Geb:** the Egyptian earth god. With Nut, one of the two members of the second generation of deities descended from the sun god Atum.

**Gigantomachy:** battle of Zeus against the Giants.

**Hathor:** a very ancient Egyptian goddess, represented as a cow, a cow-headed woman, or a human. She is usually associated with love, music, and physical pleasure, but could become violent. According to one Egyptian myth, she nearly destroyed all of humanity.

**Heliolatry:** sun worship.

**Heliopolis:** a modern suburb of Cairo. In Antiquity, it was called Iwnw and served as the cult center for the worship of Re.

**Helios:** the sun god.

**Hero Twins:** characters in the *Popol Vuh,* divine offspring of an Underworld goddess and a man later revealed in this Maya epic to be the Maize God.

**Hesiod:** in the poetry attributed to Hesiod, his birthplace is given as Ascra in Boetia. There is no credible evidence for a historical Hesiod, credited with the authorship of the *Theogony* and the *Works and Days.*

**Hesperides:** a mythical figure who dwelt in a paradisiacal garden at the western end of the known world, near Okeanos (that is, the Atlantic Ocean).

**Hewet-benben:** ("House of the Benben") sanctuary at Heliopolis dedicated to Atum in his role as creator of the universe.

**Hi:** ("sun") the Japanese ideograph signifies both "sun" and "day"; its pronunciation is the same as the pronunciation of the word for "fire."

**Hi-no-maru:** ("circle of sun") Japan's official flag.

**Homer:** many cities claim to be his birthplace, including Athens, Argos, Chios, Colophon, and Smyrna. There is no evidence, however, for a historical Homer, credited with the authorship of the *Iliad* and the *Odyssey.*

**Horus:** the divine son of Osiris and Isis. An early sky god, most frequently represented as a falcon or a falcon-headed man. He fought with his uncle Seth after the latter had murdered Osiris. Egyptian kings were thought to be the earthly manifestation of Horus.

**Hsi-ho:** the sky goddess of Chinese mythology, the "Mother of Ten Suns," each of whom represents an element of nature, such as the sun, clouds, water, stones, the stag, the tortoise, the crane, the pine tree, bamboo, and the herb of eternal life.

**Huitzilophochtli:** the "hummingbird wizard," sun god of the Aztecs. He was the ever-youthful warrior who eternally fought the night for the survival of the next day. The Aztecs nourished him with blood and the human hearts of their enemies.

**Indo-Europeans:** speakers of related languages, originally ranging from India to Europe.

**Indra:** the Hindu god of the firmament and guardian of the east. He is identified in the *Rg Veda* with Vayû (air, wind), one of the three principal deities, along with Agni (fire) and Sûrya (sun).

**Inti:** the ancestor sun god of the Incas, also called Apu-Punchau. His anthropomorphic representation is a golden mask from which sunrays and flames emanate. His sister and consort is Mama-Kilya, the moon.

**Isis:** an Egyptian goddess, the sister and wife of Osiris and the mother of Horus. After her husband's murder at the hands of Seth, she magically restored Osiris to an animate existence that resembled life. She became a model for wifely loyalty and motherly devotion.

**Ithaca:** the island home of Odysseus and the goal of the hero's many journeys in Homer's *Odyssey.*

**Kāla:** (literally, "time," "death," or "black") a demon's mask mounted above doorways and in niches.

**Kamikaze:** ("divine wind") Japanese airplane suicide units in World War II; one of these units was called "morning Sun."

**Kherpri:** one of the manifestations of the Egyptian sun, specifically, the morning sun as it emerges over the eastern horizon. Most frequently, it is depicted as a scarab beetle pushing the solar disc across the sky.

**Kin:** in Maya, "sun." Also "day."

**Kinich Ahau:** ("squint-eyed" or "sun-faced lord") for the Maya, the daytime sun.

**Kinnara, kinnari:** male and female mythical beings, half-human, half-bird. They act as heavenly musicians.

**Krishna:** ("the black one") a popular Hindu deity, with attributes similar to the Greek Dionysus or the Roman Bacchus. As the eighth incarnation of Vishnu, he obtained the fiery disc (sun symbol) through Agni, the fire deity.

**Kuvera:** a Hindu deity of wealth.

**Laksana:** a physical attribute of the Buddha, such as the *urnā*, a small curl on the forehead, or the *usnîsa*, a protuberance on the top of the Buddha's skull.

**Litany of Re:** one of a series of religious texts and images painted on the walls of the royal tombs of the Egyptian New Kingdom. The inscriptions emphasize the king's identification with the sun god.

**Loka-pâlas:** Hindu guardian deities who preside over the eight directions (that is, the four cardinal points and the four intermediate quarters). For example, Indra (god of the firmament) is the guardian of the east, while Agni (god of fire) is the guardian of the southeast quarter.

**Lotus Sûtra:** a syncretistic doctrine that includes tendencies from other strains of Mahayana Buddhism, such as Vinaya, Shingon, and Zen, as well as from Japanese Shintoism. Called T'ien-t'ai in China and Tendai in Japan, it is based on the Indian *Saddharma-pundarîka-sûtra* ("Lotus of the True Law") text.

**Makara:** a mythical aquatic beast, probably derived from the crocodile, sometimes depicted with an elephant's trunk. Together with the *kāla*, the *makara* is used to frame doorways and in niches of temples.

**Mandala:** a ritual meditation design, a diagrammatic arrangement of Buddhas and various deities of the pantheon.

**Ma-wang-dui:** Chinese archeological site uncovered in the 1960s and 1970s, located near Changsha, Hunan province. They are the burial caves for the marquis Tai of the second century BC and his immediate family. Changsha also has a specially designed museum that exhibits the relics from Ma-wang-dui.



**Mbidi Kiluwe:** cultural hero of the Luba and related peoples of southeastern Zaire; with his son, Kalala Ilunga, he established a sacred kingship and founded what would become the Luba states; he is one of a genre of cultural heroes of the Bantu-speaking peoples throughout central Africa.

**Memnon:** king of the Ethiopians, son of Eos, the dawn goddess. A hero who fought and was killed by Achilles in an epic known as the *Aithiopis.*

**Mithra:** the god of sunlight and rain, a warrior deity in Iranian mythology who was born of a rock and armed at birth with a knife and a torch. Mithraism flourished in the Roman Empire; in India, the deity is known as Mitra, but has different connotations.

**Mudra:** a symbolic gesture of the hands and fingers, in Hinduism and Buddhism.

**Naba:** a king, paramount, or lesser chief of the Mossi peoples of central Burkina Faso; a member of the ruling elite which conquered local farmers and represent the sun's powers on earth.

**Nephthys:** the divine sister of Osiris, Isis, and Seth. When Seth murdered Osiris, she assisted Isis in restoring the dead god to animate existence.

**Nihon:** ("Japan") the Japanese character combines the ideographs for "sun" and "source."

**Nioniosse:** ("the ancient ones") a farming people descended from ancestors identified with the lands inhabited by the Mossi of central Burkina Faso.

**Nkongolo Mwamba:** the primordial antihero of the origin myths of the Luba and related peoples of southeastern Zaire. He was defeated by Mbidi Kiluwe, who then founded the Luba sacred kingship; also a member of a genre of beings associated with the sun among the Bantu-speaking peoples of central Africa.

**Nommo:** a primordial being in the religion of the Dogon of westcentral Mali and northwestern Burkina Faso. One nommo defied God and stole a piece of the sun, bringing fire to earth, giving rise to human culture.

**Nostos:** ("return, homecoming, song about homecoming, return to light and life") the ultimate *nostos* is Homer's *Odyssey.*

**Nun:** a boundless ocean of dark, motionless, and inert water which held the potential for all Egyptian creation. At the moment of creation, the sun god appeared in a space he fashioned within the Nun, heralding the beginning of universal existence.

**Nut:** the Egyptian goddess of the sky. With Geb, she is one of the two members of the second generation of deities descended from the sun god.

**Nyx:** the Egyptian goddess of night.

**Odin:** one of the principal gods in Norse mythology, with ambivalent cosmic characteristics. Earlier he was known as Woden; thus Wednesday was derived from "Woden's day" by the Anglo-

Saxons. He has one eye, like the sun in later Germanic mythology.

**O-hi-sama:** the most familiar term in Japanese for "sun." It combines the ideograph for "sun" with honorifics.

**Okeanos:** the cosmic ocean surrounding the earth and the seas. According to Homeric tradition, the sun sets into its waters and rises from them.

**Olympian Dodekatheon:** the twelve Greek gods of Olympus.

**Oracle bone:** used in early China, Shang Dynasty, for divination. A question would be written on the bone, which would be heated; the answer would be read from the resulting cracks. Oracle-bone inscriptions are the earliest Chinese writing system found thus far.

**Osiris:** an early Egyptian god of agriculture and fertility. According to the legend, he was a benevolent king of Egypt who was murdered by his treacherous brother, Seth, and magically restored to an animate state by his wife-sister, Isis. Osiris subsequently ruled the Underworld as god of the dead and became the model for rebirth that all Egyptians hoped to emulate; his cult center was Abydos.

**Padadvayam:** in Indonesia, footprints.

**Padavimbadvayam:** in Indonesia, the likeness of footprints.

**Phaethon:** son of the dawn goddess Eos and a mortal man; in another version, son of Helios, the Greek sun god and a mortal woman.

***Popol Vuh:*** a sixteenth-century epic that relates the history of the Quiche Maya.

**Pradaksinā:** clockwise circumambulation; a ritual performed around stupas and other Buddhist monuments.

**Pûshan:** Hindu solar deity, with ambivalent attributes. He is associated with sunlight, but later texts (*Nirukta*) identify him with the sun. He is the "nourisher," dwelling in the sun, helping the revolution of day and night, aiding travellers on roads and journeys to the heavenly domain of the sun.

**Pyramid Texts:** a series of primitive Egyptian spells found on the interior walls of the pyramids of the late Dynasty V and VI. They were intended as a guide for the dead king during his journey through the heavens, where he would merge with the sun god and become immortal.

**Pysanki:** Easter eggs decorated in the Ukrainian style, using a batik method.

**Qu-yuan:** famous Chinese poet (c. 340–278 BC), minister of Chu, a large state in the middle valley of the Yangzi River area. He enormously influenced early Chinese poetry with his highly original and imaginative verse. His works have survived in an early anthology, the *Ch'u Tz'u* (Elegies of Ch'u), of which the most famous item is the long melancholic poem *Li Sao* ("On Encountering Sorrow").

**Quadriga:** an ancient Roman chariot drawn by four horses.

**Re:** (or Ra, "the sun") the most basic version of the Egyptian sun, the source of all light and warmth, and thus of all life. The creator of the universe who took several forms, including Atum, Khepri, and Re-Horakhty, his cult centre was Heliopolis.

**Re-Horakhty:** a conflation of the Egyptian sun god Re and the sky god Horus ("of the two horizons"). He is most commonly shown as a falcon-headed human with a sun disc on his head.

***Rg Veda:*** On of the Vedas' "divine knowing" hymns, composed by Aryan immigrants to India around 1500–1000 BC.

**Saka:** an era in Indian chronology, a calendrical system, also used in Indonesia and Indochina. The *saka* era was assumed to have started in AD 19, five hundred years after the birth of the Buddha.

**Salagrama:** a round ammonite stone, identified by Hindus as Vishnu, representing the sun.

**Sassanian:** (also, Sassenid) pertaining to the Persian Empire from the early Christian era up to the emergence of Islam, i.e. from the third to the mid-seventh century AD.

**Selene:** the Greek moon goddess.

**Seth:** the divine brother of Osiris, Isis, and Nephthys. In a fit of jealous rage, he murdered Osiris and assumed his throne. He was eventually vanquished by his nephew Horus, who assumed the kingship of Egypt. Frequently represented as a mythical, long-nosed animal, he came to represent evil and confusion.

**Shamash:** the sun god of the Semitic pantheon in the Mesopotamian region. He is often depicted seated on a horse, a symbol of the sun in pre-Islamic Arabia.

**Shôtoku Taishi:** in the early seventh century, Prince Shôtoku of Japan became famous for establishing an idealized government based on the Buddhist religious principles of peace and salvation.

**Shu:** the first male offspring of the Egyptian creator god, Atum. He represents air, light, and life. He often appears in human form, separating the sky (Nut) from the earth (Geb).

**Slavs:** an Indo-European people living in Europe in a region ranging from Russia to Bulgaria and including the following ethnic groups: Russians, Byelo-russians, Ukrainians, Sorbs, Kashubs, Poles, Czechs, Slovaks, Slovenians, Serbs, Croats, Macedonians, and Bulgarians.

**Sokar:** the terrifying Egyptian god of death. Most commonly shown as a falcon, he dwells in the lowest recesses of the Underworld and challenges the sun god during his nightly subterranean journey.

**Soma:** a fermented juice of a milky creeper-plant, identified as a deity in the Hindu *Rg Veda*.

**Sphinx:** a mythical creature combining the head of the ruling king and the body of a lion. Sphinxes served a protective role, guarding the Egyptian frontier and sacred religious areas against trespassers. The

Great Sphinx at Giza represents the Fourth Dynasty king Khafre in the image of the sun.

**Spider's web:** symbol of the sun god Sûrya's night garb, which is woven by Ushas, the Hindu goddess of dawn.

**Stambha:** column or standard.

**Stupa:** commemorative monument.

**Sûrya:** the sun. He is one of the three chief Hindu deities, with Indra, the god of rain, and Agni, god of fire.

**Sûryaprabha:** (*Nikkô* in Japanese) Buddhist sun deity who became very popular in Japan shortly after the introduction of Buddhism there, as he reflected many characteristics of the Shinto sun goddess Amaterasu.

**Taiyo:** one of the Japanese words for "sun," connoting its austere, even scientific, qualities.

**Tang-gu:** ("Warma Valley") location in Chinese myths where Fusang, the mythological mulberry tree, grows.

**Tefnut:** the first female child of the Egyptian sun god, Atum. She symbolizes moisture and heat.

**Tenga:** spirits that provide a link between autochthonous peoples and the lands inhabited by the Mossi of central Burkina Faso.

**Teocuitlatl:** ("godly excrement") gold, for the Aztecs. The Maya word *tahkin* has the same two connotations.

**Tribhanga:** (literally, "thrice bent") a flexed stand in which the line of the body changes direction twice.

**Trisula:** a trident.

**Urnā:** a small curl on the forehead, one of the *laksanas*, or bodily marks, of a Buddha.

**Ushas:** Hindu goddess of dawn.

**Utu:** the Sumerian sun god (identified with Shamash) whose pictorial sign is a disc rising from two mountains in the east, indicating the rising sun.

**Vairocana:** regarded as the oldest and the first Buddha in the Indian *Guhyasamâja* (c. AD 300). In China, Korea, and Japan, he was elevated to supreme status as Maha-Vairocan, the "Great Illuminator."

**Vajra:** thunderbolt.

**Valley of the Kings:** burial ground of most of the kings of the New Kingdom in ancient Egypt (dynasties XVII–XX). It is located on the west bank of the Nile, across from the modern city of Luxor.

**Varuma:** one of the earliest Vedic deities, personifying the all-investing sky. Later in India Varuma became the god of water, ruling the night, while Mitra ruled the day.

**Vâyu:** Hindu god of the wind whose golden chariot, drawn by a thousand horses, is driven by Indra.

**Vihāra:** monk's abode.

**Vrata:** ritual fasting during religious feasts.

**Vucub Caquix:** the "false sun" in the Maya *Popul Vuh* epic.

**Wycinanki:** Polish decorative paper cutouts.

**Xiuhcoatl:** fire serpent, the Aztec bearer of the sun through the heavens.

**Yama:** Hindu deity of the dead, the son of Vivaswat (the sun).

**Yangshao culture:** a late Neolithic and Bronze Age people of north China who lived in small settlements of circular pit houses, and practiced irrigation and loom weaving; created a fine, painted pottery and, later, practiced metallurgy.

**Yantra:** a linear diagram, used in meditation.

**Yin-Yang:** complementary forces in traditional Chinese cosmology. Yin is the feminine, negative, dark, while yang is the masculine, positive, light. They combine and interact to produce all phenomena.

**Yo domolo:** a carved wooden shoulder crook worn by members of the Yona society ("ritual thieves") among the Dogon of eastcentral Mali and northwestern Burkina Faso. The crooks refer to an episode in the Dogon creation myth in which a cultural hero steals a piece of the sun, starting off human culture.

# BIBLIOGRAPHY


**Ahmad Hasan Dani**

Banerji, J.N. *The Development of Hindu Iconography*. Calcutta, University of Calcutta, 1956.

Bisswas, T.K.; Jha, Bogendra. *Gupta Sculptures*. New Delhi, 1985.

Dani, A.H. *Chilas: The City of Nanga Parvat*. Islamabad, 1983.

—*The Historic City of Taxila*. Paris/Tokyo, 1986.

—*History of the Northern Areas of Pakistan*. 2nd ed., Islamabad, 1991.

Gardner, P. *The Coins of the Greek and Scythian Kings of Bactria and India in the British Museum*. London, 1886.

Gordon, D.H. *The Prehistoric Background of Indian Culture*. Bombay, 1960.

Kak, R.C. *Ancient Monuments of Kashmir*. New Delhi, Sagar Publications, 1971.

Majundar, R.C. (ed.). *The Classical Accounts of India*. Calcutta, 1960.

Marshall, Sir John. *Taxila*. Cambridge, 1951.

Rowland, Benjamin. *The Art and Architecture of India*. Baltimore, 1967.

**Miranda Green**

Green, Miranda. *Dictionary of Celtic Myth and Legend*. London, Thames & Hudson, 1992.

—*The Gods of Roman Britain*. London, Shire, 1983.

—*The Gods of the Celts*. London, Sutton, 1986.

—*The Sun Gods of Ancient Europe*. London, Batsford, 1991.

—*Symbol and Image in Celtic Religious Art*. London, Routledge, 1992.

**Hua Tao**

Gai Shanlin. *Yinshan Yanhua* [The Rock Paintings of Yinshan]. Beijing, Wenwu Press, 1986.

Hua Tao. The Advance of Islam. In: Chen Dezhi (ed.), *History of the Chinese Ancient Western Region*. Beijing, National Foundation for Social Studies, 1985.

Jiang Tingyu. *Tonggu Shihua* [The History of Bronze Drums]. Beijing, Wenwu Press, 1982.

Qu Yuam. *Chuci* (selected and annotated by Lu Kairu). Shanghai, 1980.

Ssu Ma Chien. *Records of the Grand Historians of China* (translated by Burton Watson). New York, Columbia University Press, 1961.

Wang Ningshen. *The Rock Paintings of Cangyuan County, Yunnan*. Beijing, Wenwu Press, 1985.

Yuan Ke (ed.). *Shanhai Jin Jaozhu* [Descriptions on Mountains and Seas]. Shanghai, Shanghai Guji Press, 1980.

Zhou Dao, et al. *Henan Hangdai Huaxiang Zhuang* [Break Carvings of Henan Province. Han Period]. Shanghai, Shanghai Meishu Press, 1985.

**Jeannine Davis-Kimball and Anatoly Ivanovich Martynov**

Allman, William. The Mother Tongue. *This World*, March 1991, pp. 11–14.

Boyce, Mary. *Zoroastrians: Their Religious Beliefs and Practices*. London/Boston, 1979.

—*A History of Zoroastrianism*. Leiden, 1989.

Chernikov, S. *The Mystery of the Golden Mound*. Moscow, 1968.

Davis-Kimball, Jeannine. *Proportions in Achaemenid Sculpture*. Ann Arbor, MI, 1989.

Martynov, Anatoly. *The Ancient Art of Northern Asia*. Bloomington, IL, 1991.

Masson, V. *The Early Civilizations*. Leningrad, 1989.

Ogibenin, B. *The Indo-European Forefatherlands*. Gorki, 1989.

Radson. *Ancient India: From the Earliest Times to the First Century AD*. Chicago, 1974.

Wilson, Thomas. *The Swastika: The Earliest Known Symbol, and Its Migration, with Observations on the Migration of Certain Industries in Pre-historic Times*. Washington, DC, 1896.

**Jacques Lacarrière**

Bardout, Michèle. *La paille et le feu. Traditions vivantes de l'Alsace*. Paris, Berger-Levrault, 1980.

Dontenville, Henri. *Mythologie française*. Paris, Payot, 1973.

*Les Evangilles des Quenouilles*. (Anonymous fifteenth-century text translated into modern French by Jacques Lacarrière.) Paris, Editions Imago, 1989.

Gennep, Arnold van. *Manuel de Folklore contemporain*. Paris, 1943.

Sebillot, Paul. *Folklore de France*. Vol. 1: *Le ciel et les esprits des airs*. 1909. Paris, Editions Imago, 1988.

Varagnac, André. *Civilisation traditionnelle et genre de vie*. Paris, 1948.

**Boris I. Marshak**

Andreev, M.S. *Tadziki doliny Khuff*. Vol. 2. Stalingrad, 1958.

Azarpay, G. *Sogdian Painting. The Pictorial Epic in Oriental Art*. Berkeley/Los Angeles/London, 1981.

Boyce, Mary *Zoroastrians. Their Religious Beliefs and Practices*. London/Boston, 1979.

Dzahonov, U. Zemledel'cheskii narodnyi kalendar' u i schet vremeni u tadzikov Sohka. In: B.A. Lituvunsky (ed.), *Ethnography of Tadjikistan*. Dushanbe, 1985.

Herzfeld, E. Die sasanidischen Quadrigae Solis et Lunae. *Archaeologische Mitteilungen aus Iran*, Vol. 2, 1930.

Lenz, W. Zeitrechnung in Nuristan und um Pamir. *Abhandlungen der preussischen Akademie der Wissenschaften*, 1938; *Phil.-hist. Klasse*, Vol. 7, Berlin, 1939.

Marshak, Boris I. *Silberschätze des Orients*. Leipzig, 1986.

—The Historico-cultural Significance of the Sogdian Calendar. *Iran*, Vol. 30, 1992.

Negmatov, N.N. O zhivopisi dvortsa afshinov Ustrushany. *Soviet Archaeology*, No. 3, 1973.

**Ramiro Matos Mendieta**

Conrad, W.G.; Demarest, A.A. *Religion and Empire: The Dynamics of Aztec and Inca Expansionism*. London/New York, Cambridge University Press, 1984.

Duviols, Pierre. Punchao, Idolo Mayor de Coricancha: Historia y Tipologia. *Antropología Andina* (Cuzco), Vol. 1/2, pp. 156–83.

Pease, Franklin. *El Dios Creador Andino*. Lima, Edición Mozca Azul, 1973.

Rowe, J.H. Religión e Imperio en el Antiguo Perú. *Antropología Andina* (Cuzco), No. 1/2, 1976, pp. 5–12.

Steward, J.H.; Faron, L.C. *Native People of South America*. New York/Toronto, McGraw-Hill, 1959.

Taylor, Gerald. *Rites et traditions de Huarochiri: Manuscrit Quechua du debut du 17ème siècle*. Paris, Editions l'Harmattan, 1980.

Zuidema, T.R. The Ceque System of Cuzco. *The Social Organization of the Capital of the Inca* (translated by E.M. Hooykass). Leiden, International Archive of Ethnography, 1964.

**Mary Ellen Miller**

Broda, Johanna; Carrasco, David; Matos Moctezuma, Eduardo. *The Great Temple of Tenochtitlan: Center and Periphery in the Aztec World*. Berkeley, University of California Press, 1987.

Clendinnen, Inga. *Aztecs: An Interpretation*. New York/London,

Cambridge University Press, 1992.
Coe, Michael D. *The Maya*. London/New York, Thames & Hudson, 1987.
Covarrubias, Miguel. *Indian Art of Mexico and Central America*. New York, Knopf, 1957.
Miller, Mary Ellen. *The Art of Mesoamerica*. London/New York, Thames & Hudson, 1986.
Miller, Mary Ellen; Taube, Karl. *The Gods and Symbols of Ancient Mexico and the Maya*. London/New York, Thames & Hudson, 1993.
Morley, S.D. *The Ancient Maya*. Palo Alto, CA, Stanford University Press, 1983.
Pasztory, Esther. *Aztec Art*. New York, Harry N. Abrams, 1983.
Schele, Linda; Freidel, David. *A Forest of Kings*. New York, Morrow, 1991.
Schele, Linda; Miller, M.E. *The Blood of Kings: Dynasty and Ritual in Maya Art*. Fort Worth/New York, Kimbell Art Museum/Braziller, 1986.
Weaver, M.P. *The Aztecs, Maya and Their Predecessors*. New York, Academic Press, 1981.

**Eduardo Matos Moctezuma**

Broda, Johanna; Carrasco, David; Matos Moctezuma, Eduardo. *The Great Temple of Tenochtitlan: Center and Periphery in the Aztec World*. Berkeley, University of California Press, 1987.
Clendinnen, Inga. *Aztecs: An Interpretation*. New York/London, Cambridge University Press, 1992.
Pasztory, Esther. *Aztec Art*. New York, Harry N. Abrams, 1983.
Townsend, Richard. *The Aztecs*. London/New York, Thames & Hudson, 1992.

**Gregory Nagy and Panos D. Valavanis**

Frame, D. *The Myth of Return in Early Greek Epics*. New Haven, CT, Yale University Press, 1978.
Hoffmann, H. Helios. *Journal of the American Research Center in Egypt*, Vol. 2, 1963, pp. 117–24.
Jessen, O. Helios. *Real Encyclopedie*. Vol. 7, 1, 1913, pp. 58–93.
—Gestirnbilder in Athen und Unteritalien. *Antike Kunst*, Vol. 5, 1962, pp. 51–64.
Nagy, G. *Greek Mythology and Poetics*. Ithaca, NY, Cornell University Press, 1990.
Sichtermann, H. Helios. *Enciclopedia dell'Arte Antica*. Vol. 3, 1960, pp. 1140–42.
Yalouris, N. Astral Representations in the Archaic and Classical Periods and Their Connection to Literary Sources. *American Journal of Archeology*, Vol. 84, 1980, pp. 313–18.
Helios. *Lexicon Iconographicum Mythologiae Classicae*. Vol. 5, 1990, pp. 1005–34.

**Jan L. Perkowski**

Conte, Francis. *Les Slaves*. Paris, Albin Michel, 1986.
Dragomonov, M.P. *Notes on the Slavic Religio-ethical Legends: The Dualistic Creation of the World*. Bloomington, Indiana University Publications, 1961.
Georgieva, Ivanichka. *Bulgarian Mythology*. Sofia, Svyat Publishers, 1985.
Gimbutas, Marija. *The Slavs*. New York, Praeger, 1971.
Guiraud, Felix (ed.). *Larousse Encyclopedia of Mythology*. London, Hamlyn, 1982.
Newall, Venetia. *An Egg at Easter*. London, Routledge & Kegan Paul, 1971.
Perkowski, J.L. Anointment of the Gods: A Solar Ritual of Renewal. *Miorita*, Vol. 7, No. 1/2, 1983, pp. 46–50.
—*The Darkling: A Treatise on Slavic Vampirism*. Columbus, OH, Slavica Publishers, 1989.
—*Vampires of the Slavs*. Cambridge, MA, Slavica Publishers, 1976.
Vana, Zdenek. *The World of the Ancient Slavs*. Detroit, Wayne State University Press, 1983.

**Allen F. Roberts and Christopher D. Roy**

Delobson, A.A. *L'Empire du Mogho-Naba*. Paris, Domat-Montchrétien, 1932.
Griaule, Marcel. *Conversations with Ogotemmeli: An Introduction to Dogon Religious Ideas*. London, Oxford University Press, 1965.
Heusch, Luc de. *The Drunken King or the Origin of the State*. Bloomington, Indiana University Press, 1982.
Jacobson-Widding, Anita. *Red-White-Black as a Mode of Thought*. Stockholm, Almqvist & Wiksell International, 1979.
—(ed.). *Body Gender and Space: African Folk Models of Social and Cosmological Order*. Stockholm, Almqvist & Wiksell International, 1991.
Mudinbe, V.Y. *Parables and Fables: Exegis, Textuality, and Politics in Central Africa*. Madison, WI, 1991.
Nooter, M. (ed.). *Art That Conceals, Art That Reveals*. New York, 1992.
Parkin, D. (ed.). *The Anthropology of Evil*. Oxford, 1985.
Roberts, Allen; Maurer, E. (eds.). *The Rising of a New Moon: A Century of Tabwa Art*. Ann Arbor, University of Michigan Museum of Art, 1985.
Skinner, E.P. *The Mossi of the Upper Volta: The Political Development of a Sudanese People*. Stanford, CA, 1961.

**James F. Romano**

Allen, J.P. *Genesis in Egypt: The Philosophy of Ancient Egyptian Creation Accounts*. New Haven, CT, Yale Egyptological Seminar, 1988.
Faulkner, R.O. *The Ancient Egyptian Book of the Dead* (ed. by Carol Andrews). London, British Museum Publications, 1985.
—The Ancient Egyptian Coffin Texts. Warminster, Aris & Phillips, 1973–78. (3 vols.)
Hart, George. *Egyptian Myths*. Austin, University of Texas Press, 1990.
Horming, Erik. *Conceptions of God in Ancient Egypt; The One and the Many*. Ithaca, NY, Cornell University Press, 1982.
—*The Valley of the Kings*. New York, Timkin Publishers, 1990.
Piankoff, Alexandre. *The Litany of Re*. New York, Pantheon Books, 1964.
—*The Shrines of Tut-Ankh-Amon* (ed. by N. Rambova). New York, Pantheon, 1955.

**James R. Russell**

Boyce, Mary. *Zoroastrians: Their Religious Beliefs and Practices*. London, 1984.
—*Textual Sources for the Study of Zoroastrianism*. Chicago, 1990.
Britt, Tilia. *Studies and Restorations at Persepolis*. Rome, IsMEO, 1978.
Cumont, Franz. *Aufstieg und Niedergang der Römischen Welt*, Vol. 2., Berlin, 1984.
—*The Mysteries of Mithra*. New York, 1956.
Ghirshman, Roman. *Persia: From the Origins to Alexander*. London, Thames & Hudson, 1964.
—*Persian Art, 249 BC–AD 651*. New York, Golden Press, 1962.
Hinnells, John. *Persian Mythology*. New York, 1985.
Russell, James. *Zoroastrianism in Armenia*. Cambridge, MA, Harvard University Press, 1987.

**Elizabeth Schultz and Fumiko Yamamoto**

De Barry, William T.; Keene, Donald; Tsunoda, Ryusaku (eds.). *Source of Japanese Tradition*. New York, Columbia University Press, 1961.
Dorson, Richard M. *Folk Legends of Japan*. Rutland, VT, Charles E. Tuttle, 1962.

Hisamatsu, Sen'ichi. *The Vocabulary of Japanese Aesthetics*. Honolulu, Center for East Asian Cultural Studies, 1963.
Muraoka, Tsunetsuju. *Studies in Shinto Thought* (translated by D.M. Brown and J.T. Araki). Tokyo, Ministry of Education, 1964.
Murasaki, Shikibu. *The Tale of Genji* (translated by E.G. Seidensticker). New York, Knopf, 1977.
Robbins-Maury, Dorothy. *The Hidden Sun: Women of Modern Japan*. Boulder, CO, Westview Press, 1983.
Reich, R.B.; Nathan, Robert. Is Japan Really Out to Get Us? *New York Times: Book Review*, February 9, 1992, pp. 22–23.
Taro, Yashima. *The New Sun*. New York, Henry Holt & Co., 1943.

### Edi Sedyawati

Ambo-Enre, Fachruddin. Kata Pengantar (Preface). In: R.A. Kern (ed.), *I La Galigo, Cerita Bugis Kuno* [I La Galigo, A Buginese Old Story]. Indonesian translation by La Side and Sagimun M.D. pp. vii–xii. Yogyakarta, Gadjah Mada University Press, 1989.
Ballard, Chris. Dudumahan: A Rock Art Site on Kai Kecil, Southeast Moluccas. *Indo Pacific Prehistory Association Bulletin*, No. 8, 1989, pp. 139–61.
Bernet-Kempers, A.J. *Ancient Indonesian Art*. Amsterdam, Van der Peet, 1959.
Fontein, Jan. *The Sculpture of Indonesia*. Washington/New York, National Gallery of Art/Harry N. Abrams, 1990.
Hadimulyo; Sedyawati, Edi. Iconographical Data from Old Javanese Kakawins. *Proceedings of the Seventh IAHA Conference, 22–26 August 1977, Bangkok*. Bangkok, Chulalongkorn University Press, 1979. Vol. 2, pp. 1151–67.
Holt, Claire. *Art in Indonesia, Continuities and Change*. Ithaca, NY, Cornell University Press, 1967.
Kosasih, S.A. Lukisan Gua Prasejaraj: Bentagan Tema dan Wilayahnya [Prehistoric Cave Painting: The Extent of Its Theme and Area]. *Diskusi Ilmiah Arkeologi II: Estetika dalam Arkeologi Indonesia* [Archaeological Discussion II: Aesthetics in Indonesian Archaeology]. Jakarta, Pusat Penelitian Arkeologi Nasional, 1987, pp. 16–37.
Lohuizen-deLeeuw, J.E. van. Sûrya in Indonesia. *The 23rd Congress of Orientalists*. 1955.
Moens, J.L. Was Pûrnavarman van Târumâ een Saura? [Was Pûrnavarman of Târumâ a Saura?]. *Tijdschrift v.h. Bataviaasch Genootschap van Kunsten en Wetenschappen*, No. 80, 1940, pp. 78–109.
Pott, P.H. *Yoga and Yantra: Their Interrelation and Their Significance for Indian Archaeology*. The Hague, Koninklijk Instituut voor Taal-, Land- en Volken-kunde, 1966.
Sedyawati, Edi. Cosmological Interpretations of Javanese Temples. *Symposium on Indonesian Views of Time and Space, October 11–12*. San Francisco, The Asian Art Museum and the Society for Asian Art, 1991.
Soekmono. *Candi: Fungsi dan Pengertiannya* [Candi: Its Function and Meaning]. Unpublished dissertation, University of Indonesia, Jakarta, 1974.
Stutley, Margaret; Stutley, James. *A Dictionary of Hinduism: Its Mythology, Folklore and Development 1500 BC–AD 1500*. London, Routledge & Kegan Paul, 1977.
Stutterheim, W.F. De Plaatsing der Rama-Reliefs van Tjandi Lara-Djonggrant en de Zonne-omloop [The Placement of the Rama Reliefs of Candi Lara Jonggrang and the Path of the Sun]. *Bijdragen v.h. Koninklijk Instituut voor Taal-, Land- en Volken-kunde*, No. 84, 1928.

### Madanjeet Singh

Bhattacharyya, Benoytosh. *The Indian Buddhist Iconography*, 1958.
Kramrisch, Stella. *Exploring India's Sacred Art*. Edited by Barbara Stoler Miller, 1983.
Singh, Madanjeet. *Indian Sculpture in Bronze and Stone*. Rome, Italian Institute of the Middle and Far East, 1951.
—*Himalayan Art*. New York, New York Graphic Society, 1968.
Coomaraswamy, Ananda K. *Svayamātrnnā: Janua Coeli. Zalmoxis*, Vol. 2, 1939.
—*The History of Indian and Indonesian Art*. 1927.
Dowson, John. *Hindu Mythology and Religion*. Calcutta, Ruper, 1991.
Hall. *Sûrya Sidhanta* (translated by Whitney and Burgess). Biblioteca Indica, 1923.
Symposium papers on Helios—from myth to solar energy—presented at the State University of New York, Albany, 1978.

### Atsuhiko Yoshida

Anesaki, Masaharu. *History of Japanese Religion*. 1930, reprinted 1963.
Bando, Shojun. *A Bibliography of Japanese Buddhism*. 1960.
Chandra, Lo Kesh. *The Esoteric Iconography of Japanese Mandalas*.
Eliot, Charles. *Japanese Buddhism*. 1935, reprinted 1959.
Getty, Alice. *The Gods of Northern Buddhism*. 1928.
Hanayama, Shiuso. *A History of Japanese Buddhism*. 1960.
Kitagawa, J.M. *Religion in Japanese History*. 1966.
Suzuki, D.T. *Essays in Zen Buddhism*. 1927–61.
Takakasu, J. *The Essentials of Buddhist Philosophy*. 1956.

### Vera N. Zalesskaya and Yuri A. Piatnitsky

Blankoff, J. Survivances du paganisme en vieille Russie. *Problèmes d'histoire du christianisme*. Brussels, 1979.
Chatzidakis, M.; Djuric, V. *Les icons dans les collections suisses*. Geneva, 1968.
Cumont, F. Il Sole vidici dei delitti ed il simbolo dele mani alzate. *Memorie della pontificia Accademia Romana di Archeologia*, Series III, Vol. 1, Part. 1, Rome, 1923.
Gabeli, G.S. Contribution to the Iconography of Saint Mamas and Saints with Attributes. *Second International Congress of Cypriot Studies*, Vol. 2, Nicosia, 1986.
Grabar, A. Un médaillon en or provenant de Mersine en Cilicie. *L'art de la fin de l'antiquité et du Moyen Age*. Vol. 1, Paris, 1968.
Moreau, J.B. *Les grands symboles méditerranéens dans la poterie algérienne*. Algiers, 1976.
Sapunov, B.V. Pamiatniki materialnoy kultury dvoevertsev. *Trudy Gos. Ermitaja*, Vol. 11, Leningrad, 1970.
Velmans. L'image de la Deisis dans les églises de Georgie et dans le reste du monde byzantin. *Cahiers archéologiques*, Vol. 31, Paris, 1983.
Yakobson, A.L. *Srednevekovuj Hersones*. Moscow/Leningrad, 1950.
Zalesskaya, V.N. Classical Symbolism in Early Byzantine Art. *East Mediterranean and the Caucasus in the Fourth to Sixteenth Centuries*. Leningrad, 1988.

# ACKNOWLEDGMENTS


Karidin Akmataliyev, Frunze, 16-18, 325–327, 333
Anaya, Madrid, 520
Archaeological Survey of India, New Delhi, 268, 273–278
Artephot, Paris, 130–131
Aurora Art Publishers, St. Petersburg, 385
Dirk Bakker, Michigan, 49, 92, 307–309, 315–324
Francisco Bedmar, 187
Christa Begall, 400
Benrido, Kyoto, 247
Victor R. Boswell, Jr., and Otis Imboden, 25, 65, 84, 133–134, 138, 141
Jack Breed, 161
Richard Carafelli, 175
Ciccione/Rapho, Paris, 56
Jeannine Davis Kimball, Berkeley CA, 339
Andris Eglitis, Riga, 132
Mihail Enev, Sofia, 395
Fabbrica di San Pietro in Vaticano, Rome, 204
Fiat Foundation, Paris, 57
David Freidel, Dallas, 490–491
Galerie Schmit, Paris, 209
Gamma, Paris, 185
George Gerster/Rapho, Paris, 77
Giraudon, Paris, 440
D.N. Goberman, Moscow, 384
Chikao Gotoh, Nara City, 249
Hidesaburo Hagiwara, Tokyo, 6
Hirmer Verlag, Munich, 40
David Joralemon, 494
Boris Kelemen, Zagreb, 389
Justin Kerr, New York, 483, 488, 495, 497
Douglas Kirkland, Los Angeles, 193
Matti Kolho, Lehtikuva, Helsinki, 415
S.A. Kosasih, 310–312
Jürgen Liepe, Berlin, 51, 102, 169, 298, 450, 460–462
I.S. Madanayake, Colombo, Sri Lanka, 101, 160
Jamshed Marzban, Bombay, 354
Roland and Sabrina Michaud/Rapho, Paris, 20, 23-24, 38, 61, 145, 170, 188
Lyubomir Mikov, Sofia, 398
Khojeste Mistree, Zoroastrian Studies, Bombay, 361
T. Okamura, 94
Krzysztof Pawlowski, Montpellier, France, 176
Photomedia, New Delhi, 107, 224, 271–272
Robert Polidori, 177–178
Réunion des Musées Nationaux, Paris, 3, 22, 33, 67–68, 89, 97, 100, 156, 351, 456, 459
James R. Russell, 358, 360
Richard Schneider, Strasbourg, 441
Shinto Shrine, Ise, Japan, 31, 127, 227, 243–244
Boris Shirokov, Aurora Art Publishers, St. Petersburg, 392
Madanjeet Singh, 1–2, 5, 8, 19, 21, 27–29, 36, 39, 44–46, 52, 54, 59, 62, 69, 74, 83, 85–86, 88, 103, 105, 108–126, 128–129, 137, 139–140, 143–144, 148–150, 152–155, 157–159, 162–166, 171–174, 181, 183–184, 187, 190, 199, 213–218, 220, 222–223, 229, 234–235, 237–238, 240, 246, 265–267, 279, 282–285, 291–297, 299–306, 329–331, 334, 338, 341, 352, 355–357, 359, 362, 365–366, 368, 393–394, 417, 447, 464–473, 477, 484, 486, 498, 500, 503–505
Stefan Slanov, Sofia, 391
Sotheby's Collection, New York, 182
Svyat Publishers, Sofia, 396
Vladimir Terebenin, St. Petersburg, 53, 63–64, 75, 93, 107, 342–345, 347–350, 353, 364, 369–378, 381–383, 406–407, 409–411, 413
Ukrainian Gift Shop, Minneapolis, Minnesota, 387
Zdenek Vana, Kiev, 386
Francesco Venturi, KEA Publishing, London, 34, 42, 106, 179–180, 514
Jacques Verroust, Paris, 445–446
Sun Yifu, China Pictorial, Beijing, 55
Michel Zabe, Mexico City, 35, 47, 50, 80, 90, 99, 142, 225–226, 485, 499, 501–502, 506–508

*We wish to express our gratitude to the numerous museums, libraries, other institutions, photographic agencies, individuals and organizations named or quoted in the book, for having provided excellent photographs for* The Sun, *and for extending the courtesy of either waiving entirely or substantially reducing the reproduction charges. Due credits are appropriately indicated. However, should there be any acknowledgment inadvertently overlooked or mentioned incorrectly, the error will be rectified in subsequent editions if brought to the attention of the publishers.*

# Index

*Italic numerals refer to captions*